Urban and Regional Models
in
Geography and Planning

Urban and Regional Models
in
Geography and Planning

A. G. Wilson

Professor of Urban and Regional Geography
University of Leeds

A Wiley–Interscience Publication

JOHN WILEY & SONS
London · New York · Sydney · Toronto

Library of Congress Catalog Card No. 73–8200

ISBN 0 471 95197 8

Reprinted December 1975

Printed in Great Britain by
J. W. Arrowsmith Ltd.,
Winterstoke Road, Bristol BS3 2NT

To
My parents

Preface

The main aim of this book is to present, in an integrated way, a body of theory on cities and regions. Important, but subsidiary, aims are to show how the resulting mathematical models can be built empirically, and how they can be used in planning studies to help solve problems. Part I consists of three introductory chapters, and a number of preliminaries, concerned mainly with the tools of model building, are presented in Part II. The core of the book is the six chapters which make up Part III. Models of population, economies, transport flows and the location of activities are presented in Chapters 7–10. These are integrated in various ways in the general models of Chapter 11. In Part IV, the use of models in planning is discussed.

Several disciplines have developed major interests in urban and regional studies in recent years. This book should be of interest in both social science disciplines, especially, perhaps, geography, economics and new 'composite' disciplines such as regional science or environmental studies, and professional disciplines such as town and regional planning; it may also be of interest as a developing field of applied mathematics. We comment on each in turn below. It is particularly intended to *begin* to meet the need for a sounder theoretical basis in urban and regional studies in these disciplines.

Fields such as geography have had their 'quantitative' revolution, but have concentrated more on statistical analysis rather than the mathematical theory building which is now needed. Fields such as economics have a better developed sense of theory in general, though disappointingly little progress has been made in the field of spatial analysis. The planners, on the other hand, are much more concerned with having effective tools to *use*, but this position can only be achieved if the basis is sound. It might be argued of fields such as applied mathematics that they have long been dominated by the problems of theoretical physics and engineering. This position may change as other disciplines become more developed mathematically—which again in effect means: 'develop a sound body of theory'.

It should be possible to use the book as a textbook for courses in 'urban and regional analysis', 'models in urban and regional planning', and so on, which are now under way in all the disciplines mentioned above. It can be used at the third year undergraduate level or at the postgraduate level. The more advanced sections in various parts have had their titles asterisked, and these sections could be omitted on a first reading or if the book is being used for an undergraduate rather than graduate course. An attempt has been made in most chapters to carry the discussion up to the research front line, and thus the book should also be of interest to research workers.

Work started on this book as long ago as 1966, though the bulk of it has been actually written in the last two years. An author is influenced by many people over such a long period of time. I hope that much of my indebtedness is acknowledged in the various papers and books cited in the references. I would particularly like to thank those who have provided my working environment for the last few years, and who offered much help and encouragement: William Walkinshaw, Christopher Foster, Henry Chilver, David Donnison and William Birch. I would also like to thank my many colleagues in the University of Oxford, the Ministry of Transport, the Centre for Environmental Studies and the University of Leeds, and many friends in a variety of institutions all over the world, who have helped and encouraged me in many ways. I should particularly mention Christine Leigh and Philip Rees in the Department of Geography in Leeds. I am grateful to Peter Hall for helpful comments on early drafts of a few chapters.

The bulk of the typing of a difficult manuscript has been effectively done by Sheila Jamieson, Ann Errington and my wife. I am also grateful to the editor at John Wiley & Sons Ltd. who has helped over a period of years and I should like to thank Gordon Bryant for drawing the bulk of the figures. Needless to say, as any author of a large book written mostly in 'spare' time will substantiate, considerable demands are made on home life, and I am most grateful for the continual support of my wife.

A. G. WILSON

Leeds
January 1973

Acknowledgments

Chapter 7 is partly based on and uses some material from the paper 'Multi-regional models of population structure and some implications for a dynamic residential location model,' in *Patterns and Processes in Urban and Regional Systems* (Ed. A. G. Wilson), Pion, London, 1972, reproduced by permission of Pion Ltd.

The quotation on p. 115 (Chapter 8) is reprinted from R. Artle, *The Structure of the Stockholm Economy: Toward a Framework for Projecting Metropolitan Community Development*. Copyright © 1965 by Cornell University. Used by permission of Cornell University Press.

The quotation on pp. 191–192 (Chapter 10) is reprinted with permission from R. U. Ratcliff, *Urban Land Economics*, McGraw-Hill Publishing Co. Ltd., 1949, pp. 347–348.

The quotation on p. 194 (Chapter 10) is reprinted with permission from W. Alonso, *Location and Land Use*, Harvard University Press, 1964, p. 37.

Table 14.1 is reproduced from *Portbury*, Ministry of Transport, 1966, Table 6. Reprinted with the permission of the Controller of Her Majesty's Stationery Office.

Tables 14.2 and 14.3 are reproduced from *S.E.L.N.E.C. Transportation Study*, 1972, Tables 40 and 46, pp. 112, 135. Reprinted with permission from S.E.L.N.E.C. Transportation Study.

Acknowledgment has also been made in the text where various Figures have been reproduced from other sources.

Contents

PART I

Models and Urban Problems

CHAPTER 1

Introduction

The aim of this book is to give a mainly elementary account of a range of mathematical models used in the analysis and planning of cities and regions. Many disciplines have interests in the study of such systems. In this presentation, the prime focus is the city or the region, and a certain style of model at a certain spatial scale. This reflects urban and regional analytical interests in social science disciplines such as geography and economics, and professional town and regional planning interests. However, in taking the city and region as the prime system of interest (together with a specific style and scale), the presentation is cross-disciplinary.

It is only in recent years that mathematical models of cities and regions have been widely developed and used and that an integrated approach has become possible for the first time. These models have their origins in a variety of disciplines (each of which ought to take on board the integrated model system as it develops). Demographers have used mathematical models for a good number of years and, rather more recently, economists have been able to develop models of urban and regional economics. It has proved more difficult to build models in which the spatial dimension plays a greater role—for example, of transport flows and the location of activities. The traditional tools of economics have been largely ineffective and members of disciplines such as geography have, until fairly recently, been too ill-equipped mathematically. The breakthrough came in the 1950s with the inauguration of the large metropolitan transport studies in the United States. Models of transport flows were developed, mainly by people with a background in civil engineering. These models 'overtook' some simple models of spatial interaction developed in the social sciences which had nineteenth century origins, with particular development by Reilly in the 1930s. More recently still, from the mid-1960s onwards, elementary models of the location of activities have been developed.

These trends in model building have been associated with another major trend of recent years: an increasing concern with the quality of life and associated problems in cities and regions. This has led to a surge of planning activity which has been increasingly comprehensive and scientific in its approach. It has been recognized that transport developments have major impacts on land use, and vice versa, and hence that it is increasingly difficult to separate planning from other branches of city and regional planning.

3

Most of these developments have originated in the town planning or regional planning professions, though with some assistance from parallel developments in broader but obviously related fields such as operational research and management science.

A model can be defined as the formal representation of some theory of a system of interest. Thus, this book is very much concerned with the theory of the structure and development processes in cities and regions. There are two possible styles of approach to the development of this body of theory: the hypotheticodeductive approach (building a model and testing the predictions against observations) or the inductive approach (starting with data and attempting to infer general laws). Although these approaches complement each other in many ways, it is the first which has been used almost universally in this book. This is partly because of the author's interests, and partly because, in the history of science, it has proved a more fruitful method of theoretical development. It should also be added that, as an approach, it has been underrepresented in the past in the analytical social sciences, and so this presentation can be seen as an attempt to redress that balance. The distinction between deductive and inductive approaches is very much the distinction between the approach of the (applied) *mathematician* and that of the *statistician*.

It is also, at the outset, worth making a general comment, on comprehensiveness, with a conclusion which then follows on scale. In this book, we have always adopted a *comprehensive* approach in the sense that the models apply to all the population of a city or region, all the transport flows, all the flows of goods to shops and so on. An alternative approach is to adopt a strictly *micro* viewpoint, and to focus on the household or the firm. Much earlier model building work on cities and regions in the social sciences has done just this, and much of it is, of course, very distinguished and interesting work. However, it has turned out that micro-theorizing does not easily aggregate into comprehensive theory. It has only proved possible to build comprehensive models by using different approaches. In this book, then, we largely focus on the comprehensive approach, though where appropriate (as in the study of transport flows and the theory of residential location) we discuss the connection of micro-theory to comprehensive theory. The study of this connection—the so-called aggregation problem—remains one of the outstanding problems in the field and will be discussed again in Chapter 15.

The structure of the book is as follows: it has fifteen chapters which are grouped together into four parts, which will briefly be described here in turn.

Part I provides the general introduction on models and urban problems. In Chapter 2, the relationships of models to problems and methods of planning are explored. Within this chapter, a conceptual framework for planning processes is developed to facilitate this. One of the underlying themes in the book is that, although it is often necessary to do so, it is difficult to study aspects of cities and regions in isolation, because 'everything depends on everything else'. In Chapter 3, therefore, we present a framework for a general model at the outset, partly to emphasize the interdependence of the sub-models and the need for an integrated model, and partly to provide a framework for the presentation of the main models in Part III.

Some preliminaries are dealt with in Part II. In Chapter 4, rules for model design are presented and discussed in relation to an example in order to give the reader a preliminary feel for what is to follow. Chapter 5 contains a discussion of mathematical prerequisites for potential readers who may feel that their mathematical background is inadequate. It is emphasized that most of the book can be read given a knowledge of elementary algebra and functions and an ability to deal with subscripts and superscripts in the notation. Members of a family of spatial interaction models turn up at frequent intervals during the book, and this family is described to facilitate later discussion in Chapter 6.

Part III is the main core of the book. Chapters 7–10 are concerned with the different sub-models, 7 and 8 particularly at the regional (or 'whole city') scale, and Chapters 9 and 10 at the intra-urban (or intra-regional) scale. Demographic models are outlined in Chapter 7 and models of urban and regional economies in Chapter 8. Chapter 9 is concerned with transport flows, and Chapter 10 with the spatial distribution of activities. In Chapter 11, these models are integrated, and a detailed presentation is made of different kinds of general model. Chapter 12 describes methods of calibration and testing for the different kinds of model.

Part IV is mainly concerned with the use of models in planning. In Chapter 13, there is a general discussion of the use of models in the different parts of the planning process, and two case studies are presented and critically reviewed in Chapter 14. A number of concluding comments are made in Chapter 15 on the applicability of the models presented in wider fields, connections to ongoing research and the prospects for the future.

CHAPTER 2

Planning, models and urban problems

2.1. URBAN PROBLEMS

It is clear from casual observation that many problems can be identified in cities and city regions. Many (usually oversimplifying) accounts of these problems are available. It is important to note at the outset that observed problems are very much functions of the observer, who should be distinguished in this context by (at least) his life style and his location: both in terms of 'which city' and 'where in the city'. We shall return to some of these viewpoints shortly, but firstly let us note some obvious urban problems on a broad-brush basis.

The urbanite resides in some sort of dwelling; he (which always means 'he or she') often works in gainful employment; he travels, to work and for other purposes; he consumes goods and services; he has various social and recreational activities. In respect of each of these types of activities, we can identify problems. For example:

(1) There is often a housing shortage. This means either that some families are homeless, or some families would like to move to improved housing which is unavailable, or both.

(2) Family networks are upset by relocation due to slum clearance.

(3) Some recreational facilities, such as golf courses in London, are hopelessly oversubscribed.

(4) There may be a job shortage; excess labour with certain skills and retraining capability; conversely, there may be a shortage of workers with certain skills, for example, typically at present, secretaries and 'mathematically-based' town planners!

(5) There are problems with all kinds of services: schools may be overcrowded in one part of a city and half empty in another part, and of varying quality; some shopping centres may be in decline because people find them increasingly inaccessible due to increasing restriction on car parking and/or declining public transport services—while others in accessible areas may not offer a fully attractive range of goods and so on.

(6) Most cities are congested at some time of day; transport services may be poor for those individuals who do not have cars available (and this includes many individuals *within* car-owning households).

Most of us, especially if we live in a big city, have a wide range of experience of difficulties which illustrate the kinds of problems mentioned above, and it often seems to be getting worse at an increasing rate. The above list has been put together with British problems in mind. Some of the problems can be found in a more acute form in wealthier countries, such as the United States, coupled with other problems, such as those of racial segregation and economic deprivation which literally cause major civil disturbances and threaten disorder throughout the community. Other problems, of course, are much worse in poorer countries.

The natural tendency is to try to 'solve' these problems, but usually in an oversimplistic way, without any detailed understanding of the problems and their *interdependence*, and without any ability to predict the consequences of implementing the 'solutions'. In this book we shall try to indicate ways of achieving deeper understanding and foresight. As a preliminary, however, it is worth exploring some elementary notions of urban structure and producing a more detailed 'shopping list' of urban problems which relates to this.

2.2. URBAN STRUCTURE AND THE INCIDENCE OF PROBLEMS

It is useful to refer to three traditional theories of urban structure, partly because this will be a useful background in relation to the urban and regional models to be introduced later, but mainly for the immediate purpose of helping us to get a more detailed understanding of urban problems by examining their incidence. The three theories are the *concentric ring* theory of Burgess (1927), the *sector* theory of Hoyt (1939) and the *polynuclear* theory of Harris and Ullman (1945).

Burgess noted that cities expand from a centre, forming a structure of concentric annules with the following characteristics (from the centre outwards).

(1) A Central Business District (CBD).

(2) A zone of transition, in which residences are 'invaded' by businesses and industry from the CBD.

(3) A working-class residential district.

(4) A district of better residences.

(5) A suburban 'commuting zone', including the possibility of ex-urban satellites.

We shall distinguish only four annules for convenience, below, allocating the zone of transition partly to the CBD and partly to the working-class residential district. We shall use the categories (i) CBD, (ii) the inner residential area, (iii) the inner suburbs, (iv) the outer suburbs. Typically, in a large British city, the CBD and the inner residential area consist of the old, or at least the 'Industrial Revolution', city. The inner suburbs are the inter-war suburbs (often with a ring road forming an outer boundary), and the outer ones are the post-war suburbs.

Hoyt noticed that in many cases it seemed that particular types of people could be identified as living within a *sector* of a city rather than a concentric annule. In this model, as the city grows, the character of a sector takes on the character of inner parts of the same sector.

Harris and Ullman argued that it was an oversimplification to assume that cities were based on a single centre. They consider cities to be multi-nuclear systems, with some centres containing a wide range of functions, others being more specialized. There must also be many versions of an urban central place theory suggesting polynucleation. (For a bibliography on central place theory, see Berry and Pred (1961).)

Quite often in urban studies, when different theories about some pheno-menon are proposed, as above, it is usually possible to argue that a mixture of the various theories would be nearer the truth. In this case, we can expect urban structure to incorporate from all three of the Burgess/Hoyt and Harris/Ullman theories. This had already been suggested in an even earlier account by Hurd (1911), as discussed by Marble in Garrison *et al.* (1959).

We can now elaborate our knowledge of this structure in terms of the kind of infrastructure, people and activities we find in the four annules, but noting that there will be sector differentiation and polynuclear development. We discuss the CBD as a special case, and then the location characteristics of residences, manufacturing industry and the services in turn. Then, given this basis, we return to our examination of urban problems. This discussion will be based on casually observable characteristics of British cities. The reader can make appropriate amendments for cities in other countries.

The CBD contains almost no residential use (London being perhaps a minor exception) and at one time contained most of the economic activity. There has been much decentralization of economic activity, but the CBD still has an important proportion of the total, even though its relative share may be declining. Manufacturing industry has decentralized from the CBD faster than service industry and the CBD usually remains much the most important area for services of all kinds. There is usually good access by public transport, especially in the very biggest cities—an inheritance from post-Industrial Revolution public transport system building—while road access is typically poor because of congestion in the high-density areas near to the CBD and the difficulty of highway building in such areas. The areal extent of the CBD will have spread in a Burgess-like way, but less so in recent years as decentralization has taken its toll. The density of CBD activity is high: the bigger the city the higher the density.

The dominant land use in the areas outside the CBD is residential. We arrive at progressively newer physical stock in general as we move outwards from the centre, though this statement is qualified by the effects of infilling and redevelopment (which are going to be increasingly important). We also observe declining densities, increasing family incomes and increasing family size. In general, poorer families will live in the oldest housing nearer the centre. There are notable exceptions to these Burgess-like generalizations which can be explained by Hoyt-like sector differentiation, or Hoyt–Burgess patterns being reproduced within the city-region area round local centres in a Harris–Ullman kind of way. Typically, work trips to the CBD will be by public transport, while non-CBD trips *by car-owners* will be by car. The quality of various services is likely to be poorer in inner areas, for example because of poor physical stock and unattractiveness to staff, but can be poor again in outer areas because of the difficulty of supplying services at low density.

It is much more difficult to give a broad generalized account of how manufacturing industry locates than it is for households. Particular industries behave very differently: manufacture of clothes, for example, usually takes place on the edge of the CBD, while a newer industry, such as electronics, is likely to be very decentralized. We can simply note at this point that there has been a lot of decentralization on average, and that a lot is known about trends within particular industries.

We have already noted that the CBD retains its importance for the service sector, but also, implicitly, that service activities are located in relation to the residential 'market'. Again, however, there has been considerable decentralization, as in the trend, for example, to the development of major 'out-of-town' (that is, suburban) shopping centres. It is particularly important to note the so-called 'post-service' sector. Economies are assumed to have been dominated by agriculture; then by manufacturing industry; then by the service sector. What might constitute the post-service sector? What is it that will increasingly offer 'employment' opportunities as the economy as we now know it becomes increasingly automated? The answer, which is probably already observable in the Californias of the world, is in the 'information processing industry', particular aspects of which are education and research. Such activities are probably relatively footloose in their locational characteristics. It is also worth noting at this stage something which is already implicit in the above notes: that classification is increasingly difficult. A firm classified as manufacturing industry may supply its own services and generate post-service type activity, for example.

We have now made sufficient progress with our sketch to return to the task of elaborating our account of urban problems, particularly considering the *incidence* of problems.

We can elaborate on our earlier list, which was concerned with such things as housing, job supply, services and transport, while still grossly over-simplifying, by considering three household income categories (low, medium and high) and noting the correlation between these categories and the spatial categories: inner residential, inner suburban and outer suburban. It is convenient at this point to generalize what we called the transport problem area to the problem of 'getting linkages right', which is a matter of land-use planning and overall spatial organization as much as transport network design.

We can then represent problem areas in relation to their incidence as in Figure 2.1. A large cross represents a major problem area, a small cross a

Socio economic group	Problem area			
	Housing	Jobs	Services	Linkages
Low income	X	X	X	X
Middle income	x	x	x	X
High income			x	X

Key:

X = major problem areas
x = minor problem areas

Figure 2.1 A problem map

minor one. Major problem areas involve a reasonably large percentage of the group concerned; minor problem areas involve a significant number of people of the group concerned. The concepts of 'reasonably large' and 'significant' are loose but will suffice for this preliminary sketch.

The first thing to note is that low-income households have major problems on all counts, and that all income groups have major linkage problems. Let us begin by considering these main problem areas.

Low-income households have major housing problems because available housing supply at a price which they can afford is poor quality old stock near city centres. This is an oversimplified generalization made on the implicit assumption that all households seek housing in a free market. Poorer households who are supplied with Council (public) houses may have less acute problems—though even in these cases, the problems of poorer families are often underestimated. (For example, some households in 'slum' accommodation have a life style based on a very low rent; if and when they are moved to Council housing redevelopment, it is often at a much higher rent, and they may then find it difficult to buy food or other necessities. See, for example, the case of the Moore family in Birmingham, whose rent increased from £1 7s. 0d. to £6 4s. 10d. in these circumstances (*Birmingham Evening Mail*, 23 February, 1970).) Of course, this is probably as much an income problem as a housing shortage problem. On the job front, problems can be discussed in the context of some linkage problems: we have seen that many low-income households only find housing opportunities near the CBD; clearly, if this phenomenon is coupled with the decentralization of jobs, there is decreasing accessibility to jobs for low-income households. There is also the possibility of a declining number of low-income job opportunities in manufacturing industry, though it is not clear at present what is happening in this respect in the service sector. Problems associated with the service sector near the centre have already been mentioned, and we can now see that they will apply particularly acutely to low-income households. One very severe problem arising from the spatial concentration of poorer people, and the associated relatively poor services, is that opportunities for development—one might almost say 'escape'—are limited.

We have said that everyone has linkage problems. The emphasis on linkages shows the *interdependence* of other problem areas. We have already seen the possibility of major linkage problems for low-income households because of the increasing amount of out-commuting, for example (and, of course, the transport system is not designed for out-commuting). Middle and high income workers who have jobs out of the CBD will usually have to travel by car, and this leads to congestion problems, especially in the inner suburbs. Congestion is further exacerbated by the relatively small number of people who commute by car to the CBD. But the journey to work is only part of 'getting linkages right'. Thus, even assuming that the head of the household has a 'reasonable' work journey, we must consider, for example, children going to school, the wife's access to job opportunities, older children's access to job opportunities and higher education, access to services, recreational facilities and a social network for all members of the family and so on, through all the activities of each member of the household: some activities being carried out singly, some together. Typical problems are: in one-car households, if one member uses the car for a work journey, other members do not have a car available for their work journey, or other activities; high-income wives and children in outer suburbs only have activity opportunities available at low densities, so they either have a low activity rate or long journeys on average.

It is clear that all of this stops a very long way short of 'understanding urban problems'. However, it serves to remind us of the sort of thing we should be aiming to 'understand with models' throughout this book. It tells us something in a preliminary way about the level of detail at which we should be working. We can then move towards solving these problems with new planning methods. We shall find opportunities from time to time to formalize and deepen the discussion of many of the concepts introduced, rather loosely, so far.

2.3. A CONCEPTUAL FRAMEWORK FOR PLANNING

Urban planners are faced with a wide range of difficult problems. It is appropriate at this stage to examine the activities of planners more formally and to establish a conceptual framework. It has been argued in an earlier paper (Wilson, 1968) that there are three main kinds of activity in planning which can. be designated *policy*, *design* and *analysis*. (These terms have a similar meaning to those used by Harris (1965), though his are perhaps more vivid: *prediction*, *invention* and *choice*.) These activities, with an indication of what they comprise, are shown in a hierarchical relationship in Figure 2.2.

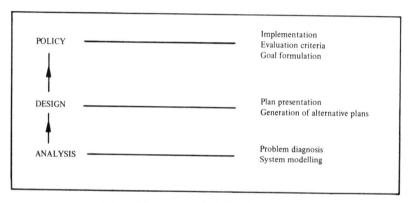

Figure 2.2   The principal planning activities

The hierarchical relationship arises as follows: the designer needs a good analytic capability so that he can diagnose problems and predict the impact of his designs; the policy maker needs good design capability to ensure that he really has a good range of alternative plans presented to him, and he needs an additional analytical capability (i.e. over and above that used by the designer) to help establish evaluation criteria for choosing between alternatives.

The breakdowns of the three activities shown on the right-hand side of Figure 2.2 are more or less self-explanatory, but again a hierarchical relationship is retained. At the top end of the hierarchy, planners are concerned with *implementation* in the sense that this represents the final decision; they are concerned with establishing *evaluation criteria* in order to be able to choose between alternative plans; and such criteria are based on explicitly formulated *goals*. (Note that a goal may be 'to solve some particular problem', though we shall explore the relation between goals and problems more closely later.) The designer must be concerned with various ways of *plan presentation*,

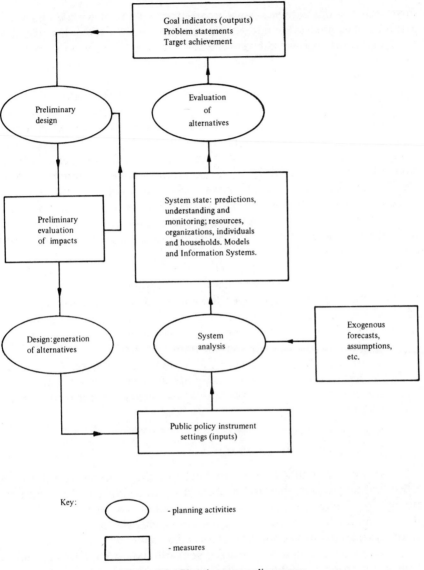

Figure 2.3   Planning as a cyclic process

though his principal activity is the *generation of alternative plans.* The analyst should be capable of *problem diagnosis* (an exercise we began, imperfectly, in the previous section) and he will build *system models* (the main subject of this book) to help develop a predictive capability.

Policy, design and analysis will be discussed in more detail in the following three sub-sections of this Chapter. However, it should be emphasized that this is only one way of presenting a broad conceptual framework for planning, and the reader must eventually develop and use one which is to his own taste. It is important to have a broad framework so that particular aspects of planning, and particular problems, can be seen in context, and so that aspects of planning which are important to a particular problem area are not forgotten. Secondly, the state of development of the planning field is such that not only is there no single agreed conceptual framework, but there is no agreed vocabulary. For example, the concept of 'model' is used in a wide variety of ways. In the conceptual framework presented here, it can be given a clear meaning. A model is a formal representation of our understanding of system behaviour, and can be used under appropriate conditions to make conditional predictions. The planner can use it in design and policy-making activities. This definition does not leave open the possibility of talking about 'optimizing models', for example. This term is sometimes used to describe the situation where a model (on our definition) is used *within an optimizing process* to solve a problem in an optimal way. In the conceptual framework presented here, this *process*—in which an analytical model may be used—can be presented in terms of design and policy-making activities.

This sub-section may have given the impression that planning is a rather tidy and even sequential process. In fact, it is more realistic to consider planning as a continuing cyclic process in which the knowledge gained at each step is used as the basis for making improvements in the next step. Such a representation is shown in Figure 2.3. Activities are represented in ovals, while measures produced by these activities are represented by rectangles. The figure should then be self-explanatory in the light of the earlier discussion in this chapter.

2.4. GOALS AND URBAN POLICY

So far, we have implicitly discussed urban policy in terms of what were called 'casually observable urban problems' in Section 2.1. We shall now attempt to relate urban policy to a first-principles study of goals: to look at urban planning from a positive what-are-our-goals viewpoint rather than a more negative how-do-we-solve-these-*casually-observed*-problems viewpoint. (The italics are important, as a study of goals should lead to a deeper understanding of problems and hence, possibilities of solution.)

As with some other relevant concepts, the notion of a goal is used in a variety of ways in the urban literature. Other concepts, like 'objective' for example, are often used more or less synonymously. It will be convenient here to distinguish carefully the concepts of *goals* and *objectives* by using our own definitions. This is done as follows: the concept of a goal will be used to represent the aspirations of individuals and households. It will be assumed that *organizations* are *resources* which exist ultimately for the benefit of

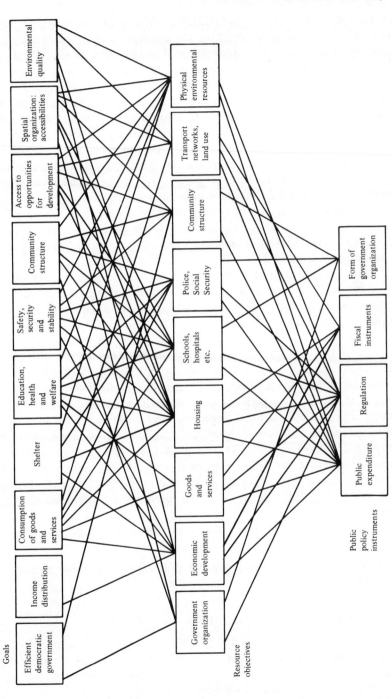

Figure 2.4   Conceptual inter-relationships of goals, objectives, and policy instruments

individuals and households (though many of them, of course, may exist to serve each other). Then, we shall use the concept of *objectives* to relate to organizations and other resources. We will usually refer to *social* goals on the one hand and *resource* objectives on the other. Planners are usually interested in manipulating resources (conceived in this wide sense) in their plans and hence with objectives, though they need ultimately to consider the impact of their plans in terms of goals. Objectives are often discussed in a rather long-term kind of way and it is sometimes convenient to introduce the concept of *targets* as statements of short-run objectives. What the planner actually does is to decide how to use *public policy instruments* in the ways open to him to achieve resource objectives and hence social goals. These concepts, elaborating part of the notion of policy introduced earlier, can themselves be exhibited in a hierarchy, and this is done in Figure 2.4. The Figure shows that the manipulation of a single policy instrument could contribute to several resource objectives and each objective, typically, contributes to several goals. This kind of presentation shows why confusion is often abundant in this kind of discussion: if the concepts of policy instruments, resource objectives and societal goals are confused, then it becomes that much more difficult to understand and explore the complex relationships exhibited in Figure 2.4.

The next step is to illustrate the kind of goals, objectives and policy instruments involved. Targets are usually taken to mirror objectives and, while the concept may be useful as an operational device, there is no need to elaborate the notion any further at this stage. As a preliminary, it is useful to introduce the concept of goals as *goals-as-areas-of-concern* rather than as anything more specific. For example 'income distribution' is an area of concern and we will discuss goals associated with it but we shall not at this stage be much more specific. This facilitates discussion of the theory of planning. Otherwise, we become bogged down in discussions about the extent to which one particular income distribution is better than another and we are postponing this discussion in the interests of progressing with the theory.

Social goals can thus be listed under a number of broad headings:

(1) *Political*
   (a) The maintenance and organization of efficient and democratic government.

(2) *Economic*
   (a) Equity issues associated with income distribution.
   (b) Consumption of goods and services.

(3) *Economic/social*
   (a) Shelter.
   (b) Education, health and welfare.

(4) *Social*
  (a) Safety, security, stability.
  (b) Community structure.
  (c) Access to opportunities for development and mobility.

(5) *Environmental*
  (a) Spatial organization—accessibilities.
  (b) Environmental quality.

The distinction between the economic and social headings is that between needs which can be more or less met with markets and those which cannot— hence the 'mixed' economic/social heading. The other headings are self-explanatory. The items in the list are intended to cover the main items which make up the life-style of individuals and households in (or indeed, out of) cities, and could represent the variables of some socio-economic welfare function. *It is obviously particularly important to consider these headings as they apply to different individuals and households, in different income levels, in different community groups and in different locations.* It can be left as an exercise for the reader, for the time being, to elaborate this list, to note any omissions and to relate it to the earlier discussion of urban problems.

Related objectives, under similar broad headings, might be listed as follows:

(1) *Political*
  (a) Forms of governmental organization.

(2) *Economic*
  (a) The economy and economic development, especially in relation to jobs and skills needed for different jobs and related wages.
  (b) Range of goods and services on offer.

(3) *Economic/social*
  (a) Housing supply, noting the variety of types involved.
  (b) Schools, colleges, universities, hospitals, health centres, welfare institutions and so on.

(4) *Social*
  (a) Resources for policing, reducing accidents, social security and so on.
  (b) Resources for encouraging the development of 'balanced' communities.

(5) *Planning*
  (a) Transport networks, land-use control and other resources (organizational and physical) for bringing about an efficient spatial organization.
  (b) Environmental resources.

This list does not correspond exactly with the goals list and, even where it does, congruence is not to be expected because of the network of inter-relationships in Figure 2.4. As we saw, developments leading towards the achievement of an objective can affect the achievement of several goals. For example, an expanding economy with more job opportunities provides increased income (and possibly a more equitable distribution) and so allows the purchase of more goods and services; indirectly it provides more government income for the development of social services and efficient spatial organization; in some circumstances, a combination of these effects may, for example, have an impact on health. Once again, we shall leave it as an exercise to the reader to elaborate these notions at this stage, though we shall be returning to them in Chapter 13, when we are better equipped and have a number of models at our disposal.

The main types of public policy instrument seem to be:

(1) Public expenditure.
(2) Regulation, e.g. land use control.
(3) Fiscal measures.
(4) Changing the form of government organization.

These headings are self-explanatory, and need no further elaboration at this stage.

If the planning process is seen as setting certain inputs to achieve certain outputs, then the public policy instruments are the *inputs* while any measurements of achievement of objectives and goals can be considered as different measures of *outputs*. Thus, the type of planning process described in this chapter can be identified to a fair extent with so-called *output-budgeting*, or PPBS procedures. (Planning, Programming and Budgeting Systems. See, for example, Rose (1970), through there is a vast literature on the subject.) By not forming a rigid correspondence, we avoid some of the rigidities of the latter.

So far, we have not seriously considered the problem of *measurement* of goal achievement. This can be considered initially in two ways. Firstly, we could simply try to identify *indicators* of goal achievement, in the hope that the value of an indicator would tell us whether situation B, developed using public policy instruments out of situation A, is 'better than' A. This is sometimes useful, and is probably always worth attempting in the absence of anything better. However, it does not deal well with questions of value: the use of indicators does not always help select the 'best' projects when not all good projects can be done because of, for example, budget constraints. To tackle questions of value, it is better to turn to the framework of welfare economics, as hinted by the mention of the concept of utility function earlier in this section. We shall return to this question again in Chapter 13.

As a final preliminary point, but an important one, note that when social goals and resource objectives are specified in relation to different individuals and households, and different community groups, and given budget constraints in relation to possible developments, then many conflicts arise. One of the roles of policy making in planning will be to find ways where possible of resolving such conflicts.

2.5. DESIGN

In terms of the framework of the previous section, the designer's task is to generate alternative settings of the public policy instruments which lead to the achievement of objectives and goals, and this is what was meant earlier by the generation of alternative plans. In our case, we will mainly be concerned with public expenditure and the regulation of spatial organization as the main instruments of policy. Of course, a plan as presented may, and should, contain an account of the expected system state which would result from the preferred scheme but this should not be confused with the main part of the plan as such: the generation of alternatives and the selection of a preferred plan from amongst them.

The designer's main problem is that usually he has an extremely large number of possibilities open to him. Consider the sub-problem of designing a transportation network for example: if there are N nodes in the network, there are $2^{\frac{1}{2}N(N+1)}$ ways of joining links and this becomes a very large number, even for quite small values of N. What the designer does is attempt to develop a number of organizing concepts to find a systematic way of avoiding the need to evaluate all possible alternatives (which is called a *combinatorial problem*). For example, in the transport network case, he may be able to convince himself that the only combination of links which make 'sensible' networks are those which form a grid, a radial-ring or an essentially linear system (as argued by Buchanan and Partners (1966)), and this obviously considerably simplifies the problem.

It is not always possible to be systematic in such a way, even when the designer can still not enumerate *all* the possibilities because of the combinatorial problem. In this case, the designer has to rely on his inventiveness to produce a wide range of 'good' plans for evaluation. This approach stems from an essentially artistic tradition, while attempts to be more systematic stem from a more scientific tradition. Both methods are likely to be necessary and useful, given our present state of knowledge, for a long time to come. This is another point where it is appropriate to mention 'optimizing models': an optimizing procedure, such as a linear-programming procedure, offers a systematic method for searching the scope of possibilities to find the optimum. With most urban problems, inherent complexity coupled with the difficulty of specifying an objective function, the thing to be optimized, means that this sort of procedure is rarely feasible.

2.6.   ANALYSIS AND MODELLING

We have implicitly described in previous sections why planners need analytical capability. For example, given a planner's job of designing a transport network to improve linkages and accessibility and to reduce congestion, he needs to know how traffic is generated and distributes itself on the network, how much accessibility is improved in different parts of the city and so on. He can use a model to make a prediction (which is *conditional* on his proposals).

It is clear from our earlier sections on problems and goals that we are interested in population demand for housing (by locations in relation, for example, to the distribution of jobs and services), in the development of the economy (and hence in the distribution of jobs and services and inter-industry linkages) and in transport patterns. There is a sense in which organizations can be considered to create the 'supply' to meet these demands. We summarize this in Figure 2.5.

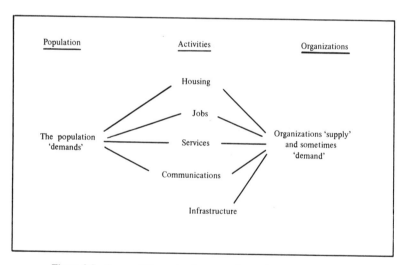

Figure 2.5   Some of the main elements of an urban-regional system

This suggests that we shall also be interested in demographic models of urban population structures (including inter-urban migratory flows, for example) and models of urban economies, in each case irrespective of the spatial distribution of associated activities. Thus, we can list a number of areas where we would like to have models:
(1) Spatially aggregated population models.
(2) Spatially aggregated economic models.
(3) Transport models.
(4) Models of residential location and housing supply.

(5) Models of workplace choice.

(6) Models of service usage and supply.

In Chapters 7–10 in Part III of this book, examples of models in each of these sectors will be presented. However, as a preliminary the next chapter outlines the model building task in more detail, and Part II contains three chapters which tell the reader how to set about model building.

2.7. CONCLUDING COMMENTS

We have tried to emphasize in this chapter that it is useful to make a systematic study of the concerns of urban and regional planning, both in terms of problems and an overall conceptual framework. Generally to date, planners have tended to concern themselves with what we have called design and policy making (though not in a systematic way) and have not striven to develop an analytical capability. This book, being essentially about models, is mostly about the development of this analytical capability and the intention of this chapter is to establish the context within which models are used in planning processes.

2.8. REFERENCES

(* Indicates that this work was not cited in the text, but is useful for further reading.)

* C. Alexander (1964) *Notes on the synthesis of form*, Harvard University Press, Cambridge, Mass.

* E. C. Banfield (1968) *The unheavenly city*, Little Brown, Boston.

B. J. L. Berry and A. Pred (1961) *Central place studies: a bibliography*, Regional Science Research Institute, Philadelphia.

Colin Buchanan and Partners, in association with Economic Consultants Ltd. (1966) *South Hampshire Study*, Ministry of Housing and Local Government, London.

E. W. Burgess (1927) The determination of gradients in the growth of the city, *Publications of the American Sociological Society*, **21**, pp. 178–84.

* G. Chadwick (1971) *A systems view of planning*, Pergamon, Oxford.

* P. Cowan (Ed.) (1970) *Developing patterns of urbanization*, Oliver and Boyd, Edinburgh.

* P. Cowan (Ed.) (1973) *The future of planning*, Heinneman, London.

* H. Gans (1972) *People and plans*, Penguin, London.

W. L. Garrison, B. J. L. Berry, D. F. Marble, J. D. Nystuen and R. L. Morrill (1959) *Studies of highway development and geographic change*, University of Washington Press, Seattle.

* T. Hagerstand (1970) What about people in regional science? *Papers, Regional Science Association*, **24**, pp. 7–21.

* P. Hall (1970) *The theory and practice of regional planning*, Pemberton, London.

B. Harris (1965) Urban development models: a new tool for planners, *Journal of the American Institute of Planners*, **31**, pp. 90–95.

* B. Harris (1967) Quantitative models of urban development: their role in metropolitan policy making, in H. Perloff and L. Wingo (Eds.) *Issues in urban economics*, John Hopkins Press, Baltimore.

C. D. Harris and E. L. Ullman (1945) The nature of cities, *Annals, American Academy of Political and Social Science*, **242**, pp. 7–17.

* D. Harvey (1971) Social processes, spatial form and the redistribution of real income in an urban system, in M. Chisholm, A. E. Frey and P. Haggett (Eds.) *Regional forecasting*, Butterworths, London.

H. Hoyt (1939) *The structure and growth of residential neighbourhoods in American cities*, Federal Housing Administration, Washington D.C.

R. M. Hurd (1911) *Principles of city land values*, The Record and Guide, New York.

* J. Jacobs (1970) *The economy of cities*, Jonathan Cape, London.

* J. B. McLoughlin (1969) *Urban and regional planning: a systems approach*, Faber and Faber, London.

* R. E. Pahl (1970) *Whose city?* Longmans, London.

K. E. Rose (1970) Planning and P.P.B.S. with particular reference to local government, *Environment and Planning*, **2**, pp. 203–10.

* A. J. Scott (1971) *Combinational programming, spatial analysis and planning*, Methuen, London.

A. G. Wilson (1968) Models in urban planning: a synoptic review of recent literature, *Urban Studies*, **5**, pp. 249–76.

* A. G. Wilson (1972) Understanding the city of the future, *University of Leeds Review*, **15**, pp. 135–66.

CHAPTER 3

Towards a framework for a general model

3.1. INTRODUCTION

In Chapter 2 we were mainly concerned with the need for models to use in planning processes to help solve problems. Clearly, the planner may be directly involved in such model building, but it is a more primary activity in such disciplines as urban and regional geography and corresponding aspects of economics and sociology. There is a happy coincidence of interest between the social scientist (the analyst) and the planner in model building. The task of building a general model is, of course, likely to involve contributions from many disciplines.

In Section 2.5, we began to specify the list of models we would be interested in. We can now examine this shopping list in more detail, though still in a preliminary way.

3.2. THE MAIN ELEMENTS OF A GENERAL MODEL

We are interested in all the activities within cities and regions, and the resources created and consumed by these activities. Human beings are involved in most activities and it is convenient at the outset to distinguish between the private behaviour of people, as individuals or as households, and the social behaviour of people in organizations. This distinction will not always be obvious and clear, but it will serve as a useful first approximation. We will also be interested in interaction and linkages between activities. So, in summary, we are concerned with:
(1) Population and population activites.
(2) Organizations and organizational activities.
(3) Interactions and linkages between activities.
(4) The resources created and used by the various activities.
The main population activities are those concerned with residence, working, shopping, the use of other services, and social and recreational activities. Nearly all of these activities also involve organizational activities: the supply of housing, jobs, shops, services and recreational facilities. Indeed, it is sometimes convenient to think of the population as creating a *demand* for facilities for their activities, and of organizations as creating the *supply* of such

facilities. Again, however, this is an oversimplification: some facilities, for example, result from the demand of organizations themselves; it will also be convenient to retain concepts such as 'organizations' and 'demand for labour' (other than 'supply of jobs'). Even at this stage, it is clear that there are strong interactions between activities.

It is important to distinguish different scales at which we can view these main elements of urban and regional systems. (This is one of the aggregation questions to be discussed in Chapter 4.) At least four useful scales can be distinguished: national, regional, urban (defined loosely, as usual, to mean a 'city region') and intra-urban. In the case of the first three scales, we will usually, though by no means always, be primarily interested in one nation, one region or one urban area, and such models at these scales can be referred to as spatially aggregated models. At the intra-urban scale, on the other hand, we are usually interested in all the sub-areas or *zones* of the urban area, and the distribution of activities among these zones; models at this scale can be referred to as spatially disaggregated models.

We must also decide how to classify our main elements (the second aggregation question to be discussed in Chapter 4). It is common to classify people by age, sex, social class, income and so on with a whole range of such characteristics, and we have to decide which sort of classification is needed in any particular case. Organizations, unlike people, are commonly classified by the activities they undertake. For example, we speak of the 'motor industry': classifying a car-producing organization by its activity. It is worth noting, however, that organizations could be classified in other ways, according to functional type, as with factory, main office, branch office and so on, and that ultimately it may be more useful to do this and then to go on to note the range of activities of each organizational type within such a classification. A further restriction will also be made for the purposes of this book: we are primarily interested in the role of organizations in *economies* and we will use concepts such as 'the economy' as more or less synonymous with 'organizations in general'. This is a restriction, but unless we impose it we shall be taken into realms of sociology and organization theory beyond the scope of this book.

Interactions and linkages between activities show themselves as transport flows, as money flows or as various kinds of information flows (face-to-face contact, exchange of letters, telephone calls and so on). We shall be primarily concerned with transport flows in this book, though occasionally we shall refer to other forms of interaction and studies of these other forms. We shall not usually refer to resources explicitly: having stated our primary concern with *economic* organizations and with population activities, we shall usually consider resources in the context of organizational and population behaviour. Organizations themselves, of course, as we saw earlier, can often be usefully considered as resources.

The main measures of population and population activity are fairly obvious; in the case of organizational activity, the main measures with which we shall be concerned in this book are jobs, product, infrastructure use and land use. In taking this view of the main elements of any general model, we have implicitly taken two major decisions. Firstly, we have decided to take a *comprehensive* view; secondly, we therefore exclude the possibility of what might be called micro-behavioural model building. There are mathematical problems which make it very difficult to aggregate from a micro-behavioural to a comprehensive view (Wilson, 1972). It is not appropriate to develop this argument in detail at this point, though we shall return to it briefly in the final chapter.

3.3. PICTURE AND PROCESS

If we begin to define variables to characterize the main elements of the urban and regional system described in Section 3.2, then we begin to develop a quantitative picture of the system at any one point in time. When we relate and explain these variables in a set of linked sub-models, then we begin to have a general model of an urban and regional system. If we believe that the system is an equilibrium system, then we could attempt to build a model of the static picture: that is, to relate and explain the variables at one point in time, without time appearing as an explicit variable. Many of the models to be described are of this form, and we can represent diagrammatically the set of interlinked models which would form this kind of picture (Figure 3.1). The intra-urban part of Figure 3.1 can be expanded to show the main population activities, the main economic activities using a crude classification, and the main interaction represented as transport flows. This is done in Figure 3.2.

Figures 3.1 and 3.2 are more or less self-explanatory. In order to take the discussion a stage further, it is useful to discuss the notion of process or change. The simplest notion of process in this context arises from imagining a time series of pictures of the forms implied by Figures 3.1 and 3.2. However, it is perhaps worth attempting to go a stage further and to introduce an elementary idea of the mechanisms of the process of change.

Consider organizational behaviour first. Suppose it is possible to assume that organizations take decisions about their policy for the coming year, and then review progress and take another lot of decisions for the following year and so on. The decision-taking process can be crudely conceived as follows: each organization reviews the alternatives open to it (depending on the state of technology, assumptions about the cost of resources, estimates of demand for its goods or services etc.); it then considers the resources needed for each alternative, and enters a 'market bargaining' process about the possibility of gaining access to these; then it takes firm policy decisions (recorded in our

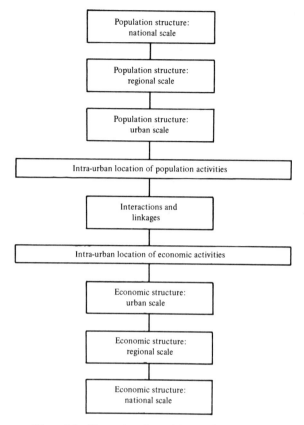

Figure 3.1 The main sub-models, at different scales

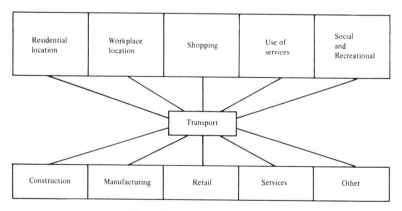

Figure 3.2 Intra-urban models

measures as jobs, produce, infrastructure and land use, perhaps also capital use). The public do not directly perceive this set of decisions by all organizations. They perceive, imperfectly, a set of job opportunities, sets of goods offered through retail establishments and other services, sets of houses which they might live in, and other factors. They then make their choices, possibly interacting and competing through another 'market bargaining' process, of jobs, houses and 'purchase' of goods and services. These steps are represented diagrammatically in Figure 3.3 which shows two feedback loops. Public

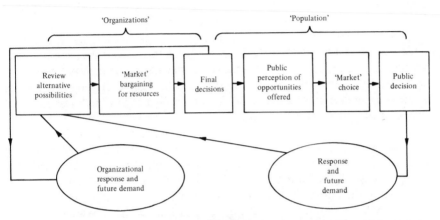

Figure 3.3   Process

response to the outcome of the process helps to create future demand and the organizations themselves have a response which also helps to create future demand.

In this book most of the models will be presented in relation to variables which can be related to the pictures of Figures 3.1 and 3.2. However, it will be important to identify the role of these variables in elaborations of the kind of process indicated in Figure 3.3, so that, eventually, adequate predictions of change can be made. In particular, we must note the possibility of what Forrester (1969) calls 'counter-intuitive behaviour' in such a complex system as a city or a region. In other words, if we are able to represent all the sub-system linkages at a level of detail which adequately represents the mechanisms of change, then the resulting whole, our general model, may be in a very real sense greater than the sum of its parts.

3.4. TOWARDS A GENERAL MODEL

There is a great temptation to specify a general urban and regional model at an early stage in our work. However, we have already seen that a general model will consist of a set of linked sub-models. Some of these sub-models are much more highly developed than others, therefore if we concentrate on a prescription for a general model at this stage, the parts will be out of balance. It has consequently been decided to concentrate on describing sub-models in separate chapters, or sections, of the book, but always bearing in mind the need to study the *ways* in which they can be linked in a more general model. There will be large numbers of ways in which sub-models can be linked together and it will be useful to maintain a variety of options. These will be explored in Chapter 11, when examples of general models will be presented. Further, most of the sub-models (hereafter referred to simply as 'models') are valuable and useful in their own right.

Part III of this book, which describes some of the models, has a structure which can be simply related to Figure 3.1. Chapter 7 outlines some demographic models which can be applied at the national, regional or urban scales and thus account for the top third of the figure. Chapter 8 describes some economic models which can also be applied at national, regional and urban scales covering the bottom third of the figure. Chapter 9 describes transport models, and hence flows between activities, and has intra-urban (the very centre of the figure) as well as inter-urban applications. Chapter 10 is concerned with all the locational models required by the middle third of Figure 3.1, as expanded in Figure 3.2. Chapter 11 further explores the task of assembling the sub-models into a general model. In all these chapters, the models will be presented as simply as possible, without reference to the problems of calibration and testing (which are discussed separately as part of Chapter 12). A discussion of the possible applications of these models is postponed to Part IV, which also contains descriptions of a number of case studies.

3.5. REFERENCES

J. W. Forrester (1969) *Urban dynamics*, M.I.T. Press, Cambridge, Mass.
* A. G. Wilson (1968) Models in urban planning: a synoptic review of recent literature, *Urban Studies*, **5**, pp. 249–76; reprinted in A. G. Wilson (1972) *Papers in urban and regional analysis*, Pion, London, pp. 3–30.
  A. G. Wilson (1972) Behavioural inputs to aggregative urban system models, pp. 71–90 in *Papers in urban and regional analysis*, Pion, London.

PART II

Techniques for Constructing Urban and Regional Models

CHAPTER 4

How to construct a model, with an example

4.1. RULES FOR MODEL DESIGN

It helps to have a check list of questions to help in model design. These are given below and then discussed in turn.

(1) What is the *purpose* behind the particular model building exercise?
(2) What should be represented as *quantified variables* within the model?
(3) Which of these variables are under the *control* of the planner?
(4) How *aggregated* a view can be taken?
(5) How should the concept of *time* be treated?
(6) What *theories* are we trying to represent in the model?
(7) What *techniques* are available for building the model?
(8) What relevant *data* are available?
(9) What methods can be used for the *calibration* and *testing* of the model?

(This list is a development of that presented in an earlier paper (Wilson, 1968-A); it is heavily influenced by papers by Harris (1965), Lowry (1965) and Steger (1965).) The question about *purpose* is closely connected to some of the other questions and may provide answers to them. Typical purposes might be:

(a) To help predict the impact of alternative strategies in a local authority development plan.
(b) To see how traffic would redistribute itself if a particular new road were to be built.
(c) To investigate the consequences of introducing a new public transport facility, such as a new bus route or a new underground railway.
(d) To investigate the pressure on land for residential development and likely directions of growth.
(e) To predict the sales in a new shopping centre.

The reader could considerably extend this list by referring back to the earlier discussion of planning problems. Thus, the purpose could relate to a major exercise (like the development plan) or something much more partial (like the new bus route). The effort devoted to the model-building exercise, especially if the model-building work is to start from scratch, should be related to the importance of the purpose in hand. Note, however, that one of the advantages of broadly-based model-building exercises within a continuous planning framework is that it becomes relatively easy, at low marginal

31

cost, to carry out small projects. We shall see as this discussion proceeds that different purposes *in the same general problem area* demand different types of model.

The second question is about *quantified variables* to be represented in the model and is, of course, closely linked to the question about theory. We can discuss this concurrently with the third question about variables which the planner can control. Suppose our purpose is (b) in the last list: to predict the effect of building a new road. In this case, the only things directly under the model builder's control are the characteristics of the transport network and we are considering one possible change in these characteristics—building a new road. We obviously have to be interested in trips, in the people making the trips and in the vehicles being used. If there are several transport modes, we have to consider them all because of the possibility of mode-switching. We have to consider the origins of trips and their destinations.

The next question is about *aggregation* and takes the discussion on variable definition a step further. There are two main aggregation questions: sectoral aggregation and spatial aggregation. 'Sectors' are commonly used, for example, in relation to economies: how many sectors do we have to distinguish to get a good understanding, and possibly to form the basis of a model? If we continue the discussion of the previous paragraph, we need to know about people making trips and, by implication, which types of people. How many types do we have to distinguish to get a good understanding? Suppose, for example, people have fairly constant trip-making behaviour within income groups: how many income groups do we need? (In another model where income is important, it may be appropriate to introduce income directly as a variable.) The spatial aggregation problem is best illustrated by recalling the concepts of origins and destinations in the earlier discussion. People usually make trips from one address (that is, a rather precisely defined spatial location) to another and to retain maximum information we should record trip origins and destinations by these addresses. However, this creates problems both computationally and statistically, as we shall see in Chapter 9, and trip origins and destinations have to be grouped into zones. The aggregation question then is: how large should zones be, and what criteria should be used to define them? This question is closely connected to question (8) in our list, as quite often data are only available for some administratively determined zone system and if the data are vital this may force the answer to the aggregation question.

We then asked how *time* should be treated. This is partly a planning question ((1) above), how far ahead are we trying to look (i.e. what is our time horizon?) and partly a model design question: to what extent is behaviour in the system being modelled such that it should be explicitly dynamic with time appearing as a variable, or can comparative static equilibrium techniques be used? The first question has been partly tackled under (1) above and we cannot really take the discussion any further until Part IV. The second question itself raises the question of technique: it is often preferable to develop a fully dynamic model, but very much more difficult in terms of technique.

The next question, what *theories* are we trying to represent in the model? is perhaps the most important of all. As the present concern with quantification has developed, there has been a disturbing trend in some quarters suggesting that assembling quantitative *data* in some kind of information system, and perhaps carrying out elementary statistical analysis on these data, is sufficient. This may occasionally give useful insights, but if we are to develop a predictive capability it must be based on theories about system behaviour, formally represented in models, and our degree of belief in our predictions will depend upon our degree of belief in our theories. However, it is much easier to deliver a homily than to produce the theories! It will suffice to note at this point that many disciplines contribute to theory building in urban and regional studies and that the model builder should be capable of utilizing this literature when appropriate.

The discussion on *techniques* is postponed until the next chapter, when an attempt will be made to explain the mathematical basis of much urban and regional model building. The main aim will be to demonstrate that the reader can get a long way with elementary mathematical techniques, though of course more advanced techniques are needed from time to time, and perhaps increasingly so as skills develop.

The question about data connects closely to those questions which define variables. Since a model will predict a number of (endogenous) variables given other (exogenous) variables, if the model is to be fully tested data should exist to match each variable. This restriction can be weakened slightly, as we shall see in later discussion.

Model *calibration* and model *testing* are closely connected: calibration involves estimating any parameters of the model in such a way as to get the best fit between model prediction and the data representing the real world; testing involves deciding whether such fits are good ones. The two are closely related because it is common to calibrate by maximizing appropriate indicators of goodness-of-fit. The theory of goodness-of-fit statistics is rather obscure: it is complicated by the fact that the data representing the real-world state itself have associated errors. It is only for linear models that the theory of error and goodness-of-fit is anything like satisfactory. However, this question forms the subject matter of Chapter 12 and further discussion will be postponed until then.

4.2. EXAMPLE: A MODEL OF RETAIL SALES

The discussion so far probably seems rather abstract, especially to the reader who has had little contact with urban and regional models. It is, however, appropriate in relation to the overall structure of the book to continue with rather abstract discussions on model building techniques. However, to fix ideas on Section 4.1 and to ensure that the reader has seen a real model against which he can match the more abstract ideas, this seems to be an appropriate point at which to present an example. We will work, more or less, through the list of questions given at the beginning of Section 4.1.

Suppose our problem is this: in some large city-region, it is intended to build a large new shopping centre: which is the 'best' of the possible sites? Our first job is to identify the quantified variables we should like to see represented in the model. One of the arts of good model building is to do this well, though, since it is an art, it is not usually possible to be entirely systematic about how best to do so. For example, we are obviously mainly interested in total *sales* in the shopping centre in each possible site. This means that we are interested in the *market area* of the shopping centre. Now, each of these concepts gives us a possible variable and much work on the problem in hand has been based directly on such concepts—parts of central place theory, for example, which incorporate concepts of non-overlapping market areas; some formulation of the theory of consumer behaviour in economics also leads to the notion of non-overlapping market areas. In fact, once one focuses on market areas as such, it is difficult to find analytical tools to deal with *overlapping* market areas which casual observation suggests are evident in the real world. The trick in this case is to define the main variable differently: it is achieved by looking directly at what we should be interested in given that our main requirement is to predict sales. We want to look at the *flow of cash* from its origin (usually residences and let us assume only residences for this example) to its destination (a shopping centre). Even if our main interest is in a single shopping centre, we shall have to consider all homes and all shopping centres, since we need to assess the effect of competition of other shopping centres on the one we are interested in. Thus, it is clear that we shall have to have one variable which represents the distribution of population as a source of the cash flow, and another to characterize the 'attractiveness' of each shopping centre as a potential sink. It is also likely that the 'distance' between homes and shopping centres will be important. So, to summarize, our main variables seem likely to be concerned with:

(1) Flow of cash from homes to shopping centres.
(2) Population distribution.
(3) Shopping centre 'attractiveness'.
(4) Home-shopping centre 'distance'.

Which of these variables are under the planner's control? The planner has partial control over all the variables in this case, but let us assume that, for the problem as we have posed it, his only real instrument of control is the determination of the *site* of the shopping centre and possibly its size.

We are now in a position to consider the aggregation questions. Our main variable is flow of cash and since this is cash to buy goods, the first question is: should we disaggregate by types of goods and if so, how many types should we have? The answer to the first part of this question is clearly yes: we know from our individual experiences that our behaviour when buying groceries is different from when we are buying furniture. However, *for the purpose of his illustration*, let us assume we can deal with all goods as a single bundle. This is not too bad an approximation if we are only interested in total sales in *large* shopping centres.

Now let us consider our 'people' variable. Since we are interested in cash and expenditure on consumer goods, the natural assumption is that we should somehow incorporate different income groups into our 'people' variable. We shall soon see how to do this.

A more difficult task is the definition of the 'attractiveness' of a shopping centre; a concept which is intended to measure the rate at which shoppers visit one centre rather than another, other things being equal. We find that it is a reasonable approximation to assume that attractiveness is proportional to some indicator of size. Again, casual observation suggests that this is so and there are also economic arguments in terms of scale economies.

The 'distance' variable is also tricky. Straight-line distance between home and shopping centre, or even road distance, is not good enough: it is necessary to take account of modes of travel available and congestion and time costs as well as various money costs of travel. This is a kind of sector disaggregation and we shall see that there is a way of achieving this.

Only one thing now stands between us and the full definition of variables: the question of spatial aggregation. For the reasons mentioned in Section 4.1, we cannot deal with individual homes and so we aggregate to *zones*. In principle, we could have different sets of zones for households and shopping centres. This could be necessary, as it is obviously appropriate to group households into aggregates of similar incomes and to define zones which do not contain more than a single major shopping centre (as we will be predicting flows of cash to *zones* and hence implicitly to shopping centres). However, let us assume that we can define a single zone system to meet both criteria. Consider the zone system shown in Figure 4.1(a) below. The next task is to give the zones names. It would be possible to give them geographical or administrative names, as illustrated for a couple of zones in Figure 4.1(b). However, for a large number of zones this is clumsy. If there are 100 zones, it is simpler to number them consecutively from 1 to 100 as shown in Figure 4.1(c). The next step in developing a good notation is to be able to talk about *any* zone easily, instead of particular zones by number only. This is done by using letters, and talking about *any zone* i, *or any zone* j, *or a flow from any zone* i *to any zone* j. This is shown in Figure 4.1(d).

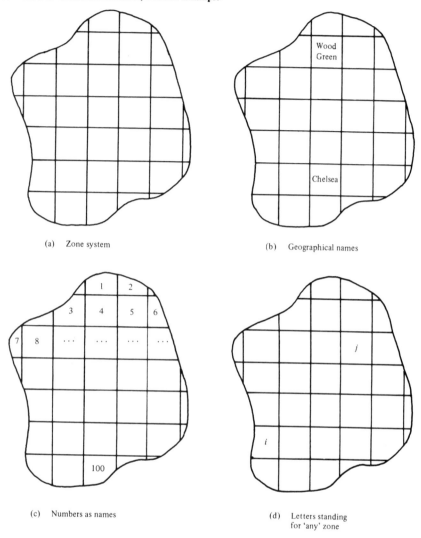

(a)   Zone system

(b)   Geographical names

(c)   Numbers as names

(d)   Letters standing
       for 'any' zone

Figure 4.1   Zone systems and names for zones

It seems that we have progressed through a simple sequence of steps, from names to numbers, and to letters which stand for *any* number, but it is worth emphasizing the increase in convenience and economy of description. If we had numbers only and there were 100 zones and if we were interested in flows, then we would have to list 100 × 100 (equals 10,000) pairs of numbers, but by using letters we can simply discuss the flow from zone i to zone j and set i and j equal to particular numbers only when necessary.

Taking account of the previous discussion, we can now define our variables
in relation to the zone system just defined. Let i be any residential zone and
j any shopping centre zone. Then we could write $S_{i \to j}$ to represent the flow
of money from zone i to zone j: that is, the sales in j to residents of i, measured
in money units. However, it is inconvenient to write the arrow all the time, so
we will use the symbol S_{ij}. Let P_i be the population of zone i, and we can
introduce the income effect by introducing a variable e_i as the average
expenditure per resident of zone i on shopping goods. Hence, the product
$e_i P_i$ is the total amount of money spent on shopping goods by residents of i.
Let W_j be the size of the shopping centre in zone j (say measured in square
footage) and recall that we shall use this as a proxy for attractiveness. Finally,
we need a variable for the 'distance' between zone i and zone j. It is convenient
to introduce the concept of 'generalized cost' which will incorporate the
several components of distance mentioned in the earlier discussion. Assume,
for simplicity, that we need only consider one mode of transport (or that all
modes have similar cost characteristics). Assume further that the main components of generalized cost are travel time (the variation of which will allow
for congestion effects) and out-of-pocket money costs. Let the zone i to zone j
travel time be t_{ij} and the out-of-pocket money cost be m_{ij}. Then, we can
define the generalized cost to be c_{ij}, where

$$c_{ij} = at_{ij} + m_{ij} \tag{4.1}$$

where a is a constant which values time in money units. Thus, in summary:
S_{ij} = sales in shops in zone j to residents of zone i;
P_i = population of zone i;
e_i = mean expenditure on shopping per person in zone i.
So:
$e_i P_i$ = money spent on shopping goods by residents of i;)
W_j = 'size' of shopping centre in j, measured in square feet;
c_{ij} = generalized cost of travel from zone i to zone j.
Including components
t_{ij} = travel time from zone i to zone j;
m_{ij} = money cost of travel from zone i to zone j.)
These variables are shown in relation to the zone system in Figure 4.2.

We now have to consider the questions of time and theory. Let us assume,
again for simplicity in this illustration, that we are primarily interested in the
immediate impact of a new shopping centre, that this is all we are trying to
predict and we are not trying to make any other forecasts through time. We
can now begin to consider questions of theory. What kinds of assumptions
do we want to build into our model? Our main task is to predict sales, using
the variable S_{ij}, in terms of the other variables we have defined, which we
assume to be given. Three assumptions seem sensible:

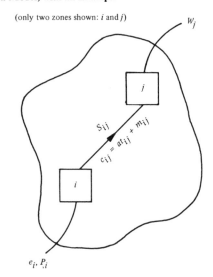

(only two zones shown: i and j)

Figure 4.2   Variables, in relation to
the zone system

(1) The flow of cash from i to j is proportional to the total amount of cash available for shopping expenditure in zone i.

(2) The flow of cash from i to j is proportional to the attractiveness of the shopping centre in zone j.

(3) The flow of cash from i to j decreases in relation to increasing travel cost from zone i to zone j; that is, the flow is proportional to something like the *inverse* of travel cost.

The mathematical sign which represents the relationship 'is proportional to' is $\propto$, so these assumptions can be written in a mathematical notation as follows:

$$(1) \ S_{ij} \propto e_i P_i \tag{4.2}$$

$$(2) \ S_{ij} \propto W_j \tag{4.3}$$

$$(3) \ S_{ij} \propto 1/c_{ij} \tag{4.4}$$

and once again, the economy of the mathematical notation can be appreciated. Now, if

$$X \propto Y$$

then

$$X = KY$$

where K is a constant of proportionality. So, on the basis of relations (4.2)–4.4), we can write

$$S_{ij} = \frac{K(e_i P_i) W_j}{c_{ij}} \qquad (4.5)$$

where K is a constant of proportionality. Equation (4.5) now represents a very simple model; it predicts S_{ij} in terms of the other variables and one parameter, the constant of proportionality K. It is the simplest example of a *gravity model*.

In physics, if there are two bodies with masses m_1 and m_2 and the distance between them is d_{12}, then there is an *interaction* between them, which is the gravitational force, F_{ij} say. Then Newton's law of gravity is

$$F_{ij} = \frac{K^m{}_1 m_2}{d_{12}^2} \qquad (4.6)$$

where K is a constant. The similarity between equations (4.5) and (4.6) is evident: we can interpret S_{ij} as a spatial interaction, $(e_i P_i)$ and W_j as the masses, and c_{ij} as the distance. Note that in equation (4.6), the distance is squared—the famous inverse squared law. Obviously the nature of the relationship depends on the particular circumstances, and this suggests that we should raise c_{ij} in equation (4.5) to some power, say n, and amend the equation to

$$S_{ij} = \frac{K(e_i P_i) W_j}{c_{ij}^n} \qquad (4.7)$$

We can also use a similar argument in relation to our attractiveness index, W_j: we raise it to a power α so that we can later investigate empirically the exact form of relationship. Thus, the model is further modified to

$$S_{ij} = \frac{K(e_i P_i) W_j^\alpha}{c_{ij}^n} \qquad (4.8)$$

This model is similar to Reilly's law of retail gravitation which was propounded as long ago as 1931. (See Reilly, 1931). The history of the model will be presented in greater detail in Chapter 10.

Note that we have implicitly answered the 'techniques' question by building a simple algebraic model. We would now like to have real-world data corresponding to each of the variables we have defined, so that we can set about calibrating and testing the model. This means finding values of the parameters K, n and α to obtain a best fit between S_{ij} as predicted by the model and the 'real-world S_{ij}', which we might write S_{ij}(observed) or S_{ij}(obs). We shall consider ways of doing this when we have further elaborated the model.

So far, we have not taken the step of calculating the total sales predicted by the model in each shopping centre. This is done by adding, for each zone

j, all the flows from each zone i. This sum, exhibited diagrammatically i Figure 4.3, is

$$S_{1j} + S_{2j} + S_{3j} + \ldots + S_{Nj}$$

where N is the total number of zones. We adopt a special notation for suc a sum: it can be written as

$$\sum_{i=1}^{N} S_{ij}$$

where $\sum$ is a summation sign and, in this case, implies summation over th subscript i for all values from i equals 1 up to N. It is also convenient t

(Illustrative flows only—one flow *from* each zone)

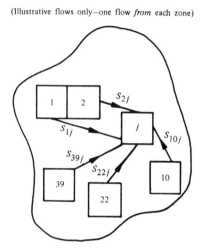

Figure 4.3 Flows to the shopping
centre in zone j

introduce the notation that if a subscript or other index is replaced by a asterisk, summation is implied. Clearly, this notation can only be used if th range of summation is obvious, as it is in this case over all zones. Thus,

$$S_{*j} = \sum_{i=1}^{N} S_{ij} = S_{1j} + S_{2j} + S_{3j} + \ldots + S_{Nj} \tag{4.9}$$

and we can refer to S_{*j} as the total sales in the shopping centre in j rather thar introducing a distinct variable.

This is an appropriate point to note that, with a doubly subscripted vari able, we may sometimes have a double summation S_{*j} could be summed over j, and

$$\sum_{j=1}^{N} S_{*j} = \sum_{j=1}^{N} \sum_{i=1}^{N} S_{ij} = S_{**}$$

We can also carry out the summation on the other subscript and form the sum

$$S_{i1} + S_{i2} + S_{i3} + \ldots + S_{iN}$$

shown diagrammatically in Figure 4.4. Using the notation introduced earlier, this sum can be written

$$S_{i*} = \sum_{j=1}^{N} S_{ij} = S_{i1} + S_{i2} + S_{i3} + \ldots + S_{iN} \qquad (4.10)$$

We interpreted S_{*j} as the total sales in the shopping centre in j; how do we interpret S_{i*}? A little thought, and an examination of Figure 4.4 and equation

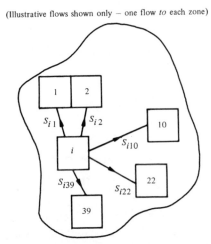

(Illustrative flows shown only – one flow *to* each zone)

Figure 4.4   Flows from residential zone i

(4.10), shows that S_{i*} is the total flow of cash out of residential zone i. We have already hypothesized that this sum is $e_i P_i$, so we can write

$$S_{i*} = \sum_{i=1}^{N} S_{ij} = e_i P_i \qquad (4.11)$$

Thus S_{i*} is of a different character to S_{*j}. The latter is a prediction of the model; the former is equal to a quantity which we have postulated. This enables us to develop the model a stage further.

Let us, for convenience, write the Reilly-type equation (4.8) in the form

$$S_{ij} = K(e_i P_i) W_j^{\alpha} c_{ij}^{-n} \qquad (4.12)$$

using the form c_{ij}^{-n} instead of $1/c_{ij}^{n}$. We can form the sum S_{i*} as follows, using equation (4.12):

$$S_{i*} = \sum_{j=1}^{N} S_{ij} = \sum_{j=1}^{N} K(e_i P_i) W_j^{\alpha} c_{ij}^{-n}$$

So,

$$S_{i*} = K(e_i P_i) \sum_{j=1}^{N} W_j^{\alpha} c_{ij}^{-n} \qquad (4.13)$$

since any term not dependent on j can be taken outside the summation sign as a factor. To see this, consider

$$\sum_{i=1}^{N} ax_i = ax_i + ax_2 + \ldots + ax_N$$

$$= a(x_1 + x_2 + \ldots + x_N)$$

$$= a \sum_{i=1}^{N} x_i$$

However, we know from equation (4.11) that $S_{i*} = e_i P_i$, so we obtain from this relationship and equation (4.13)

$$K(e_i P_i) \sum_{j=1}^{N} W_j^{\alpha} c_{ij}^{-n} = e_i P_i \qquad (4.14)$$

$e_i P_i$ cancels from either side of the equation and with some rearrangement, we get

$$K = 1 \Big/ \sum_{j=1}^{N} W_j^{\alpha} c_{ij}^{-n} \qquad (4.15)$$

We now see that we have unearthed an inconsistency in the Reilly model relative to one of our assumptions: the right-hand side of equation (4.15) is dependent on i, and so it is impossible to solve equation (4.15) for K, as there are N (one for each i) possible values of the right-hand side. We shall see later in the book just how this sort of inconsistency should be handled. (Chapter 6 and Appendix 1.) For the present, assume we can replace the constant of proportionality K by a set of constants, K_i, dependent on i. Then equation (4.12) can be written

$$S_{ij} = K_i(e_i P_i) W_j^{\alpha} c_{ij}^{-n} \qquad (4.16)$$

and the argument can be repeated from equation (4.13) through to equation (4.15) with K_i replacing K, and then equation (4.15) gives for K_i

$$K_i = 1 \Big/ \sum_{j=1}^{N} W_j^{\alpha} c_{ij}^{-n} \qquad (4.17)$$

and we now have a free index i on each side of the equation. (An index is 'free' if there is no summation over it. Conversely, an index which is summed over is known as a 'dummy' index, because it can be replaced without changing the meaning of the expression within which it occurs, e.g. $\sum_{i=1}^{N} x_i = \sum_{k=1}^{N} x_k$.)

Thus equations (4.16) and (4.17) give a revised model which is consistent with our initial assumption represented by equation (4.11). We can consolidate the two equations of the model by substituting for K_i from equation (4.17) into (4.16) to give

$$S_{ij} = (e_i P_i) \frac{W_j^\alpha c_{ij}^{-n}}{\sum_{j=1}^N W_j^\alpha c_{ij}^{-n}} \tag{4.18}$$

and this will help in interpretation later. This form of model is known as the Lakshmanan–Hansen model or the Huff model [Lakshmanan and Hansen (1965), Huff (1964)]. Since this model *is* internally consistent in a way in which the Reilly model is not, we will work with it for the rest of this chapter. Later, in Chapter 6, a full discussion of the whole family of spatial interaction models will be presented.

We can now start to interpret the model and to explain how it works and what it does. Firstly, let us concentrate on the prediction for a particular shopping centre designated as J. Equation (4.18) can be written for this shopping centre as

$$S_{iJ} = (e_i P_i) \frac{W_J^\alpha c_{iJ}^{-n}}{\sum_{j=1}^N W_j^\alpha c_{ij}^{-n}} \tag{4.19}$$

and there is one such equation for each residential zone i. For this shopping centre, the flows predicted by the model could be plotted as we have already illustrated for a general zone j in Figure 4.3. (So, set $j = J$ in Figure 4.3).

Note that, according to the model, there will *be* a flow from each residential zone, though that flow could be very small (and effectively zero) if any of the following conditions held:

(1) $e_i P_i$ was very small;
(2) W_J was very small;
or (3) c_{iJ} was very large (and hence c_{iJ}^{-n} was very small).

Thus, although the whole study area contributes to sales in J, in practice a large proportion of the sales may well come from a relatively small number of residential zones. We can go on to define the *market area* of J, though there are many ways in which this could be done. Consider some alternatives:

i is in the market area of J if

(1) $S_{iJ} > A$, where A is some constant;
(2) $S_{iJ}/S_{i*} > B$, where B is a constant;
(3) Either of (1) and (2) above, *or* there exists a zone i' such that i' is in the market area of J and $c_{iJ} < c_{i'J}$.

The first condition is based on the absolute magnitude of the flow; the second condition uses the relative proportion of money leaving i and going to J. Either of these could reasonably be chosen, but it leaves the possibility of 'holes' in the market area, so if this is considered undesirable, then either of (1) and (2) should be chosen in conjunction with (3). Note, however, that all this simply helps to interpret the model in terms of a more traditional concept—but we have no need to define the concept of market area to use the model. Note, however, that market areas defined in this way can *overlap*.

It can easily be seen how the variable S_{ij} varies with $(e_i P_i)$, W_j and c_{ij}^{-n}, at least in terms of the principal effects, for they are recognized in our original hypotheses (the relations (4.2)–(4.4)). However, we cannot see as easily how the term K_i in equation (4.16), that is the denominator $\sum_{j=1}^{N} W_j^\alpha c_{ij}^{-n}$ in equation (4.18), affects the prediction. In looking at equation (4.19) and thinking specifically about J, the interesting thing is that the term $W_J^\alpha c_{iJ}^{-n}$ in the numerator is of the same form as the term which is summed in the denominator.

We can take this discussion a stage further by fixing on a particular residential zone, designated I. The flows from the zone can be plotted, as in Figure 4.4, with $i = I$. The term $W_J^\alpha c_{IJ}^{-n}$ can be considered to measure the joint attractiveness (because of W_J^α)/accessibility (because of C_{IJ}^{-n}) of the shopping centre in J *as perceived from I*. If this is summed over all zones j, we can define

$$X_I = \sum_{j=1}^{N} W_J^\alpha c_{Ij}^{-n} \tag{4.20}$$

to be the total attractiveness/accessibility, or *accessibility* for short, offered to residents of I. So, we can now see that S_{IJ} will be large, relatively, if $W_J^\alpha c_{IJ}^{-n}$ is large *relative* to the sum $\sum_{j=1}^{N} W_j^\alpha c_{Ij}^{-n}$.

Now, returning to the original discussion about the significance of the denominator for the shopping centre at J, we can see that this term represents the *competition* of other shopping centres: J will get a high proportion of the total amount of money leaving i if $W_J^\alpha c_{ij}^{-n}$ is large relative to the sum $\sum_{j=1}^{N} W_j^\alpha c_{ij}^{-n}$.

Thus, in summary, we have now introduced three concepts which help us to interpret the model: market area, accessibility and competition; and we note that the term $\sum_{j=1}^{N} W_j^{-\alpha} c_{ij}^{-n}$, which plays a significant role in the model, has a dual interpretation: as *accessibility* from the viewpoint of residents of i, and as *competition* from the viewpoint of a particular shopping centre J, as it has to be compared to $W_J^\alpha c_{ij}^{-n}$. Next, we consider the problem of calibrating the model, and this also takes us a stage further in our interpretation of the model, since it forces us to understand the role of the parameters of the model. As formulated in equation (4.18), the model has two parameters, n and α. A little thought shows the role of these parameters. As n increases, c_{ij}^{-n} will *decrease* increasingly rapidly as c_{ij} increases. Thus, other things being equal, larger values of n imply shorter mean trip lengths. For larger values of α, W_j^α increases more rapidly as W_j increases. Recall that W_j is size, and W_j^α is our index of attractiveness thus, the greater α, the greater are the scale economies for the shopper, associated with size. If we take S_{ij} as the prediction of the model, and $S_{ij}(\text{obs})$ as observed values from some survey, then we need a measure of correspondence between the two sets of quantities. The simplest such measure is the so-called sum of squares:

$$S = (S_{11} - S_{11}(\text{obs}))^2 + (S_{12} - S_{12}(\text{obs}))^2 + \ldots + \ldots + (S_{NN} - S_{NN}(\text{obs}))^2$$

and this can be written with a *double* summation sign as

$$S = \sum_{i=1}^{N} \sum_{j=1}^{N} (S_{ij} - S_{ij}(\text{obs}))^2 \qquad (4.21)$$

For an exact correspondence, it is easy to see that S is zero, and that it increases steadily as the correspondence gets worse.

The simplest calibration procedure is to run the model for a range of values of n and α, and to calculate S for each pair of values. The values of S can be recorded at points of a grid, as shown in Figure 4.5. The n and α values

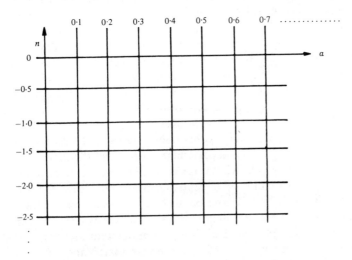

Figure 4.5 A grid of possible parameter values

which give the minimum value of S are then our best estimates of the parameters and they are used henceforth in any runs of the model for planning purposes. However, only if S is 'reasonably small' can we accept the best fit as a good fit. This all begs many questions, but they will be postponed until Chapter 12 so as not to complicate this simple presentation.

Suppose, for the sake of illustration, that $n = 2\cdot5$, $\alpha = 0\cdot75$ give the best fit. We now have the model

$$S_{ij} = (e_i P_i) \frac{W_j^{0\cdot75} c_{ij}^{-2\cdot5}}{\sum_{j=1}^{N} W_j^{0\cdot75} c_{ij}^{-2\cdot5}} \qquad (4.22)$$

How do we use this model? Let us return to the original problem: we have three possible sites for a major shopping centre development, how do we choose the 'best' one? Suppose the possible sites are J_1, J_2 and J_3 and we call the development of each plan 1, 2 and 3; e_i, P_i and c_{ij} are taken as fixed as are all the W_js (say size in square feet of shopping centre) except for a change from, say, W_{J_1} to V from plan 1, W_{J_2} to V for plan 2 and W_{J_3} to V for plan 3, where V is the planned square footage of the new centre. We can then run the model for each plan, and obtain a set of cash flows $S_{ij}(1)$ say, $S_{ij}(2)$ and $S_{ij}(3)$, in turn.

Suppose we are interested only in the effect on the shopping centre being planned. Then we can calculate the total sales in the new centre:

$$S_{*J_1} = \sum_{i=1}^{N} S_{iJ_1}(1) \tag{4.23}$$

for plan 1, and similarly S_{*J_2} and S_{*J_3}. We could then simply choose the site for which S_{*J}/V, the sales per square foot, was a maximum. This is obviously valuable information for the developer. However, it allows the developer and/or planner to go further: they may have a minimum sales per square foot criterion, and if S_{*J}/V is less than this figure, they can decrease V and run the model again. Or if S_{*J}/V is particularly high, they may feel that they have *underestimated* V and correspondingly increase it. So, the developer and/or the planner can run the model on a trial and error basis until they get the best site and the 'optimum' square footage.

There are, of course, many other considerations, at least for the planner if not for the developer of the particular centre, and the model can also help with these. For example, what is the effect of the new centre on other centres? S_{*j} can be calculated for other centres j, and the decrease (for there will be a decrease in most if not all cases because of the loss of trade to the new centre) can be taken into account in any overall plan. Or, what is the impact on the level of accessibility offered to shoppers in different locations? The accessibility term, X_i in equation (4.20), can be calculated and any changes taken into account.

The discussion of this example of a model may seem too lengthy and discursive from some points of view and too condensed, omitting many important points of detail, from others. The point to note at this stage, especially for readers to whom this is completely new, is that a reasonably realistic and useful model can be presented using only concepts of elementary algebra from the mathematical point of view. Note, however, that by using subscripts and a general notation, which may seem rather frightening at first, a tremendous economy has been achieved. We can talk of S_{ij}, for example, almost as though it were a single variable; but if there are 100 zones in our study area ($N = 100$), then there are 100×100 possible S_{ij}s. In writing down one equation, say (4.18), in S_{ij}, we are actually writing down 10,000 equations.

Thus, this kind of model is conceptually straightforward, but clearly involves large computational problems which can usually be handled with an electronic computer.

4.3. REFERENCES

B. Harris (1965) Urban development models: new tools for planners, *Journal of the American Institute of Planners*, **31**, pp. 90–95.

D. L. Huff (1964) Defining and estimating a trading area, *Journal of Marketing*, **28**, pp. 34–38; reprinted in P. Ambrose (Ed.) (1970) *Analytical human geography*, Longman, London, pp. 161–71.

T. R. Lakshmanan and W. G. Hansen (1965) A retail market potential model, *Journal of the American Institute of Planners*, **31**, pp. 134–43.

I. S. Lowry (1965) A short course in model design, *Journal of the American Institute of Planners*, **31**, pp. 158–66.

W. J. Reilly (1931) *The law of retail gravitation*, G. P. Putman and Sons, New York.

W. Steger (1965) A review of analytical techniques for the C.R.P., *Journal of the American Institute of Planners*, **31**, pp. 166–72.

A. G. Wilson (1968) Models in urban planning: a synoptic review of recent literature, *Urban Studies*, **5**, pp. 249–76; reprinted in A. G. Wilson (1972) *Papers in urban and regional analysis*, Pion, London, pp. 3–30.

CHAPTER 5

Mathematical prerequisites

5.1. INTRODUCTION

This book could be considered to belong in part to an applied mathematics' field, and the reader from such a field should have no difficulty in understanding it from a mathematical point of view; in part, it also belongs to social science and professional fields such as geography, economics and planning. In the latter field, there will be readers whose mathematical knowledge is poor and inadequate for the book, but who very much need to assimilate the material. This chapter is aimed at those readers. It aims only to sketch out a syllabus, not to teach the appropriate mathematical background. And it also aims to reassure, since the most essential mathematical prerequisties for the bulk of the book are not at all demanding: they amount to little more than can be acquired by 'brushing up' what is already known from an earlier school mathematical education.

Most of the book can be read by anyone with an elementary knowledge of *algebra* and some notion of what a *function* is. Most chapters call for this sort of knowledge, and for the ability to put up with what may occasionally appear at first sight to be a complicated notation. The next most important topic is elementary *matrix algebra*, which plays a significant role in Chapters 7 and 8 and a minor role in Chapter 11. Some knowledge of *calculus* is required, but the reader with no previous knowledge of this subject should be able to get by with the notion that the calculus provides a procedure for finding the maximum or minimum value of some function and so on. At a similar level, some knowledge is required of various *algorithms*; shortest path through a network, linear programming and search algorithms, but the book is largely self-contained in this respect. The prerequisite knowledge in the fields mentioned above is outlined in Sections 5.2–5.5 below; in 5.6 we mention statistics, in 5.7 some useful 'black boxes' and in 5.8 computing.

In this Introduction we have emphasized the minimum mathematical prerequisite for effectively reading the book, and the fact that most people should be able to get by with their memories of school mathematics. It should also be emphasized, however, that for effective ongoing research in this field, a much deeper mathematical background is desirable, and that effort spent in this direction is likely to be well worthwhile. There are many standard textbooks available as reference works for the first kind of reader and as first textbooks for the second. They include those by Allen (1938), Morley (1972),

48

)'Brien and Garcia (1971), Parry Lewis (1959, 2nd Edition, 1970) and
Yamane (1962), but the reader should be prepared to search his library and
bookshop shelves until he finds books best suited to his own style and
purposes.

5.2. ALGEBRA AND FUNCTIONS

Elementary algebra is conducted with variables, $x, y, z, \ldots$, which represent
measured quantities. They are related through equations:

$$x = a + b \tag{5.1}$$

If our prime interest is in a variable x which is not given explicitly as in
equation (5.1), then we can 'solve' the equation for x. For example, if

$$a = b - 2x \tag{5.2}$$

we can solve to obtain

$$x = \frac{b - a}{2} \tag{5.3}$$

When large numbers of variables are involved, it is more convenient to
distinguish them with subscripts and superscripts rather than different letters,
as $x_1, x_2, x_3, \ldots$, for example, which we can write as $x_i, i = 1, 2, 3, \ldots$. This
also allows us to develop a convenient notation for summation and products:

$$\sum_{i=1}^{n} x_i = x_1 + x_2 + \ldots + x_n \tag{5.4}$$

or

$$\prod_{i=1}^{n} x_i = x_1 x_2 \ldots x_n \tag{5.5}$$

We can have double subscripts, $x_{ij}, i = 1, 2 \ldots, j = 1, 2, \ldots$, and double
summations:

$$\sum_{i=1}^{m} \sum_{j=1}^{n} x_{ij} = \sum_i (x_{i1} + x_{i2} + \ldots + x_{in}) \tag{5.6}$$

$$= x_{11} + x_{21} + \ldots + x_{12} + x_{22} + \ldots + x_{13} + x_{23} + \ldots$$
$$\vdots$$
$$+ x_{12} + \ldots + x_{mn} \tag{5.7}$$

Most of the elementary algebra used in this book is of this form, and the
reader has already had examples in Chapter 4.

We have already referred to variables as being related by an equation these can be called functional relationships. A *function* is then some specific kind of relationship between two variables. The function 'squaring' relates variables x and y by

$$y = x^2 \qquad (5.8)$$

for example. In this relationship, y is known as the dependent variable and x as the independent variable. More generally, we have the power function

$$y = x^n \qquad (5.9)$$

for any value of the constant or 'parameter' n. Functions can be plotted graphically on a Cartesian coordinate system, as in Figure 5.1. For each

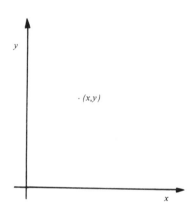

Figure 5.1   A Cartesian coordinate
system

permitted value of x, the corresponding value of y is calculated, and the 'point (x, y)' is plotted as shown. Plots of $y = x$ and $y = x^2$ are shown on Figure 5.2. This is a convenient way of obtaining a visual picture of the form of any function. Often, we do not want to specify a particular function, but only to say that y is 'some function of x', and this can be written

$$y = f(x) \qquad (5.10)$$

A large range of functions exists and the reader should familiarize himself with these as they arise. Of particular importance at the outset are the power functions of equation (5.9), the exponential functions

$$y = e^{\beta x} \qquad (5.11)$$

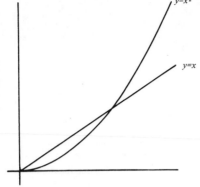

N.B. Plots in this and following figures are rough sketches to indicate 'shape' only.

Figure 5.2 $y = x, y = x^2$

for a range of values of β, and the log function, usually to base e

$$y = \log_e x \qquad (5.12)$$

Plots of these are shown in Figures 5.3–5.5.

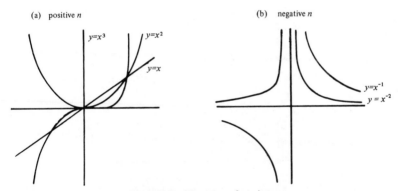

Figure 5.3   The power function

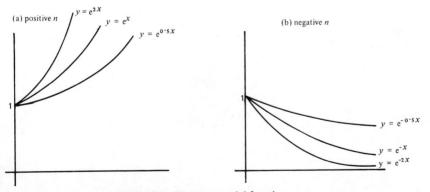

Figure 5.4   The exponential function

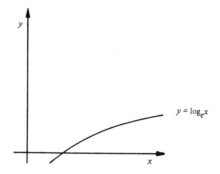

Figure 5.5 The log function

The notion of plotting functions graphically in a Cartesian coordinate system also gives the reader the basis of coordinate geometry, and the basis of the definition of the trigonometric functions which are used occasionally In Figure 5.6,

$$a = \sqrt{x^2 + y^2} \tag{5.13}$$

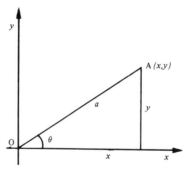

Figure 5.6 Basis for definition of trigonometric functions

from Pythagoras' theorem, and the definitions of the main trigonometric functions are

$$\sin \theta = \frac{y}{a} \tag{5.14}$$

$$\cos \theta = \frac{x}{a} \tag{5.15}$$

$$\tan \theta = \frac{y}{x} \tag{5.16}$$

tan θ is probably the most familiar as the gradient of the line OA on Figure 5.6.

A dependent variable y may be a function of several independent variables $x_1, x_2, \ldots x_n$. A simple example would be

$$y = x_1 + x_2 + \ldots + x_n \tag{5.17}$$

and in general we could write

$$y = f(x_1, x_2, \ldots x_n) \tag{5.18}$$

A great variety of functions can be built up by combining standard functions using the basic operation of addition, subtraction, multiplication or division for both single or multi-variable functions.

5.3. MATRICES

Only the barest bones are presented below. A specialist textbook for social scientists in this field is that by Mills (1968).

An $m \times n$ matrix is a set of doubly subscripted variables, $a_{ij}, i = 1, 2 \ldots m$, $j = 1, 2, \ldots n$ arranged as follows:

$$\mathbf{a} = \begin{bmatrix} a_{11} & a_{12} & \cdots & a_{1n} \\ a_{21} & a_{22} & \cdots & a_{2n} \\ \vdots & & & \\ a_{m1} & a_{m2} & \cdots & a_{mn} \end{bmatrix} \tag{5.19}$$

$\mathbf{a}$ is the name of the array. We can develop algebra of matrices, defining operations of addition, multiplication and division for the matrices themselves; a_{ij} is known as the (i, j)th element of $\mathbf{a}$—indeed the matrix is sometimes written $\{a_{ij}\}$. Matrix operations are defined by giving formulae for the (i, j)th element of the matrix $\mathbf{c}$ where

$$\mathbf{c} = \mathbf{a} + \mathbf{b} \tag{5.20}$$

$$\mathbf{c} = \mathbf{a} - \mathbf{b} \tag{5.21}$$

$$\mathbf{c} = k\mathbf{a} \tag{5.22}$$

$$\mathbf{c} = \mathbf{ab} \tag{5.23}$$

We deal with division later. In equations (5.20) and (5.21) all the matrices must be of the same size. In (5.22) the matrices are of the same size and k is a number, a scalar quantity, and the operation is known as 'multiplication by a scalar'. In equation (5.23) if $\mathbf{a}$ is an $m \times n$ matrix, the operation is defined if $\mathbf{b}$ is an $n \times l$ matrix for any l. That is, $\mathbf{a}$ must have the same number of columns as $\mathbf{b}$ has rows. $\mathbf{c}$ is then an $m \times l$ matrix. The definitions are: for addition, equation (5.20),

$$c_{ij} = a_{ij} + b_{ij} \qquad (5.24)$$

for subtraction, equation (5.21),

$$c_{ij} = a_{ij} - b_{ij} \qquad (5.25)$$

for multiplication by a scalar, equation (5.22)

$$c_{ij} = ka_{ij} \qquad (5.26)$$

and for multiplication, (5.23),

$$c_{ij} = \sum_k a_{ik}b_{kj} \qquad (5.27)$$

For division, we have to proceed in stages as follows. We can define the unit matrix I as that which multiplies into a square matrix ($m \times m$), a, such that

$$Ia = aI = a \qquad (5.28)$$

(Note that, in general, $ab \neq ba$ in matrix algebra.) In fact,

$$I = \begin{bmatrix} 1 & 0 & 0 & \ldots & 0 \\ 0 & 1 & 0 & \ldots & 0 \\ 0 & 0 & 1 & \ldots & 0 \\ \vdots & & & & \\ 0 & 0 & 0 & \ldots & 1 \end{bmatrix} \qquad (5.29)$$

That is, I is the matrix with 1s down the diagonal and 0s elsewhere. The inverse of a number x is the number x^{-1} such that

$$xx^{-1} = x^{-1}x = 1 \qquad (5.30)$$

Similarly, under suitable conditions, we can define the inverse of a square matrix a as that matrix a^{-1} such that

$$aa^{-1} = a^{-1}a = I \qquad (5.31)$$

No procedure will be given here for the calculation of the elements of the inverse matrix as it is fairly complicated. We only need to know that, under suitable conditions, it exists. Division is then pre- or post-multiplication by a^{-1}.

In this book, matrices are most useful for obtaining a shorthand notation for such things as sets of simultaneous linear equations, and for obtaining the solution to such equations in terms of the inverse matrix. For example, the reader can check that the equations

$$a_{11}x_1 + a_{12}x_2 + \ldots + a_{1n}x_n = b_1$$
$$a_{21}x_1 + a_{22}x_2 + \ldots + a_{2n}x_n = b_2$$
$$\vdots$$
$$a_{n1}x_1 + a_{n2}x_2 + \ldots + a_{nn}x_n = b_n$$

(5.32)

can be written

$$\mathbf{ax} = \mathbf{b}$$ (5.33)

where **a** is the $n \times n$ matrix with elements a_{ij}, **x** is the $n \times 1$ matrix

$$\mathbf{x} = \begin{bmatrix} x_1 \\ x_2 \\ \vdots \\ x_n \end{bmatrix}$$ (5.34)

(which is known as a *vector*) and **b** is the $n \times 1$ matrix

$$\mathbf{b} = \begin{bmatrix} b_1 \\ b_2 \\ \vdots \\ b_n \end{bmatrix}$$ (5.35)

The *solution* of the equations can be obtained by pre-multiplying each side by $\mathbf{a}^{-1}$ and using equation (5.31), as

$$\mathbf{x} = \mathbf{a}^{-1}\mathbf{b}$$ (5.36)

5.4. CALCULUS

The two main branches of the calculus are the *differential calculus* and the *integral calculus*. Expressed in the simplest possible way, differentiation is concerned with finding the gradient of a curve at any point. In terms of Figure 5.7, this means finding the gradient of the tangent to the curve at the point $P(x, y)$.

If the relationship is

$$y = f(x)$$ (5.37)

the gradient, as calculated in the differential calculus, at (x, y), is written in various notations as dy/dx, df/dx, $df(x)/dx$, $y'(x)$, $f'(x)$, and so on.

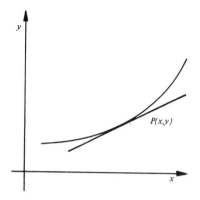

Figure 5.7   The gradient at a point on a
curve

Differentiation provides a procedure for calculating the gradient and, in most standard cases, it provides a formula. For example, if

$$y = x^n \tag{5.38}$$

$$\frac{dy}{dx} = nx^{n-1} \tag{5.39}$$

Since the derivative is itself a function of x, we can also define the second- and higher-order derivatives. These are written, for the second-order d^2y/dx^2, d^2f/dx^2, $d^2f(x)/dx^2$, $y''(x)$, y'', $f''(x)$, and for the third-order, d^3y/dx^3, and so on. For example, if we apply the result of equation (5.39) to x^{n-1} in (5.39), then we see that if y is given in equation (5.38) then

$$\frac{d^2y}{dx^2} = n(n-1)x^{n-2} \tag{5.40}$$

Integration is the reverse of differentiation. If we know the gradient of some curve at every point, then the equation of the curve itself is known as the integral. Thus if

$$y = g(x) \tag{5.41}$$

is the gradient, the equation of the curve is written

$$y = \int^x g(x')\,dx' \tag{5.42}$$

It is always arbitrary up to an additive constant. Thus, if

$$y = g(x) = nx^{n-1} \tag{5.43}$$

e know from equations (5.38) and (5.39) that

$$y = \int^x nx'^{n-1} \, dx' = x^n + C \qquad (5.44)$$

where C is an arbitrary constant of integration.

The most practical elementary use of integration is to obtain the *area under a curve* as a definite integral, as shown in Figure 5.8.

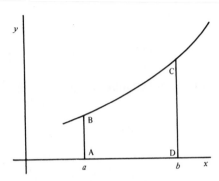

Figure 5.8   The area under a curve

$$\text{Area ABCD} = \int_a^b y \, dx = \int_a^b f(x) \, dx \qquad (5.45)$$

If

$$f(x) = nx^{n-1} \qquad (5.46)$$

then

$$\text{ABCD} = \int_a^b nx^{n-1} \, dx = [x^n]_a^b \qquad (5.47)$$

$$= b^n - a^n \qquad (5.48)$$

A specific use of the differential calculus is to find maximum and minimum values of functions. Consider Figure 5.9 for example. The function shown has a maximum at the point P. This is characterized by the gradient of the curve being zero at that point. The values of (x, y) at which this occurs can be found by solving the equation

$$\frac{dy}{dx} = 0 \qquad (5.49)$$

Whether it is a maximum, minimum or point of inflexion is determined by

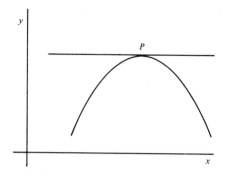

Figure 5.9 Maximum

the *second* derivative. For a maximum,

$$\frac{d^2y}{dx^2} < 0 \tag{5.50}$$

For a minimum,

$$\frac{d^2y}{dx^2} > 0 \tag{5.51}$$

while for a point of inflexion

$$\frac{d^2y}{dx^2} = 0 \tag{5.52}$$

These cases are illustrated in Figure 5.10.

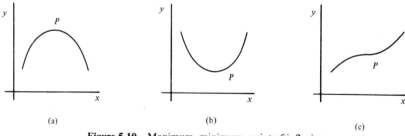

Figure 5.10 Maximum, minimum, point of inflexion

Finally, it is useful to note what happens to the concepts of differential and integral calculus if they are applied to functions of more than one variable. Suppose

$$y = f(x_1, x_2, \ldots x_n) \tag{5.53}$$

Then the derivative of y with respect to one of these variables is calculated for given values of the other variables which are supposed constant during the calculation. This is known as the *partial* derivative and is written $\partial y/\partial x_i$ or $\partial f/\partial x_i$. For example, if

$$y = x_1^2 x_2^2 \tag{5.54}$$

$$\frac{\partial y}{\partial x_1} = 2x_1 x_2^2 \tag{5.55}$$

or

$$\frac{\partial y}{\partial x_2} = 2x_1^2 x_2 \tag{5.56}$$

It can be shown that maximum or minimum of a function such as that in equation (5.53) can now be found by setting all the partial derivatives to zero:

$$\frac{\partial y}{\partial x_i} = 0, \quad i = 1, 2, \ldots n \tag{5.57}$$

and so this gives a set of simultaneous equations to solve. We can also briefly consider the case of the restricted maximum or minimum: say, maximize

$$y = f(x_1, x_2, \ldots x_n) \tag{5.58}$$

subject to

$$\left. \begin{array}{l} g_1(x_1, x_2, \ldots x_n) = b_1 \\ g_2(x_1, x_2, \ldots x_n) = b_2 \\ \quad \vdots \\ g_m(x_1, x_2, \ldots x_n) = b_m \end{array} \right\} \tag{5.59}$$

This can be done by defining Lagrangian multipliers, $\lambda_1, \lambda_2, \ldots, \lambda_m$, one for each of the equations (5.59) in turn, and maximizing

$$L = f(x_1, x_2, \ldots x_n) + \sum_{k=1}^{n} \lambda_k(g_k(x_1, \ldots x_n) - b_k) \tag{5.60}$$

as a function of $x_1, x_2, \ldots x_n$ and $\lambda_1, \lambda_2, \ldots \lambda_n$. Thus, we solve

$$\frac{\partial L}{\partial x_i} = 0, \quad i = 1, 2, \ldots n \tag{5.61}$$

and

$$\frac{\partial L}{\partial \lambda_k} = 0, \quad k = 1, 2, \ldots m \tag{5.62}$$

The equations (5.62) are simply the constraint equations (5.59) in another guise, and thus this device of introducing the multipliers as additional variables enables the restricted maximum to be found.

In the integral case, multiple integrals can be defined. For example, given the definition in equation (5.53), we might have

$$I = \int \int \dots \int f(x_1, x_{2'}, \dots x_n)\, dx_1\, dx_2 \dots dx_n \qquad (5.63)$$

with n integral signs. Consider the two-dimensional case. If

$$y = f(x_1, x_2) \qquad (5.64)$$

then y may be considered as defining a surface in the three-dimensional Cartesian system defined in Figure 5.11.

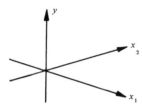

Figure 5.11   Three-dimensional   Cartesian   coordinate system

Then,

$$I = \int \int f(x_1, x_2)\, dx_1\, dx_2 \qquad (5.65)$$

measures a *volume* under this *surface* in a similar way to the single variable integral measuring an area under a curve.

5.5. ALGORITHMS

Algorithms are mathematical procedures which cannot be expressed in the kinds of algebra or calculus discussed so far. They have become particularly important since the advent of computers, since they can often be easily programmed for such machines. Three examples will be mentioned here. Again, as with inverse matrices, the important thing to know is that the algorithms exist and work, not any detail as to how they work.

The first example is concerned with finding the *shortest path through a network*, and it turns up implicitly throughout the book. Consider the shopping model in Chapter 4. This contains the variable c_{ij}, the cost of travel from i to j. How is c_{ij} measured? i and j will be 'points' on some transport network. The cost will be known for each *link* of the network. The problem is to find the least-cost route (set of links) through the network between i and

'; c_{ij} can then be obtained by adding the link costs for links in the shortest route. There is a good computer algorithm for doing this, which produces minimum-cost *trees*: the set of minimum-cost paths from one point to all other points. One form of this algorithm is explained in Haggett and Chorley (1969). Examples of trees are shown in later chapters: in diagrammatic form in Figure 9.9 and a real example in Figure 14.3.

Another example of a major field of algorithmic mathematics is *linear programming*. We have shown how the methods of the calculus can be used to obtain maxima or minima of functions of several variables subject to constraints. A special case is when the objective function and the constraints are linear. This is special in two senses: first, the linearity suggests an elementary case but second, the calculus methods are inapplicable in this case. Algorithmic procedures have been developed in a variety of ways for solving this problem. A good introductory book is that by Beale (1968). Linear programming concepts are only used once in this book, in Chapter 10.

The third example turns up in Chapter 12 and is fully described there, therefore it will only be mentioned here for completeness: the use of search algorithms as an alternative procedure on the computer for finding maxima and minima of functions of several variables.

5.6. STATISTICS

We have already, in the introductory chapters, emphasized that the approach is very much a mathematical rather than a statistical one. Nonetheless, even mathematical models have parameters which have to be estimated from data: an essentially statistical exercise. Most of our work on this is concentrated into Chapter 12 where it is explained in the necessary detail. However, there are some basic statistical concepts which are perhaps taken for granted in the rest of the book. For example, we assume that the reader is familiar with the principles of regression analysis to estimate coefficients of linear models such as

$$y = a_0 + a_1 x_1 + a_2 x_2 + \dots \quad (5.66)$$

(mainly for Chapters 9, 10, 11 and 12) and with some of the basic distribution functions which turn up in statistics, such as the normal distribution

$$y = k\,e^{-\mu x^2} \quad (5.67)$$

(again mainly for Chapters 9, 10, 11 and 12).

5.7. A NOTE ON 'BLACK BOXES'

We are arguing, in effect, that the reader needs to know very basic elementary mathematics, and enough of certain other branches of mathematics to be able to treat them in a 'black box' manner. For example, consider:

(1) The inverse of a matrix and the corresponding solution of linear simultaneous equations.

(2) The shortest path through a network.

(3) Linear programming.

(4) Search routines.

(5) Multiple regression analysis.

The bare bones of the meanings of these concepts have been explained above and the reader has been referred to other texts. For the five fields cited above he should then be able to find computer programmes available to him which carry out the necessary tasks and which he can treat as black boxes. Basic model programmes, such as the shopping model of Chapter 4 and the spatial interaction programmes in general, should also be available to him.

5.8. COMPUTING

Computer programming languages such as FORTRAN (see, for example, McCracken, 1968) are easy to learn. A reader with even the minimum mathematics for this book should be able to acquire such a language. Actual programming ability within the language, however, is probably determined by the programmer's mathematical level. It is a straightforward matter to programme up to that level. The advantage of learning the language whatever the level, and above all of learning how to use computer programmes on the machine, is that, as a minimum, a whole range of model and analysis facilities then become available in a black box way as discussed in the preceding section.

5.9. REFERENCES

* R. L. Ackoff and N. W. Sasieni (1968) *Fundamentals of operations research*, John Wiley, London.

R. G. D. Allen (1938) *Mathematical analysis for economists*, Macmillan, London.

* W. J. Baumol (1965) *Economic theory and operations analysis*, Prentice Hall, Englewood Cliffs, New Jersey.

E. M. L. Beale (1968) *Mathematical programming in practice*, Pitman, London.

P. Haggett and R. J. Chorley (1969) *Network analysis in geography*, Arnold, London.

D. D. McCracken (1965) *A guide to Fortran IV programming*, John Wiley, New York.

G. Mills (1968) *Introduction to linear algebra for social scientists*, Allen and Unwin, London.

R. Morley (1972) *Mathematics for moden economics*, Fontana, London.

R. J. O'Brien and G. G. Garcia (1971) *Mathematics for economists and social scientists*, Macmillan, London.

J. Parry Lewis (1959, 2nd edition, 1970) *Mathematics for students of economics*, Macmillan, London.

* G. Polya (1945) *How to solve it*, Princeton University Press, Princeton, New Jersey.

* A. A. Walters (1968) *An introduction to econometrics*, Macmillan, London.

T. Yamane (1962) *Mathematics for economists*, Prentice-Hall, Englewood Cliffs, New Jersey.

CHAPTER 6

The theory of spatial interaction

6.1. A FAMILY OF SPATIAL INTERACTION MODELS

We have so many examples of spatial interaction phenomena and spatial interaction models within the various models which are described in the subsequent chapters of Part III that it seems worthwhile to begin by developing a general theory of spatial interaction. We have already had one example of a spatial interaction model in Chapter 4: the model of retail sales, within which we represented the interaction between the purchasing power of residents in each zone of the study area and shopping centres within the zone. The reader will recall that the purchasing power of the residents of zone i was defined to be $e_i P_i$, the attractiveness of shops in j was defined to be W_j and the interaction between them was defined to be S_{ij}, the proportion of the purchasing power of residents of zone i which was spent in shops in zone j.

Since we are trying to develop a general theory, it is appropriate to begin by defining a more abstract notation. As in the case of the shopping model, however, we can assume that our study area has been divided up into zones which are numbered sequentially, and that we can use the indices i and j to refer to 'any zone i' and 'any zone j'. We can define the interaction between zone i and zone j to be T_{ij}. It is usually of interest to define interaction-end totals: that is, we will be interested in the total volume of interaction flows leaving zone i (the origin total of interaction flows out of i) and the total of interaction flows into zone j (the volume of interaction flows with a destination in zone j). We can call these totals O_i and D_j respectively. Since W_j represents the relative attractiveness of shops in j in the more general case we might also have an attractiveness term associated with the origin zone as well as with the destination zone: thus we define two attractiveness terms, $W_i^{(1)}$ for the origin zone i and $W_j^{(2)}$ for the destination zone j. As before, we can define c_{ij} to be the cost of travel between zone i and zone j.

We can now proceed, in the first instance rather loosely, and by analogy with our shopping model procedure, and make three assumptions rather like those represented in equations (4.2)–(4.4). That is, we assume that the interaction is proportional to the total of interaction flows leaving zone i, the total of interaction flows terminating at zone j, and proportional to some decreasing function of travel cost. In the case of the shopping model, this function was c_{ij}^{-m}. Thus, we have our three hypotheses:

(1) $T_{ij} \propto O_i$

$$\tag{6.1}$$

(2) $T_{ij} \propto D_j$ (6.2)

(3) $T_{ij} \propto f(c_{ij})$ (6.3)

We can introduce a constant of proportionality K and write

$$T_{ij} = KO_iD_jf(c_{ij}) \qquad (6.4)$$

This is the analogue of the Reilly model in the general notation. It is then appropriate at this stage, as with our analysis of the shopping model in Chapter 4, to examine the interaction flow totals. We can form the sum

$$T_{i1} + T_{i2} + T_{i3} + \ldots + T_{iN}$$

which is the sum of all interaction flows leaving zone i. N is the total number of zones. Using a summation sign and the convention introduced in Chapter 4 that an asterisk replacing an index denotes summation, then this sum can be written

$$T_{i1} + T_{i2} + \ldots + T_{iN} = \sum_{j=1}^{N} T_{ij} = T_{i*} \qquad (6.5)$$

Similarly, we can consider the sum

$$T_{1j} + T_{2j} + \ldots + T_{Nj}$$

which can be written using a similar notation as in equation (6.5) above as

$$T_{1j} + T_{2j} + \ldots + T_{Nj} = \sum_{i=1}^{N} T_{ij} = T_{*j} \qquad (6.6)$$

Note, however, that we have already defined variables to represent these interaction sums, O_i and D_j and *if these are known*, then we can write

$$\sum_{j=1}^{N} T_{ij} = O_i \qquad (6.7)$$

and

$$\sum_{i=1}^{N} T_{ij} = D_j \qquad (6.8)$$

then we shall find, as in the case of the shopping model, that if either or both of the quantities O_i and D_j are known, then we cannot choose K in the model given by equation (6.4) so that (6.7) and/or (6.8) hold. Suppose, for example, that equation (6.7) holds. Then we could substitute for T_{ij} from equation (6.4) into equation (6.7) and we obtain

$$\sum_{j=1}^{N} KO_iD_jf(c_{ij}) = KO_i \sum_{j=1}^{N} D_jf(c_{ij}) = O_i \qquad (6.9)$$

the O_i in this equation cancels and we are left with

$$K = 1 \bigg/ \sum_{j=1}^{N} D_jf(c_{ij}) \qquad (6.10)$$

and we see that the right-hand side of equation (6.10) is dependent on i while K is on the left-hand side is not, and once again we have an inconsistency. However, it is not quite as easy to resolve in the general case as it was in the shopping model in Chapter 4. As a preliminary to resolving the inconsistency, we have to decide whether we know O_i and D_j in the particular case being considered.

We can distinguish four cases:

(1) Neither the set of totals O_i nor the set of totals D_j is known.

(2) The set of totals O_i is known.

(3) The set of totals D_j is known.

(4) Both sets of totals, O_i and D_j are known.

It is convenient to introduce another aspect of spatial interaction terminology at this point: the quantity O_i can be considered to be the total *production* of interaction flows out of zone i, while the quantity D_j can be associated with the *attraction of* interaction flows into zone j. (This makes our notation consistent with transportation study notation as we shall see in Chapter 9.) Then, we can say that the case (2) in the above list, for example, is *production-constrained*, since all the O_is are given. A complete list of names for the various cases might well be:

(1) Unconstrained case.

(2) Production-constrained case.

(3) Attraction-constrained case.

(4) Production-attraction-constrained case, sometimes called the doubly constrained case in contrast to the singly constrained cases (2) and (3).

We can now return to the problem of how to patch up the model equation (6.4) to take account of the internal inconsistencies of the equation (6.4) model when there are production and/or attraction constraints.

The first thing to note is that if either O_i or D_j is not known, then the corresponding term in equation (6.4) is replaced by an attractiveness term, either $W_i^{(1)}$ or $W_j^{(2)}$ as appropriate. Then we can consider each case in turn.

Case (1): *unconstrained*

In this case, O_i should be replaced by $W_i^{(1)}$ and D_j by $W_j^{(2)}$, and the constant K in this case suffices because neither equation (6.7) nor (6.8) holds. Thus, we have

$$T_{ij} = K W_i^{(1)} W_j^{(2)} f(c_{ij}) \qquad (6.11)$$

Case (2): *production-constrained*

In this case, O_i is known, while D_j is not, and so D_j in equation (6.4) is replaced by $W_j^{(2)}$. Also, we have to calculate a proportionality factor to ensure that equation (6.7) is satisfied. In fact, we have to resolve the inconsistency represented by equation (6.10) above. The problem there arose because of the free subscript i on the right-hand side of that equation. Thus, we can remove the inconsistency if we replace K by a proportionality factor which is dependent on i. (This is exactly analogous to the procedure used for the shopping model in Chapter 4 where K was replaced by K_i and equations (4.16) and (4.17) were developed.) In this case we proceed with our development of a more general notation, and replace K by the set of factors A_i. We can then calculate A_i so that equation (6.7) is automatically satisfied. In this case, we have already done the work, because we can see from equation (6.10) that if we replace K by A_i in that equation, and D_j by $W_j^{(2)}$, then (6.10) gives us an expression for A_i. This is written out explicitly in equation (6.13) below. Meanwhile, let us note that equation (6.4) has become

$$T_{ij} = A_i O_i W_j^{(2)} f(c_{ij}) \tag{6.12}$$

where

$$A_i = 1 \bigg/ \sum_{j=1}^{N} W_j^{(2)} f(c_{ij}) \tag{6.13}$$

Case (3): *attraction-constrained*

This case is the mirror image of case (2). We know D_j but not O_i, and therefore we replace O_i in equation (6.4) by $W_i^{(1)}$. Now, equation (6.8) has to be satisfied rather than (6.7). We can achieve this by replacing the proportionality factor K by a set of factors B_j. We can proceed in exact analogy in case (2) above, and the new form of equation (6.4) appropriate to this case becomes

$$T_{ij} = B_j W_i^{(1)} D_j f(c_{ij}) \tag{6.14}$$

where

$$B_j = 1 \bigg/ \sum_{i=1}^{N} W_i^{(1)} f(c_{ij}) \tag{6.15}$$

and the reader can check that equation (6.8) is then satisfied.

Case (4): *production-attraction-constrained*

This case turns out to be slightly more complicated in relation to the proportionality factor. In equation (6.4) we do not have to replace either O_i or D_j because both are postulated to be known, but now both equations (6.7) and (6.8) hold. The inconsistencies in this case can be resolved if K is replaced by a product of proportionality factors $A_i B_j$ which are then calculated to ensure that equations (6.7) and (6.8) are satisfied simultaneously. We can replace K in equation (6.4) to give us the model equation for this case as

$$T_{ij} = A_i B_j O_i D_j f(c_{ij}) \tag{6.16}$$

where A_i and B_j are obtained by substituting for T_{ij} from equation (6.16) into (6.7) and (6.8) respectively. This gives

$$A_i = 1 \bigg/ \sum_{j=1}^{N} B_j D_j f(c_{ij}) \qquad (6.17)$$

and

$$B_j = 1 \bigg/ \sum_{i=1}^{N} A_i O_i f(c_{ij}) \qquad (6.18)$$

Thus, we have now derived a whole family of spatial interaction models to fit a variety of circumstances. We can perhaps by two further comments make this argument more understandable to the reader who has found it rather abstract. Firstly, the reader will probably recognize that the shopping model of Chapter 4 is simply a production-constrained model. If we identify T_{ij} as the flow of retail sales, S_{ij}, the purchasing power, $e_i P_i$, with interaction flow total O_i at the origin (and assume that this is given) and our old attractiveness term W_j with the attractiveness term $W_j^{(2)}$ in the above general notation, then we see that the production-constrained equations can be written

$$S_{ij} = A_i(e_i P_i) W_j^{(2)} f(c_{ij}) \qquad (6.19)$$

where

$$A_i = 1 \bigg/ \sum_{j=1}^{N} W_j^{(2)} f(c_{ij}) \qquad (6.20)$$

The only difference between equations (6.19) and (6.20) and the earlier equations (4.16) and (4.17) is that we are now using A_i instead of K_i, which is simply a matter of notation, and we have replaced c_{ij}^{-n} by a more general function of travel cost, $f(c_{ij})$.

The second observation is that, in each of the four cases, we can still see an identifiable 'gravity model structure'. We have one or more factors, multiplied by a mass term, multiplied by a second mass term, multiplied by a decreasing function of travel cost. In fact, each basic model equation is of the form

$$\text{Interaction} = \text{factor(s)} \times \text{mass} \times \text{mass} \times \text{distance function} \qquad (6.21)$$

This is an easy form of equation to remember. It is also convenient to summarize the four cases by listing in Table 6.1 the factors, the mass terms and the distance function in each case.

6.2. RANGE OF APPLICATION

In the subsequent chapters of Part III, we shall find opportunities to apply this general spatial interaction model in a variety of ways. When we are

Table 6.1

Case	Interaction	Factors	Mass	Mass	D.F.
(1)	T_{ij}	K	$W_i^{(1)}$	$W_j^{(2)}$	$f(c_{ij})$
(2)	T_{ij}	A_i	O_i	$W_j^{(2)}$	$f(c_{ij})$
(3)	T_{ij}	B_j	$W_i^{(1)}$	D_j	$f(c_{ij})$
(4)	T_{ij}	$A_i B_j$	O_i	D_j	$f(c_{ij})$

studying demographic models in Chapter 7, we shall be interested in migration between regions and will have cause to develop a production-attraction-constrained model of migration flows. In Chapter 8 at one point we shall consider interaction between regions as represented by the flows of goods and services. We shall be able to use the same kinds of models again, in this case each of the four types of model being relevant at different times. In Chapter 9, on transport models, we are mainly concerned with various person flows and, again, the production-attraction-constrained model. In Chapter 10 we discuss in general how spatial interaction models are relevant to locational analysis, and we briefly consider the retail sales model (already discussed in detail in Chapter 4) and discuss how interaction models can help us in the study of residential location; in the latter case we shall use an attraction-constraint model. Thus, we have already seen how one member of the family of interaction models can be applied in the analysis of patterns of retail sales and we now note that we shall see other examples in subsequent chapters. Meanwhile, the reader is asked to bear with a general notation and a general discussion of the concepts of the model for the rest of this chapter. This will provide the tools for model building in later chapters.

6.3. A DISCUSSION OF BASIC MODEL CONCEPTS

It is appropriate to begin this section with a qualification. We are discussing the basic concepts of the family of spatial interaction models introduced above as though each model can be reasonably described as a gravity model. In particular, we speak of the mass terms and the travel cost function (sometimes called the impedance function) as though these were terms of a gravity model. We shall continue to do this because of the convenience of the terminology and because it is in accord with historical precedence. We shall note in Section 6.5, however, that it is better to derive this particular family of models using entropy-maximizing methods, and that it is then clear that a statistical analogy is rather more appropriate than the more deterministic gravity model analogy. This general comment has a particular relevance to subsequent discussion in this section. In the physics' gravity model, the mass terms have well-defined dimensions and the cost function is a power function: in fact an inverse-square function. The very earliest gravity models in the social sciences utilized an inverse-square function, and even today there is the feeling in some quarters that the gravity model cost function should be a power function. Equally, there has been a reluctance to use some kind of composite index to measure certain kinds of mass terms. Now we can feel confident that another analogy is more appropriate, then we can discuss ways of measuring 'mass' and the form of the cost function without having to worry about the corresponding situation, with respect to the physics' gravity model. It remains convenient, however, to consider that the basic terms of the model are the mass terms, the measure of travel cost and the form of the cost function, and we now discuss each of these in turn.

We have seen that the mass terms can each be one of two kinds: either some measure of total interaction flow out of or into a zone or some kind of attractiveness factor. In the first case, the mass obviously has a clearly defined dimension—as a number of trips or whatever flow is measured in. Since this quantity has been defined to be known outside the spatial interaction model itself, then this external information supplies an appropriate measure of mass. For example, we shall see in Chapter 9 that in transportation studies trip origins and trip destinations are estimated in generation sub-models which are independent of the spatial interaction model. The units, however, are well-defined and in that case are trips. In the second case, where the mass term is a measure of attractiveness, it is difficult to associate a dimension with the term, and from the point of view of the model unnecessary, as the reader will note that any attractiveness mass term appears in both numerator and denominator (that is, in the A_is and/or B_js as well as in the model numerator) of the expression on the right-hand side of the main model of the equation. This means that the measure which is adopted for attractiveness can always be multiplied by a scale factor without changing the model prediction. This creates all kinds of possibilities for constructing composite indices for this kind of mass term, which we shall pursue in relation to particular examples that occur later in Part III. It is also important, especially for attractiveness-type mass terms, to try to ensure that the models do not make estimates and predictions which are dependent on zone size if the zones of the study areas are of unequal size. If some measure of 'size' is being used as a proxy for attractiveness, then biases can easily enter the model if all the zones are not of equal size. In this case, the definitions of the attractiveness terms should be carefully scrutinized and possibly amended, for example, by dividing by the area of the zone. So far, we have assumed that mass terms can be estimated outside the interaction model. In particular, we have at least implicitly assumed that the mass term is independent of the ease of inter-action. In effect, we have assumed that total interaction is inelastic with respect to ease of interaction. There are various ways of modifying this assumption.

Further, in particular cases, an interaction flow total estimated within the model itself may be used as a measure of mass. In the shopping model of Chapter 4, for example, S_{*j} is a measure of total retail sales in shops of j and may itself be used as a measure of attractiveness. That is, we might replace $W_j^{(2)}$ in equation (6.19) by S_{*j}. In this case, of course, the model equation has to be solved iteratively, but occasionally this will be a reasonable hypothesis to make.

We can now turn our attention to the problem of measuring travel cost. It seems intuitively clear that often there are several components to what we call travel cost. If any one of us makes a journey, for example, then we might well take account of the money cost, the different kinds of time expended (such as travelling and waiting time) and possibly other features like comfort and convenience. It seems reasonable, therefore, to try to develop some composite measure of travel cost appropriate to the kind of spatial interaction which is being represented in the model. This usually leaves us with the problem of estimating the relative weight of various components. We shall see an example of this kind of composite measure of travel cost in Chapter 9.

In the case of the cost function itself, it would seem better to try to find empirically the shape of cost function which gives the best fit between model predictions and observations, rather than simply to assume that one member of the family of power functions will fit best. There are various ways of doing this which will be discussed in Chapter 12 on the calibration and testing of models. If an analytical function is required, there are good theoretical reasons (associated with the entropy-maximizing derivation of spatial inter-action models—Wilson, 1970) for first trying the negative exponential func-tion, say in the form $e^{-\beta c_{ij}}$. It is argued elsewhere (Wilson, 1970) that if this function fits well, then the traveller is perceiving cost linearly. This is more likely to be true for short trips than for longer ones: it may be that an extra ten miles on a hundred mile trip is perceived quite differently to an extra ten miles on a one mile trip. If the marginal ten miles is perceived as 'worth less', or 'less bother' after the traveller has already covered a hundred miles, then an approximation to the way in which he is perceiving cost may be logarith-mic. Then, if c_{ij} in $e^{-\beta c_{ij}}$ is replaced by $\log c_{ij}$ the function transforms into the power function, $c_{ij}^{-\beta}$. Thus, even within the entropy-maximizing framework, it is appropriate to test a range of cost functions and the one which fits best may say something about the traveller's perception.

The negative exponential function is convenient to manipulate analytically and in subsequent chapters we shall frequently use it instead of the general function, $f(c_{ij})$. The reader should always bear in mind, however, that it could be replaced by some other function.

In Chapter 4, following equation (4.20), we introduced concepts of accessi-bility and competition and earlier we defined the associated concept of market area. These concepts can also be given a meaning in relation to the more general spatial interaction framework set up in this chapter.

6.4. A SPATIAL INTERACTION MODEL-BUILDING KIT

We can summarize the argument so far by presenting a check list of steps for the spatial interaction model builder. This can be done as follows:

(1) The first task is to specify the spatial interaction variable itself. In general terms, this is written as T_{ij}. In the shopping model example it was written as S_{ij}.

(2) The nature of the mass terms should next be investigated, and in particular whether they are known interaction flow totals or attractiveness terms. The answers to these questions will determine which member of the family of spatial interaction models is selected (and hence the nature of the balancing factors).

(3) It is now necessary to decide how to measure the mass terms. It will be clear how to do this for those which are interaction flow totals, but for attractiveness terms there will be a considerable degree of choice, with the possibility of developing composite indices and so on.

(4) The next task is to measure interaction cost: this will be straightforward in principle, but it has been noted that there may be several components and in this case some way will have to be found of estimating the relative weights of such components.

(5) We have noted that there is in principle a very wide choice of cost functions. Several functions should be tried and that which best fits model prediction to observation should be used.

(6) It is necessary to design a zone system for this kind of spatial analysis and we have noted that if the zones are of unequal sizes then the measure of attractiveness may have to be modified.

We should attempt to follow this procedure later on as models are developed. Also, in Section 6.5, we shall be introducing a number of further modifications and developments of spatial interaction models which imply that the above check list should be extended.

* 6.5. FURTHER DEVELOPMENTS

An attempt has been made above to keep the discussion relatively simple and straightforward. The price paid for this is that a number of comparatively recent refinements (and some older alternative ways of developing spatial interaction models) have not been discussed. This section outlines such developments, which can be discussed under four headings. Firstly, a number or practical extensions associated with this kind of model building are mentioned. Secondly, there has been some development in the basic theory of these models. Thirdly, other kinds of development of spatial interaction models enable us to cope with more complex situations. Fourthly, there are alternative approaches to this kind of model building which might be adopted. Each of these is discussed in turn below.

First, then, we discuss a number of practical extensions. So far we have assumed that it is possible to define a study area which is a closed system. This is rarely possible, of course, and we must consider various ways of handling the interactions between the study area and its environment. The most common way of handling this problem is to define a zone system for the study area environment, calling these zones external zones, then to model the interaction between study area zones and external zones without modelling interactions between the external zones themselves. (There is a minor exception to this last remark in the case of transport models, where one is interested in trips which pass right through the study area with an external origin and an external destination.) The external zones which are defined in this way are usually much larger in size than zones of the study area.

A theoretically better way of tackling the external zones problem is shown in Figure 6.1. In that Figure the study area is shown as area I. This is surrounded by area II which is designed to be of such a size that no interaction

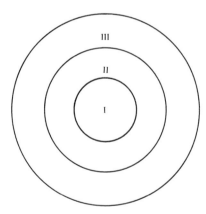

Figure 6.1   A system for handling external
zones

takes place between zones outside area II and the study area I. Interaction can, however, take place between area II and area III (whose dimensions are defined in an analogy with those of area II) which has an impact on area I because interaction flows originating in area II, which might have gone to area I, could be attracted to area III, depending on the attractiveness values of zones in that area. However, it is often not practically possible to develop n external zone system of this kind because of the size of areas II and III cf. Wilson, 1970, Chapter 5).

In our earlier discussion we assumed that in any study of a spatial inter-action phenomenon it would be a straightforward task to classify that phenomenon into one of the four model cases which we have defined. In act, this is not always so: we will occasionally find cases where, for one kind of interaction, some of the flows fall into one type, say production-constrained, while others fall into another, say production-attraction-constrained. How-ever, in this case it is possible to develop a hybrid model to deal adequately with the situation. An example occurs below in Chapter 10.

The family of spatial interaction models can be further extended to account for multi-stage interaction. For example, consider the flow of goods from exporting regions i in one country, through a set of ports j with destinations at a set of importing countries, k. In this case, let O_i be the exportable produce of zone i, X_j the capacity of the port at j and D_k the imports of k. Let c_{ijk} be the cost of getting a unit of goods from i to k via the port at j. Then in this case we have defined three mass terms and we might also demand that three kinds of constraint on the spatial interaction variable, which can be written T_{ijk}, may hold as follows:

$$\sum_j \sum_k T_{ijk} = O_i \tag{6.22}$$

$$\sum_i \sum_k T_{ijk} = X_j \tag{6.23}$$

$$\sum_i \sum_j T_{ijk} = D_k \tag{6.24}$$

the corresponding spatial interaction model might then be

$$T_{ijk} = A_i B_j C_k O_i X_j D_k f(c_{ijk}) \tag{6.25}$$

where

$$A_i = 1 \Big/ \sum_j \sum_k B_j C_k X_j D_k f(c_{ijk}) \tag{6.26}$$

$$B_j = 1 \Big/ \sum_i \sum_k A_i C_k O_i D_k f(c_{ijk}) \tag{6.27}$$

$$C_k = 1 \Big/ \sum_i \sum_j A_i B_j O_i X_j f(c_{ijk}) \tag{6.28}$$

thus we now see at least the formal possibility of a spatial interaction model with three mass terms and three balancing factors (which will incidentally ensure that overall dimensionality is correct). In the particular example cited, of course, it would probably be more appropriate to develop some kind of hybrid model.

The development in basic theory mentioned above refers to the entropy-maximizing methodology (Wilson, 1970). When spatial interaction phenomena are viewed in this light, flows are seen essentially as statistical averages of a variety of micro behaviour. The mathematics of entropy maximizing is outlined briefly for the interested reader in Appendix 1. We can simply note, however, that the entropy-maximizing methodology does offer more satisfactory interpretation of the basic concepts of the spatial inter action models developed in this chapter. For example, when a mass term is an attractiveness term this can be related to the notion of scale economies.

Thirdly, we mentioned that spatial interaction models have been developed so that they can handle more complex problems. This refers to the definition and level of understanding of the interaction phenoma which are being modelled. Consider a specific example of passenger flows in a transport system. At one level of resolution we can look at more passenger flow between each pair of zones in our study area and build a spatial interaction model utilizing the appropriate member of the family of spatial interaction models introduced above. However, suppose we increase our power of resolution. We then notice that passengers travel by different modes of transport. In effect, then, we have several kinds of interaction phenomena passenger trips by different modes. However, it will not suffice simply to build a spatial interaction model for each particular type of interaction. If we are considering the journey to work, for instance, then the passengers making the trips are perhaps competing for a common set of opportunities at their destinations, in this case jobs. In other words the different types of interaction flow are linked. When we attempt to solve this problem in Chapter 9, we shall see that it is possible to develop a set of linked spatial interaction models, and that this further extends the family of models which have been introduced in this chapter. The entropy-maximizing methodology is also particularly helpful in developing disaggregated multi-sector models of this kind. (It is useful to designate the type of model introduced directly in this chapter a single-sector models relative to the multi-sector model just outlined). In many of the areas where we use spatial interaction models as part of the model system, this kind of disaggregation into multi-sector models is possible Because of the variety of ways of doing it, it is not appropriate to develop and formally extend the family of models derived above. Instead, we will develop in *ad hoc* fashion in subsequent chapters below.

Finally, we mentioned above that there were alternative approaches to spatial interaction modelling. In particular, perhaps the most frequently used alternative to a gravity model type of interaction model is the intervening opportunities model. Rather than interrupt the presentation in this book, the intervening opportunities model is described in detail in Appendix 2. Many of the concepts developed in this chapter, which will be further developed in subsequent chapters, can be applied to the original intervening opportunities mode. The methods of doing this are made clear in the Appendix.

5.6. REFERENCES

G. A. P. Carrothers (1956) An historical review of the gravity and potential concepts of human interaction, *Journal of the America Institute of Planners*, **22**, pp. 94–102; also reprinted in P. Ambrose (Ed.) (1970) *Analytical human geography*, Longman, London, pp. 226–42.

M. Cordey Hayes and A. G. Wilson (1971) Spatial interaction, *Socio-economic planning sciences*, **5**, pp. 73–95.

G. Olsson (1965) *Distance and human interaction*, Regional Science Research Institute, Philadelphia.

A. G. Wilson (1970) *Entropy in urban and regional modelling*, Pion, London.

A. G. Wilson (1971) A family of spatial interaction models, and associated developments, *Environment and Planning*, **3**, pp. 1–32; reprinted in A. G. Wilson (1972) *Papers in urban and regional analysis*, Pion, London, pp. 170–201.

PART III

Urban and Regional Models

CHAPTER 7

Demographic models

7.1. THE SINGLE-REGION COHORT SURVIVAL MODEL

A cohort is defined as a group of people born in a given time period. The essence of cohort survival demographic models, as the name implies, is that cohorts 'survive' from one time period to the next. Suppose $w(t)$ is the size of a population at time t. Then, in the simplest kind of cohort survival model, a birth rate, a survival rate and a net in-migration rate would be defined for the period t to $t + T$, say as $b(t, t + T)$, $s(t, t + T)$ and $m(t, t + T)$. Then, clearly

$$w(t + T) = [b(t, t + T) + s(t, t + T) + m(t, t + T)]w(t) \qquad (7.1)$$

This extremely simple model of population change has some of the characteristics of a cohort survival model in that the rates are a function of calendar time, t. It is obvious, however, that such a model is too simple: births are to females in certain age groups and the rates vary with age; survival rates for different segments of the population vary with age; migration rates vary with age and other characteristics. The first step, then, in the development of a more realistic model is to work with a population divided into age groups. Two possible definitions are shown in Table 7.1, one based on five year

Table 7.1   Age groups

(a)		(b)	
Age group	Years	Age group	Years
1	0–4	1	0–4
2	5–9	2	5–14
3	10–14	3	15–19
.		4	20–24
.		5	25–44
.		6	45–59
	95–99	7	60–64
21	100+	8	65+

intervals, the other on the intervals most frequently used for the presentation of data in the British Census. For convenience, we have given each group of years, which we shall call an age-group interval, a number. In general, we can now refer to $w_r(t)$ as the population in age group r at time t in some region. Thus, we have defined a *vector* quantity which can also be written as $\mathbf{w}(t)$.

We can again define birth, survival and net in-migration rates, and apply them to this age-group-disaggregated population. We must now note, however, that in the period from t to $t + T$, the population ages. In order to make the presentation of the model simple at this stage, we can make the assumption that our age-group intervals are so defined as to be each equal and further, each equal to the projection period. We could achieve this, for example, by adopting the Table 7.1(a) definition of age-group intervals and assuming that $T = 5$. We shall retain the general notation—age groups and projection period T—but, for the time being, with this restrictive assumption holding. Then, during the projection period, it can easily be seen that the survivors of one age group 'age' into the next higher age group. We can now define our rates. Suppose there are R age groups in all. Let $b_k(t, t + T)$ be the rate at which children are born (into the first age group, of course) to population in age group k from t to $t + T$; let $s_{rr-1}(t, t + T)$ be the rate of survival of the age group $r - 1$ population at t into the r population at $t + T$; let $m_{rr-1}(t, t + T)$ be the rate of net immigration of population in age group $r - 1$ at t into age group r at $t + T$. Then,

$$w_1(t + T) = \sum_{k=\alpha}^{\beta} b_k(t, t + T)w_k(t) \tag{7.2}$$

where α and β are the age group limits of the child-bearing age groups, and for $r > 1$,

$$w_r(t + T) = s_{rr-1}(t, t + T)w_{r-1}(t) + m_{rr-1}(t, t + T)w_{r-1}(t) \tag{7.3}$$

This is the single-region cohort survival model. It has been elegantly stated in matrix form by Rogers and developed by him in a number of ways. A substantial part of the rest of this chapter is based on his work (Rogers, 1966, 1967, 1968). For convenience, we will now drop the time indices which relate to the rate-variables (though it should be remembered that they are still implicitly present, rates vary with calendar time and projection period). The model given by equations (7.2) and (7.3) can then be written in matrix form as follows

$$
\begin{bmatrix} w_1(t + T) \\ w_2(t + T) \\ \vdots \\ w_R(t + T) \end{bmatrix} = \begin{bmatrix} 0 & 0 \dots b_\alpha \dots b_\beta \dots 0 \dots 0 \\ s_{21} + m_{21} & 0 \dots\dots\dots\dots\dots\dots\dots 0 \\ 0 & s_{32} + m_{32} \dots\dots\dots\dots 0 \\ \vdots & \\ 0 & \dots\dots\dots\dots s_{RR-1} + m_{RR-1} 0 \end{bmatrix} \begin{bmatrix} w_1(t) \\ w_2(t) \\ \vdots \\ w_R(t) \end{bmatrix} \tag{7.4}
$$

The process which is implicit in this model can be shown more clearly, perhaps, if the matrix in equation (7.4) is broken down into three component matrices.* **B** is all zeros, except for a first row which is

$$[0 \quad 0 \quad \ldots \quad b_\alpha \quad \ldots \quad b_\beta \quad \ldots \quad 0] \tag{7.5}$$

$$\mathbf{S} = \begin{bmatrix} 0 & 0 & \ldots & & 0 \\ s_{21} & 0 & \ldots & & 0 \\ 0 & s_{32} & \ldots & & 0 \\ \ldots\ldots\ldots\ldots & & s_{RR-1}0 \end{bmatrix} \tag{7.6}$$

and

$$\mathbf{M} = \begin{bmatrix} 0 & 0 & \ldots & & 0 \\ m_{21} & 0 & \ldots & & 0 \\ 0 & m_{32} & \ldots & & 0 \\ 0 & \ldots\ldots\ldots & & m_{RR-1}0 \end{bmatrix} \tag{7.7}$$

which are the birth, survival and migration matrices respectively. We can then define the growth matrix **G**, such that

$$\mathbf{G} = \mathbf{B} + \mathbf{S} + \mathbf{M} \tag{7.8}$$

and the reader can easily check that equation (7.4) can be written

$$\mathbf{w}(t + T) = \mathbf{G}\mathbf{w}(t) \tag{7.9}$$

This model could, in principle, be applied to any kind of region: a nation, an economic planning region, a city, or even a zone of a city, if estimates of the appropriate rates existed.

7.2. THE MULTI-REGION MODEL

It would obviously be an advantage if we could develop the model further so that it is applicable to a system of several regions (which may be nations, regions of a nation, cities within a region or zones within a city). In the single-region model, migration in and out of the region is estimated simply as net in-migration as a rate which is applied to the region's population. This is less than satisfactory, and a multi-region model will provide the framework within which we can make a more careful study of migration flows.

We will now use the superscript i (and sometimes j) as a regional label $(i = 1, 2, \ldots N)$ for a system of N regions; for example, $w_r^i(t)$ is the population

---

* Rogers (1966) breaks it down into two, a survivorship matrix which includes the birth terms, **B** + **S** in our notation, and a migration matrix.

of region i in age group r at time t. We now have a population vector for each region which can be written $\mathbf{w}^i(t)$. These vectors can be combined together to form one larger vector of population for the whole system, written simply as $\mathbf{w}(t)$. But this now has a different meaning from the case of the single-region system. We have

$$\mathbf{w}^i(t) = \begin{bmatrix} w_1^i(t) \\ w_2^i(t) \\ \vdots \\ w_R^i(t) \end{bmatrix}. \tag{7.10}$$

$$\mathbf{w}(t) = \begin{bmatrix} \mathbf{w}^1(t) \\ \mathbf{w}^2(t) \\ \vdots \\ \mathbf{w}^N(t) \end{bmatrix} = \begin{bmatrix} w_1^1(t) \\ w_2^2(t) \\ \vdots \\ w_R^1(t) \\ \vdots \\ w_1^N(t) \\ w_2^N(t) \\ \vdots \\ w_R^N(t) \end{bmatrix} \tag{7.11}$$

As usual, in order to build the model we need a careful definition of the various rates which are involved. We define* $b_k^i(t, t + T)$ to be the rate of births per population in age group k in region i from t to $t + T$; $s_{rr-1}^i(t, t + T)$ to be the survival rate of population in age groups $r - 1$ at t to age group r at $t + T$ for the population of region i, *this time allowing for out-migration as well as deaths*; and $m_{rr-1}^{ij}(t, t + T)$ to be the rate of migration from population in age group $r - 1$ in region j at time t to age group r in region i at time $t + T$. Then, the multi-region form of the model given by equations (7.2) and (7.3) is

$$w_1^i(t + T) = \sum_{k=\alpha}^{\beta} b_k^i(t, t + T) w_k^i(t) \tag{7.12}$$

and, for $r > 1$

$$w_r^i(t + T) = s_{rr-1}^i(t, t + T) w_{r-1}^i(t) + \sum_{j \neq i} m_{rr-1}^{ij}(t, t + T) w_{r-1}^j(t) \tag{7.13}$$

---

* With the same restrictive assumption of equal age-group intervals equal to the projection period of the preceding section.

This model has a similar structure to the single-region model. However, only an out-migration rate (implicitly included in the survival rate) is applied to the i-region population and the in-migration rates are applied to the sending j-region populations. This is an obvious improvement.

This model can also be written in matrix form. It can be done as follows: define a birth matrix and a survival matrix for each region by analogy with equations (7.5) and (7.6), but with regional subscripts. Then, $\mathbf{B}$ has a first row

$$[0 \quad 0 \quad \ldots \quad b_\alpha^i \quad \ldots \quad b_\beta^i \quad \ldots \quad 0] \tag{7.14}$$

$$\mathbf{S}^i = \begin{bmatrix} 0 & 0 & \ldots & 0 \\ s_{21}^i & 0 & \ldots & -0 \\ 0 & s_{32}^i & \ldots & 0 \\ 0 & 0 & \ldots & s_{RR-1}^i 0 \end{bmatrix} \tag{7.15}$$

and a regional growth matrix $\mathbf{G}^i$ (which allows for out-migration only), so that

$$\mathbf{G}^i = \mathbf{B}^i + \mathbf{S}^i \tag{7.16}$$

We can now also define an inter-regional migration matrix of the form

$$\mathbf{M}^{ij} = \begin{bmatrix} 0 & 0 & \ldots & 0 \\ m_{21}^{ij} & 0 & \ldots & 0 \\ 0 & m_{32}^{ij} & \ldots & 0 \\ 0 & m_{32}^{ij} & \ldots & 0 \\ 0 & \ldots & & m_{RR-1}^{ij} 0 \end{bmatrix} \tag{7.17}$$

and then we can write the growth matrix for the whole system as

$$\mathbf{G} = \begin{bmatrix} \mathbf{G}^1 & \mathbf{M}^{12} & \mathbf{M}^{13} & \ldots \\ \mathbf{M}^{21} & \mathbf{G}^2 & \mathbf{M}^{23} & \ldots \\ \vdots & & & \\ \mathbf{M}^{N1} & \mathbf{M}^{N2} & \mathbf{M}^{N3} & \ldots & \mathbf{G}^N \end{bmatrix} \tag{7.18}$$

and then the model can be written in the form

$$\mathbf{w}(t + T) = \mathbf{G}\mathbf{w}(t) \tag{7.19}$$

This is, of course, exactly equivalent to equations (7.12) and (7.13).

7.3. THE MULTI-REGION MODEL, DISTINGUISHING MALE AND FEMALE POPULATIONS

The cohorts defined so far have been structured by age group only. Since children of either sex can be born only to females, and since survival rates differ considerably by sex, it seems sensible further to sub-divide the population by sex. This is a straightforward task, and the method presented here follows Rogers and MacDougal (1968). We now further amend our notation by adding male (M) and female (F) superscripts. Thus $w_r^{iF}(t)$ and $w_r^{iM}(t)$ are the female and male populations in age group r in region i. We can define rates $b_k^{iF}(t, t + T), b_k^{iM}(t, t + T), s_{rr-1}^{iF}(t, t + T), s_{rr-1}^{iM}(t, t + T), m_{rr-1}^{ijF}(t, t + T)$ and $m_{rr-1}^{ijM}(t, t + T)$, which are obvious extensions of those defined in the preceding section. We can now easily build the extended model by writing down the obvious developments of equations (7.12) and (7.13). This gives

$$w_1^{iF}(t + T) = \sum_{k=\alpha}^{\beta} b_k^{iF}(t, t + T)w_k^{iF}(t) \tag{7.20}$$

$$w_1^{iM}(t + T) = \sum_{k=\alpha}^{\beta} b_k^{iM}(t, t + T)w_k^{iF}(t) \tag{7.21}$$

(Note in this equation that the male birth rates are applied to *female* populations).

For $r > 1$,

$$w_r^{iF}(t + T) = s_{rr-1}^{iF}(t, t + T)w_{r-1}^{iF}(t) + \sum_{j \neq i} m_{rr-1}^{ijF}(t, t + T)w_{r-1}^{jF}(t) \tag{7.22}$$

$$w_r^{iM}(t + T) = s_{rr-1}^{iM}(t, t + T)w_{r-1}^{iM}(t) + \sum_{j \neq i} m_{rr-1}^{ijM}(t, t + T)w_{r-1}^{jM}(t) \tag{7.23}$$

Equations (7.20)–(7.23) provide a good model for making multi-region population projections provided the appropriate data can be assembled. The estimation of *historical* birth and survival rates is not easy, in spite of a wealth of information being available, and the problem of forecasting these is even more fraught with danger. There are similar difficulties in obtaining appropriate empirical estimates of migration rates. In this case, however, given a data base it is possible to build models of migration flows, and these models help with the task of projecting rates. The subject of migration models is tackled in the next section of this chapter.

To conclude this section we note that the model given by equations (7.20)–(7.23) can be written very compactly in matrix form. We can more or less work by analogy with the previous section, but we have to be careful about the way in which male births are incorporated into the system growth matrix. Define matrices $\mathbf{B}^{iF}, \mathbf{B}^{iM}, \mathbf{S}^{iF}, \mathbf{S}^{iM}, \mathbf{M}^{ijF}$ and $\mathbf{M}^{ijM}$ by disaggregating the definitions of equations (7.14), (7.15) and (7.17) by sex. We have to be more careful in defining regional growth matrices by sex, however,

$$G^{iF} = B^{iF} + S^{iF} \tag{7.24}$$

but

$$G^{iM} = S^{iM} \tag{7.25}$$

Then, we can define a system growth matrix $\mathbf{G}$ by

$$
\mathbf{G} = \begin{bmatrix}
\mathbf{G}^{1F} & 0 & \mathbf{M}^{12F} & 0 & \cdots \\
\mathbf{B}^{1M} & \mathbf{G}^{1M} & 0 & \mathbf{M}^{12M} & \cdots \\
\mathbf{M}^{21F} & 0 & \mathbf{G}^{2F} & 0 & \cdots \\
0 & \mathbf{M}^{21M} & \mathbf{B}^{2M} & \mathbf{G}^{2M} & \cdots \\
\vdots & & & &
\end{bmatrix} \tag{7.26}
$$

and

$$
\mathbf{w}(t) = \begin{bmatrix}
\mathbf{w}^{1F}(t) \\
\mathbf{w}^{1M}(t) \\
\vdots \\
\mathbf{w}^{NF}(t) \\
\mathbf{w}^{NM}(t)
\end{bmatrix} \tag{7.27}
$$

and then the model can be written

$$\mathbf{w}(t + T) = \mathbf{G}\mathbf{w}(t) \tag{7.28}$$

7.4. MIGRATION MODELS

A considerable amount of development work has been carried out on models of migration flows (see, for example, Lowry, 1966 and Masser, 1969). In this section, however, a formalized and general spatial interaction model of migration will be presented rather than a description of all this work. It will then be possible for the reader to transform this into almost any specific model of migration if required.

Models have been developed of net flows, gross flows and directional flows. It is obviously most general to attempt to build a model of directional flows and we begin by defining $M_{ij}(t, t + T)$ to be the migration flow from region i to region j in the time period t to $t + T$. (Note that the flow is i to j; in the previous sections of this chapter, the flows implied by the rates m^{ij} were from j to i to facilitate building the matrix form of the model.) This will be written M_{ij} for short, though reference to the time period should always be implicitly understood. The same applies to most other variables to be defined. Clearly, migration flows will depend on age, on characteristics such as occupation and so on. Thus, we shall sub-divide M_{ij} from time to time for example, we might employ M_{ij}^r as the flow of migrants who were in age group r at time t. For the time being, however, we will use M_{ij} and then disaggregate later.

We will begin by building a production-constrained model. This is based on the assumption that propensity to leave, to out-migrate, will be predictable as a function of the region and its population. We might proceed as follows let μ_i be the propensity to migrate per thousand population from region i let P_i be the population of i, let O_i be the number of migrants leaving i, let λ be the system-wide propensity to migrate, let X_i^k be the number of variables which characterize region i (unemployment, etc.) and let Y_j^k be a number of factors which characterize region j. Then we might hypothesize that

$$\mu_i = \lambda + \sum_k a^k X_i^k \tag{7.29}$$

$$O_i = \mu_i P_i \tag{7.30}$$

and that an attractiveness to migrants term for each region j exists of the form

$$W_j = \sum_k b^k Y_j^k \tag{7.31}$$

Then for some given period, $\mu_i - \lambda$ can be measured, and the coefficients a^k in equation (7.29) estimated by regression analysis; we can assume

$$W_j = K M_{*j} \tag{7.32}$$

for the same period, and estimate the coefficients b^k by regression analysis. Then we can build a spatial interaction model of the form

$$M_{ij} = A_i O_i W_j \, e^{-\beta c_{ij}} \tag{7.33}$$

where

$$A_i = 1 \Big/ \sum_j W_j \, e^{-\beta c_{ij}} \tag{7.34}$$

and estimate β in the usual way (see Chapter 12).

If we were particularly interested in migration flows by age group, then we could carry out such an analysis for the model

$$M_{ij}^r = A_i^r O_i^r W_j^r \, e^{-\beta^r c_{ij}} \tag{7.35}$$

where

$$A_i^r = 1 \Big/ \sum_j W_j^r \, e^{-\beta^r c_{ij}} \tag{7.36}$$

using obvious extensions of the definitions of the variable for age group r.

Clearly, there is a wide variety of choice of the variables X_i^k and Y_j^k, and in this way many models can be developed and tested. Further, the relationship between these variables need not necessarily be additive as in equations (7.29) and (7.31), though log linear regression or other methods of estimation would then have to be used.

If migration flows can be estimated in this way then we can use them to estimate rates which then form inputs to the demographic model. We would have relationships of the form

$$m_{rr-1}^{jiF}(t, t + T) = \frac{M_{ij}^{r-1F}(t, t + T)}{W_{r-1}^{jF}(t)} \qquad (7.37)$$

and

$$m_{rr-1}^{jiM}(t, t + T) = \frac{M_{ij}^{r-1M}(t, t + T)}{W_{r-1}^{jM}(t)} \qquad (7.38)$$

(assuming that we could estimate migration models disaggregated by age group and sex). Thus, if equations (7.37) and (7.38) and associated migration model equations are added to the demographic model equations (7.20)–(7.23), then a more complete demographic-migration model is obtained.

*7.5. FURTHER DEVELOPMENTS I: GENERALIZING THE THE ROGERS' MODEL

The demographic models developed in previous sections of this chapter all rely on Rogers' assumption of equal age-group intervals, each equal to the projection period. As is clear from Table 7.1(b), most available demographic data do not conform with this restriction; in any case, it would be good to have a model sufficiently general that it could be run for an arbitrary projection period, T. It is possible, of course, to manipulate available data to get them into Rogers' form, by employing various kinds of interpolation, but even this does not deal with the problem of then being tied to a single projection period, usually one of five years. Accordingly, a generalized demographic model has been developed (Wilson 1972) which will permit the definition of population age groups of arbitrary length, and an arbitrary projection period, T.

Let $\Delta_1, \Delta_2, \ldots \Delta_R$ be the age group intervals covering age ranges (0, $\Delta_1 - 1$), ($\Delta_1, \Delta_1 + \Delta_2 - 1$), ($\Delta_1 + \Delta_2, \Delta_1 + \Delta_2 + \Delta_3 - 1$),... and so on. Let T be the projection period, but note that it can bear an arbitrary relationship to the Δ_is. In the Rogers' case, during a projection period T, people always aged from one age group to the next, or were born into the first age group. In the general case, there are many additional possibilities, as illustrated in Figure 7.1. The Rogers' case is shown as Figure 7.1.(a). Figures 7.1(b) and 7.1(c) show a variety of other cases. In Figure 7.1(b), the arrow A

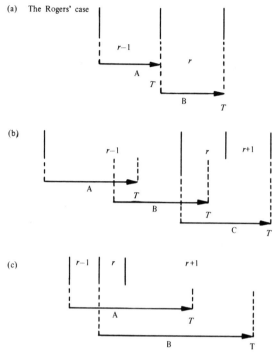

Figure 7.1 Ageing in the Rogers' and generalized demographic models

Figure 7.2 Births in the generalized model

shows that someone whose age group puts him at the 'beginning' of age group $r - 1$ will remain in $r - 1$ at the end of time T when Δ_{r-1} and T bear the relationship shown in the Figure. Arrow B shows someone surviving from age group $r - 1$ to age group r, but because Δ_r is short compared to T, it is also possible (arrow C) for someone to survive into age group $r + 1$ from $r - 1$ in time t. Arrows A and B in Figure 7.1(c) show that if T is large compared to Δ_{r-1} *and* Δ_r, then survivors from age group $r - 1$ may jump age group r and survive directly into age group $r + 1$. Many other cases are possible.

Figure 7.2 shows that if T is large compared to $\Delta_1, \Delta_2, \ldots \Delta_m$, then children may be first recorded as being 'born' into any of the age groups $1, 2, \ldots m$ during the projection period T.

We can set up a number of variables so that we can handle this variety of cases as follows (in most cases, time period t to $t + T$ should be understood). Let b_{rk}^{iF}, b_{rk}^{iM} be female and male birth rates to females in age group k which are first recorded in age group r; let s_{rr-k}^{iF} and s_{rr-k}^{iM} be female and male survival rates from age group $r - k$ ($k = 0, 1, 2, \ldots n_r$) into age group r; let m_{rr-k}^{ijF} and m_{rr-k}^{ijM} be female and male migration rates of people from age group $r - k$ ($k = 0, 1, 2, \ldots n_r$) in j to age group r in i. $r - n_r$ is the most distant age group from age group r from which people can survive into age group r in the projection period. It is illustrated in Figure 7.3. n_r is the largest

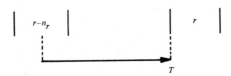

Figure 7.3 Survivorship into age group r

integer to satisfy

$$\Delta_{r-n^r+1} + \ldots + \Delta_{r-1} < T \tag{7.39}$$

provided

$$r - n_r \geqslant 1 \tag{7.40}$$

If the value of n_r obtained from the inequality (7.39) infringes the inequality (7.40), then it should be set to

$$n_r = r - 1 \tag{7.41}$$

This simply ensures that no-one survives from an age group earlier than the first.

There is one other special case: if

$$\Delta_{r-1} \geqslant T \tag{7.42}$$

then we also get

$$n_r = r - 1 \tag{7.43}$$

Note that some of the s_{rr-k}s and m_{rr-k}s for $k = 0, 1, 2, \ldots n_r$ may be zero because of the 'jumping' situation illustrated by arrows A and B of Figure 7.1(c).

We also calculate m (see Figure 7.2) as the smallest integer such that

$$\Delta_1 + \Delta_2 + \ldots + \Delta_m \geqslant T \tag{7.44}$$

and this gives the age groups which people can be born into.

The birth rates, survival rates and migration rates for the generalized model will typically be calculated from data on total births, survivors and migrants in the same period T. We now show how to calculate the model rates from this kind of information. The method turns on the notion of finding the proportion of survivors (or migrants) who pass from one given age group at the beginning of the period into one of a number of age groups by the end of the period. Consider Figure 7.4. This shows that survivors of

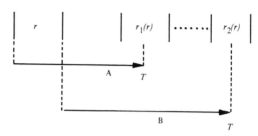

Figure 7.4　Survivorship from age group r

age group r end up in an age group in the range $r_1(r)$ to $r_2(r)$. $r_1(r)$ is the largest integer such that

$$\Delta_r + \Delta_{r+1} + \cdots + \Delta_{r_1(r)-1} \leqslant T \tag{7.45}$$

with the special case

$$r_1(r) = r \tag{7.46}$$

if

$$\Delta_r > T \tag{7.47}$$

$r_2(r)$ is the largest integer such that

$$\Delta_{r+1} + \cdots + \Delta_{r_2(r)-1} < T \tag{7.48}$$

with special cases that

$$r_2(r) = r + 1 \tag{7.49}$$

if

$$\Delta_{r+1} > T \tag{7.50}$$

and

$$r_2(r) = R \tag{7.51}$$

if

$$r = R \tag{7.52}$$

The non-zero values of the rates of the form s_{rr-k} and m_{rr-k} can now be expressed as $s_{r'r}$ and $m_{r'r}$ for $r' = r_1(r), \ldots r_2(r)$. We can then calculate quantities p_{rr-k}, $k = 0, \ldots n_r$ which give the proportion of survivors (or migrants) who are in age group r at time $t + T$. These proportions can be expressed as follows: p_{rr-k} is zero, the 'jumping' case of Figure 7.1(c), except for terms of the form $p_{r'r}$, $r' = r_1(r), \ldots r_2(r)$, and these are given in the general case (see Figure 7.4) by

$$p_{r_1(r)r} = \frac{\Delta_r + \Delta_{r+1} + \cdots + \Delta_{r_1(r)-1} - T}{\Delta_r} \tag{7.53}$$

$$p_{r'r} = \frac{\Delta_{r'}}{\Delta_r}, \qquad r_1(r) < r' < r_2(r) \tag{7.54}$$

$$p_{r_2(r)r} = \frac{T - (\Delta_{r+1} + \cdots + \Delta_{r_2(r-1)})}{\Delta_r} \tag{7.55}$$

In the special case where

$$r_1(r) = r \tag{7.56}$$

then equation (7.53) is to be interpreted as

$$p_{r_1(r)r} = \frac{\Delta_r - T}{\Delta_r} \tag{7.57}$$

and in the special case

$$r_2(r) = r + 1 \tag{7.58}$$

then equation (7.55) is to be interpreted as

$$p_{r_2(r)r} = \frac{T}{\Delta_r} \tag{7.59}$$

Finally, in the special case where

$$r_1(r) = r_2(r) \tag{7.60}$$

then

$$p_{r_1(r)r} = p_{r_2(r)r} = 1 \tag{7.61}$$

Births are easier to allocate to age groups. Define quantities π_r, $r = 1, \ldots m$, and then (see Figure 7.2) we have

$$\pi_r = \frac{\Delta_r}{T}, \qquad r < m \tag{7.62}$$

$$\pi_m = \frac{T - (\Delta_1 + \Delta_2 + \cdots + \Delta_{m-1})}{T} \tag{7.63}$$

as the proportions being 'born' into different age groups.

Suppose now that we are given our data in the form $B_k^{iF}(t, t + T)$ and $B_k^{iM}(t, t + T)$, the total number of female and male births to mothers in age group k in region i from t to $t + T$, $S_r^{iF}(t, t + T)$ and $S_r^{iM}(t, t + T)$ the number of female and male survivors in period t to $t + T$ who were in age group r at time t, and $M_r^{ijF}(t, t + T)$ and $M_r^{ijM}(t, t + T)$, the number of migrants from region i to region j who were in age group r at time t in t to $t + T$. Then using the quantities $p_{rr-k}, k = 0, \ldots n_r$ and $\pi_r, r = 1, \ldots m$, we can calculate the model rates as follows:

$$b_{rk}^{iF} = \frac{\pi_r B_k^{iF}(t, t + T)}{w_k^{iF}(t)} \tag{7.64}$$

$$b_{rk}^{iM} = \frac{\pi_r B_k^{iM}(t, t + T)}{w_k^{iF}(t)} \tag{7.65}$$

$$s_{rr-k}^{iF} = \frac{p_{rr-k} S_{r-k}^{iF}(t, t + T)}{w_{r-k}^{iF}(t)} \tag{7.66}$$

$$s_{rr-k}^{iM} = \frac{p_{rr-k} S_{r-k}^{iM}(t, t + T)}{w_{r-k}^{iM}(t)} \tag{7.67}$$

$$m_{rr-k}^{ijF} = \frac{p_{rr-k} M_{r-k}^{jiF}(t, t + T)}{w_{r-k}^{jF}(t)} \tag{7.68}$$

and

$$m_{rr-k}^{ijM} = \frac{p_{rr-k} M_{r-k}^{jiM}(t, t + T)}{w_{r-k}^{jM}(t)} \tag{7.69}$$

It is then a simple step to present the generalizations of equations (7.20)–(7.23) for this more general case. The differences are that 'survival' and 'migration' are possible in 'birth' age groups, and there may now be several of these instead of just the first, and that all terms involving survival and migration rates are summed over the age groups from which people might survive into the age group under consideration. Thus the four model equations are:

$$w_r^{iF}(t + T) = \sum_{k=\alpha}^{\beta} b_{rk}^{iF} w_k^{iF}(t) + \sum_{k=0}^{n_r} s_{rr-k}^{iF} w_{r-k}^{iF}(t)$$

$$+ \sum_{j \neq i} \sum_{k=0}^{n_r} m_{rr-k}^{ij} w_{r-k}^{jF}(t), \qquad r \leqslant m \tag{7.70}$$

$$w_r^{iM}(t + T) = \sum_{k=\alpha}^{\beta} b_{rk}^{iM} w_k^{iF}(t) + \sum_{k=0}^{n_r} s_{rr-k}^{iM} w_{r-k}^{iM}(t)$$

$$+ \sum_{j \neq i} \sum_{k=0}^{n_r} m_{rr-k}^{ijM} w_{r-k}^{jM}(t), \qquad r \leqslant m \tag{7.71}$$

$$w_r^{iF}(t + T) = \sum_{k=0}^{n_r} s_{rr-k}^{iF} w_{r-k}^{iF}(t)$$

$$+ \sum_{j \neq i} \sum_{k=0}^{n_r} m_{rr-k}^{ijF} w_{r-k}^{jF}(t), \qquad r > m \qquad (7.72)$$

$$w_r^{iM}(t + T) = \sum_{k=0}^{n_r} s_{rr-k}^{iM} w_{r-k}^{iM}(t)$$

$$+ \sum_{j \neq i} \sum_{k=0}^{n_r} m_{rr-k}^{ijM} w_{r-k}^{jM}(t), \qquad r > m \qquad (7.73)$$

To use the model it would have to be calibrated, with some estimates of the various rates being made from data for one or more 'historical' projection periods, and then these rates themselves have to be projected forward before the model can be used for future-oriented projections. The migration model described in Section 7.4 can be used to help do this for the migration rates. The birth rates and survival rates for the future must be estimated by trend projections of historical data combined with detailed demographic work.

*7.6. FURTHER DEVELOPMENTS II: A CONTINUOUS VARIABLE MODEL

In the models built in previous sections of this chapter, we have had considerable difficulty in handling age groups, and especially in the generalized case where people may survive into more than one age group in a projection period. One way of overcoming this difficulty is to treat time as a continuous variable: both in the sense of age, and as calendar time. In a continuous variable model, birth is to be interpreted as being born in the next infinitesimal interval of time, while survival and migration are to be interpreted as 'surviving into' and 'surviving into and migrating during' the next period of time.

Since we are going to treat age as a continuous variable, as well as calendar time, we no longer read it as a subscript and we write our populations as $w^{iF}(r, t)$ and $w^{iM}(r, t)$, the female and male populations in region i age r at time t. (Strictly, these are population density functions, and we should speak of $w^{iF}(r, t) \, \delta r$ as the female population of region i aged between r and $r + \delta r$). If we now define $b^{iF}(r, t)$ and $b^{iM}(r, t)$ to be the female and male birth rates to females age r at time t, then the birth equations are simply

$$w^{iF}(0, t) = \int_\alpha^\beta b^{iF}(r, t) w^{iF}(r, t) \, dr \qquad (7.74)$$

$$w^{iM}(0, t) = \int_\alpha^\beta b^{iM}(r, t) w^{iF}(r, t) \, dr \qquad (7.75)$$

where α and β are the limits of the child-bearing age ranges. Then, approximately, $w^{iF}(0, t)\,\delta t$ and $w^{iM}(0, t)\,\delta t$ are the number of births between t and $t + \delta t$.

In order to obtain the survival and migration equations, let us manipulate equation (7.72) from the generalized discrete model. It is repeated here for convenience:

$$w_r^{iF}(t + T) = \sum_{k=0}^{n_r} s_{rr-k}^{iF} w_{r-k}^{iF}(t) + \sum_{j \neq i} \sum_{k=0}^{n_r} m_{rr-k}^{ijF} w_{r-k}^{jF}(t) \qquad (7.72)$$

We transform this to the continuous notation for an increment t to $t + \delta t$ in which the population age r age to $r + \delta r$. Of course,

$$\delta r = \delta t \qquad (7.76)$$

in this case. Recall that the survival and birth rates were functions of t and $t + T$ as well as r, and so we now define them to be $s^{iF}(r, \delta t, t)$ and $m^{ijF}(r, \delta t, t)$: the rate of survival of r age people to $r + \delta r$ in projection period $\delta t (= \delta r)$, and the corresponding migration rate. We can expand these rates about $\delta t = 0$:

$$s^{iF}(r, \delta t, t) = s^{iF}(r, 0, t) + \delta t \cdot \frac{\partial s^{iF}}{\partial \delta t} + O(\delta t^2) \qquad (7.77)$$

$$m^{ijF}(r, \delta t, t) = m^{ijF}(r, 0, t) + \delta t \cdot \frac{\partial m^{ijF}}{\partial \delta t} + O(\delta t^2) \qquad (7.78)$$

However, by definition

$$s^{iF}(r, 0, t) = 1 \qquad (7.79)$$

since everyone survives in a zero time interval, and

$$m^{ijF}(r, 0, t) = 0 \qquad (7.80)$$

since no-one migrates in a zero time interval. Equation (7.72) can be written, using the continuous variables as

$$w^{iF}(r + \delta r, t + \delta t) = s^{iF}(r, \delta t, t)w^{iF}(r, t) + \sum_{j \neq i} m^{ijF}(r, \delta t, t)w^{jF}(r, t) \qquad (7.81)$$

We can now substitute from equations (7.79) and (7.80) into (7.77) and (7.78) and then from the latter pair into (7.81). This gives

$$w^{iF}(r + \delta r, t + \delta t) = w^{iF}(r, t) + \delta t \frac{\partial s^{iF}}{\partial \delta t} \cdot w^{iF}(r, t)$$

$$+ \sum_{j \neq i} \delta t \frac{\partial m^{ijF}}{\partial \delta t} \cdot w^{jF}(r, t) \qquad (7.82)$$

Define

$$\sigma^{iF}(r, t) = \frac{\partial s^{iF}}{\partial \delta t}(r, \delta t, t)|_{\delta t = 0} \tag{7.83}$$

$$\mu^{ijF}(r, t) = \frac{\partial m^{ijF}}{\partial \delta t}(r, \delta t, t)|_{\delta t = 0} \tag{7.84}$$

and substitute in equation (7.82):

$$w^{iF}(r + \delta r, t + \delta t) = w^{iF}(r, t) + \delta t \cdot \sigma^{iF}(r, t)w^{iF}(r, t)$$
$$+ \sum_{j \neq i} \delta t \cdot \mu^{ijF}(r, t)w^{jF}(r, t) + O(\delta t^2) \tag{7.85}$$

This can be rearranged as

$$\frac{w^{iF}(r + \delta r, t + \delta t) - w^{iF}(r, t)}{\delta t} = \sigma^{iF}(r, t)w^{iF}(r, t)$$
$$+ \sum_{j \neq i} \mu^{ijF}(r, t)w^{jF}(r, t) + O(\delta t) \tag{7.86}$$

Now let $\delta t \to 0$, and equation (7.86) becomes

$$\frac{\partial w^{iF}}{\partial t}(r, t) = \sigma^{iF}(r, t)w^{iF}(r, t) + \sum_{j \neq i} \mu^{ijF}(r, t)w^{jF}(r, t) \tag{7.87}$$

so that we now have a set of simultaneous linear differential equations in $w^{iF}(r, t)$. An exactly similar equation could be written down for $w^{iM}(r, t)$.

This is a tricky equation system to handle, for it contains two time variables, r and t, but $\delta r = \delta t$. The next step is to write the equation in terms of a single time variable. Put

$$r = r_0 + \hat{t} \tag{7.88}$$

and

$$t = t_0 + \hat{t} \tag{7.89}$$

so that $\hat{t}$ represents elapsed time from some base t_0. We can later consider the equation system for a range of values of r_0. Equation (7.87) can now be written in full (dropping the $\hat{}$ on $\hat{t}$ and the 0 on r_0) as

$$\frac{\partial w^{iF}}{\partial t}(r + t, t_0 + t) = \sigma^{iF}(r + t, t_0 + t)w^{iF}(r + t, t_0 + t)$$
$$+ \sum_{j \neq i} \mu^{ijF}(r + t, t_0 + t)w^{jF}(r + t, t_0 + t) \tag{7.90}$$

The equivalent equation for males is

$$\frac{\partial w^{iM}}{\partial t}(r + t, t_0 + t) = \sigma^{iM}(r + t, t_0 + t)w^{iM}(r + t, t_0 + t)$$

$$+ \sum_{j \neq i} \mu^{ijM}(r + t, t_0 + t)w^{jM}(r + t, t_0 + t) \quad (7.91)$$

These equations can be solved as linear simultaneous differential equations in a function of t for a (continuous) set of values of r. At $t = 0$, the solution has to satisfy the boundary condition $w^{iF}(r, t_0)$ and $w^{iM}(r, t_0)$ which are assumed to be given. The values of $w^{iF}(0, t_0 + t)$ and $w^{iM}(0, t_0 + t)$ are given for all t by equations (7.74) and (7.75) with t replaced by $t_0 + t$.

The next step is to explore the nature of the coefficients $\sigma^{iF}(r, t)$ and $\mu^{ijF}(r, t)$. We shall see that they are not rates in the usual manner, but derivatives of rates. Consider $s^{iF}(r, \delta t, t)$ as a function of δt and r for given t. The δt and r dimensions are shown in Figure 7.5; s^{iF} can be considered to be plotted as a

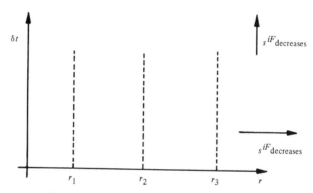

Figure 7.5   Survival rates' surface, with time as a
continuous variable

surface in a third dimension at right angles to these. As shown on the Figure, s^{iF} decreases as r increases and as δt increases. If we fix r and cut a section through the Figure 7.5 surface, say at $r = r_1, r_2$ and r_3, then we can show a plot of $s^{iF}(r, \delta t, t)$ against δt for given values of r. This is shown in Figure 7.6. We now see that $\sigma^{iF}(r, t)$ is the gradient of one of these curves at $\delta t = 0$.

Similarly, we can plot $m^{ijF}(r, \delta t, t)$ against δt as shown in Figure 7.7. μ^{ijF} is the gradient of these curves (for given r) at $\delta t = 0$. Note that in the case shown in Figure 7.7, r_1 represents an age group with a higher migration propensity than r_2, and r_2 a higher propensity than r_3. They are not necessarily in any particular numerical order of course.

Now assuming that $\sigma^{iF}(r, t)$, $\sigma^{iM}(r, t)$, $\mu^{iF}(r, t)$ and $\mu^{iM}(r, t)$ can be estimated from empirical studies and then projected forward on the basis of trends or a

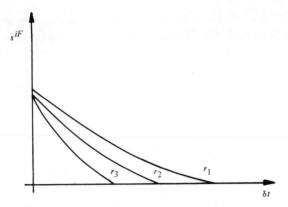

Figure 7.6 Cross-section through the survival rates'
surface

range of assumptions, how do we solve the differential equation system given by equations (7.90) and (7.91)? They are a very unusual set of differential equations since, although t is the main independent variable, r and t_0 can vary also. The first task is to *organize* the solution of the equations. We do this by noting that r and t_0 between them determine the cohort structure of the population. If we assume we are given the initial distribution of population $w^{iF}(r, t_0)$ and $w^{iM}(r, t_0)$, and that we are given births at all future times from equations (7.74) and (7.75), that is $w^{iF}(0, t_0 + t)$ and $w^{iM}(0, t_0 + t)$ for all t, then we see that our task is to solve the differential equation system for each cohort in turn for $t > 0$: that is, to project $w^{iF}(r, t_0)$, $w^{iM}(r, t_0)$ $w^{iF}(0, t_0 + t)$ and $w^{iM}(0, t_0 + t)$ forward. In the case of future births, we start from $t = t_1 > 0$, not $t = 0$, for a full range of t_1. Although r and t_1 and t vary continuously, it will perhaps help fix understanding if we consider them to

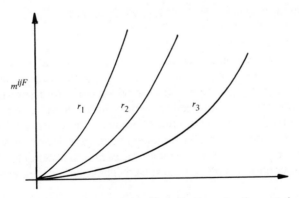

Figure 7.7 Cross-section through the migration rates'
surface

vary in one year intervals and then we can exhibit the cohorts which are being modelled as in Table 7.2 shown for the female population. A similar table could be drawn up for males. It can then easily be seen that Table 7.2

Table 7.2   Cohorts in the continuous variable formulation

	Initially		Predicted		
$t_1 = 0$	$w^{iF}(0, 0)$	$w^{iF}(1, 1)$	$w^{iF}(2, 2)$	$w^{iF}(3, 3)$	...
	$w^{iF}(1, 0)$	$w^{iF}(2, 1)$	$w^{iF}(3, 2)$	$w^{iF}(4, 3)$	...
	$w^{iF}(2, 0)$	$w^{iF}(3, 2)$	$w^{iF}(4, 3)$	$w^{iF}(5, 4)$	...
	$\vdots$				
$t_1 = 1$	$w^{iF}(0, 1)$	$w^{iF}(1, 2)$	$w^{iF}(2, 3)$	$w^{iF}(3, 4)$	...
$t_1 = 2$	$w^{iF}(0, 2)$	$w^{iF}(1, 3)$	$w^{iF}(2, 4)$	$w^{iF}(3, 5)$	...
$t_3 = 3$	$w^{iF}(0, 3)$	$w^{iF}(1, 4)$	$w^{iF}(2, 5)$	$w^{iF}(3, 6)$	...
	$\vdots$				

exhibits a number of discrete (r, t) points from a continuous array which shows that estimates will be made for all the population for all combinations of r and $t > 0$, and without repetition. The equations (7.90) are solved for r and t_0 (or t_0 and t_1) given for each row of Table 7.2 in turn. The first population shown in each row of the Table is given and provides a boundary condition.

For a given (r, t_0, t_1) combination, and a given sex, the differential equation system takes the form

$$\frac{\partial y_i(t)}{\partial t} = \sum_j a_{ij}(t) y_j(t) \tag{7.92}$$

and such equation systems are well known, for example, in the literature of theoretical biology and control engineering. Much of the discussion in this literature relates to equations systems of the form of (7.92), but in which the coefficients a_{ij} are time-independent. This could be useful for us if we are projecting forward for relatively short periods, in which case we may obtain a set of a_{ij}s for each (r, t_0, t_1) combination which could be assumed independent of t. How short the projection period would have to be before the approximation was sound is a matter of empirical investigation. In general, though, we will be interested in the time-dependent case. However, we indicate for time-independent and time-dependent cases in turn how equation systems of the form of equation (7.92) can be solved. The time-independent case is

$$\frac{\partial y_i}{\partial t} = \sum_j a_{ij} y_j \tag{7.93}$$

general solution can be obtained in this case. Our first task is to transform the matrix a_{ij} to a particular canonical form using the contragredient transformation (and in this we are following Rosen, 1970 and Birkhoff and Maclane, 1953). Write equation (7.93) in an obvious matrix notation, dropping the subscripts:

$$\frac{\partial \mathbf{y}}{\partial t} = \mathbf{a}\mathbf{y} \tag{7.94}$$

We wish to find a non-singular transformation $\mathbf{T}$ so that we have new variables $\mathbf{y}^*$ given by

$$\mathbf{y}^* = \mathbf{T}\mathbf{y} \tag{7.95}$$

and a matrix of coefficients $\mathbf{a}^*$ given by

$$\mathbf{a}^* = \mathbf{T}\mathbf{a}\mathbf{T}^{-1} \tag{7.96}$$

Then equation (7.94) can be written

$$\frac{\partial}{\partial t}\mathbf{T}^{-1}\mathbf{y}^* = \mathbf{a}\mathbf{T}^{-1}\mathbf{y}^* \tag{7.97}$$

and so pre-multiplying by $\mathbf{T}$, and using equation (7.96),

$$\frac{\partial \mathbf{y}^*}{\partial t} = \mathbf{a}^*\mathbf{y}^* \tag{7.98}$$

Our task is to choose $\mathbf{T}$ so that $\mathbf{a}^*$ takes an appropriately simple form. This task is dealt with in an Appendix where it is shown that we can find a vector α, a cyclic vector of $\mathbf{a}$, such that $\alpha, \mathbf{a}\alpha, \mathbf{a}^2\alpha, \ldots \mathbf{a}^{n-1}\alpha$ can be taken as a new basis leading to a coordinate transformation $\mathbf{T}$, the contragredient transformation, which gives

$$\mathbf{a}^* = \mathbf{T}^{-1}\mathbf{a}\mathbf{T} = \begin{bmatrix} 0 & 0 & \ldots & -\beta_n \\ 1 & 0 & \ldots & -\beta_{n-1} \\ 0 & 1 & \ldots & -\beta_{n-2} \\ \vdots & \vdots & & \\ 0 & 0 & \ldots & 1-\beta_1 \end{bmatrix} \tag{7.99}$$

The β_ns are given by

$$\beta^n = A_{N-n+1} \tag{7.100}$$

where the A_ns are the coefficients of the characteristic polynomial of $\mathbf{a}$. Then, substituting from equation (7.99) into equation (7.98), the transformed equation system can be written out in full as

$$
\left.
\begin{aligned}
\frac{\partial y_1^*}{\partial t} &= y_2^* \\[2mm]
\frac{\partial y_2^*}{\partial t} &= y_3^* \\[2mm]
&\;\;\vdots \\[2mm]
\frac{\partial y_N^*}{\partial t} &= \sum_{i=1}^{N} A_i y_i^*
\end{aligned}
\right\}
\tag{7.101}
$$

We can then substitute for y_2^* from the first of equations (7.101) into the second and so on, and these N first-order differential equations are then seen to be equivalent to a single Nth order differential equation

$$
\frac{d^n y_1^*}{dt^n} + A_1 \frac{d^{n-1} y_1^*}{dt^{n-1}} + \cdots + A_N y_1^* = 0
\tag{7.102}
$$

The general solution of this equation can then be obtained in the usual way. Write D for the operator d/dt, and write equation (7.102) in the form

$$
f(D) y_1^* = 0
\tag{7.103}
$$

Then we note

$$
f(D)\, e^{at} = f(a)\, e^{at}
\tag{7.104}
$$

and so

$$
y_1^* = e^{at}
\tag{7.105}
$$

is a solution if

$$
f(a) = \sum_{i=1}^{N} A_i a^i = 0
\tag{7.106}
$$

and this is the characteristic polynomial of a. If $\lambda_1, \lambda_2, \lambda_3 \ldots \lambda_n$ are the possible solutions for a, then

$$
y_1^* = \sum_{i=1}^{N} c_i\, e^{\lambda_i t}
\tag{7.107}
$$

is the general solution; $y_2^*, y_3^*, \ldots y_N^*$ can be obtained from equations (7.101) and $\mathbf{y}^*$ from equation (7.95), given $\mathbf{T}$ from the Appendix. If some of the λ_is are equal, special steps must be taken (Rosen, 1970, p. 101). In general, some of the values of λ_i may be complex and then the imaginary parts of $e^{\lambda_i t}$ cause damped oscillations.

We can now deal with the time-dependent case. Since the functions $a_{ij}(t)$ are to be determined empirically and we have no reason to think that they

:an be well fitted by simple analytical functions, at this stage we look for general formal solutions to the equation.

As with most differential equation systems of this kind, the general solution is usually expressed as a function of a number of particular solutions. Rosen (1970), for example, notes that if $\mathbf{y}^{(n)}(t)$ form N linearly independent particular solutions, and we form the matrix $\equiv(t)$ whose columns are the vector $\mathbf{y}^{(n)}$, then the general solution is

$$\mathbf{y}(t) = \equiv(t)\equiv^{-1}(t_0)\mathbf{y}(t_0) \tag{7.108}$$

where $\mathbf{y}(t_0)$ is the boundary condition. It is also sometimes convenient to apply the contragredient transformation. Rosenbrook and Storey (1970), from another field, give a similar general solution in a different notation. They go on to discuss the *stability* of solutions, which has obvious implications in the study of populations.

An alternative approach is to convert the differential equation system into integral equations, following Bellman (1970). Equation (7.94) integrates to

$$\mathbf{y} = \mathbf{y}(t_0) + \int_{t_0}^{t} \mathbf{a}(t^1)\mathbf{y}(t^1)\,dt^1 \tag{7.109}$$

and this can be solved by successive approximations. Given $\mathbf{y}(t_0)$, then the $(n + 1)$th approximation is

$$\mathbf{y}^{(n+1)} = \mathbf{y}(t_0) + \int_{t_0}^{t} \mathbf{a}(t^1)\mathbf{y}^{(n)}(t^1)\,dt^1 \tag{7.110}$$

This procedure obviously lends itself to numerical analysis more easily than does the search for particular solutions to the differential equation.

*7.7. FURTHER DEVELOPMENTS III: USE OF AN ACCOUNTING FRAMEWORK

It has recently been argued that demographic models are best placed on a sound analytical footing if they are developed in relation to an accounting framework, and that this also facilitates certain rate estimation tasks in relation to commonly available data (Rees and Wilson, 1973, Wilson and Rees, 1973, Rees and Wilson, 1974). The main ideas involved are briefly sketched here, though the reader is referred to the papers and the book cited above for details. First, the principles involved in this kind of accounting are explained and then they are applied to the same situation as the multi-region Rogers' model of Section 7.2. This leads to some new suggestions for that model.

The general ideas on accounting are presented here in relation to 'people', but they could be applied to all kinds of 'populations'. We begin by defining a set of state labels (such as 'age', 'location') 1, 2, 3,... N. Then we define K^{ij} as the number of people who were in state i at time t and state j at time $t + T$. Thus, using an asterisk to denote summation, K^{i*} is the original population in state i and K^{*j} the final population in stage j. These are the row

$$
\begin{array}{cccccc}
& & & & & \text{Row} \\
& & & & & \text{sums} \\
K^{11} & K^{12} & K^{13} & \dots & K^{1N} & K^{1*} \\
K^{21} & K^{22} & K^{23} & \dots & K^{2N} & K^{2*} \\
\vdots & \vdots & \vdots & & \vdots & \vdots \\
K^{M1} & K^{M2} & K^{M3} & \dots & K^{MN} & K^{M*}
\end{array}
$$

$$\text{Column sums} \quad K^{*1} \quad K^{*2} \quad K^{*3} \quad \dots \quad K^{*N}$$

Figure 7.8 The basic accounting scheme (The matrix need not be square, but for convenience we shall take $M = N$ unless otherwise stated.)

and column totals of the *accounting scheme* set out in Figure 7.8. We can define the matrix

$$\mathbf{K} = \{K^{ij}\} \tag{7.111}$$

as the accounting matrix, where $\{K^{ij}\}$ denotes the matrix whose (i, j)th element is K^{ij}. We can then define a matrix of rates, $\overline{\mathbf{G}}$, obtained from $\mathbf{K}$ by dividing each element by its row sum. Thus, an element K^{ij}/K^{i*} is the rate at which population in state i at t move to state j at $t + T$.

$$\overline{\mathbf{G}} = \{K^{ij}/K^{i*}\} \tag{7.112}$$

Suppose $'$ denotes transposition of a matrix, so if $\mathbf{A} = \{A_{ij}\}$, $A' = \{A^{ji}\}$. Then

$$\mathbf{G} = \overline{\mathbf{G}}' \tag{7.113}$$

is the matrix operator which turns the 'old' population into the 'new'. In full,

$$
\begin{bmatrix}
K^{11}/K^{1*} & K^{21}/K^{2*} & \dots & K^{N1}/K^{N*} \\
K^{12}/K^{1*} & K^{22}/K^{2*} & \dots & K^{N2}/K^{N*} \\
\vdots & & & \\
K^{1N}/K^{1*} & K^{2N}/K^{2*} & & K^{NN}/K^{N*}
\end{bmatrix}
\begin{bmatrix}
K^{1*} \\
K^{2*} \\
\vdots \\
K^{N*}
\end{bmatrix}
=
\begin{bmatrix}
K^{*1} \\
K^{*2} \\
\vdots \\
K^{*N}
\end{bmatrix}
\tag{7.114}
$$

if we denote by $\mathbf{K}^{\wedge *}$ the vector $\{K^{i*}\}$, and by $\mathbf{K}^{*\wedge}$ the vector $\{K^{*j}\}$, then equation (7.114) can be written more concisely as

$$\mathbf{GK}^{\wedge *} = \mathbf{K}^{*\wedge} \tag{7.115}$$

The reader can easily check that this equation is identically true. It becomes useful as a *model* equation when the rates K^{ij}/K^{i*} can be estimated directly in some way.

We can apply it to the situation for which we stated the Rogers' model in Section 7.2. We need to construct a state label which distinguishes region of residence, and an age group. We do this by letting (i, r) be the (region, age group), with a special notation for births and deaths: let $(\beta(i), 1)$ denote birth in region i into age group 1 in the period t to $t + T$, and $(\delta(i), r)$ be death in region i at age r during t to $t + T$. Thus the possible initial states are (i, r), $i = 1, 2, \ldots N$, $r = 1, 2, \ldots R$, say, and $(\beta(i), 1)$, $i = 1, 2, \ldots N$ and the possible final states are (j, s) $j = 1, 2, \ldots N$, $s = 1, 2, \ldots R$ and $(\delta(j), s)$, $j = 1, 2, \ldots N, s = 1, 2, \ldots R$. We write the element of the accounting matrix as K^{ij}_{rs}, for $(i, r) \to (j, s)$ in t to $t + T$, and $K^{\beta(i)j}_{11}$, $K^{i\delta(j)}_{rs}$ if births or deaths are involved as initial or final states. We also have $K^{\beta(i)\delta(j)}_{11}$ for infant mortality. If $i \neq j$, then K^{ij}_{rs} is a migration element, $K^{\beta(i)j}_{11}$ is a birth followed by a migration, and $K^{i\delta(j)}_{rs}$ is migration followed by a death. The accounting matrix $\mathbf{K}$ can be written as

$$\mathbf{K} = \left[\begin{array}{c|c} \{K^{ij}_{rs}\} & \{K^{i\delta(j)}_{r\delta(j)}\} \\ \hline -\{K^{\beta(i)j}_{11}\} & \{K^{\beta(i)\delta(j)}_{11}\} \end{array} \right] \tag{7.116}$$

using an obvious notation for sub-matrices. This can usefully be written as follows, with additional rows of zeros added as indicated:

$$\mathbf{K} = \left[\begin{array}{cccc|cccc} \mathbf{K}^{11} & \mathbf{K}^{12} & \ldots & & \mathbf{K}^{1\delta(1)} & \mathbf{K}^{1\delta(2)} & \ldots & \\ \mathbf{K}^{21} & \mathbf{K}^{22} & \ldots & & \mathbf{K}^{2\delta(1)} & \mathbf{K}^{2\delta(2)} & \ldots & \\ \vdots & \vdots & & & \vdots & \vdots & & \\ \hline \mathbf{K}^{\beta(1)1} & \mathbf{K}^{\beta(1)2} & \ldots & & \mathbf{K}^{\beta(1)\delta(1)} & \mathbf{K}^{\beta(2)\delta(2)} & \ldots & \\ \mathbf{K}^{\beta(2)1} & \mathbf{K}^{\beta(2)2} & \ldots & & \mathbf{K}^{\beta(2)\delta(1)} & \mathbf{K}^{\beta(2)\delta(2)} & \ldots & \\ \vdots & \vdots & & & \vdots & \vdots & & \end{array} \right] \tag{7.117}$$

where $\mathbf{K}^{ij}$ is the matrix whose (r, s)th element is K^{ij}_{rs}, $\mathbf{K}^{i\delta(j)}$ that whose (r, s)th element is $K^{i\delta(j)}_{rs}$, $\mathbf{K}^{\beta(i)j}$ that whose (r, s)th element is $K^{\beta(i)j}_{rs}$, and $\mathbf{K}^{\beta(i)\delta(j)}$ that whose (r, s)th element is $K^{\beta(i)\delta(j)}_{rs}$. Note that $K^{\beta(i)j}_{rs}$ and $K^{\beta(i)\delta(j)}_{rs}$ are defined to be zero unless $r = s = 1$ (and in that sense, rows of zeros have been added). $\mathbf{K}$ is now a $2NR \times 2NR$ matrix. We should also note that with the Rogers' assumption of equal age groups and those equal to T, $K^{ij}_{rs} = 0$ unless $s = r + 1$ and $K^{i\delta(j)}_{rs} = 0$ unless either $s = r$ or $s = r + 1$.

The row sums K^{i*}_{r*} are the number of people in age group r in region i at the time t, and $K^{\beta(i)*}_{1*}$ are the number of births in region i in t to $t + T$. The column sums are K^{*j}_{*s}, the number of people in age group s in region j at time $t + T$, and $K^{*\delta(j)}_{*s}$ is the number of people who die in age group s in region j in t to $t + T$. Thus, the rates to be defined are of the form (for the four 'quadrants' of $\mathbf{K}$ in equation (7.117))

$$K^{ij}_{rs}/K^{i*}_{r*}, \ K^{i\delta(j)}_{rs}/K^{i*}_{r*}, \ K^{\beta(i)j}_{11}/K^{\beta(i)*}_{1*}$$

and $K_{11}^{\beta(i)\delta(j)}/K_{1*}^{\beta(i)*}$. Transposition involves r and s as well as i and j, and so the matrix **G** can be defined as

$$
\mathbf{G} = \left[
\begin{array}{cccc|cccc}
\mathbf{G}^{11} & \mathbf{G}^{21} & \dots & & \mathbf{G}^{\beta(1)1} & \mathbf{G}^{\beta(2)1} & \dots \\
\mathbf{G}^{12} & \mathbf{G}^{22} & \dots & & \mathbf{G}^{\beta(1)2} & \mathbf{G}^{\beta(2)2} & \dots \\
\hline
\mathbf{G}^{1\delta(1)} & \mathbf{G}^{2\delta(1)} & \dots & & \mathbf{G}^{\beta(1)\delta(1)} & \mathbf{G}^{\beta(2)\delta(1)} & \dots \\
\mathbf{G}^{1\delta(2)} & \mathbf{G}^{2\delta(2)} & \dots & & \mathbf{G}^{\beta(1)\delta(2)} & \mathbf{G}^{\beta(2)\delta(2)} & \dots \\
\vdots & \vdots & & & \vdots & \vdots
\end{array}
\right] \tag{7.118}
$$

where

$$
G_{sr}^{ij} = \begin{cases} K_{rs}^{ij}/K_{r*}^{i*}, & s = r + 1 \\ 0 & s \neq r + 1 \end{cases} \tag{7.119}
$$

$$
G_{sr}^{\beta(i)j} = \begin{cases} K_{rs}^{\beta(i)j}/K_{1*}^{\beta(i)*}, & r = s = 1 \\ 0 & \text{otherwise} \end{cases} \tag{7.120}
$$

$$
G_{sr}^{i\delta(j)} = \begin{cases} K_{rs}^{i\delta(j)}/K_{r*}^{i*}, & s = r, s = r + 1 \\ 0 & \text{otherwise} \end{cases} \tag{7.121}
$$

$$
G_{sr}^{\beta(i)\delta(j)} = \begin{cases} K_{rs}^{\beta(i)\delta(j)}/K_{r*}^{\beta(i)*}, & r = s = 1 \\ 0 & \text{otherwise} \end{cases} \tag{7.122}
$$

In other words, in defining the sub-matrices of **G**, the i–j transposition was carried out, but not the r–s transposition. The model equation, then, is

$$
\mathbf{GK}\hat{}* = \mathbf{K}*\hat{} \tag{7.123}
$$

where

$$
\mathbf{K}\hat{}* = \begin{bmatrix} K_{1*}^{1*} \\ K_{2*}^{1*} \\ \vdots \\ K_{1*}^{2*} \\ K_{2*}^{2*} \\ \vdots \\ K_{1*}^{\beta(1)*} \\ 0 \\ \vdots \\ K_{1*}^{\beta(2)*} \\ 0 \\ \vdots \end{bmatrix} \tag{7.124}
$$

$$(7.126)$$

$$
\begin{bmatrix}
K_{12}^{11}/K_{1*}^{1*} & 0 & \cdots & 0 & 0 & \cdots & 0 & K_{11}^{\beta(1)1}/K_{1*}^{\beta(1)*} & 0 & \cdots & 0 & K_{11}^{\beta(2)1}/K_{1*}^{\beta(2)*} & 0 \cdots 0 \\
0 & K_{23}^{11}/K_{2*}^{1*} & & 0 & K_{12}^{21}/K_{1*}^{1} & 0 & & 0 & \cdots & 0 & 0 & \cdots \\
0 & & K_{23}^{21}/K_{2*}^{2*} & & & & & & & & & \\
\hline
0 \cdots 0 & & 0 & K_{12}^{12}/K_{1*}^{1} & 0 & \cdots & 0 & K_{11}^{\beta(1)2}/K_{1*}^{\beta(1)*} & 0 \cdots 0 & & K_{11}^{\beta(1)\delta(1)}/K_{1*}^{\beta(1)*} & 0 \cdots 0 \\
0 & K_{23}^{12}/K_{2*}^{1*} \cdots 0 & & & & & & & & & & \\
\hline
K_{11}^{1\delta(1)}/K_{1*}^{1*} & 0 \cdots 0 & & K_{11}^{2\delta(1)}/K_{2*}^{2*} & 0 \cdots 0 & & K_{11}^{\beta(1)\delta(1)}/K_{1*}^{\beta(1)*} & 0 \cdots 0 & & K_{11}^{\beta(2)\delta(1)}/K_{1*}^{\beta(2)*} & 0 \cdots 0 \\
K_{12}^{1\delta(1)}/K_{1*}^{1*} & K_{22}^{1\delta(1)}/K_{2*}^{1*} & 0 \cdots 0 & K_{12}^{2\delta(1)}/K_{2*}^{2*} & & & & & & & \\
\hline
K_{11}^{1\delta(2)}/K_{1*}^{1*} & 0 \cdots 0 & & & & & & & & & \\
K_{12}^{1\delta(2)}/K_{1*}^{1*} & & & & & & & & & & \\
\end{bmatrix}
\begin{bmatrix}
K_{1*}^{*1} \\
K_{2*}^{*1} \\
\vdots \\
K_{1*}^{2*} \\
K_{2*}^{2*} \\
\vdots \\
K_{1*}^{\beta(1)*} \\
0 \\
\vdots \\
0 \\
K_{1*}^{\beta(2)*} \\
0 \\
\vdots \\
0 \\
\vdots
\end{bmatrix}
=
\begin{bmatrix}
K_{*1}^{*1} \\
K_{*2}^{*1} \\
\vdots \\
K_{*1}^{*2} \\
K_{*2}^{*2} \\
\vdots \\
K_{*1}^{*\delta(1)} \\
K_{*2}^{*\delta(1)} \\
\vdots \\
K_{*1}^{*\delta(2)} \\
K_{*2}^{*\delta(2)} \\
\vdots \\
\vdots
\end{bmatrix}
$$

and

$$\mathbf{K^{*\wedge}} = \begin{bmatrix} K^{*1}_{*1} \\ K^{*1}_{*2} \\ \cdot \\ \cdot \\ K^{*2}_{*1} \\ K^{*2}_{*2} \\ \cdot \\ \cdot \\ K^{*\delta(1)}_{*1} \\ K^{*\delta(1)}_{*2} \\ \cdot \\ \cdot \\ K^{*\delta(2)}_{*1} \\ K^{*\delta(2)}_{*2} \\ \cdot \\ \cdot \end{bmatrix} \qquad (7.125)$$

For clarity, equation (7.123) is written out in full as equation (7.126).

The 'model' represented by equations (7.123) or (7.126) does not yet look very like the Rogers' model of Section 7.2. We can make it more directly comparable with the following series of manipulations. First, we need to record births by age of mother. This can be done by extending the terms in the $\{G^{\beta(i)j}_{rs}\}$ and $\{G^{\beta(i)\delta(j)}_{rs}\}$ sub-matrices as follows. Re-define $K^{\beta(i)j}_{11}$ to be $K^{\beta(i)j}_{11}(k)$ where k is age of mother (we refer to 'age of mother' even though, in this model, there is no sex disaggregation); similarly define $K^{\beta(i)\delta(j)}_{11}(k)$. Examples of the corresponding changes in the sub-matrices of $\mathbf{G}$ in equation (7.126) are

$$\begin{bmatrix} K^{\beta(1)1}_{11}/K^{\beta(1)*}_{1*} & 0\ldots\ldots 0 \\ 0\ldots\ldots\ldots\ldots 0 \\ 0\ldots\ldots\ldots\ldots 0 \end{bmatrix} \rightarrow$$

$$(7.127)$$

$$\begin{bmatrix} K^{\beta(1)1}_{11}(1)/K^{\beta(1)*}_{1*}(1) & K^{\beta(1)}_{11}(2)/K^{\beta(1)*}_{1*}(2) & \ldots \\ 0\ldots\ldots\ldots\ldots\ldots\ldots 0 \\ 0\ldots\ldots\ldots\ldots\ldots\ldots 0 \end{bmatrix}$$

$$
\begin{bmatrix} K_{11}^{\beta(1)\delta(1)}/K_{1*}^{\beta(1)*} & 0\ldots\ldots 0 \\ 0\ldots\ldots\ldots\ldots\ldots 0 \\ 0\ldots\ldots\ldots\ldots\ldots 0 \end{bmatrix} \rightarrow
$$

$$
\begin{bmatrix} K_{11}^{\beta(1)\delta(1)}(1)/K_{1*}^{\beta(1)*}(1) & K_{11}^{\beta(1)\delta(1)}(2)/K_{1*}^{\beta(1)*}(2) & \ldots \\ 0\ldots\ldots\ldots\ldots\ldots\ldots\ldots\ldots\ldots\ldots 0 \\ 0\ldots\ldots\ldots\ldots\ldots\ldots\ldots\ldots\ldots\ldots 0 \end{bmatrix} \qquad (7.128)
$$

The second half of the old population vector is changed correspondingly:

$$
\begin{bmatrix} K_{1*}^{\beta(1)*} \\ 0 \\ 0 \\ \vdots \\ K_{1*}^{\beta(2)*} \\ 0 \\ 0 \\ \vdots \end{bmatrix} \rightarrow \begin{bmatrix} K_{1*}^{\beta(1)*}(1) \\ K_{1*}^{\beta(1)*}(2) \\ \\ \vdots \\ K_{1*}^{\beta(2)*}(1) \\ K_{1*}^{\beta(2)*}(2) \\ \\ \vdots \end{bmatrix} \qquad (7.129)
$$

The birth-rate terms in equation (7.126), such as those shown in the sub-matrix in (7.127), multiply into total birth terms in the old population vector. It is more customary to express these rates in terms of base population in one age group. This can be achieved as follows: in each birth-rate term in equation (7.126), replace total births in the denominator by the equivalent total population, and simultaneously replace the total birth term in the old population vector by total population terms. Thus, the first row of the sub-matrix shown on the right-hand side of (7.127) now becomes

$$
[K_{11}^{\beta(1)1}(1)/K_{1*}^{\beta(1)*}(1) \quad \ldots] \rightarrow [K_{11}^{\beta(1)1}(1)/K_{1*}^{1*} \quad \ldots] \qquad (7.130)
$$

and the birth part of the old population vector, shown in (7.129), becomes

$$
\begin{bmatrix} K_{1*}^{\beta(1)*}(1) \\ K_{1*}^{\beta(1)*}(2) \\ \vdots \\ K_{1*}^{\beta(2)*}(1) \\ K_{2*}^{\beta(2)*}(2) \\ \vdots \end{bmatrix} \rightarrow \begin{bmatrix} K_{2*}^{1*} \\ K_{2*}^{1*} \\ \vdots \\ K_{1*}^{2*} \\ K_{2*}^{2*} \\ \vdots \end{bmatrix} \qquad (7.131)
$$

Thus, the second half of the population vector now duplicates the first. We can take advantage of this by converting **G** from a $2NR \times 2NR$ matrix to a $2NR \times NR$ matrix by adding the $(NR + i)$th column to the ith column, and taking the right-hand side of (7·131) as the whole of the new population vector. Call the matrix obtained from re-arranging **G** in this way $\hat{\mathbf{G}}$. Then, the model has become

$$
\hat{\mathbf{G}}
\begin{bmatrix}
K^{1*}_{1*} \\
K^{1*}_{2*} \\
\vdots \\
K^{2*}_{1*} \\
K^{2*}_{2*} \\
\vdots
\end{bmatrix}
=
\begin{bmatrix}
K^{*1}_{*1} \\
K^{*1}_{*2} \\
\vdots \\
K^{*2}_{*1} \\
K^{*2}_{*2} \\
\vdots \\
\hline
K^{*\delta(1)}_{*1} \\
K^{*\delta(1)}_{*2} \\
\vdots \\
K^{*\delta(2)}_{*1} \\
K^{*\delta(1)}_{*2} \\
\vdots
\end{bmatrix}
\tag{7.132}
$$

which can be written out in full as:

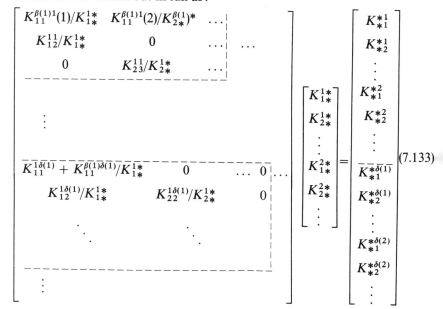

$$
\tag{7.133}
$$

f we are not interested in recording deaths explicitly, we can form $\hat{\hat{G}}$ from by deleting the final NR rows from G, and correspondingly amend the model equation by deleting the final NR rows from the new population vector. The model then becomes

$$\hat{\hat{G}} K^{\wedge *} = K^{*\wedge} \qquad (7.134)$$

where, now,

$$K^{\wedge *} = \begin{bmatrix} K^{1*}_{1*} \\ K^{1*}_{2*} \\ \cdot \\ \cdot \\ K^{2*}_{1*} \\ K^{2*}_{2*} \\ \cdot \\ \cdot \end{bmatrix} \qquad (7.135)$$

and

$$K^{*\wedge} = \begin{bmatrix} K^{*1}_{*1} \\ K^{*1}_{*2} \\ \cdot \\ \cdot \\ K^{*2}_{*1} \\ K^{*2}_{*2} \\ \cdot \\ \cdot \end{bmatrix} \qquad (7.136)$$

Equation (7.134) in full, is the 'top half' of equation (7.133). At this stage, we have an account-based model which is directly comparable with the Rogers' model of Section 7.2. What features emerge from the comparison? $\hat{\hat{G}}$ is equivalent to Rogers' growth matrix. The first point to note is that the non-zero terms are in the same place—as birth, survival and migration rates, with one exception: in the new model, terms such as $K^{\beta(1)2}_{11}/K^{1*}_{1*}$ appear, to represent migrating infants. These should therefore be added to the original Rogers' model. The second point is a more important one: the accounting framework has provided us with an explicit definition of all the rates. Survival, birth and migration rates can be written

$$s^{ii}_{rr+1} = K^{ii}_{rr+1}/K^{i*}_{r*} \qquad (7.137)$$

$$b^{i}(k) = K^{\beta(i)i}_{11}(k)/K^{\beta(i)*}_{1*}(k) \qquad (7.138)$$

$$m^{ij}_{rr+1} = K^{ij}_{rr+1}/K^{i*}_{r*} \qquad (7.139)$$

It is unlikely that most users of Rogers' model use these definitions for th various rates. For birth rates, for example, it is much more likely that the take

$$\text{birth rate} = \frac{\text{recorded births}}{\text{total population}} \qquad (7.14\text{0})$$

i.e.,

$$b^i(k) = K_{1*}^{\beta(i)*}(k)/K_{1*}^{1*} \qquad (7.141)$$

and these are analogous problems for the other rates. This is because i is terms such as $K_{1*}^{\beta(i)*}$ and $K_{*s}^{*\delta(i)}$ which are directly available from statistic As it happens, because of the way migration is measured, by questionin *surviving* migrants in a Census, K_{rr+1}^{ij} in equation (7.139) is directly availabl and this information can also be used to obtain a direct estimate of K_{rr+1}^{ii} However, there are many pitfalls in rate estimation from data which can b avoided if the accounting framework is used. The full details are availabl in the papers and book by Rees and Wilson cited at the beginning of thi section.

7.8. REFERENCES

R. Bellman (1970) *Methods of non-linear analysis*, Vol. 1, Academic Press, New York

G. Birkhoff and S. MacLane (1953) *A survey of modern algebra*, Macmillan, London

* N. Keyfitz (1968) *Introduction to the mathematics of population*, Addison-Wesley Reading, Mass.

I. S. Lowry (1966) *Migration and metropolitan growth*, Chandler, San Francisco.

I. Masser (1969) A test of some models for predicting intermetropolitan movement o population in England and Wales, University Working Paper 9, Centre fo Environmental Studies, London.

* R. Pressat (1972) *Demographic analysis*, Arnold, London.

P. H. Rees and A. G. Wilson (1973) Accounts and models for spatial demographic analysis I: age–sex-aggregated populations, *Environment and Planning*, **5**, pp. 61–90.

P. H. Rees and A. G. Wilson (1974) *Spatial demographic analysis*, to be published.

A. Rogers (1966) Matrix methods of population analysis, *Journal of the American Institute of Planners*, **32**, pp. 40–44.

A. Rogers (1967) Matrix analysis of inter-regional migration, *Papers, Regional Science Association*, **18**, pp. 177–196.

A. Rogers (1968) *Matrix analysis of inter-regional population growth and movement,* University of California Press, Berkeley.

* A. Rogers (1969) On perfect aggregation in the matrix cohort-survival model of interregional population growth, *Journal of Regional Science*, **9**, pp. 417–424.

* A. Rogers (1972) *Matrix methods in urban and regional analysis*, Holden Day, San Francisco.

A. Rogers and S. McDougall (1968) An analysis of population growth and change in Slovenia and the rest of Yugoslavia, Working Paper 81, Centre for Planning and Development Research, University of California, Berkeley.

R. Rosen (1970) *Dynamical systems theory in biology*, Vol. 1, John Wiley, New York.

H. H. Rosenbrook and C. Storey (1970) *Mathematics of dynamical systems*, Nelson, London.

R. Stone (1967) *Mathematics in the social sciences*, Chapman and Hall, London.

R. Stone (1970) *Mathematical models of the economy*, Chapman and Hall, London.

R. Stone (1971) *Demographic accounting and model building*, O.E.C.D., Paris.

A. G. Wilson (1972) Multi-regional models of population structure and some implications for a dynamic residential location model, in A. G. Wilson (ed.) *Patterns and processes in urban and regional systems*, Pion, London, pp. 217–240.

A. G. Wilson and P. H. Rees (1973) Accounts and models for spatial demographic analysis II: age–sex disaggregated populations, *Environment and Planning*, to be published.

CHAPTER 8

Models of urban and regional economies

8.1. THE INPUT–OUTPUT MODEL FOR A SINGLE REGION

In this chapter we shall study models of urban or regional economies, which we may refer to simply as the 'urban economy', or the 'economy' for short. This economy is the set of organizations of the city or region which produce goods and services. We shall be studying the economy in an aggregated sense: groups of organizations with similar characteristics will be collected together and called an industry, and we shall model the inter-relationships and products of these industries.

The input–output model, as the name implies, is concerned with the inputs and outputs of each industry and their inter-relationships. The products of an industry can be used as industrial inputs (in other industries, or in that in which it was produced) or can be consumed by what is defined to be the final demand sector. Typically, by final demand is meant household, export, governmental or investment demand. We should also note at this stage, to complete the picture, that each industry may have a number of inputs supplied from outside what we have defined as the industries of our system. These exogenous inputs include primary factors of production such as labour and capital, imports from outside the system, governmental subsidies and so on.

The structure thus described can be formally assembled as a set of accounts. Let X^m be the total product of industry m in some time period, say one year. This is used either as inputs to other industries or is consumed by the final demand sector. Let Z^{mn} be the amount of X^m used as an input to industry n, and let Y^m be the amount consumed by the final demand sector. We assume that the products of each industry m can be allocated between so-called intermediate demand and final demand in this way. Note that as m varies, Z^{mn} gives the inputs to industry n. However, we have already noted that there are also exogenous inputs and, for industry n, we shall lump these together for the time being and call them Z^{0n}. We can then form the set of accounts shown in Table 8.1.

We see immediately that for each row we must have

$$\sum_{n=1}^{s} Z^{mn} + Y^m = X^m \tag{8.1}$$

as the total output of industry m, where S is the total number of sectors.

Table 8.1.   System of accounts for a single region.

		Inputs to industry 1, 2, ...					Exogenous sector: final demand	Total output
		1	2	3	4 ... n ...			
Outputs of industry 1, 2, ...	1	Z^{11}	Z^{12}	Z^{13}	$Z^{14} \dots Z^{1n}$ ...		Y^1	X^1
	2	Z^{21}	Z^{22}	Z^{23}	$Z^{24} \dots Z^{2n}$ ...		Y^2	X^2
	3	Z^{31}	Z^{32}	Z^{33}	$Z^{34} \dots Z^{3n}$ ...		Y^3	X^3
	4							
	⋮							
	m	Z^{m1}	Z^{m2}	Z^{m3}	$Z^{m4} \dots Z^{mn}$ ...		Y^m	X^m
	⋮							
Exogenous sector (Labour, capital, imports, etc.)		Z^{01}	Z^{02}	Z^{03}	$Z^{04} \dots Z^{0n}$ ...			

It is also useful to form the column sums of the set of accounts, $\sum_{m=0}^{s} Z^{mn}$. However, this is only meaningful if the same units are used for each item in a column. It seems natural to suppose that the same units are used in each row, which is simply an apportionment of the product of a single industry, but not necessarily in each column, given the usual data deficiencies. We shall see later that this is a useful distinction to make.

So far, we have made a number of definitions and built a set of accounts. In order to build a model, we now have to make some hypotheses and to construct the input–output model we proceed as follows. Consider the ratio Z^{mn}/X^n: this is the amount of the produce of industry m which is used to make a unit of the product of industry n. Our main hypothesis is that the coefficient

$$a_{mn} = \frac{Z^{mn}}{X^n} \tag{8.2}$$

is a constant. Then we can note from equation (8.2) that Z^{mn} can be replaced by $a_{mn}X^n$ in the accounting equation (8.1) to give

$$\sum_{n=1}^{s} a_{mn}X^n + Y^m = X^m \tag{8.3}$$

This can be written

$$\sum_{n=1}^{s} (\delta_{mn} - a_{mn})X^n = Y^m \tag{8.4}$$

where δ_{mn} is a kronecker delta ($\delta_{mn} = 1$ if $m = n$, 0 otherwise). We now see equation (8.4) as a set of simultaneous linear equations in X^m: given a set of final demands Y^n and a set of *technical coefficients* a_{mn} then we can solve for total product X^m. We can write equations (8.4) in matrix notation as

$$(\mathbf{I} - \mathbf{a})\mathbf{X} = \mathbf{Y} \qquad (8.5)$$

and we can solve for $\mathbf{X}$ by pre-multiplying by $(\mathbf{I} - \mathbf{a})^{-1}$:

$$\mathbf{X} = (\mathbf{I} - \mathbf{a})^{-1}\mathbf{Y} \qquad (8.6)$$

This is the usual statement of the input–output model. We can interpret this equation effectively if we expand $(\mathbf{I} - \mathbf{a})^{-1}$. It is a standard result that, for $x < 1$, then

$$(1 - x)^{-1} = 1 + x + x^2 + x^3 + \dots \qquad (8.7)$$

This relationship can be applied to matrices also and equation (8.6) can then be written

$$\mathbf{X} = (\mathbf{I} + \mathbf{a} + \mathbf{a}^2 + \mathbf{a}^3 + \dots)\mathbf{Y} \qquad (8.8)$$

$\mathbf{IY}\,(= \mathbf{Y})$ is the amount of the product directly demanded by the final demand sector; $\mathbf{aY}$ is the amount of products directly demanded by the intermediate demand sector; the rest of the sum may be referred to as the indirect demand (products for industries to provide the inputs to make the intermediate demand and so on—an infinite regress). Of course, we do not have to sum the infinite series in equation (8.8) in practice, as we can invert the matrix $(\mathbf{I} - \mathbf{a})$ and use equation (8.6) to estimate total product.

We can now return briefly to the question of units and the utility of the column sums in the accounts of Figure 8.1: so far we have utilized only the row sums in the accounts. Suppose we can find a common unit for rows and columns—which would almost certainly have to be money. Suppose though, that Z^{mn}, X^m and Y^m still referred to appropriate physical units for each good, and that p^m was the price for such a unit of good m. Then, we can define quantities $\hat{Z}^{mn}$, $\hat{X}^m$ and $\hat{Y}^m$ which are Z^{mn}, X^m and Y^m measured in monetary units:

$$\hat{Z}^{mn} = Z^{mn}p_m \qquad (8.9)$$

$$\hat{X}^m = X^m p_m \qquad (8.10)$$

$$\hat{Y}^m = Y^m p_m \qquad (8.11)$$

Suppose we now assume that row sums and column sums balance for each industry. We must have

$$\sum_{n=1}^{s} a_{mn}\hat{X}^n/p_n + \hat{Y}^m/p_m = \hat{X}^m/p_m$$

$$= \sum_{m=1}^{s} a_{mn}\hat{X}^n/p_n \qquad (8.12)$$

We can use the second two relationships and multiply through by $p^m p^n$ and re-arrange:

$$\sum_{m=1}^{s} a_{mn} X^n p_m = X^m p_n \qquad (8.13)$$

and this is a set of simultaneous linear equations in the prices which we can solve, taking one of the prices, say p_0, the money price of factor *etc* inputs, as numeraire. To do this empirically, we can see from equation (8.13) that we need to know the technical coefficients a_{mn}, and the total products X^m in money units. In studies of urban and regional systems we rarely have such data. We recall that we can use the input–output equation (8.6) with any set of units provided they are consistent within a row. One case of interest to us, for example, is the use of employment units.

It is already clear that the input–output model represents interaction between industries in a useful way. In particular, we note that the matrix $(\mathbf{I} - \mathbf{a})^{-1}$ in equation (8.6) can be interpreted as a *matrix multiplier*: given final demand $\mathbf{Y}$, this is scaled up by one matrix, in a way which takes account of all the terms in the infinite series in equation (8.8), to give a total product sector for the economy. The model will be useful insofar as we can forecast final demand and insofar as our knowledge of the technical coefficients a_{mn}, and the way in which they might change, is sound. There are special problems also at the urban and regional scale. Artle (1959) remarks that, for the United States, he believes that 40% of the total product is final demand and 60% intermediate. He goes on: 'This percentage distribution changes drastically when the object of our study is a region within the United States. Generally speaking, the smaller the region, the higher is the percentage allocated to final demand. To understand why this is so, it may be sufficient to think of the division of labor, and other forms of specialisation which occur within the nation, and which reflect themselves in one item of final demand, namely, in "exports" to the rest of the nation. This item, which is of course non-existent in a national study, usually becomes quite important in the regional study.' Thus, he goes on to argue the need to disaggregate the final demand sector not only into household, export and governmental sectors, but also to disaggregate the household sector itself.

In summary then, we can say that to build an input–output model we need a detailed set of accounts of inter-industry relations; to make forecasts of the technical coefficients (which turns on having good definitions of industries, each of organizations with common and relatively stable input profiles); and to obtain forecasts of exogenous inputs and the final demand sectors. The matrix multiplier of equation (8.6) can then be used to forecast total economic product for each industry.

In the following sections of this chapter we discuss the economic base model (8.2), a particularly simple but often used version of the input–output model, the mechanisms of growth (8.3), multi-region input–output models (8.4), econometric approaches to modelling (8.5), and conclude with a review c problems and the import of some recent developments on these problem (8.6).

8.2. THE ECONOMIC BASE MODEL

In an urban or regional system, an economic base model is developed b assuming that there is a single sector, which includes a basic sector to mee export demand. If we denote the single industrial sector by X and the expor demand by Y, and if we assume that

$$a = \frac{X - Y}{X} \tag{8.14}$$

is constant, then the reader can easily check that the accounting identity

$$(1 - a)X = Y \tag{8.15}$$

holds, and indeed, that

$$X = (1 - a)^{-1}Y \tag{8.16}$$

This shows that the economic base model is a scalar version of the input–output model: with one industrial sector and one final demand sector which is supposed to be wholly concerned with exports from the system. In principle this model can be used in the same way as the input–output model: given Y we can obtain X from equation (8.16). In practice, it is clearly such a poor representation of an urban or regional economy that it is a very dangerous model to use. Unfortunately it is frequently used, probably because it is relatively easy to obtain data for it, though it is not easy to make the basic-export distinction adequately (Massey, 1970) compared to the input–output model. It is, of course, possible to improve the economic base model by introducing more sectors but, since it relies on the theory of export-led growth entirely, it still seems more general to use the input–output model framework directly.

8.3. THE MECHANISMS OF GROWTH

There is a vast economic literature on models of economic growth (for a review of such models, see Bergstrom, 1967). All that we can attempt to do here is to note that there is a variety of mechanisms of growth, many of, if not most of, which can be incorporated into the input–output model. For a particular economy, we might note the possibility of growth (or decline, of course) brought about by changing demand for its goods from outside (that is, changing exports), changing demand for ex-system goods by its own

ndustry and consumers (imports and import substitution), changing pattern
of demand of its own consumers (changing income and preferences of households and government sectors) and, finally, changing technology (new
products, changing inter-industry relations). Note immediately how difficult
it is to incorporate this range of effects into something like the economic base
model. In the case of the input–output model, however, all of these effects,
at least in theory, can be incorporated with ease. The mechanisms outlined
above are concerned with (using the terms introduced in Section 8.1):
exogenous demand (exports, households, government), exogenous inputs
(factors of production, imports) and the structure of the inter-industry
relationships. Further aspects of the problem of building dynamic economic
models will be discussed in Section 8.6.

8.4. THE INPUT–OUTPUT MODEL FOR A SYSTEM OF SEVERAL REGIONS

So far in this chapter we have considered models of a single-region economy
relative to the rest of the world. As in the case of demographic models, it is
useful to explore corresponding models of multi-region systems. This would
be of relevance, for example, to a national government which wanted to
explore the development of its regions, and their inter-relations, or to a
regional government interested in its sub-regions.

Suppose we have a system of N regions, labelled $i = 1, 2, \ldots N$ (or $j = 1,
2, \ldots N$). Then our first task is to produce the multi-region equivalent of the
accounting equation (8.3). We do this using the method of Leontief and Strout
(1963). Let X_i^m be the total amount of m produced in region i and let Y_i^m be
the final demand for this good. Let a_{mn}^i be the set of technical coefficients for
the industries of region i. If we are to build a consistent multi-region model,
the most important aspect we have to get right is the flow of goods between
the regions of the system. Let x_{ij}^m be the flow of goods produced in industry
m in the region i to region j; they may be used in j either for consumption or
intermediate demand. In this notation, if we use an asterisk to denote
summation, then the total amount of good m used in region i is clearly
x_{*i}^m, while the total amount produced in region i is x_{i*}^m. Thus, the accounting
relationship (8.3) becomes

$$\sum_{n=1}^{s} a_{mn} x_{i*}^n + Y_i^m = x_{*i}^m \tag{8.17}$$

There is one such equation for each region $i = 1, 2, \ldots N$ in the system.
However, the basic variables in the model are x_{ij}^m, and equation (8.17) could
be written explicitly in terms of these variables as

$$\sum_{n=1}^{s} a_{mn}^i \sum_{j=1}^{N} x_{ij}^n + Y_i^m = \sum_{j=1}^{N} x_{ji}^m \tag{8.18}$$

Clearly, there are many more unknowns than there are equations, and we can only solve for x_{ij}^m if we can find a way of adding more equations in x_{ij}^m, particularly relating to the flows for which $i \neq j$. What is needed is some kind of spatial interaction model for the x_{ij}^ms. If a full-blown economic model were being developed, and a set of prices were introduced for each region, then we could build a model based on the theory of trade (usually developed as the theory of *international* trade), comparative advantage and so on. At the regional scale, this is not likely to be fruitful in the short run at least because of data deficiencies. Leontief and Strout solved their problem with a very simple spatial interaction model. They hypothesized that

$$x_{ij}^m = \frac{x_{i*}^m x_{*j}^m}{x_{**}^m} Q_{ij}^m, \qquad i \neq j \tag{8.19}$$

where Q_{ij}^m is to be estimated from empirical data and plays the role of a distance attenuation function. We then recognize equation (8.19) as a variant of the *unconstrained* spatial interaction of Chapter 6. In this case, however, it is more than usually unconstrained, as even the total flow, x_{**}^m, is estimated within the model. The interaction equations are only assumed to hold for $i \neq j$; when these equations are added to the accounting equations (8.18), we obtain a set of simultaneous equations which can be solved for the x_{ij}^ms.

Clearly, many other kinds of spatial interaction model could be developed for this problem. Rather than unduly complicate the presentation at this point, however, further comments on this problem are reserved for Section 8.6.

8.5. ECONOMETRIC APPROACHES

This chapter has leaned very heavily on the concept of the input–output model in the development of models of urban and regional economies. Even when the model is used in its simplest form, however, it makes considerable demands on data, particularly in relation to the problem of estimating the technical coefficients and imports and exports. In such a situation, it is natural that simpler methods have been developed, typically using econometric methods. If these simpler methods are applied to a single region, then they consist of a time series statistical analysis and what amounts to a trend projection, and although this may be better than nothing, it is of relatively little interest to us here. Therefore, we shall concentrate on alternative econometric approaches to the multi-region problem, and we shall concentrate on two examples: both simultaneous equation models, one based on differential shift concepts (Lakshmanan, 1968), and one not (Hill, 1965). These models are usually applied to sub-regions within a region, or even to zones within a city, and as such may be considered to have a place in Chapter 10. However, they could also be used for regions within a nation, or for urban reas within a region, and so we have chosen to begin the discussion at this stage, at least for the purpose of introducing econometric models of urban or regional economies.

It is best with econometric models to estimate shifts, that is, changes rather than totals. We begin by describing Hill's Empiric model and then introduce the concept of differential shift. We shall assume that unless we state otherwise the unit of measurement of economic activity is employment. Then these econometric models predict *changes* in employment. (There is an interesting 'stock and flow' question here: if employment is used as the unit in input–output models, it is in the sense of 'total labour in a year contributing to that activity'. One of the problems in building a dynamic input–output model, of course, is estimating changes in such inputs, due to technological changes or changes in demand; the econometric models do not contain such richness, but we see that it is appropriate that they should focus on change in employment.) Let ΔX_i^m be the change in employment in industry m in some time period, say a year. Then, the Empiric model assumes that this change can be related to changes in other changes in employment on the one hand, and to values of regional characteristics, say Z_i^k, $(k = 1, \ldots M$ say), or changes in these, ΔZ_i^k in the time period. Thus, we hypothesize

$$\Delta X_i^m = \sum_{n=1}^{s} a_i^n X_i^n + \sum_{k=1}^{M} b_i^k (Z_i^k \text{ or } \Delta Z_i^k) \qquad (8.20)$$

The coefficients a_i^n and b_i^k are estimated by regression analysis: in principle either from time series data for the whole system, or as a^n and b^k, assuming constant values for each region, in which case the regression can also cover the range of regional values. Clearly, not all variables would be included in the right-hand side of equation (8.20); the ones to be used can be chosen on the basis of a combination of theoretical expectation for particular industries and contribution of the variable to goodness-of-fit following a series of statistical tests. Clearly, the coefficients a_i^n have some of the characteristics of technical coefficients in the input–output matrix, while the Z_i^ks or ΔZ_i^ks represent some kind of measure of comparative advantage.

The change in employment used in the Empiric model is the net shift in employment. Lakshmanan's (1968) model uses the same principles but employs the concept of differential shift. In order to define this concept, it is useful to introduce time explicitly into our notation, and so $X_i^m(t)$ is now the employment in region i in industry m at time t. We can retain the symbol Δ for net shift in a period from 0 to t, so

$$\Delta X_i^m(t) = X_i^m(t) - X_i^m(0) \qquad (8.21)$$

We use an asterisk, as usual, to denote summation, so that the net shift for the whole system is given by

$$\Delta X_*^m(t) = X_*^m(t) - X_*^m(0) \qquad (8.22)$$

We can then define the *proportionate shift for the whole system for industry m* to be α^m given by

$$\alpha^m = \frac{X_*^m(t)}{X_*^m(0)} \tag{8.23}$$

Then the differential shift (denoted by the operator DS) for region i is given by

$$DS \cdot X_i^m(t) = X_i^m(t) - (1 + \alpha^m)X_i^m(0) \tag{8.24}$$

It is the difference between expected change if the amount of employment in industry m in region i had grown at the same rate as the whole system, and what has actually occurred. The argument is that it is more likely that this shift rather than the net shift is closely related to regional characteristics and so these shifts are estimated by regression analysis. Typically, the variables used as independent variables in the regression analysis can be classified into the same groups as those used in equation (8.20), but using differential shifts instead of net shifts. Thus one might write

$$DS \cdot X_i^m(t) = \sum_{n=1}^{s} a_i^n DS \cdot X_i^{(n)}(t) + \sum_{k=1}^{M} b_i^k (Z_i^k \text{ or } \Delta Z_i^k) \tag{8.25}$$

Note that the Z_j^ks may include such terms as total population or total employment, or total employment in particular industries, at the beginning of the time period, or indeed in earlier time periods; it would be easy to introduce lagged variables in this way. Again, variables can be chosen on the basis of a mixture of theoretical expectation and contribution to goodness of fit.

One point must be emphasized at an early stage in relation to both of these models: the reader will have already noted that some of the dependent variables, the shifts, in some equations will appear as independent variables in others. This means special care must be taken when the coefficients of these equations are estimated: the usual regression analysis techniques lead to biased estimates, and something like two-stage least-squares or maximum-likelihood methods must be used (cf. Lakshmanan, 1968 or Johnson, 1961). It is also important from an econometric point of view not to mix variables which vary directly with zone size (such as population or land area) with those which do not (such as density); this can usually be easily achieved by careful variable definition.

The models which have been built of this form have typically also included population as a dependent variable and have estimated either net shift or differential shift in population using equations of the form of (8.20) or (8.25). This is of no direct concern to us here, but it is important to note that, for economic sectors, the shift terms on the right-hand side of the equation typically involve population shift terms. (And, of course, we may view these as alternative population forecasting models to the demographic models of Chapter 7).

We have already mentioned that the Z_j^k terms might include total population and employment figures. They usually also include measures of accessibility to population and to various kinds of employment, but such measures are probably most useful for finer spatial scales, as we shall see later.

8.6. FURTHER DEVELOPMENTS

As already indicated, an enormous literature exists in the economic field and it is impossible in the space available in a book of this nature to indicate in detail the many possible kinds of refinement which can be applied to the models described in this chapter. What is attempted here is only an indication of some of these refinements and alternative methods which are available in relation to a number of headings. The reader can pursue these lines of enquiry further in the references which are cited. The headings to be used are: classification problems, model improvements, model dynamics and optimization models.

Classification problems

Input–output models only work if it is possible to group organizations into industries within which the organizations have similar input structures and which produce commodities more or less peculiar to that activity. One of the biggest problems is that it is known empirically that most industries (on any reasonably aggregated classification scheme) produce a variety of commodities and that very few commodities are produced by one industry alone. To meet this difficulty, Stone (1970) has described a set of accounts in which entries are made both for commodities and for industries (or activities). A number of coefficients are defined which relate commodities and industries, and it is then possible to utilize the information in these accounts to build input–output models *either* using commodities *or* using industries. Stone also makes it elegantly clear that great care has to be taken to record all taxes separately in such accounts, otherwise errors can arise if input–output models are used to forecast employment generation, for example.

Artle (1965), whose achievement in building the input–output model of Stockholm in the late 50s remains outstanding, made particularly important advances in relation to the final demand sector, particularly in introducing a number of categories of household by income. This serves two major purposes: it enables better estimates of final demand to be made, since the form of demand functions will certainly vary with income; and secondly, since the model generates the income accruing to households in each category, it makes the model useful in a policy-making context in which it may be desirable to set goods on the distribution of income.

There is a perennial problem of relating the rather aggregative classifications for either industry or household to the corresponding micro-behavioural units of firms and households. This problem is tackled in an interesting way by Isard *et al.* (1969) who manage to write down a comprehensive set of accounts built on just such a basis. Of course, the very essence of the input-output model approach is that it is based on a set of accounts, and since we will always have aggregation/disaggregation problems, it is useful to develop a facility for manipulating the accounts—aggregating to cover data defi-ciencies, disaggregating where possible—to ensure that which model is developed makes maximum use of available information and yet is internally consistent. Stone (1967) shows how to aggregate multi-regional accounts in this way to allow for the fact that inter-region transaction data is rarely available. If accounts are used in this way then, in a sense, classification problems become less severe, as we realize that maximum available informa-tion is incorporated in them.

Model improvements

The point reached above in the discussion of classification problems is an appropriate point at which to discuss improvements in the model. As we aggregate our accounts to avoid data deficiencies, is it then always possible to build something which looks like an input–output model? The answer must be: not always! However, Artle (1965), for example, introduces some ingenious devices for handling the difficulties associated with this problem. In a single-region model he introduces (using *our* earlier notation) a quantity Z^{mn}, but then makes great use of quantities Z^{mm}, which he defines to be m-inputs to all industries, and Z^{**}, the total product. This leads him to a pro-cedure for building a consistent and useful model in spite of some data deficiencies.

In section 8.4, we described the Leontief and Strout approach to building multi-regional models. This turned on the definition of a spatial interaction model of flows x_{ij}^m for $i \neq j$. The present author has shown (Wilson, 1970) that it is possible to consider the regional input–output equation (8.24) as *constraints* on flows in an entropy-maximizing procedure. This leads to the development of a multi-regional model which has all the properties of the Leontief–Strout model, but which has improved spatial interaction models and which is internally consistent. (Consistency, of course, is a property whose achievement is facilitated by entropy-maximizing methods as well as by careful account building.)

Another area for improvement in any of these models is in relaxing the implicit assumption of aggregative *linear* production functions for each industry. This is straightforward enough in theory (see, for example, Dorfman, Samuelson and Solow, 1958), but difficult in practice because of the usual data deficiencies.

There is another interesting field of work with multi-regional models which attempts to model regional incomes and their inter-relationships directly. In effect, such models are based on sets of accounts which are extremely aggregated for each region so that only the total income of the region, and its apportionment to sources in other regions, is involved. This can be pursued in the work of Metzler (1950), for example, whose paper also indicates what the theory of international trade offers us in the development of multi-regional models.

We have not so far discussed improvements to the econometric models. We saw that in these models the shift in one industry was related to other shifts and to regional variables. One possibility which is currently being explored is that of using input–output tables in studies where empirical work has been possible to improve econometric models for other study areas. This involves carrying out the sort of analysis which Nystuen and Dacey (1961) suggested for flows in space to an input–output table, to identify the model structure of the economy, which then tells us something about dependent and independent variables in regression equations.

How can we summarize this rather sketchy account of what is a wide range of possible improvements to and developments of the models described earlier in this chapter? There is a sense, in this field of urban and regional analysis, that theory has run ahead of practice simply because of the difficulty of obtaining data to test new theoretical ideas, or even old ones. This may mean that we are in a situation where the theoretician has to play a new kind of role. We have available to us models which can be calibrated, but which have been aggregated in different ways because of data deficiencies. An interesting theoretical problem is then to ask : how do these different analyses constrain each other? For example, if an Empiric-type model or a differential shift model is estimated econometrically, then the values of the coefficients in such models *have a bearing on* the values of coefficients in an input–output model which cannot themselves be directly estimated. Further, we will have empirical estimates of *national* input–output coefficients, and these also have a bearing on the values of the regional ones (Hewings, 1971). Can we devise techniques which would enable us to put bounds on such coefficients by bringing all the relevant information to bear?

Model dynamics

In Section 8.3, we outlined briefly the mechanisms of growth in urban and regional economies and how these could be incorporated into the input–output model framework. Of course, a lot of work has been done on this and it has been reported in a large body of literature. We will content ourselves here with three observations on the problem of building dynamic models from the sort of basic models we have outlined in the rest of the chapter.

Firstly, the models which have been outlined are essentially *flow* models: the associated accounts represent transactions in some period such as a year, and the associated production processes depend on the existence of capital stock. Thus, a dynamic model must involve the representation of use of stock and its replacement. The first step is to incorporate stocks into the accounting framework, and Stone (1970) shows us how to do this by adding the balance sheet to the usual kind of transaction accounts. Dorfman, Samuelson and Solow (1958) present a range of dynamic linear models which can be built using this kind of principle. Most of these, while theoretically enlightening, are not empirically practicable at the urban and regional scale. This leads to our second observation.

Artle (1965) shows how to build a dynamic model in relatively simple fashion, particularly in relation to the difficult problem of estimating changes in the input–output coefficients. If a is a typical coefficient in his model, he usually assumes that it takes the form $a_0 + a_1 t$ for the sort of future time periods in which he is interested. Even this method, of course, requires some data to be available for two points in time.

Thirdly, we note that so far in this chapter we have worked implicitly with discrete time periods. It is possible, as it was in the demographic case, to treat time as a continuous variable. Indeed, Leontief, the inventor and doyen of input–output modelling, always preferred to do this. Dynamic models can then be represented in differential equation form. (Dorfman, Samuelson and Solow, 1958).

Optimization

So far we have assumed that our models are to be used for forecasting, given certain exogenous assumptions. As always in the urban-modelling field, we can turn this situation around and ask: can we use the model to help us achieve a particular desired end state at some point in the future? Or, alternatively, can we maximize some objective function? This involves us in optimization processes.

Usually, the task implied by the first question is not an easy one and heuristic methods have to be employed. However, Artle (1965) in his work on Hawaii has shown that the model can be used to test whether particular end states are feasible, and what kind of policies might bring them about.

The second question can be dealt with more systematically. Activity analysis developed partly because of the commodity/industry classification question which can bedevil input–output analysis, and partly solve the second question (for a detailed description, see Baumol, 1958). In essence, inputs and outputs are associated with activities, and the state of the economy is determined by the levels of these activities. It is possible to choose these levels so as to maximize some objective function subject to a number of constraints on resource inputs using linear-programming techniques.

3.7. REFERENCES

R. Artle (1959) *Studies in the structure of the Stockholm economy*, The Business Research Institute of the Stockholm School of Economics; republished in 1965 by the Cornell University Press, Ithaca, New York.

* R. Artle (1961) On some methods and problems in the study of metropolitan economics, *Papers, Regional Science Association*, **8**, pp. 71–87.

R. Artle (1965) External trade, industrial structure, employment mix and the distribution of incomes, a simple model of planning and growth, *The Swedish Journal of Economics*.

W. J. Baumol (1958) Activity analysis in one lesson, *American Economic Review*, **48**, pp. 837–873.

A. R. Bergstrom (1967) *The construction and use of economic models*, English Universities Press, London.

* B. Cameron (1968) *Input-output analysis and resource allocation*, Cambridge University Press, London.

R. Dorfman, P. A. Samuelson and R. Solow (1958) *Linear programming and economic analysis*, McGraw-Hill, New York.

G. J. D. Hewings (1971) Regional input–output models in the U.K. some problems and prospects for the use of non-survey techniques, *Regional Studies*, **5**, pp. 11–22.

D. M. Hill (1965) A growth allocation model for the Boston region, *Journal of the American Institute of Planners*, **31**, pp. 111–120.

* W. Hirsch (Ed.) (1962) *Elements of regional accounts*, Johns Hopkins Press, Baltimore.

* W. Hirsch (Ed.) (1964) *Regional accounts for policy decisions*, Johns Hopkins Press, Baltimore.

* W. Isard *et al.* (1960) *Methods of regional analysis*, M.I.T. Press, Cambridge, Mass.

W. Isard *et al.* (1969) *General theory: social, political, economic and regional*, M.I.T. Press, Cambridge, Mass.

* J. Jacobs (1970) *The economy of cities*, Jonathan Cape, London.

J. Johnson (1961) *Econometric methods*, Magraw-Hill, New York.

T. R. Lakshmanan (1968) A model for allocating urban activities in a state, *Socio-economic planning sciences*, **1**, pp. 283–295.

* W. Leontief (1967) *Input–output analysis*, Oxford University Press, Oxford.

W. Leontief and A. Strout (1963) Multi-regional input–output analysis, in T. Barna (Ed.) *Structural interdependence and economic development*, Macmillan, London, pp. 119–150.

D. B. Massey (1970) The basic/service categorization, Working Paper 63, Centre for Environmental Studies, London.

L. Metzler (1950) A multiple-region theory of income and trade, *Econometrica*, **18**, pp. 329–354.

* J. R. Meyer (1963) Regional economics: a survey, *American Economic Review*, **53**, pp. 19–54.

* W. H. Miernyk *et al.* (1970) *Simulating regional economic development*, Heath Lexington Book, Lexington, Mass.

* H. O. Nourse (1968) *Regional economics: a study in the economic structure, stability and growth of regions*, McGraw-Hill, New York.

J. D. Nystuen and M. F. Dacey (1961) A graph theory interpretation of nodal regions, *Papers, Regional Science Association*, **7**, pp. 29–42.

* H. W. Richardson (1969) *Regional economics*, Weidenfeld and Nicholson, London.

* J. I. Round, (1972) Regional input–output models in the U.K.: a reappraisal of some techniques, *Regional Studies*, **6**, pp. 1–9.

* H. Siebert (1969) *Regional economic growth: theory and policy*, International Textbook Co., Scranton, Pennsylvania.

R. Stone (1967) *Mathematics in the social sciences*, Chapman and Hall, London.

R. Stone (1970) *Mathematical models of the economy*, Chapman and Hall, London.

* H. Theil (1967) *Economics and information theory*, North Holland, Amsterdam.

* E. L. Ullman and M. F. Dacey (1960) The minimum requirements approach to the urban economic base, *Proceedings, Royal Society of Arts*, **6**, pp. 175–194.

A. G. Wilson (1970) Inter-regional commodity flows: entropy-maximizing approaches *Geographical Analysis*, **2**, pp. 255–282.

* C. S. Yan (1969) *Introduction to input–output economics*, Holt, Reinhart and Winston, New York.

CHAPTER 9

Transport models

9.1. PRELIMINARY DEFINITIONS

The pattern of transport flows in cities and regions is extremely complex. Trips are made by a variety of kinds of people, for a variety of purposes, on a maze of routes and by several modes. If we are to model this complex pattern, we need to take considerable care with our initial definitions.

A person trip is made from an *origin* to a *destination* by some *route*. The technological characteristics of the route chosen define the *mode* of the trip: walk on a footpath or road, car by road, various forms of public transport. The pattern of trips in the region, and the situation faced by a particular traveller, also vary by *time of day*.

Already, we have to face a number of complications. What if a family of three make the following trips: wife, husband and child leave home by car; the child is dropped at school; the husband is dropped at a railway station; the wife returns home; the husband proceeds to another station by train; finally he catches a bus to his office. How do we characterize these trips using the sort of terms we have introduced? It simplifies matters if we consider each person individually. The wife can be considered to make three origin–destination trips: home to school, school to station and station to home, by mode 'car driver' and for purpose 'serve passenger'. The child makes a journey from home to school, by mode 'car passenger', for purpose 'school'. The husband could be considered to make three trips: home to station, mode 'car passenger', purpose 'work'; station to station, mode 'rail', purpose 'work'; station to office, mode 'bus', purpose 'work'. When the greatest detail is required, the trip would have to be classified this way. An alternative is to clarify his journey as a single trip from home to office, purpose work, and with some means of recording the 'mixed mode' nature of the trip. If less detail is required, then the husband's trip might be classified as a single trip according to the *main* mode of travel, which in this case would be 'rail'. It is customary if this procedure is adopted to categorize the trip into the three categories of collection, line haul and distribution (Meyer, Kain and Wohl, 1965).

Inevitably, when we build a model there is considerable loss of information which partly helps us to resolve some of the definitional difficulties. It is obviously not possible to work with a level of detail in which trips are

127

recorded from individual address to individual address in the model. The study area will be divided into zones in the usual way, and we will model trips from zone to zone (and, to a minor extent, within a zone).

We can now proceed to introduce more formally some of the concepts which will be required in the rest of this chapter. Person trips will be classified by the type of person making the trip, the purpose of the trip, the mode used and route followed, and the time of day at which the trip was made. Commercial vehicle trips are considered separately. There are many ways in which these classifications can be made, and in this chapter we will content ourselves with describing the kind of decisions on this line which typify transport model builders of recent years.

Person type characteristics introduced into the model will typically include *household* characteristics such as car ownership, income, household size and number of workers. Again, there are problems in the exact definitions to be used; for example, 'car ownership' does not necessarily determine 'car availability' for a particular member of a household.

The trip purpose categories used rely on a distinction between home-based and non-home-based trips, and another definition related to this distinction can usefully be made as a preliminary at this stage. We have introduced the concepts of trip origins and trip destinations, which have an obvious meaning. We now introduce the concepts of trip *productions* and trip *attractions*. A trip production is the home end of a home-based trip (i.e. either origin or destination is the home), or the origin end of a non-home-based trip; a trip attraction is the non-home end of a home-based trip or the destination end of a non-home-based trip. Typically, for reasons which will become clear as we proceed, we will work with productions and attractions rather than origins and destinations.

We can now introduce typical trip-purpose categories as follows: for a home-based trip, we distinguish journey to work, shop, school, personal business, employer's business, for social and recreational purposes, and the ever present 'other'; for a non-home-based trip, we might distinguish only shop, personal business, employer's business and other.

This can be further qualified when we have commented on time period definitions. The main distinction which is usually introduced is between morning and evening peak periods and non-peak periods. In the peak periods, work is the dominant trip purpose, with only school trips forming another significant category, and it is common to build a model for peak period trips whose purposes are aggregated to home-based work, school, other home-based and non-home-based. A suitable aggregative classification for the non-peak period may be home-based work, school, shop, social/recreational, other and non-home-based.

A very detailed mode classification is possible: for example, we might consider walk, car driver, car passenger, motor cycle, cycle, taxi, bus, surface

ail and underground rail. Typically, however, walk trips and cycle trips are
gnored by transport modellers (and not always rightly, because they are
often a significant percentage of trips), and the other modes aggregated to
car' and 'public transport'. This also simplifies the network analysis part
of the modellers' work, since (again typically but not necessarily) a network
of routes has to be built for each mode.

9.2. THE STRUCTURE OF THE MODEL, WITH A SIMPLE EXAMPLE

The transport model consists of four sub-models, concerned with trip
generation, trip distribution, modal split and assignment, as shown in Figure
9.1. 'Generation' is used as a generic term for 'production' and 'attraction',

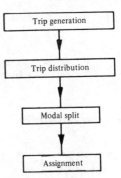

Figure 9.1   The main sub-models of the transport model

and so this part of the model predicts the total number of trips produced by
each zone, and the total number of trips attracted to each zone. The trip-
distribution model predicts how the trips leaving a zone will be distributed
among attraction zones, that is, among all other zones. At this stage, we have
a bundle of trips between each pair of zones. The modal split model then
allocates proportions of each bundle to particular modes. We now have a
bundle of trips for each mode between each pair of zones. The assignment
model then takes the bundles for each mode in turn and loads them onto
routes on the modal network, noting how many trips in all have been allocated
to each link of the network. These stages are shown diagrammatically for
typical zones i and j in Figure 9.2.

These various sub-models of the transport model correspond to a con-
ceptualization of the trip-making process as follows: shall I make a trip?
(generation); where shall I go? (distribution); by what mode? (modal split);
by what route? (assignment).

To fix ideas, we will now present a very simple transport model. We shall
then critically assess it, and go on to present an improved model in the

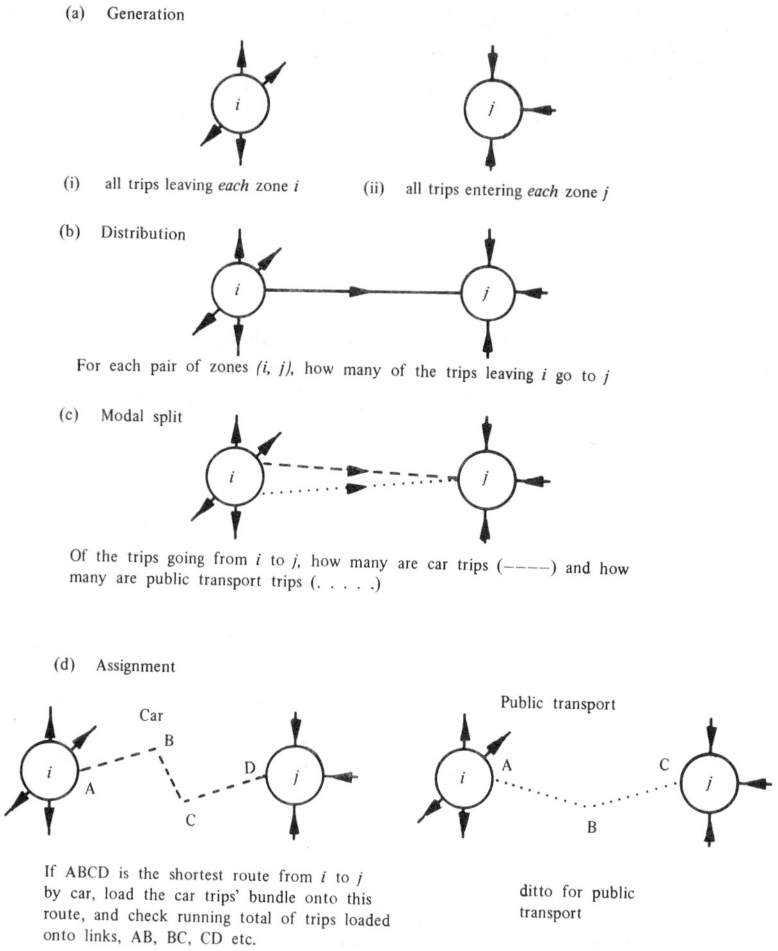
(a) Generation
i
j
(i) all trips leaving *each* zone *i*
(ii) all trips entering *each* zone *j*
(b) Distribution
i
j
For each pair of zones *(i, j)*, how many of the trips leaving *i* go to *j*
(c) Modal split
i
j
Of the trips going from *i* to *j*, how many are car trips (––––) and how many are public transport trips (. . . . .)
(d) Assignment
Car
i
A
B
C
D
j
Public transport
i
A
B
C
j
If ABCD is the shortest route from *i* to *j* by car, load the car trips' bundle onto this route, and check running total of trips loaded onto links, AB, BC, CD etc.
ditto for public transport

Figure 9.2 Diagrammatic representations of sub-model concepts

remainder of the chapter. To maintain simplicity, we will assume that we are modelling trips of a single purpose in a single time period (say the journey to work in the morning peak), and that there are only two modes, car and public transport. We can define some basic variables for this problem as follows: let O_i and D_i be the number of trips productions and attractions from zone *i* and to zone *j* respectively (*O* and *D* clearly stand for *o*rigin and *d*estination; but they *are* productions and attractions and *O* and *D* are retained as variables for historical reasons!); let T_{ij}^k be the number of trips from *i* to *j* by mode *k* ($k = 1$, car and $k = 2$ public transport, say) and note that T_{ij}^* is the total bundle of trips between *i* and *j*; let t_{ij} be the travel time between *i* and *j*; let

$R^k(i, j)$ be the set of links, l, forming the best route between i and j for mode k; let x^{lk} be the number of trips on this link. Then, we can set about building the model as follows.

The number of trip productions O_i for each zone i can be considered to be a linear function of a number M_1 of zonal variables X_i^m say (such as the number of resident workers in zone i), and the number of trip attractions D_j for each zone j can be considered a linear function of a number M_2 of other zonal variables Y_j^m (such as the number of jobs in the zone). Then

$$O_i = \sum_{m=1}^{M_1} a_m X_i^m \qquad (9.1)$$

$$D_j = \sum_{m=1}^{M_2} b_m Y_j^m \qquad (9.2)$$

The next step is to estimate T_{ij}^* in the trip-distribution model. We recognize from Chapter 6) that we have a production-attraction constrained situation, and we have a measure t_{ij} for travel time which we can use as a proxy for cost. Thus, we might hypothesize that

$$T_{ij}^* = A_i B_j O_i D_j\, e^{-\beta t_{ij}} \qquad (9.3)$$

for some parameter β. A_i and B_j are the usual balancing factors for the production-attraction constrained model.

For this simple model, we will base the modal split sub-model on an empirical result. Our task now is: given T_{ij}^* and, let us say, travel time by mode, t_{ij}^1 and t_{ij}^2, estimate T_{ij}^k for $k = 1$ (car) and $k = 2$ (public transport). This can be done as follows. Suppose from a survey we plot the proportion travelling by car against the ratio of car time to public transport time for a range of (i, j) pairs, then we would expect to obtain a plot of the form of that in Figure 9.3.

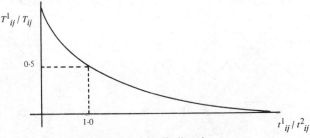

Figure 9.3   Modal split diversion curve

The curve shown in Figure 9.3 represents a function f, say, of t_{ij}^1/t_{ij}^2. It is clear that our modal split estimate can then be obtained as follows by the use

(a)   Generation

(i) Productions

(ii)   Attractions

(b)   Distribution

(c)   Modal split

(i) Car

(ii)   Public transport

(d)   Assignment

(i) Car

(ii)   Public transport

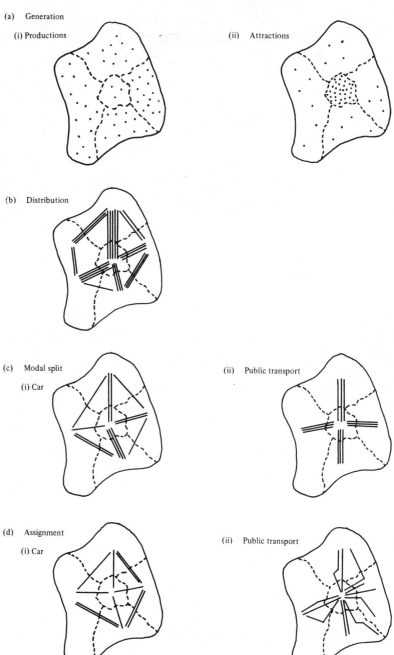

Figure 9.4   Diagrammatic representations of sub-model outputs

f this function:

$$T_{ij}^1 = f(t_{ij}^1/t_{ij}^2) \cdot T_{ij}^* \tag{9.4}$$

$$T_{ij}^2 = T_{ij}^* - T_{ij}^1 \tag{9.5}$$

The heart of the assignment problem is building the set of best paths $R^k(i, j)$. This can be accomplished in a straightforward manner on the computer using the method mentioned in Chapter 5. We can then obtain link loadings from

$$x^{lk} = \sum_{\substack{ijs.t \\ l \in R^k(i, j)}} T_{ij}^k \tag{9.6}$$

Equations (9.1)–(9.6) then represent a simple transport model. The outputs of the model can be mapped in the manner indicated diagrammatically in Figure 9.4 so that the results may be easily visualized.

Although the model presented here is a particularly simple one, it is perhaps more typical of the models used in transport studies of the last few years (and better than many so employed) than the one to be described next. We conclude this section with a number of critical observations and comments on this model which will then serve as a springboard for the discussion of an improved model in the rest of the chapter. We discuss each of the sub-models in turn, and then the model structure.

Trip generation

We did not present any detailed discussion of the variables X_i^m and Y_j^m to be used in the regression equations (9.1) and (9.2). In transport studies which have been carried out, a wide range of such variables have been used. The decision on the choice of these variables is important for two reasons: firstly, they represent the connection between the transport model and the other urban and regional models, since they are usually population or economic activity variables; secondly, trip-generation rates are found to vary quite sensitively with household characteristics, and so these must be carefully incorporated. We shall attempt to do this using an alternative trip-generation sub-model in the next section.

Trip distribution

If the estimates of O_i and D_j provided for the distribution model by the generation model are reasonable, then the main task of the distribution modeller will be to get the distance attenuation function, shown in equation (9.3) as $e^{-\beta t_{ij}}$ in a sound form. It is possible to test a range of functions, and a range of values of β. Also, as is clear from Chapter 6, it will be appropriate to use a generalized cost c_{ij}, instead of travel time t_{ij}, and to experiment with the components (and their relative weightings) of such a term.

Modal split

The modal split model is probably basically sound as it has a firm empirical foundation. We shall seek an improved theoretical formulation, which will also be useful for situations where there are more than two modes.

Assignment

For each modal network, the assignment model relies on the assumption that all trips between i and j follow the 'best' (least-time or least-cost) route. Even casual observation suggests that this is not the case, and we shall have to explore whether this assumption can be improved in a worthwhile manner.

The model structure

The main weakness in the overall model structure relates to the travel time estimates and an oversimplification of Figure 9.1. (The same comment would apply if generalized cost was being used, if only because travel time would always be one of the components.) There are two problems. First, it seems clear that travel time should be estimated on best routes in relation to link loadings of traffic; however, travel time is first used in the distribution model and link loadings are not known until after the assignment model has been run. Secondly, the distribution model uses travel time, t_{ij}, while the modal split model uses *modal* travel time t_{ij}^1 and t_{ij}^2—since the latter pair of times are the ones that are measured, how is t_{ij} obtained?

The first problem can be tackled by recognizing that the assignment sub-model does two jobs: network analysis and travel time estimation, and traffic loading, and that it is necessary to cycle through the model iteratively. The revised structure is shown in Figure 9.5.

The model is run with provisional travel time estimates which can then be revised for a second run following assignment, by the use of some speed–flow relationship on links. This solution is conceptually straightforward, but could involve a lot of computer time!

The second problem is more difficult. In the past, particular studies have used car-travel time for distribution purposes or (more rarely) a weighted sum. We shall show below that we can solve this problem with a theoretical development.

One further comment is appropriate at this stage: it would be theoretically correct to connect the network analysis box in Figure 9.5 with an arrow to

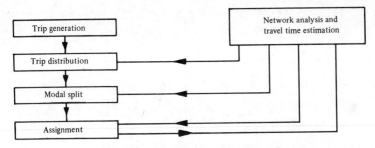

Figure 9.5   Revised model structure

he trip-generation box, since we would expect trip-generation rates to vary
with ease of travel (as represented by travel time). Unfortunately, no-one has
yet succeeded in building an effective *elastic* trip-generation model of this
kind, and so the arrow is not shown.

We now present improved versions of the various sub-models (Sections
9.3 to 9.6) and review the impact of these on overall model structure in
Section 9.7.

9.3. TRIP GENERATION

In this section, we describe a technique known as category analysis
(following Wootton and Pick, 1967). Trip productions (that is mainly trip
generation at the home end of home-based trips) are estimated as functions
of household characteristics and trip attractions as functions of economic
activity. Rather like the modal split method described in the previous section,
the method relies on a substantial empirical input from a large survey. We
concentrate initially on production, and the key assumption of the category
analysis method is the (relative) constancy of trip-making rates within a
number of household groups. It is these rates which have to be estimated
empirically. Then, of course, the related critical information is the numbers
of households in each group. The method has been devised so that these
numbers can be obtained from census data for the base year, but there always
remains a tricky forecasting problem for future years.

We can now define some variables to describe the method more formally.
We define n to be a person-type index and h to be a household-type index.
For each trip purpose and time period (we could add extra labels but we do
not do so explicitly so as to keep the notation as simple as possible), let $T(h)$
be the average number of trips made for that purpose, in the time period, by
a household of type h. If we plotted a frequency distribution of number of
trips made for this household type, we would expect something of the form of
Figure 9.6. The 'art' of category analysis, then, is to choose the household

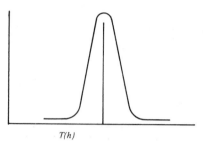

$T(h)$

Figure 9.6   Distribution of trip frequencies for a household category

categories so that the widths of such frequency distributions are extremely
small.

Let $a_i(h)$ be the number of households in zone i in household category h.
Then $a_i(h)T(h)$ is the number of trip productions made by households of
category h in zone i. For the model to be built, we require trip productions
by person type: typically, this will be car owner or non-car owner, a much
broader categorization than the household-type categorization. To facilitate
the calculation, we define $H(n)$ to be the set of households h, containing persons of type n, and we use the notation $h \in H(n)$ to denote membership of this
set. $\sum_{h \in H(n)}$ is then to be interpreted as the sum over households containing
members of type n. Thus, we can write for O_i^n, the number of trip productions
in zone i by persons of type n.

$$O_i^n = \sum_{h \in H(n)} a_i(h)T(h) \qquad (9.7)$$

The model can be tested by comparing the O_i^ns obtained from equation (9.7)
with corresponding observed values; any error arising would relate to using
average rates for $T(h)$; this test could be repeated using simulated values of
$a_i(h)$ for the base year—an important test, as simulated values must be used
for future years. There are obviously many ways in which household categories
could be defined. Wootton and Pick used 108 categories by employing three
car ownership groups, six levels of household structure and six income
groups. The 'levels of household structure' relate to family size and to number
of workers; these groups are not used separately as that would generate an
uncomfortably large number of categories overall. Wootton's and Pick's
groups were defined by:

Car ownership   0
                 1
                 more than 1

Household structure:	No. employed	Other adults
	0	1
	0	2 or more
	1	1 or less
	1	2 or more
	2 or more	1 or less
	2 or more	2 or more

Income: less than £500 p.a.
£500–£1000
£1000–£1500
£1500–£2000
£2000–£2500
over £2500

It is clearly vital to the method that it should be possible to forecast the number of households in each category, and we now outline how this is done. Essentially a number of probability distributions are defined and estimated, and these are then used to construct a joint probability distribution which can be used to allocate households to categories. These are described in turn: we need an income distribution, a car-ownership distribution, a family-size distribution and an employed-adults distribution.

A gamma function is chosen for the income distribution. Let $\phi(x)$ be the probability that a household has income x, and assume

$$\phi(x) = \frac{\alpha^{n+1}}{\Gamma(n+1)} x^n e^{-\alpha x} \tag{9.8}$$

where

$$\alpha = \bar{x}/\sigma^2 \tag{9.9}$$

$$n = \alpha\bar{x} - 1 \tag{9.10}$$

Γ is the gamma function, whose values are readily available in tabulated form; $\bar{x}$ is the mean of the distribution, σ^2 its variance; n and α are parameters —n is found by calibrating the distribution using some survey data. A value of $n = 1{\cdot}636$ was used in the West Midlands Transport study, while $n = 1{\cdot}8$ has been used in the SELNEC study. For forecasting purposes, some assumption has to be made about the rate of increase of income: if g is the growth rate per annum, then after y years $\bar{x}$ changes so that

$$\bar{x}_{\text{new}} = \bar{x}(1 + g)^y \tag{9.11}$$

n is assumed to be unchanged, and a new value of α can then be obtained from equation (9.10). Using this distribution, households can be allocated to income groups for small area units provided that $\bar{x}$ can be obtained for each area.

For car-ownership estimation, we define $P(n|x)$ to be the probability that a household owns n cars given that it has income x. Then, if $P(n)$ denotes the probability of a household owning n cars

$$P(n) = \int_0^\infty P(n|x)\phi(x)\,dx \qquad (9.12)$$

For the car-ownership categories described earlier, distributions have to be assumed for $P(0|x)$ and $P(1|x)$, and $P(>1|x)$ is then obtained from

$$P(>1|x) = 1 - P(0|x) - P(1|x) \qquad (9.13)$$

In the West Midlands study, distributions of the form

$$P(n|x) = a_n x^{b_n} e^{-c_n x} \qquad (9.14)$$

were assumed for $n = 0$ and 1. The coefficients were estimated as

$$a_0 = 1\cdot15, \quad b_0 = 0, \quad c_0 = 0\cdot8; \quad a_1 = 1\cdot64; \quad b_1 = 2\cdot29, \quad c_1 = 1\cdot31.$$

However, alternative assumptions could easily be made. For forecasting purposes, it is assumed that $P(n|x)$ will remain stable. Care should be taken though, in estimating $\phi(x)$ for use in equation (9.12): for the future, this should record the increase in income relative to car prices. So, for this purpose only, equation (9.11) should be replaced by

$$\bar{x}_{new} = \bar{x}(1 + g - i)^y \qquad (9.15)$$

where the variables are as before, and i is the annual increase in car prices.

The family-size distribution is assumed to be a Poisson distribution. An assumed distribution is needed for families of 1 or 2 adults, $p(1)$ and $p(2)$ say, and then

$$p(>2) = 1 - p(1) - p(2) \qquad (9.16)$$

The assumptions made in the West Midlands study are

$$p(1) = e^{-(F-1)} \qquad (9.17)$$

$$p(2) = (F - 1)e^{-(F-1)} \qquad (9.18)$$

where F is mean family size.

The distribution of employees per household is assumed to be binominal. We assume

$$E(0) = \left(1 - \frac{R}{N}\right)^N \qquad (9.19)$$

and

$$E(1) = R\left(1 - \frac{R}{N}\right)^{N-1} \qquad (9.20)$$

to be the probability of 0 or 1 workers per household, where R is the mean alue and N is a parameter ($=4$ in the West Midland's Study). Then

$$E(>1) = 1 - E(0) - E(1)$$

or forecasting purposes, it is assumed that the distributions are stable; then orecasts are needed for F and R.

We can now estimate the probability of a household being in one of the ix family structure categories listed earlier. Suppose the six categories are umbers 1–6 and that $f(\rho)$ is the probability of being in category ρ. Then

$$f(1) = p(1)E(0) \tag{9.21}$$

$$f(2) = (1 - p(1))E(0) \tag{9.22}$$

$$f(3) = (p(1) + p(2))E(1) \tag{9.23}$$

$$f(4) = p(>2)E(1) \tag{9.24}$$

$$f(5) = \frac{1 + p(1) + p(2)}{2} E(>1) \tag{9.25}$$

$$f(6) = \frac{1 - p(1) - p(2)}{2} E(>1) \tag{9.26}$$

The justification of equations (9.21)–(9.24) is clear; in the case of equations 9.25) and (9.26) the first term in each on the right-hand side has been chosen to ensure that all the probabilities sum to 1.

We can now construct the joint probability distribution $\Phi(I, n, \rho)$ as follows. Let income group I be defined by upper and lower bounds a_{I+1} and a_I. Then

$$\Phi(I, n, p) = f(\rho)\int_{a_I}^{a_{I+1}} P(n|x)\phi(x)\,\mathrm{d}x \tag{9.27}$$

Note that $\phi(x)$ must use $\bar{x}$ which relates to future incomes, while $P(n|x)$ must use $\bar{x}^1$, the future mean income relative to the increase in car prices.

One further point can conveniently be tackled at this stage. It is often very difficult to obtain income data for small areas. We now show how some of the distributions defined above can be used to estimate small-area income distributions from car-ownership data.

From available data, we can usually obtain (omitting the zone subscripts) $P^0(0)$, $P^0(1)$ and $P^0(>1)$, where the superscript denotes observed value. Then, if we assume that the value of n in equation (9.8) is known $\phi(x)$ is a function of $\bar{x}$. Thus, *for an assumed* $\bar{x}$, we can calculate $P(0)$, $P(1)$ and $P(>1)$ using equations (9.12)–(9.14). We then need to set up a search process to find the $\bar{x}$ which minimizes, say,

$$S = \alpha_0(P(0) - P^0(0))^2 + \alpha_1(P(1) - P^0(1))^2 + \alpha_2(P(>1) - P^0(>1))^2 \tag{9.28}$$

and this is a relatively straightforward task.

Thus, given information on car ownership, family size and number of resident employees for each zone i, and given the total population of each zone, we can use equation (9.27) to obtain $a_i(h)$, the number of households in each zone i in category h.

We must now turn to trip attractions, which are estimated by a similar though less complicated, procedure. Activity measures, in employment or household units, are used as independent variables. We define $b_j(l)$ to be the level of activity l in zone j, and $t(l)$ to be the rate at which trips are attracted per unit. Then, if D_j is the number of trip attractions to zone j,

$$D_j = \sum_l b_j(l)t(l) \qquad (9.29)$$

The categories employed by Wootton and Pick were as follows:

	Method of estimation
1. Industries	SIC I–XVII
2. Education	School attendance
3. Utility	SIC XVIII
4. Transport and communication	SIC XIX
5. Shopping	MLH 820
6. Distribution, less shopping	SIC XX less MLH 820
7. Other employment (service)	SIC XXI–XXIV
8. Residential	Census population

* SIC = Standard industrial classification; MLH = minimum list heading within SIC main heading.

There is one minor case which we have not dealt with: the non-home-based trip. In that case, a procedure analogous to that used for attraction can be used for both production (origins) and attractions (destinations).

For both productions and attractions, there remain substantial forecasting problems: forecasting the distribution of population and economic activity. The trip-generation sub-model, as we noted earlier, is the main connection between the transport model and other urban models which will help to produce these forecasts for us.

In concluding this section, we should note that the bulk of the category analysis method is concerned with forecasting household structures rather than with trip generation *per se*, and this technique is potentially of great use in other fields of urban modelling, especially those which need household information at a fine sectoral scale for small areas. If such data is not available directly, we might then recall that a category analysis estimation technique may be an effective substitute.

9.4. TRIP DISTRIBUTION AND MODAL SPLIT

It is convenient to discuss trip distribution and modal split together. In Section 9.2 we employed in our simple example a production-attraction

onstrained model to estimate trips T_{ij} from i to j, and an empirically based
modal split model. There are two basic inconsistencies which are difficult
o eliminate in that approach: firstly, the distribution model needs a travel
ost c_{ij}, while we actually measure *modal* travel costs c_{ij}^k; secondly, the modal
plit model implicitly assumes that everyone has a choice of mode, yet if we
ave two modes, car and public transport, non-car owners have no choice.
These difficulties, as is often the case in modelling, can be resolved in part by
a more careful choice of variable. We now define T_{ij}^{kn} to be the number of
trips from i to j by persons of type n by mode k. To fix ideas, the reader can
bear in mind the example of a two-person type, two-mode situation, $n = 1$,
car owner, $n = 2$, non-car owner, $k = 1$, car, $k = 2$, public transport, though
the notation and model to be developed is quite general and is applicable
in principle to any number of person types and modes. This is why we now
discuss trip distribution and modal split together: we can estimate T_{ij}^{kn}
directly and produce a combined trip-distribution–modal split model.

We assume that trip productions can be estimated by person type, O_i^n,
while trip attractions are still estimated in total D_j. (This was the assumption
of the previous section.) We use modal costs c_{ij}^k. We mentioned in Chapter 6
that travel cost has several components: money cost, travel time, waiting
time and so on. A typical definitions used in a recent transportation study
Wilson, Hawkins, Hill and Wagon, 1969) was

$$c_{ij}^k = a_1 t_{ij}^k + a_2 e_{ij}^k + a_3^k d_{ij}^k + p_j^k + \delta^k \qquad (9.30)$$

where:

t_{ij}^k = travel time from i to j by mode k in minutes (which includes car-
parking time and walking time on the public transport system);
e_{ij}^k = excess time in the journey from i to j in minutes (waiting time on the
public transport system);
d_{ij}^k = distance from i to j in miles (used for estimating perceived operating
costs for car drivers and fares for public transport passengers, which are
assumed proportional to distance);
p_j^k = terminal cost at j in pence (car parking charges);
δ^k = a modal penalty, usually associated with travelling by public transport
over and above the other costs referred to above.

a_1, a_2 and a_3^k are parameters which, since p_j^k and δ^k are measured in money
units, value the other terms in money units.

We can now develop the Mark 1 generalized distribution modal split
model: we can build a model for each (k, n) pair by analogy with our other
spatial interaction models. We get

$$T_{ij}^{kn} = A_i^n B_j O_i^n D_j \, e^{-\beta^n c_{ij}^k} \qquad (9.31)$$

A_i^n and B_j are given by

$$A_i^n = 1 \bigg/ \sum_{j=1}^{N} \sum_{k \in \gamma(n)} B_j D_j \, e^{-\beta^n c_{ij}^k} \tag{9.32}$$

and

$$B_j = \sum_{i=1}^{N} \sum_{n} \sum_{k \in \gamma(n)} A_i^n O_i^n \, e^{-\beta^n c_{ij}^k} \tag{9.33}$$

where $\gamma(n)$ is the set of modes available to type n travellers. For our simple case $\gamma(1)$ is 1 and 2, car and public transport, while $\gamma(2)$ consists of mode 2, public transport only. A_i^n and B_j in equations (9.32) and (9.33) are calculated thus to ensure that the constraints

$$\sum_{j=1}^{N} \sum_{k \in \gamma(n)} T_{ij}^{kn} = O_i^n \tag{9.34}$$

$$\sum_{i=1}^{N} \sum_{n} \sum_{k \in \gamma(n)} T_{ij}^{kn} = D_j \tag{9.35}$$

A more detailed derivation of this model using entropy-maximizing principles (a good way of ensuring internal consistency) is available in another book by the author (Wilson, 1970, Chapter 2).

The model thus obtained, whose main equation is (9.31), is a combined distribution–modal split model, as it predicts trips by origin–destination pair, by mode. We can draw out the modal split implications explicitly as follows: we shall use our usual convention of replacing an index by an asterisk to denote summation, with the additional convention, in this case, that summations over the mode index k are restricted to $k \in \gamma(n)$. Then, we can sum T_{ij}^{kn} over k in equation (9.31) to obtain

$$T_{ij}^{*n} = A_i^n B_j O_i^n D_j \sum_{k \in \gamma(n)} e^{-\beta^n c_{ij}^k} \tag{9.36}$$

Note that the terms $A_i^n B_j O_i^n D_j$ can be taken outside the summation sign as they do not depend on k. Then, we can divide T_{ij}^{*n} from equation (9.36) into T_{ij}^{kn} from equation (9.31) to give the proportion of trips by travellers of type n between i and j made by mode k as

$$\frac{T_{ij}^{kn}}{T_{ij}^{*n}} = \frac{e^{-\beta^n c_{ij}^k}}{\sum_{k \in \gamma(n)} e^{-\beta^n c_{ij}^k}} \tag{9.37}$$

For example, in our simple case, we can write

$$\frac{T_{ij}^{11}}{T_{ij}^{*1}} = \frac{e^{-\beta^1 c_{ij}^1}}{e^{-\beta^n c_{ij}^1} + e^{-\beta^n c_{ij}^2}} \tag{9.38}$$

s the proportion of members of car-owning families who travel by car. This
an be written in the form

$$\frac{T_{ij}^{11}}{T_{ij}^{*1}} = \frac{1}{1 + e^{-\beta^n(c_{ij}^2 - c_{ij}^1)}}$$ (9.39)

f this is plotted, we get a logistic curve of the form of that in Figure 9.7.

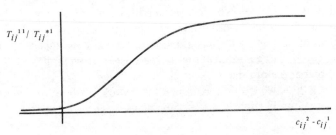

Figure 9.7   Modal split as a function of cost differences

This is the equivalent to the diversion curve presented in Figure 9.3. It looks
different, of course, because it is stated in terms of cost differences rather than
cost ratios. But, basically, we now have a theoretical explanation for the
diversion curve. We thus see that we have a powerful model.

The Mark 2 model arises from an observation that the parameter β^n is
made to do a lot of work in the model. Its value, for each person type n,
determines the average distance travelled by that person type, and also, in
the modal split equation, it determines the sensitivity of that person type to
differences in cost between modes. The model can be generalized if we replace
β^n in the modal split equation by another set of parameters, λ^n. We can then
use equation (9.36), with one amendment, as a distribution model equation
for persons of type n. To make it look like a more conventional distribution
model we put

$$e^{-\beta^n C_{ij}^n} = \sum_{k \in \gamma(n)} e^{-\beta^n c_{ij}^k}$$ (9.40)

and write equation (9.36) in the form

$$T_{ij}^{*n} = A_i^n B_j O_i^n D_j e^{-\beta^n C_{ij}^n}$$ (9.41)

which now looks like a conventional distribution model for person of type n.
A_i^n and B_j can be obtained by substituting from equation (9.40) into equation
(9.32) and (9.33) to give

$$A_i^n = 1 \bigg/ \sum_{j=1}^{N} B_j D_j e^{-\beta^n C_{ij}^n}$$ (9.42)

$$B_j = 1 \bigg/ \sum_{i=1}^{N} \sum_{n} A_i^n O_i^n e^{-\beta^n C_{ij}^n}$$ (9.43)

The modal split equation is

$$\frac{T_{ij}^{kn}}{T_{ij}^{*n}} = \frac{e^{-\lambda^n c_{ij}^k}}{\sum_{k \in \gamma(n)} e^{-\lambda^n c_{ij}^k}}$$ (9.44)

Equations (9.41)–(9.44) form the Mark 2 model. The Mark 1 model is a special case obtained by setting $\lambda^n = \beta^n$. Whether λ^n really is equal to β^n is a matter of empirical investigation which is pursued further in Chapter 12. Note, at this point, that with the introduction of C_{ij}^n in equation (9.40), we have solved the problem of finding an $i - j$ cost made up as a composite cost out of the modal costs. C_{ij}^n can be interpreted as the cost of travelling from i to j as perceived by people of type n.

In general, then, we would recommend the Mark 2 model, and in any case it is computationally slightly more convenient.

9.5. COMMERCIAL VEHICLE TRIPS: AN INTRODUCTION TO GROWTH FACTOR METHODS

So far, we have only considered passenger trips. In principle, the same methods of model building can be applied to commercial vehicle trips. However, information on commercial vehicle trips is often less satisfactory than that for passenger trips and this makes trip-generation models (of regression analysis or category analysis types) and trip-distribution models difficult to calibrate. If survey data is good enough to calibrate such models then of course they should be used; if not, then a simpler method such as a growth factor method must be used. (These were once used for passenger trips as well.) This involves taking the survey trip matrix as given and applying zonal growth factors in order to obtain forecasts. Suppose that T_{ij}^s is the survey commercial vehicle trip matrix, and that

$$O_i^s = \sum_{j=1}^{N} T_{ij}^s$$ (9.45)

and

$$D_j^s = \sum_{i=1}^{N} T_{ij}^s$$ (9.46)

are the associated trip ends. Suppose that a_i and b_j are sets of factors such that the new trip ends are

$$O_i = a_i O_i^s$$ (9.47)

and

$$D_j = b_j D_j^s$$ (9.48)

t some future time. These would be estimated from forecasts of zonal ctivity levels derived from planning assumptions or from activity models. hen we assume that the new trip matrix, say T_{ij}, is proportional to the old ne, and to some combination of the growth factors. One of the simplest nethods, for example, is the so called *average factor method* which would efine the inter-zonal trip growth factor to be

$$K_{ij} = \frac{a_i + b_j}{2} \tag{9.49}$$

nd

$$T_{ij} = K_{ij}T_{ij}^s \tag{9.50}$$

Whatever is chosen for K_{ij}, the likelihood of T_{ij} satisfying

$$\sum_{j=1}^{n} T_{ij} = O_i \tag{9.51}$$

and

$$\sum_{i=1}^{n} T_{ij} = D_j \tag{9.52}$$

is small. We can adjust the value of T_{ij} given by equation (9.50) by the kind of balancing factors A_i and B_j used in spatial interaction models. Equation (9.50) then becomes

$$T_{ij} = A_iB_jK_{ij}T_{ij}^s \tag{9.53}$$

where

$$A_i = O_i \bigg/ \sum_{j=1}^{N} B_jK_{ij}T_{ij}^s \tag{9.54}$$

and

$$B_j = D_j \bigg/ \sum_{i=1}^{N} A_iK_{ij}T_{ij}^s \tag{9.55}$$

to ensure that equations (9.51) and (9.52) are satisfied.

In the author's view it would be preferable to use a multiplicative assumption for K_{ij} rather than the additive assumption of equation (9.49) such as

$$K_{ij} = a_ib_j \tag{9.56}$$

(It may be appropriate to take the square root of the product for dimensional reasons but, provided the A_iB_j factors are used, the dimensions look after themselves.)

In this case, equations (9.53)–(9.55) take a simpler form: we can substitute for O_i and D_j from equations (9.47) and (9.48) and for K_{ij} from equation (9.5?) to obtain

$$T_{ij} = A_i B_j a_i b_j T_{ij}^s \qquad (9.5?)$$

where

$$A_i = O_i^s \bigg/ \sum_{j=1}^{N} B_j b_j T_{ij}^s \qquad (9.5?)$$

$$B_j = D_j^s \bigg/ \sum_{i=1}^{N} A_i a_i T_{ij}^s \qquad (9.5?)$$

A host of such growth factor methods exist. They are reviewed in Martin Memmott and Bone (1961). A detailed discussion of the $A_i B_j$ adjustment process in relation to growth factor methods is presented in the paper by Evans (1970).

9.6. ASSIGNMENT

The problem faced by the builder of an assignment model is shown symbolically in Figure 9.8. Two zones, i and j, of a study area are shown together with the relevant parts of a modal network, say the highway network.

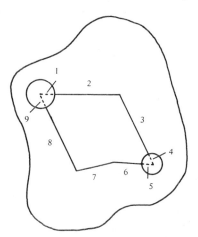

Figure 9.8 Two possible routes between zones in a network

Each zone is connected to the network by dummy links from the zone centroid, shown in the Figure as dotted lines; the links have been numbered including the dummy links. Given link travel costs c_l^1 the shortest-path

rogramme can be used to find the shortest path between zone centroids.
This is the set $R^k(i, j)$. Thus, if the upper route is the best path and $k = 1$
represents the car mode, $R^1(i, j)$ would be the set of links 1, 2, 3, 4. A bundle
of trips T_{ij}^1 could then be loaded onto these links. Some of the links will be
on best paths between other pairs of zones, and so the assignment computer
programme must keep a running check of the total number of trips loaded
onto each link. Thus, at the end of the process, we have the link loadings.
The public transport assignments can be made in the same way, though the
task of building the network is more difficult: the main links and associated
costs must take account of routes and timetables; the subsidiary dummy
links must be used to simulate waiting time and transfer times between routes,
as well as walking links from zone centroids to terminals. This can be done.
However, special algorithms have been developed to deal with these problems,
such as the TRANSITNET algorithm (Freeman, Fox, Wilbur Smith, 1967).

   The minimum cost paths, $R^k(i, j)$, are known as trees because of the way
they are developed and stored in the computer. The shortest path from one
origin zone to all other zones forms a tree-like structure as shown diagrammatically in Figure 9.9. Of course, every sub-section of such a tree is also a

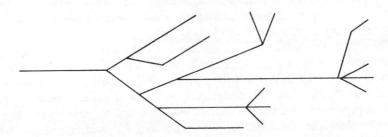

Figure 9.9   Diagrammatic representation of a tree in a network

tree. For a given node k, the c_{ij}^ks are worked out by adding up the link costs
for each link on the best path from i to j. In the computer such a process is
known as tree-skimming and so the c_{ij}^ks are sometimes known as skimmed
trees.

   So far, we are still describing the so-called 'all or nothing' assignment
method in which the whole bundle of trips is loaded onto a single best path.
We criticized this for being an unrealistic assumption earlier and we must
now proceed to improve it. The tests to be satisfied by a good assignment
model are the following:

   (1) the final traffic loads which are produced must be reasonably close to
survey totals and,

   (2) traffic loads must be in reasonable accord with the travel-cost characteristics assumed for each link; in particular, travel time, and hence speed

must be linked with flow through a known speed–flow relationship for each link.

The second of these conditions is saying, in essence, that traffic flows should be compatible with the 'capacity' of a link, with capacity being defined as the speed–flow relationship rather than as a fixed absolute number. An assignment algorithm which satisfies these conditions is known as a *capacity restraint procedure* and we shall see that, in passing, such procedures modify the all-or-nothing algorithm in such a way that our earlier criticisms of all-or-nothingness are alleviated.

The simplest form of capacity restraint procedure is simply to carry out a series of all-or-nothing assignments, at the end of each one adjusting travel times on links to be in accordance with assigned flows as implied by Figure 9.5. On each iteration, some of the minimum paths will differ from those of earlier iterations. If the final iteration is accepted as the solution, then, clearly, this still has 'all-or-nothing' characteristics, a single best path for each origin-destination pair. However, it is sometimes appropriate to take an average of the last few iterations and this has the effect of assigning traffic to more than one 'best' path for each pair.

It is possible to devise multi-path algorithms, such as that of Burrell (1968). However, there is a fundamental mathematical problem associated with the task of finding the nth best path (Sakarovitch, 1968).

To obtain the traffic loadings, assuming a balanced all-or-nothing algorithm, we proceed in a similar manner to Section 9.2, except that now we convert person trips to vehicle trips. Further, note that whereas statements on generation distribution and modal split models were made in terms of trips for one purpose at one time of day, *we must now add all purposes together in order to obtain link loadings*. Suppose, then, that T_{ij}^{11} is the number of trips by car, *for all purposes* in some time period, between zones i and j. Then, if s is the average occupancy,

$$v_{ij} = T_{ij}^{11}/s \qquad (9.60)$$

is the number of vehicle trips. Suppose that the number of commercial vehicle trips is V_{ij}, and then the all-or-nothing loadings are

$$x_l = \sum_{ijs.t.l \,\in R^1(i,\,j)} (v_{ij} + V_{ij}) \qquad (9.61)$$

If the results of several iterations are being used, then average values must be taken. A final adjustment must then be made to add bus loadings on each highway link: these will be known directly from route and timetable information. The public transport loadings are obtained similarly, but in terms of person trips only. (Buses (and commercial vehicles) are usually counted in p.c.u's (passenger car units), say three for one bus, to take account of the fact that a bus affects traffic flows more than a car.)

.7. ASSEMBLING COMPLETE MODELS

The model described in Sections 9.3–9.6 is essentially that used in the
;ELNEC (*South East Lancashire, North East Cheshire*) Transportation
tudy (Wilson, Hawkins, Hill and Wagon, 1969; Wagon and Wilson, 1971).
¯he complete model is assembled by putting the pieces together in accordance
vith Figure 9.5. Figure 9.10 shows in more detail how this is done; one symbol

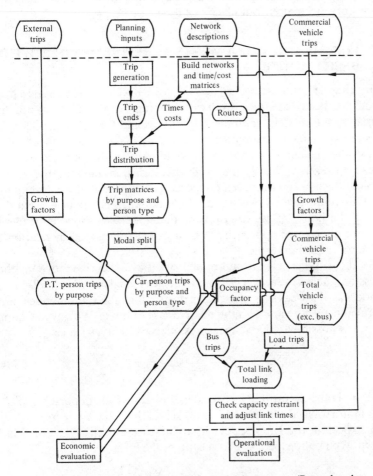

Figure 9.10 An example of a complete model structure. (Reproduced
with permission from Wilson, Hawkins, Hill and Wagon, *Regional
Studies* **3**, p. 340, Figure 1 (1969)).

is used for computer operations, another for the numbers which form the
inputs and outputs to and from these operations. The intermediate outputs
are often just as important to the model builder as the final outputs, as he

needs to check them and to use them for calibration purposes. However,
is usually possible to arrange the modules of the associated computer packag
so that a run of the model is achieved with relatively few runs on the compute

Of course, the very great advantage of the modular construction of th
computer package is that any one module can easily be replaced. This mean
that if the model builder wants to use an alternative sub-model, say th
intervening opportunities model instead of a gravity model, then it is
straightforward matter to replace one by the other.

*9.8. FURTHER DEVELOPMENTS I: REFINEMENTS TO THE BASIC MODEL

This chapter has described models in a field in which a tremendous amoun
of work has been done. As a result of this volume of effort, a large number o
alternative sub-models, computer algorithms and further refinements of a
kinds are available to the model builder. Any reader who wishes to pursu
such studies in depth should immerse himself in the publications of th
Highway Research Board: the Highway Research *Bulletin*, the Highwa
Research *Record*, and the *Special Reports*. To describe all these development
in detail would involve writing a whole book, rather than a section of .
chapter of a book. All we can do here, therefore, is to show the reader tha
there are alternative approaches which can be developed in relation to
number of important topics.

For the trip-generation sub-model, we have described two methods
regression analysis (Section 9.2) and category analysis (Section 9.3). Eacl
method has the weakness of being inelastic since the total number of trip
generated does not vary with the relative ease of travel. We saw in Chapter
that it was possible to derive measures of accessibility, such as

$$X_i = \sum_{j=1}^{n} D_j e^{-\beta c_{ij}} \qquad (9.62$$

where X_i is the accessibility of residents of zone i to 'opportunities' D_j.
some motorways are built and c_{ij}s decrease, then the X_is increase, and w
might expect the total number of trips to increase, as well as their distribution
pattern. We might expect a relationship of the form

$$O_i(t) = O_i(0) . \left(\frac{X_i(t)}{X_i(0)} \right)^\alpha \qquad (9.63$$

where $O_i(t)$ is trip productions at time t, $X_i(t)$ is accessibility at time t and
is a parameter. In other words, it is easy to envisage and construct an elasti
trip-generation model. Unfortunately, it is very difficult to calibrate on
because of the lack of time series data. One model which has been developed

eally as a joint generation–distribution model, is that of Quandt and Baumol
1966), which has some of the characteristics of the elastic model outlined
bove.

In the above comment on trip generation, no person-type distinction was
nade. It would be easy, of course, to re-introduce this and to produce a
uitably modified form of equations (9.62) and (9.63). The different acces-
ibility (patterns and quantities) of car owners and non-car owners would be
very important in such a context. The construction of amended equations
s left as an exercise for the reader.

An important refinement connected to the definition of person types can
be outlined at this stage. In the generalized distribution-modal split model
our main variable was T_{ij}^{kn}: trips between zones i and j by mode k by persons
of type n. Trip productions were categorized by person type as O_i^n. For this
point, we will restrict ourselves to the two mode–two person type situation
in which we took $k = 1$ to be car, $k = 2$ to be public transport, $n = 1$ to be
member of car-owning household, $n = 2$ to be member of non-car-owning
household. The difficulty is that the real distinction we wish to make for
modal split purposes is between people who have a car available and those
who do not, and then 'car-available' people have the real choice. There will
be many members of car-owning families who do not have a car available
(because it is being utilized by another member of the family) and there will
be members of non-car-owning families who do have a car available (in the
form of lifts from friends and so on). And yet our category analysis trip-
generation estimates are based on the car-owning–non-car-owning household distinction. We need to find a way of converting from one to the other,
and this can be done as follows.

Let α_i be the proportion of members of car-owning households in zone i
travelling by public transport who had a choice of travelling by car, and let
$(1 - \beta_i)$ be the corresponding proportion of members of non-car-owning
households travelling by public transport. We will use $k = 1$ and 2 for modes
as usual, but we will now use $n = co$ and nco for membership of car-owning
and non-car-owning households and $n = ca$ and nca for 'car-available' and
'non-car-available' people, and we shall show how to convert from one
system to the other. We have

$$O_i^{1/ca} = O_i^{1/co} + O_i^{1/nco} \tag{9.64}$$

$$O_i^{2/ca} = \alpha_i O_i^{2/co} + (1 - \beta_i)O_i^{2/nco} \tag{9.65}$$

$$O_i^{2/nca} = (1 - \alpha_i)O_i^{2/co} + \beta_i O_i^{2/nco} \tag{9.66}$$

as a consequence of these definitions. It is useful to aggregate these equations
over modes; we use an asterisk to denote summation as usual:

$$O_i^{*/ca} = O_i^{1/co} + O_i^{1/nco} + \alpha_i O_i^{2/co} + (1 - \beta_i)O_i^{2/nco} \tag{9.67}$$

and

$$O_i^{*/nca} = (1 - \alpha_i)O_i^{2/ca} + \beta_i O_i^{2/nca} \tag{9.68}$$

The reader can check that the implicit assumption we have been making hitherto is

$$\alpha_i = \beta_i = 1 \tag{9.69}$$

We shall now give a method of estimating α_i and β_i from survey data. Firstly however, we write equations (9.68) and (9.69) in the form

$$O_i^{*/ca} = \rho_i O_i^{*/co} + \tau_i O_i^{*/nco} \tag{9.70}$$

and

$$O^{*/nca} = O_i^{**} - O_i^{*/ca} \tag{9.71}$$

where

$$\rho_i = \frac{O_i^{1/co} + \alpha_i O_i^{2/co}}{O_i^{*/co}} \tag{9.72}$$

and

$$\tau_i = \frac{O_i^{1/nco} + (1 - \beta_i)O_i^{2/nco}}{O_i^{*/nco}} \tag{9.73}$$

We now derive α_i and β_i as follows. Suppose we take a modal split equation of the form of (9.44) and apply it separately to car available for each mode. We can then divide $T_{ij}^{1/ca}$ into $T_{ij}^{2/ca}$ and obtain

$$\frac{T_{ij}^{2/ca}}{T_{ij}^{1/ca}} = e^{-\lambda(c_{ij}^2 - c_{ij}^1)} \tag{9.74}$$

* We do not bother to superscript the λ-parameter as there is only one such parameter in this case.

We now make the assumption that the proportion of people who can choose, in car-owning households, is the same proportion who actually do choose to travel by car in the car-available population. In words, this is:

Those members of car-owning households who can choose to travel and choose public transport	Number of car-available people choosing public transport
Those who can choose and choose car	Number of car-available people choosing car

That is
$$\frac{\alpha_i T_{ij}^{2/co}}{T_{ij}^{1/co}} = \frac{T_{ij}^{2/ca}}{T_{ij}^{1/ca}} = e^{-\lambda(c_{ij}^2 - c_{ij}^1)} \tag{9.76}$$

This equation gives a value of α_i for each j—since $T_{ij}^{2/co}$, $T_{ij}^{1/co}$, c_{ij}^2 and c_{ij}^1 will all be known from the survey (λ would have to be guessed initially, or a value taken from another similar study; it could then be iteratively refined). An average can be obtained by multiplying through in equation (9.76) by $T_{ij}^{1/co}$ and summing over j to give

$$\alpha_i O_i^{2/co} = \sum_{j=1}^{n} T_{ij}^{1/co} \, e^{-\lambda(c_{ij}^2 - c_{ij}^1)} \tag{9.77}$$

which we can solve for α_i. A similar argument gives

$$(1 - \beta_i)O_i^{2/nco} = \sum_{j=1}^{N} T_{ij}^{1/nco} \, e^{-\lambda(c_{ij}^2 - c_{ij}^1)} \tag{9.78}$$

Thus, given $O_i^{1/co}$, $O_i^{2/co}$, $O_i^{1/nco}$, and $O_i^{2/nco}$ and the corresponding matrix elements, we can obtain α_i and β_i from equations (9.77) and (9.78), and hence $\rho_i(0)$ and $\tau_i(0)$, where the (0) signifies at time $t = 0$, from equations (9.72) and (9.71) to obtain $O_i^{*/ca}$ and $O_i^{*/nca}$. The model can then be run using car-available/non-car-available as the person-type categories.

The intermediate variables ρ_i and τ_i have been introduced to help in forecasting; ρ_i being the proportion of members of car-owning households who have a car available, τ_i the same proportion for members of non-car-owning households. (Recall that α_i and $1 - \beta_i$ were defined in relation to members of these households travelling by public transport.) α_i and β_i are easier to estimate from data than ρ_i and τ_i, but the latter pair are easier to forecast. Thus, we use the procedure outlined above to obtain $\rho_i(0)$ and $\tau_i(0)$ and then add a further procedure for estimating $\rho_i(t)$ and $\tau_i(t)$ for when the model is used to make forecasts. We assume that $\rho_i(t)$ will change with the proportion of cars available in car-owning households, and that $\tau_i(t)$ will change with the proportion of car-owning households. Let $C_i(t)$ be the number of cars owned in zone i at time t. Then we can assume

$$\rho_i(t) = \rho_i(0) \frac{C_i(t)}{O_i^{*/co}(t)} \frac{O_i^{*/co}(0)}{C_i(0)} \tag{9.79}$$

and

$$\tau_i(t) = \tau_i(0) \frac{O_i^{*/co}(t)}{O_i^{**}(t)} \frac{O_i^{**}(0)}{O_i^{*/co}(t)} \tag{9.80}$$

We now have the basis for a complete model run whose main person-type classification is car-available/non-car-available. We can now proceed to look at other refinements of distribution, modal split and assignment procedures, most of which can be dealt with briefly by reference to Chapter 6 and related books and papers.

Firstly, although we have used the negative exponential form of cost function in the models of this chapter, the reader will recall the remarks of

Section 6.3 that other functions can also be used. For example, although negative exponential functions seem to fit as well as anything in urban studies, a power function may be more appropriate for inter-urban studies. More details will emerge below in Chapter 12 on calibration. We note also that the form of function used in the modal split equation (9.44) could also be changed from negative exponential to something else. Indeed, it was found in the SELNEC study (Wilson, Hawkins, Hill and Wagon, 1969) that different measures of generalized cost were appropriate also, as between the two sub-models.

Perhaps the biggest single weakness of the cost function, however, is that it averages too many different kinds of individual behaviour within (in the case of a particular study) a single functional form and a single β. There is much scope for disaggregation here: a kind of category analysis of types of traveller by their distribution behaviour would seem to be appropriate. There are a number of straws in the wind. Hyman (1970) has explored the form which the distribution model takes when the population is disaggregated by income, and notes that if β in $e^{-\beta c_{ij}}$ is replaced by β_i, so that the function becomes $e^{-\beta_i c_{ij}}$, then some of the necessary effects can be incorporated into the model as an approximation. Harris (1964) showed how the function $e^{-\beta c_{ij}}$ transforms into something more like c_{ij}^{-n} if β is assumed to have a distribution (he assumed a gamma distribution) in the population. Dickey and Hunter (1970) have investigated methods of grouping trips to obtain similar travel-time distributions in order to define trip purposes; it might be appropriate to test such methods on traveller types. Archer (1970) has tested a function of the form $e^{-\beta(1-\alpha c_{ij})c_{ij}}$ with some success. This is equivalent to assuming that β decreases with increasing cost of trip, relative to the usual assumption. This all indicates the existence of a rich field of research which has hardly been tapped. Further discussion of this point arises in another context below.

The measurement of generalized cost, and the form of the cost function, have an impact on the transport model through to the assignment stage. We showed in Section 9.4 how an inter-zonal travel cost C_{ij}^n could be constructed out of the modal costs c_{ij}^k and interpreted as the inter-zonal travel cost perceived by type n people. Even with this achievement, a problem remains: we do not measure modal costs directly, but only *route* costs, which we might call γ_{ij}^r for the rth route between zones i and j. A group of routes by road form the car mode for getting from i to j, and a group of public transport routes form the public transport mode. Thus we have another composite impedance problem: how to construct c_{ij}^ks out of γ_{ij}^rs. The solutions to this problem are outlined in Wilson (1970). Since 'route split' is essentially what we have called the assignment problem, the above solutions have a bearing on the assignment sub-model. In principle, we could build a combined distribution–route split model in relation to a network in which all links were coded irrespective of mode, and then we would have no need of a modal split sub-model. However, it is shown in the reference cited that this is unlikely to be a successful strategy for the transport modeller.

We should also note another assumption: we have assumed implicitly that a system of interest is closed, or that external zones are defined in some particularly simple way. Methods of closing systems through different ways of defining external zones were outlined in Chapter 6, and a detailed account of an entropy-maximizing method which is particularly suitable for transport models is given in Chapter 5 of Wilson, 1970.

*9.9. FURTHER DEVELOPMENTS II: ALTERNATIVE MODELS, LEADING TO FURTHER REVISION OF THE BASIC MODEL

In Section 9.8 we concentrated mainly on the task of developing the model as presented in the earlier part of the chapter. We should also consider other types of recent development. To do this we proceed as follows: we note the interest in building better behavioural models of transport, particularly models which are more soundly based on the theory of consumers' behaviour in economics; we consider the search for greater consistency in transport modelling; and finally, we review again the main thread of the argument of this chapter against these new strands of work, and note some possible revisions to the model of Sections 9.3 to 9.6 which may begin to emerge.

There is a general, and reasonable, feeling that the traditional transport model is too aggregative, but there is less agreement about how to respond to this situation, and so a variety of alternative models is now available, few, if any, necessarily any better than the one their proponents are trying to replace.

It is generally agreed that a suitable framework for behavioural modelling is provided by the utility-maximizing theory of consumers' behaviour. The simplest possible response is then to argue that each member of the population has a more-or-less identical utility function, and then to derive a model based on this. Not surprisingly, a popular form of function is the entropy function, and such approaches produce, in the end, an aggregative model which is not very distinguishable from the original and is in some ways inferior. Examples of such approaches are the works of Beckmann and Golob (1971), who include the entropy function as one of their functions, and Neidercorn and Bechdolt (1969), who adopt a more general stance. The essential problem with this straightforward approach to building utility-maximizing models lies in aggregation: given a large population, one has to assume the existence of a variety of utility functions. It is this variety, unless handled in some very simple form, together with (in the transport case) the presence of a large number of independent variables in each function, which makes aggregation difficult. (For a detail discussion, see Wilson (1970), Chapter 6.)

The task of building such models has been made both easier and more interesting by the new formulation of consumers demand theory by Lancaster (1965). This has led to a number of approaches to transport modelling, many of which are described in the recent book edited by Quandt (1970). Put very simply, the essence of Lancaster's approach is that demand should be a function of the attributes and characteristics of the goods rather than the goods themselves. In transport modelling, this had led to the search for a so-called *abstract mode model*: where demand by mode is a function of modal attributes but, hopefully, not dependent on the modes as such. This facilitates the analysis of the introduction of new modes and estimation of resulting generation and substitution effects. Models based (sometimes rather loosely) on Lancaster's work are also sometimes called *direct demand models*.

The first model to be both an abstract mode model and a direct demand model was that of Quandt and Baumol (1966):

$$T_{kij} = \alpha_0 P_i^{\alpha_1} P_j^{\alpha_2} Y_i^{\alpha_3} Y_j^{\alpha_4} M_i^{\alpha_5} M_j^{\alpha_6} N_{ij}^{\alpha_7} f_1(H) f_2(C) f_3(D) \qquad (9.81)$$

where

T_{kij} = trips from i to j by mode k;

P_i = population of zone i;

Y_i = mean income at zone i;

M_i = industrial character index for zone i;

N_{ij} = number of modes serving i and j, and where

$$f_1(H) = (H_{ij}^b)^{\beta_0}(H_{kij}^r)^{\beta_1} \qquad (9.82)$$

$$f_2(C) = (C_{ij}^b)^{\gamma_0}(C_{kij}^r)^{\gamma_1} \qquad (9.83)$$

$$f_3(D) = (D_{ij}^b)^{\delta_0}(D_{kij}^r)^{\delta_1} \qquad (9.84)$$

where

H_{ij}^b = least travel time between i and j;

H_{kij}^r = relative travel time for mode k;

C_{ij}^b = least travel cost;

C_{kij}^r = relative travel cost for mode k;

D_{ij}^b = best departure frequency;

D_{kij}^r = relative departure frequency for mode k.

The parameters of the model are estimated simultaneously. This procedure will be discussed and contrasted with alternative procedures in Section 12.7 on the calibration of transport models. This model has some interesting properties. The number of trips, for example, is elastic with respect to the provision of facilities. However, it is not really an abstract mode model, in the sense that including 'best' time, costs and so on involves implicitly noting the existence of modes. Indeed, in a later paper, Quandt and Young (1969) note that 'the "abstract mode model" in its simplest form may not be all that abstract.'

Another example of a recent model is provided by the Charles River Associates (1972). This is also an example of a *disaggregate* model in that it is estimated directly from household data rather than zonal aggregates, and stated in terms of household probabilities. The model equations are stated in terms of four sub-models in reverse of the usual order. Modal choice is

$$\frac{p_{ija}^M}{1 - p_{ija}^M} = \exp\left[a + \sum_l b_l(L_{ijal} - L_{ijtl}) + \sum_l c_l S_{il} \right] \qquad (9.85)$$

where

p_{ija}^M = fraction of trips by household i to destination j by auto (a) rather than transit (t);

L_{ijal}, L_{ijtl} = auto, transit level of service variables;

S_{il} = socio-economic variables.

The levels of service variables used were waiting time, in-vehicle travel time, operating, parking and fare costs, and the socio-economic variables were car-ownership per worker, race and occupation.

Time-of-day choice (a potentially useful innovation) was modelled as

$$\frac{p_{ij}^o}{1 - p_{ij}^o} = \exp\left[a' + b'(IP_{ij}^o - IP_{ij}^p) + \sum_l c_l' S_{il}' \right] \qquad (9.86)$$

where

p_{ij}^o = fraction of trips made by household i to destination j during off-peak period;

S_{il}' = socio-economic variables;

IP_{ij}^o, IP_{ij}^p = inclusive prices for off-peak and peak trips.

The socio-economic variables in this case were sex of head of household, number of workers per resident in the household and number of pre-school children in the household. IP_{ij}^o is taken as

$$IP_{ij}^o = \sum_l b_l L_{ijkl}^o \qquad (9.87)$$

where L_{ijkl}^o are the off-peak service variables for mode k, as previously defined, the b_ls are the parameters which appear in equation (9.85) and a', b' and c_l' are parameters to be estimated.

Destination choice is modelled as

$$\frac{p^D_{ij}}{p^D_{im}} = \exp\left[a''_1(IP_{ij} - IP_{im}) + a''_2(A_j - A_m) + a''_3(IP_{ij}S_j - IP_{im}S_m)\right] \quad (9.88)$$

where

$$P^D_{ij} = \text{probability of household } i \text{ going to } j;$$
$$IP_{ij} = \text{inclusive price of household } i \text{ going to } j;$$
$$A_j = \text{activity system variables for destination } j;$$
$$S_i = \text{socio-economic variables for household } i.$$

IP_{ij} is taken from equation (9.87), using peak or off-peak service variable values as appropriate; a''_1, a''_2 and a''_3 are new parameters to be estimated.

Finally, trip frequency choice is modelled as

$$\frac{p^F_i}{1 - p^F_i} = \exp\left[a'''_1 IP_i + a'''_2 IE_i + a'''_3 Y_i\right] \quad (9.89)$$

where

$$P^F_i = \text{probability that household } i \text{ will make a trip};$$
$$IP_i = \text{index of inclusive costs of trips for } i;$$
$$IE_i = \text{access to shops for household } i;$$
$$Y_i = \text{family income of household } i.$$

IP_i is taken as

$$IP_i = \sum_j IP_{ij} p^D_{ij} \quad (9.90)$$

and IE_i is taken as

$$IE_i = \sum_j A_j p^D_{ij} \quad (9.91)$$

The sub-models can be collected together as

$$p^t_{ijk} = p^F_i p^D_{ij} p^t_{ij} p^M_{ijk} \quad (9.92)$$

giving the probability that household i will travel to j in period t (peak or off-peak) by mode k.

The sub-models are estimated in reverse order to the usual one: that is, modal choice first, because coefficients turn up in later sub-models which are estimated in earlier ones. In effect, this means that the cost coefficients, the b_is, retain the same values in the different sub-models. This model is not perhaps as different from the traditional model as appears at first sight. P^F_i is an elastic trip-generation model. P^D_{ij} is not unlike a singly constrained gravity model in that competition *is* represented. To obtain P_{ij}^D for equation (9.92) from equation (9.88), we would have to proceed as follows: rewrite equation (9.88) as

$$\frac{p_{ij}^D}{p_{im}^D} = \frac{\exp\,[a_1'' IP_{ij} + a_2'' A_j + a_3'' IP_{ij} S_j]}{\exp\,[a_1'' IP_{im} + a_2'' A_m + a_3'' IP_{im} S_m]} \tag{9.93}$$

Sum over j:

$$\frac{\sum_j p_{ij}^D}{p_{im}^D} = \frac{\sum_j \exp\,[a_1'' IP_{ij} + a_2'' A_j + a_3'' IP_{ij} S_j]}{\exp\,[a_1'' IP_{im} + a_2'' A_m + a_3'' IP_{im} S_m]} \tag{9.94}$$

Substitute j for m and vice versa, and rearrange to give

$$p_{ij}^D = \frac{\exp\,[a_1'' IP_{ij} + a_2'' A_j + a_3'' IP_{ij} S_j]}{\sum_m [a_1'' IP_{im} + a_2'' A_m + a_3'' IP_{im} S_m]} \tag{9.95}$$

since $\sum_j p_{ij}^D$ can be taken as 1.

We have already noted that the time-of-day model is a potentially useful innovation, and finally we note that the model split sub-model is the standard one. Further issues associated with this model will also be discussed under the calibration heading in Chapter 12.

We give a final example of an alternative model by Ben-Akiva (1972) which illustrates the problem of making the distribution and modal split models simultaneous:

$$\frac{p_{ijk}}{p_{ij'k'}} = \exp\left[\sum_l a_l(A_{jl} - A_{j'l}) + \sum_l b_l(M_{kl}^1 - M_{k'l}^1) + \sum_l c_l Y_i(M_{kl}^2 - M_{k'l}^2)\right.$$

$$\left. + \sum_l d_l(L_{ijkl}^1 - L_{ij'k'l}^1) + \sum_l \frac{e_l}{Y_i}(L_{ijkl}^2 - L_{ij'k'l}^2)\right] \tag{9.96}$$

where

P_{ijk} = fraction of total trips from household i going to destination j by mode k;

A_{jl} = activity system variables at j;

M_{kl}^1, M_{kl}^2 = modal variables;

L_{ijkl}^1, L_{ijkl}^2 = level of service variables;

Y_i = household income.

The activity variables used were the number of jobs in wholesale and retail establishments in the zone of destination j and an indicator for CBD destinations. The modal variables were indicators for auto usage, one used in association with income, one without. The L^1 level of service variables were out-of-vehicle travel time and in-vehicle travel time, and the L^2 service variable was out-of-pocket cost, the last named being divided by income.

The model was estimated by Ben-Akiva only for shopping trips, and for a given number of trips in each household. An expression could, of course, be derived from P_{ijk} directly using the same method as that which produced equation (9.95) from (9.88) in the previous example.

In summary then, we note that the three examples of models presented above indicate the following kinds of recent development. The Quandt–Baumol model is simultaneous and direct in its demand estimation, and attempts to achieve an abstract mode formulation. The Charles River Associates' model is sequential rather than simultaneous, but is associated with a reverse-order estimation procedure which ensures, in effect, simultaneous parameter estimations—or at least values of coefficients which remain the same between, and are transmitted between, the different sub-models. This also illustrates the development of disaggregate models, since it is applied directly to household data, rather than zone-aggregated data. Both the Quandt–Baumol and the Charles River Associates' model have elastic trip generation. The third example, Ben-Akiva's model, illustrates a simultaneous disaggregate model, though it deals with distribution and model split only, not trip generation.

There is another thread of work, due to Manheim (1970), which can now usefully be introduced into the discussion. He discusses a class of models which he calls *general share models* (G.S.M.s). These take the form

$$T_{ij}^{kr} = T_i P_{ij}^{(1)} P_{ij}^{(2)k} P_{ij}^{(3)kr} \tag{9.97}$$

where

T_{ij}^{kr} = number of trips from i to j by mode k by route r;
T_i = number of trips generated in i;
$P_{ij}^{(1)}$ = share of T_i to destination j;
$P_{ij}^{(2)k}$ = share of $T_i P_{ij}^{(1)}$ by mode k;
$P_{ij}^{(3)kr}$ = share of $T_i P_{ij}^{(1)} P_{ij}^{(2)k}$ by route r.

G.S.M.s have the advantage that they are internally consistent. Manheim shows that direct models which are internally consistent can be expressed as G.S.M.s, and hence as sequential models. Thus for good models (internally consistent ones in particular) the distinction between direct and simultaneous models on the one hand, and sequential models on the other, is *not* a fundamental one. (There is a more fundamental distinction in relation to the way in which the parameters of such models are estimated, and this will be discussed further in Chapter 12.) Such consistency issues, and the possibility of setting up an axiomatic foundation for transport models is also interestingly discussed in a paper by Mayberry (1970). He lists some of the invariance properties which a good model should have: the prediction should be independent of the way in which the modes are *named*, for example. Such properties, and possible desirable invariance properties of models, are also investigated by McLynn (1972). One of the main reasons for the interest in model consistency in the United States has been that the 'authorized' transport model used by many planning agencies is demonstrably inconsistent. It should be made clear that the equivalent model as used in the U.K., for example in the SELNEC study (Wagon and Wilson, 1971), *is* internally consistent; and could be expressed as one of Manheim's G.S.M.s. The achievement of internal consistency is one of the main benefits of constructing models using entropy-maximizing methods (Wilson, 1970) and this was the basis of the consistency of the SELNEC model.

The concluding part of this 'further developments' discussion is to study possible modifications to the Section 9.3–9.6 model of this chapter as a result of some of the other new ideas discussed above. Many of these possible modifications have been discussed in a recent paper (Wilson, 1973). The reader is referred to that paper for details, and only the basic argument, together with some newer ideas, is presented here.

Since one of the main concerns of recent work has been to improve the behavioural basis of transport models, we begin with a discussion of the characterization of travel behaviour at the individual level and related aggregation questions. We will take the 'individual' as the basic unit, though this could be taken to mean a person or a household according to the preference of the analyst. It is customary, and probably preferable, to use the household as the basic unit.

We must first characterize transport as a good. Usually, we speak of the quantity x_i purchased at price p_i of some good i. But for transport as a good, we need two variables to describe 'quantity': number of trips in some time period and expenditure. We could only avoid having two such variables if we had number of trips *to each destination* in the time period (and the associated cost) but, typically, this involves a large number of variables. However, it will turn out that both types of description of transport as a good will have their place in the scheme to be presented.

For an individual, r, resident in zone i, trip-making behaviour can be described at four levels of detail, I–IV, as indicated in Figure 9.11 on p. 162. The variables displayed on the Figure employ an obvious notation: C_i^r, O_i^r are total expenditure and number of trips for individual r resident in zone i, C_i^{pr}, O_i^{pr} are similar quantities split by purpose; T_{ij}^{pr} is the number of trips now further split by destination, and now that destination is specified we revert to having the cost of a single trip, c_{ij}^{pr} instead of total expenditure; T_{ij}^{pkr} and c_{ij}^{pkr} are similar quantities further split by mode. There could be further disaggregation to route split, but we shall ignore that here. The reader can easily add the appropriate extension if desired. The quantities defined above

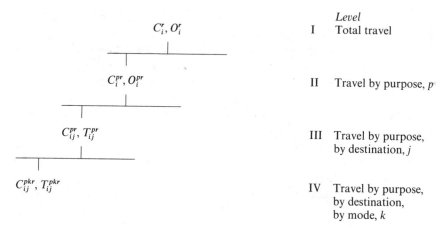

$$\qquad\qquad C_i^r, O_i^r \qquad\qquad\qquad\qquad\qquad \text{I} \quad \text{Total travel}$$

$$\qquad\qquad\qquad C_i^{pr}, O_i^{pr} \qquad\qquad\qquad \text{II} \quad \text{Travel by purpose, } p$$

$$\qquad C_{ij}^{pr}, T_{ij}^{pr} \qquad\qquad\qquad\qquad \text{III} \quad \text{Travel by purpose,}$$
$$\qquad\qquad\qquad\qquad\qquad\qquad\qquad\qquad\qquad \text{by destination, } j$$

$$C_{ij}^{pkr}, T_{ij}^{pkr} \qquad\qquad\qquad\qquad\qquad \text{IV} \quad \text{Travel by purpose,}$$
$$\qquad\qquad\qquad\qquad\qquad\qquad\qquad\qquad\qquad \text{by destination,}$$
$$\qquad\qquad\qquad\qquad\qquad\qquad\qquad\qquad\qquad \text{by mode, } k$$

Figure 9.11   Alternative levels of resolution

are related as follows:

$$\sum_p C_i^{pr} = C_i^r \qquad\qquad (9.98)$$

$$\sum_p O_i^{pr} = O_i^r \qquad\qquad (9.99)$$

$$\sum_j T_{ij}^{pr} c_{ij}^{pr} = C_i^{pr} \qquad\qquad (9.100)$$

$$\sum_j T_{ij}^{pr} = O_i^{pr} \qquad\qquad (9.101)$$

$$\sum_k T_{ij}^{pkr} c_{ij}^{pkr} = T_{ij}^{pr} c_{ij}^{pr} \qquad\qquad (9.102)$$

$$\sum_k T_{ij}^{pkr} = T_{ij}^{pr} \qquad\qquad (9.103)$$

and these relationships must be preserved (possibly aggregated over r or sub-sets of r) as part of any internal consistency conditions.

The distribution–modal split model of Section 9.4 is obtained by aggregating over r to produce persons of type n (where n is some characteristic of r, usually car-ownership, but it could be any set of characteristics), denoted by $r \in R(n)$ say. That is, $R(n)$ is the set of individuals r with characteristics n. In such aggregation, if we assume that i is a zone label, we also imply aggregation of individuals of type n in each zone. We usually assume as given quantities:

$$O_i^{pn} = \sum_{r \in R(n)} O_i^{pr} \tag{9.104}$$

which is obtained from the trip generation sub-model, and

$$C^{pn} = \sum_i \sum_{r \in R(n)} C_i^{pr} \tag{9.105}$$

which determines β^n in the distribution model, and we usually obtain this from survey data. Usually, we also assume that the numbers of trip attractions, D_j are given.

We simply note at this point, to discuss again later, that it seems odd that in the existing model we treat the O-quantity O_i^{pn} and the C-quantity C^{pn} at different levels of aggregation.

Next, though, we consider how a utility-maximizing theory could be developed. Hitherto, it has been applied at the III or IV level of aggregation of Figure 9.11. However, this leads to a form of utility function which contains a very large number of variables, about which there is relatively little hope of obtaining empirical information. Another possibility is to try and apply utility theory at the II level of aggregation. Then, C_i^{pr} and O_i^{pr} could be determined as demand variables as functions of other prices. The important practical consequence at this stage of theoretical development is that whatever methods are used to estimate O_i^{pr} could in principle be used to estimate C_i^{pr}, and then O-variables and C-variables would be treated at the same aggregation level. We shall discuss how to do this below.

If we assert then, that the major role of utility theory is at the II level, then we can proceed to model T_{ij}^{pkn} and T_{ij}^{pkn} by the same methods as before. Suppose we aggregate over $r \in R(n)$ and to origin zones. Define

$$O_i^{pn} = \sum_{r \in R(n)} O_i^{pr} \tag{9.106}$$

and

$$C_i^{pn} = \sum_{r \in R(n)} C_i^{pr} \tag{9.107}$$

Suppose also that instead of taking D_j as given, we define a set of X_j^ps as attractiveness factors for each zone. Suppose further that c_{ij}^{pr} and c_{ij}^{pkr} are 'averaged' to c_{ij}^{pn} and c_{ij}^{pkn} and are related by

$$c_{ij}^{pn} = c_{ij}^{p2}(c_{ij}^{p1n}, c_{ij}^{p2n}, \ldots) \tag{9.108}$$

(Specifically, this may take the form of equation (9.40), the relationship used when this situation arose earlier). The distribution and modal split models would then be*

$$T_{ij}^{pn} = A_i^{pn} O_i^{pn} X_j^p e^{-\beta_i^{pn} c_{ij}^{pn}} \qquad (9.109)$$

where

$$A_i^{pn} = 1 \bigg/ \sum_j X_j^p e^{-\beta_i^{pn} c_{ij}^{pn}} \qquad (9.110)$$

$$T_{ij}^{pkn} = T_{ij}^{pn} \frac{e^{-\lambda_i^{pn} c_{ij}^{pkn}}}{\sum_{k \in \gamma(n)} e^{-\lambda_i^{pn} c_{ij}^{pkn}}} \qquad (9.111)$$

For the modal split model, it may still be desirable to assume that the parameter is independent of i and to replace λ_i^{pn} in equation (9.111) by λ^{pn}. Our aggregation discussion, however, has certainly shown us that β_i^{pn} should remain i-dependent. We explore the corresponding calibration issues in Chapter 12.

In summary then, we are arguing that a level of aggregation has been identified at which it is best to apply economic theory, to estimate C_i^{pr} and C_i^{pn} as well as O_i^{pr} and O_i^{pn}. If equation (9.100) is summed over $r \in R(n)$, we then get

$$\sum_j T_{ij}^{pn} c_{ij}^{pn} = C_i^{pn} \qquad (9.112)$$

and, with known C_i^{pn}, this allows β_i^{pn} to be calculated so that, in effect, it is no longer a parameter. The parameters of the model would become those of the C_i^{pn} sub-model which, incidentally, could be a category analysis model exactly analogous to the O_i^{pn} model, but with trip costs instead of frequencies. This revised model can be embodied in the usual framework, with a trip-generation model which may be elastic, and an assignment model, the whole system being iterated until equilibrium is achieved. As before, n can be car-ownership/non-car-ownership, but a more disaggregated scheme could be adopted. Further, the model is internally consistent in most of, indeed possibly all, the ways advocated by Manheim (1970) and Mayberry (1970). Thus, this revised model reflects most of the new trends discussed earlier, except two: it would probably not be simultaneously estimated, though perhaps it could be on the lines of the Charles River Associates' model (this issue is discussed in Chapter 12) and it is not fully disaggregate. This last issue we explore now.

---

* If capacity constraints, D_j^p, are known to apply at the destination end (or even D_j^{pk}, constraints by mode), then methods can easily be developed to build these into the model, see Wilson (1970) and Wilson (1973), so there is little loss of generality in discussing only the singly constrained model below.

Often, the model will have to be aggregated as above since only aggregate data will be available for calibration. However, there is no theoretical reason why we should not explore the disaggregate version of the above model, and sometimes household or person data would be available to calibrate it.

Essentially, we are now arguing that the aggregation in equations (9.106) and (9.107) need not take place. Trip generation is already estimated for much finer household categories in the category analysis sub-model and we aggregate in a manner analogous to equations (9.106) and (9.7). This suggests that we can build disaggregate models in two ways: using something like the one categories h of equation (9.7), or using individuals r. We will start with the latter.

We would then need trip-generation and trip-cost sub-models to estimate O_i^{pr} and C_i^{pr} for each individual r, probably on a probabilistic basis. A utility-maximizing model may be appropriate. Note that now, i is being carried as a label only and implies no aggregation. O_i^{pr} and C_i^{pr} may be functions of i-variables, though in the sense that location is a characteristic of r. Formally, we may write

$$O_i^{pr} = O_i^{pr}(X_i^{p1}, X_i^{p2}, \ldots Y_1^r, Y_2^r, \ldots x_1, x_2 \ldots) \qquad (9.113)$$

where the X_i^{pl}'s characterize the location (accessibilities etc), and the Y_i^r's the individuals; $x_1, x_2 \ldots$ are other external or random variables. Similarly,

$$C_i^{pr} = C_i^{pr}(X_i^{p1}, X_i^{p2}, \ldots Y_1^r, Y_2^r, \ldots x_1, x_2 \ldots) \qquad (9.114)$$

The terms to be estimated could perhaps conveniently be rewritten as $\Omega_i^{pr}(m)$ and $\Gamma_i^{pr}(c)$ the probability of making m trips and spending amount c. Then

$$O_i^{pr} = \frac{\sum_m \Omega_i^{pr}(m)m}{\sum_m \Omega_i^{pr}(m)} \qquad (9.115)$$

and

$$C_i^{pr} = \frac{\sum_c \Gamma_i^{pr}(c)c}{\sum_c \Gamma_i^{pr}(c)} \qquad (9.116)$$

In equation (9.116) the summation signs would be, of course, replaced by integral signs if c were defined as a continuous variable.

Suppose then that, one way or another, we obtain a model estimate of O_i^{pr} and C_i^{pr} for an r described by characteristics $(Y_1^r, Y_2^r, \ldots)$. Then $p_{ij}^{(1)pr}$ could be taken as the probability of j being a destination, and $p_{ij}^{(2)pkr}$ as the probability of using mode k. These terms are defined so that

$$\sum_j p_{ij}^{(1)pr} = 1 \qquad (9.117)$$

and

$$\sum_{k\in\gamma(r)} p_{ij}^{(2)pkr} = 1 \tag{9.11}$$

The usual entropy-maximizing models would be

$$p_{ij}^{(1)pr} = \frac{X_j^p \, e^{-\beta^{pr} C_{ij}^{pr}}}{\sum_j X_j^p \, e^{-\beta^{pr} C_{ij}^{pr}}} \tag{9.11}$$

$$p_{ij}^{(2)pkr} = \frac{e^{-\lambda_{ij}^{pr} C_{ij}^{pkr}}}{\sum_{k\in\gamma(r)} e^{-\lambda_{ij}^{pr} C_{ij}^{pkr}}} \tag{9.120}$$

We may, of course, wish to assume that the travel costs were independent of r and λ of j. Thus, the probable number of trips for individual r would be

$$T_{ij}^{pkr} = O_i^{pr} p_{ij}^{(1)pr} p_{ij}^{(2)pkr} \tag{9.121}$$

Note that there is a trip-end balancing term, but it is explicitly part of $p_{ij}^{(1)p}$

A more convenient way of developing such a model may be to assume that a set of indices h characterizes individuals. Then, for one individual with characteristics h,

$$T_{ij}^{pkh} = O_i^{ph} p_{ij}^{(1)ph} p_{ij}^{(2)pkh} \tag{9.122}$$

At the finest level of disaggregation, there would be a unique h for each individual. At coarser levels, we may assume $a_i(h)$ individuals *in zone i* with characteristics h. The number of trips made by these individuals would be

$$T_{ij}^{pkh} = a_i(h) O_i^{ph} p_{ij}^{(1)ph} p_{ij}^{(2)pkh} \tag{9.123}$$

Thus, we now have a distribution and modal split model which operates at any desired level of disaggregation (and in particular can easily be made compatible with the usual category analysis level).

We illustrate this new model by showing how it would work at the category analysis level of aggregation; O_i^{ph} is the trip rate for a given purpose, effectively the $T(h)$ of equation (9.107). It is considered that the variance is carried by h and the zone label i could be dropped. A similar argument could be applied to C_i^{ph} in one way but not in another: category analysis could be used to estimate C_i^{ph} but, in this case, the i should not be dropped. Thus, the full model would become

$$T_{ij}^{pkh} = a_i(h) O^{ph} p_{ij}^{(1)ph} p_{ij}^{(2)pkh} \tag{9.124}$$

where

$$p_{ij}^{(1)ph} = \frac{X_j^p \, e^{-\beta_i^{ph} c_{ij}^{pkh}}}{\sum_j X_j^p \, e^{-\beta_i^{ph} c_{ij}^{pkh}}} \tag{9.125}$$

nd

$$p_{ij}^{(2)pkh} = \frac{e^{-\lambda_{ij}^{ph}c_{ij}^{pkh}}}{\sum_{k \in \gamma(h)} e^{-\lambda_{ij}^{ph}c_{ij}^{pkh}}} \qquad (9.126)$$

ould be estimated from

$$\sum_j \sum_k T_{ij}^{pkh} c_{ij}^{ph} = a_i(h) C_i^{ph} \qquad (9.127)$$

nd λ_{ij}^{ph} (a full explanation of this is given in Chapter 12) from

$$\sum_k p_{ij}^{(2)pkh} c_{ij}^{pkh} = C_{ij}^{ph} \qquad (9.128)$$

The relationship between c_{ij}^{ph} and c_{ij}^{pkh} would have to be specified, of course, by an equation of the form (9.108).

Another way of progressing from the finest level of disaggregation (individuals) to groups, is to assume that individuals r in a set $R(h)$ have trip-making and expenditure characteristics according to some known distributions. Such a scheme is, however, considerably more difficult to handle mathematically.

9.10. REFERENCES

* S. Angel and G. M. Hyman (1972) Urban spatial interaction, *Environment and Planning*, **4**, pp. 99–118.

E. Archer (1970) An investigation of a rider prediction technique for a demand-scheduled bus system, M.A.Sc. Dissertation, Department of Civil Engineering, University of Waterloo, Ontario.

M. J. Beckmann and T. Golob (1971) On the metaphysical foundation of traffic theory; entropy revisited, paper presented to the Fifth International Symposium on the Theory of Traffic Flow and Transportation, Berkeley, California.

M. Ben-Akiva (1972) Passenger transport demand: theory and models, mimeo, Department of Civil Engineering, M.I.T.

D. Brand (1972) The state of the art of travel demand forecasting: a critical review, paper presented to the Highway Research Board Conference on Travel demand forecasting, Williamsburg, Virginia; to be published.

J. E. Burrell (1968) Multiple route assignment and its applications to capacity restraint, paper presented to the Fourth International Symposium on the Theory of Traffic Flow, Karlsruhe.

Charles River Associates (1972) A disaggregated behavioural model of urban travel demand, report to the U.S. Department of Transportation, Washington, D.C.

J. W. Dickey and S. P. Hunter (1970) Grouping of travel time distribution, *Transportation Research*, **4**, pp. 93–102.

* F. X. de Donnea (1971) *The determinants of transport mode choice in Dutch cities*, Rotterdam University Press, Rotterdam.

A. W. Evans (1970) Some properties of trip-distribution models, *Transportation Research*, **4**, pp. 19–36.

Freeman, Fox, Wilbur Smith and Associates (1967) *T.A.P. Manual*, London.

B. Harris (1964) A note on the probability of interaction at a distance, *Journal c Regional Science*, **5**, pp. 31–35.

* K. W. Heathington and E. Isibor (1972) The use of dummy variables in trip generatio. analysis, *Transportation Research*, **6**, pp. 131–142.

G. M. Hyman (1970) Trip distribution and modal split by categories of households *Transportation Research*, **4**, pp. 71–76.

* G. Kraft and M. Wohl (1967) New directions for passenger demand analysis an forecasting, *Transportation Research*, **1**, pp. 205–230.

K. J. Lancaster (1965) A new approach to consumer theory, *Journal of Politica Economy*, **74**, 132–157; also reprinted in R. E. Quandt (Ed.) (1970) *op. cit.*, pp 17–54.

* R. Lane, T. J. Powell and P. Prestwood Smith (1971) *Analytical transport planning* Duckworth, London.

J. M. McLynn (1972) private communication.

M. L. Manheim (1970) Fundamental properties of systems of demand models, mimeo Department of Civil Engineering, M.I.T., Cambridge, Mass.

* B. V. Martin, F. W. Memmott and A. J. Bone (1961) Principles and techniques o predicting future demand for urban area transportation, Research Report No. 38 M.I.T., Cambridge, Mass.

J. P. Mayberry (1970) Structural requirements for abstract-mode models of passenge transportation, in R. E. Quandt (Ed.) (1970) *op. cit.*, pp. 103–125.

J. R. Meyer, J. F. Kain and M. Wohl (1965) *The urban transport problem*, Harvar University Press, Cambridge, Mass.

J. A. Neidercorn and B. V. Bechdolt (1969) An economic derivation of the 'gravit law' of spatial interaction, *Journal of Regional Science*, pp. 273–282.

R. E. Quandt (Ed.) (1970) *The demand for travel: theory and measurement*, Heath Lexington Books, Lexington, Mass.

R. E. Quandt and W. J. Baumol (1966) The demand for abstract modes: theory and measurement, *Journal of Regional Science*, **6**, pp. 13–26; also reprinted in R. E Quandt (Ed. 1970) *op. cit.* pp. 83–101.

R. E. Quandt and K. H. Young (1969) Cross-sectional travel demand models: estimates and tests, *Journal of Regional Science*, **9**, pp. 201–214; reprinted in R. E. Quand (Ed.) (1970) *op. cit.*, pp. 129–162.

* D. A. Quarmby (1967) Choice of travel mode for the journey to work: some findings, *Journal of Transport Economics and Policy*, **1**, pp. 273–314; also reprinted in R. E. Quandt (Ed.) (1970) *op. cit.*, pp. 235–295.

* E. Ruiter (1972) Analytical structures, paper prepared for H.R.B. Conference on Travel demand forecasting, Williamsburg, Virginia; to be published.

M. Sakarovitch (1968) The *k* shortest chains in a graph, *Transportation Research*, **2**, pp. 1–11.

* J. O. Tressider, D. A. Meyers, J. E. Burrell and T. J. Powell (1968) The London Transportation Study: methods and techniques, *Proceedings, Institute of Civil Engineers*, **39**, pp. 433–464.

D. J. Wagon and A. G. Wilson (1971) The mathematical model, Technical Working Paper 5, SELNEC Transportation Study, Town Hall, Manchester.

A. G. Wilson (1967) A statistical theory of spatial distribution models, *Transportation Research*, **1**, pp. 253–269; also reprinted in R. E. Quandt (Ed.) *op. cit.*, pp. 55–82.

A. G. Wilson (1970) *Entropy in urban and regional modelling*, Pion, London.

* A. G. Wilson (1972) Travel demand forecasting: achievements and problems, paper presented to the H.R.B. Conference on Travel demand forecasting, Williamsburg, Virginia; to be published.

A. G. Wilson (1973) Further developments of entropy maximizing transport models, *Transportation Planning and Technology*, **1**, pp. 183–193.

A. G. Wilson, D. Bayliss, A. J. Blackburn and B. G. Hutchinson (1971) New directions in strategic transportation planning, in *The urban transportation planning process*, O.E.C.D., Paris, pp. 227–351.

A. G. Wilson, A. F. Hawkins, G. J. Hill and D. J. Wagon (1969) Calibrating and testing the SELNEC transport model, *Regional Studies*, **2**, pp. 337–350; reprinted in A. G. Wilson (1972) *Papers in urban and regional analysis*, Pion, London, pp. 202–215.

H. J. Wootton and G. W. Pick (1967) A model for trips generated by households, *Journal of Transport Economics and Policy*, **1**, pp. 137–153.

CHAPTER 10

The spatial distribution of activities

10.1. INTRODUCTION

In Chapters 6 to 9 we have worked with a fairly restricted set of techniques, mainly building on matrix operator-probability, or spatial interaction concepts. In the field of locational analysis (the study of the spatial distribution of urban activities) a much wider range of techniques is available, and it is useful to return to the model-builder's check list of Chapter 4 by way of introduction.

Models of the distribution of activities can be built for a wide variety of purposes. We emphasized earlier that it was important to be clear about purpose, and we shall see here that this issue can indeed affect choice of technique for model development.

The next item on the check list related to choice of variables. Clearly, we are interested in variables which describe activities by location, and the determinants of the associated patterns and processes. We have to be particularly clear as to whether the prime interest is in the activities themselves, the associated physical stock, or both. An example from the population-residential-housing sector will illustrate the issues involved here. We may be primarily interested in residential activity, the spatial distribution of different types of people, the types of houses they live in and so on, or we may be interested in housing primarily in order to set up a house-building programme. Ideally, we should be interested in both simultaneously, but available time and effort may prohibit this. It is extremely easy to confuse the two interests, especially since, at any one time, the population cross-section coincides in some way with the housing stock cross-section. However, the behaviour in time of people and stock is quite different: people move around more frequently than the pattern of the housing stock changes. Typically, one home will be utilized by many families during its lifetime. The distinction which is being made can usefully be conceived as relating to aspects of an economic supply and demand system: people demand housing at a location and some houses are supplied there; what is observed at one point in time is the intersection of supply and demand curves. This discussion is beginning to anticipate that under the heading of 'theory' below, however, and will be pursued further there. Once again, we can observe that choice of variables in relation to the prime system of interest may affect the model-building techniques to be used.

At this point, it is convenient to discuss another distinction between types of variable which is particularly crucial in a *spatial* distribution model: this relates to whether we focus primarily on the distribution of an activity (or stock) across the zones of our spatial system, or on the set of activities which use up the capacity of a particular zone. In relation to Figure 10.1, it is a

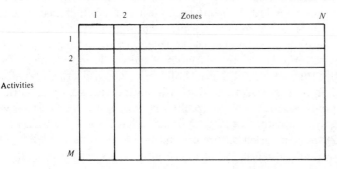

Figure 10.1 Zone-activity cross-tabulations. (Based, with permission, on I. S. Lowry, *Urban Development Models*, Special Report 97, Highway Research Board, Washington, D.C., U.S.A., p. 128, Figure 2, 1968).

matter of whether we focus primarily on rows or on columns. Generally speaking, we will adopt the row or activity location focus as distinct from the column or land-use focus. In any partial study of one activity, we should bear in mind that we should not neglect the fact that it is competing for land (and possibly other resources) with other activities. Each activity location model should ideally be part of a more general model which incorporates a set of land-use accounts. Such issues are taken further in Chapter 11 where we discuss the building of general models.

The third item on the model-builder's check list was the identification of variables which were under the planner's control. This is partly a matter of planning powers in relation to the system in which the model builder is interested, partly a matter of the model-builder's purpose and interest, and partly a matter of interpretation. These matters cannot be resolved except in relation to particular examples. However, one matter can be usefully recalled at this stage: the question as to whether our models are to be normative or positive. The convention adopted in this book is that it is better to think of all models as positive models, built for analysis, which may be capable of (conditional) predictions which can be utilized within some essentially normative planning process. This argument simply recapitulates that of Chapter 2, but it is particularly appropriate to mention it in relation to location models. In practical terms, the model builder has to decide which variables are *endogenous* to the model and which *exogenous*.

The fourth item in the check list referred to aggregation issues. Since we are interested in the spatial distribution of activities, our urban system must be divided into zones. These may be very small, or larger, depending on the purposes of the exercise, and once again, this decision relates to other decisions which will finally decide the model-building technique to be used. It is the sectoral aggregation/disaggregation question which is a more tricky one for the locational analyst. This is the question as to whether an essentially micro or macro approach should be adopted. Throughout this book we have attempted to develop a *comprehensive* approach to model building in the sense of trying to represent all the activities of the whole study area in their entirety. Within this, we would like to build in as much detail as possible; indeed, in the limit, it is possible to deal with all individuals, organizations and units of physical stock in a comprehensive micro approach. However, this is practically impossible for large systems. It has been argued elsewhere (Wilson, 1972) that an *essentially* micro approach involves modelling the behaviour of an individual (or other micro unit) *in his environment*, taking this environment as given. Such an approach inevitably ceases to be comprehensive and so, in this sense, we are primarily interested in macro or aggregative models. We should note, however, as we shall see in relation to specific examples below, that such models can be given micro-scale interpretations, usually in probabilistic terms, and much can be learned by insisting that the theories which underpin our models are maximally consistent with corresponding micro-behavioural theories. One further comment on this point is in order: micro-analysis at the individual level may often be a powerful tool for the identification of problems. But, when policies are implemented to solve problems, however they were identified, then it is usually important to treat the system-wide impacts of these policies and this can only be accomplished in a comprehensive framework. This is perhaps one of the main reasons for the stance adopted in this book. A deeper discussion would take us beyond the scope of this book, but the interested reader can pursue it further in the paper cited earlier (Wilson, 1972). For the time being, however, we shall assume that we are concerned with macro or aggregative models, and the techniques presented are chosen with this in mind. In some associated fields, such as the study of industrial location, much of the model building has been what we have called essentially micro, and will be largely neglected in this chapter.

The fifth item in the check list concerned the treatment of time. In the building of location models, the important 'time' question relates to whether the model builder is attempting to represent the total cross-section of one or more activities at some point(s) in time, or the marginal change between two points in time. This again turns out to have a fundamental bearing on technique. The perfect answer to the question would be to seek a fully dynamic model in which time was a continuous variable which had been applied over a very long time period, so that both cross-sections and marginal changes were predicted by the model. This is rarely possible in practice, if only because of the lack of suitable time series data. In fact, many cross-section models have been developed for data which refer to one point in time only, and thus are not even tested on a comparative static equilibrium basis, while the rarer marginal models usually relate to only a small number of points in time, often only two. However, the answer to the question depends to some extent on the interest and purpose of the model builder. It is good to be able to model a total cross-section, and sometimes lack of time series data means that that is the only possibility, but a model builder may be interested only in the development of new housing in the next five years, in which case a marginal model would be more appropriate.

A model is a formal representation of a theory and, as ever, the most important task for the model builder is to seek out and develop an adequate and appropriate theoretical basis for his model. We have already discussed a number of preliminary theoretical questions: questions of a prime interest in people or stock, in activity or land use, the micro–macro question and so on. More detail will be added in the introductory parts of each sub-section which follows, where the kinds of hypotheses and theories to be represented in the models are discussed. The discussion on this topic, therefore, will be postponed.

The next item in the check list related to techniques for model building. A number of techniques can be distinguished, though, as we shall see, they overlap and complement each other in various ways. They include

(1) algebraic models, including as special cases spatial interaction models and entropy maximizing models,
(2) matrix operator models,
(3) linear programming models,
(4) differential equation/difference equation models,
(5) simulation models,
(6) econometric models,
(7) models based on economic theory,
(8) ecological models,
(9) models based on the theory of games.

These are not listed in any particular order. It is difficult, indeed, to think of any 'logical' order for such a list. (It is almost impossible to list them in increasing order of 'difficulty' for example, as, in most cases, there are simple and complicated models based on each technique.) The essence of each approach will be explained in broad terms in Section 10.2, and details will only be presented in relation to particular examples in later sub-sections. The preceding discussion has raised issues concerned with population activity/ physical stock foci, demand/supply relationships, micro/macro questions and cross-section/marginal foci. If particular techniques contribute to one focus rather than another, this will be noted in the next section.

10.2. SOME AVAILABLE TECHNIQUES

Algebraic models express relationships between variables using the operations of elementary algebra coupled with the notion of a function. The relationships may involve notions of causality, but this is not necessary. A specific example of algebraic models is the family of *spatial interaction models* outlined in Chapter 6. We have already discussed one such model in detail, the retail sales model in Chapter 4, which the reader will now recognize as a production-constrained spatial interaction model. The essence of using the concept of spatial interaction in a location model is that the activity which is being located has a strong interaction with some other activity. In the case of the retail sales model, the activity being located is retailing and this interacts strongly with the resident population and its spending power (which is, in this case, assumed to be given). When a spatial interaction model is used in this way, the given activity is the constrained part of a singly constrained model (it could be either production- or attraction-constrained) and the other activity, relating to the other end of the interaction, is obviously un-constrained; the total volume of that activity located in a zone is obtained by adding all the flows into (or out of) the zone.

The spatial interaction model has mostly been used to represent residential location in relation to the distribution of workplaces, and the utilization of services in relation to the distribution of population. (These two models can also be coupled together, as we shall see in Chapter 11.) Most typically, it has been used to model population activity rather than stock and the total cross-section rather than marginal change, though there is no fundamental limitation associated with the technique. In theoretical terms, it can be seen as a set of equations which represent a model of demand–supply interaction, and the modeller has to be particularly careful in his treatment of supply-side variables within the model. Further, as we noted in Chapter 6, spatial interaction models can be seen as special cases of *entropy-maximizing models* and the statistical averaging interpretation of such models helps to relate micro and macro population of associated modelling tasks (Wilson, 1972).

The class of models just briefly discussed is only a small sub-set of the class of algebraic models. Algebraic model building will always represent one of the most fruitful techniques for the representation of theories. Its main weakness relates to the treatment of time associated with such models, though this can easily be rectified by adding the tools of the differential calculus or by the use of difference equations, as we shall see later.

Matrix operator models are really special cases of algebraic models. We saw with the demographic models of Chapter 7 that the matrix formulation of the models is an optional extra. However, if matrix inversion is involved, as with the input–output model of Chapter 8, or any other special property of matrices, then it would be extremely clumsy *not* to use matrix concepts. The technique has been of relatively limited application in locational analysis, but could become increasingly important if multi-region versions of the demographic or economic models of Chapters 7 and 8 are applied to systems of interest made up of very small 'regions', or zones.

Linear programming models in locational analysis are often confusing because it is not always clear whether the resulting model is positive or normative, since, in many cases, some measure of welfare or utility is being maximized. Following our earlier comment on this question, we will consider only models in which the objective function characterizes behaviour, and the resulting distribution of activities, may or may not be optimal in some normative sense. That is a matter for separate investigation. (Linear programming techniques may be used additionally as part of a planning process in which a behavioural model has been used separately to assess impact, but the term 'model' will not be used in this context.) The technique can be employed when it is possible to construct an objective function which, when maximized subject to linear constraints, reproduces behaviour. It has been used most commonly in studies of residential location and industrial location, but also in relation to land use.

Differential equations or *difference equations* are concerned with change, with the period of change being measured by some independent variable, the variable being continuous in the first case, discrete in the second. Typically, that variable will be time in our case, though it could in principle be a spatial variable. In effect, the body of mathematics associated with these concepts simply enables us to handle time properly; when we are otherwise capable of doing this. (We may be fundamentally incapable of it, because of data limitation, for example.)

There are circumstances when a model can be specified as a set of rules which enable numbers to be operated on, usually in the computer, though the rules and the consequences of applying them cannot be written down as a set of algebraic equations. Such mathematics was called algorithmic in Chapter 5. When a model is assembled in this way, it is algorithmic, but not necessarily *an* algorithm: it may consist of several algorithms, or algorithms plus equations, and it can usefully be called a *simulation* model, though the term 'simulation' is sometimes used much more widely. Sometimes, the simulation technique lends itself naturally to a problem. This happens, for example, when the underlying theory consists of a set of statements involving conditional probabilities. More generally, we might say that we resort to simulation techniques for situations which are too complicated to be handled by more straightforward algebraic techniques. We shall see examples below, from the residential location field. Of course, the notion of using simulation techniques has recently been given a substantial boost in the urban and regional modelling field with the work of Forrester (1968, 1969).

Econometric modelling techniques are used to study relationships between variables using the methods of statistical analysis. The relationships usually have some basis in economic theory, though 'econometric' seems to be used more widely now to describe a certain kind of statistical analysis. The relationship between the variables are often of a rather simple kind: they are usually either linear, or can be transformed into linear form by taking logs, for example. It is this simplicity (mainly linearity, and additiveness) which limits their usefulness in locational analysis, but examples will be presented below.

Of the remaining three technique areas listed at the end of Section 10.1 each represents a way of looking at a problem in locational analysis: *economic ecological* and *game-theoretical*. The resulting models use a combination of the techniques mentioned earlier, but are each constrained by the rules of the viewpoint adopted. In some cases, the rules and viewpoints are so highly developed that it is useful to consider them as a model-building technique. The economist's method of locational analysis is typically based on the theory of consumer's behaviour, suitably aggregated; the ecologist's approach (in the somewhat old-fashioned Chicago sense in which we are using the notion here) is based on such concepts as invasion and succession; the game theorist hypothesizes a locator playing a game against other locators, or against the market. Each approach has been used, and examples will be presented below of all but the last. The difficulty of the economic approach is that of aggregation from an essentially micro viewpoint to a comprehensive one without losing the essence of the economic theory by turning it into an oversimplified econometric model. The ecological approach has been hampered by the difficulty of formalizing and mathematicizing it. The game theory approach is hamstrung by the virtual impossibility of obtaining an effective aggregation, which is why no example is given here.

Finally, we should note that the techniques can be obtained in various ways, indeed we have already had examples of this in the way in which the 'viewpoint' techniques can be combined with the rest.

10.3. METHOD OF PROCEDURE

In Chapter 3 (in Figures 3.1 and 3.2), we identified an interest in the location of population activities and the location of economic activities, and (in Figure 3.3) set these in a demand/supply relationship with each other. There are various ways in which we could proceed. We could take particular population activities and particular economic activities and discuss the associated models. Alternatively, we could define sub-systems which incorporated both demand and supply mechanisms; for example, we could take a residential system which incorporated the population's demand for residences *and* the mechanms of housing supply. There are other ways of cutting up the whole system, of course, and some methods of locational analysis do not fit into either of he frameworks which have been mentioned. In the last analysis, we must e concerned with the total system, the general model, and we shall return o this in Chapter 11. Meanwhile, we will adopt the first of the two frameworks and consider in turn the demand side, the location of population ctivities, in several sections, and then the supply side, the location of economic activities, in one section only. Several sections are devoted to residential ocation (10.4–10.8), and three to the utilization of services (10.9–10.11). The supply side, about which less is known in modelling terms, is discussed in Section 10.12.

This division has the substantial advantage that it clarifies at the outset wo of the issues raised in Section 10.1, concerned with population activity/ physical stock foci and demand/supply relationships. Although there is some overlap, and occasionally supply considerations will be mentioned in a demand section, and vice versa, in the main Sections 10.4–10.11 are concerned with population activity and demand, and stock is one aspect of all supply aspects in Section 10.12. In relation to the third (macro/micro) issue, we have already decided that our goal of comprehensiveness forces us to accept an aggregative position, though macro/micro relationships will be discussed whenever possible. This leaves us with the cross-sectional/marginal and choice-of-techniques issues and these are discussed in particular sections as appropriate.

10.4. RESIDENTIAL AND WORKSHOP LOCATION: BASIC HYPOTHESES

We can begin our discussion of the hypotheses to be built into our models by focusing on individuals or households. We assume that the appropriate micro-unit for the study of residential location is the household (more or less by definition), and for the study of workplace location, the individual. Occasionally, we shall have difficulty in reconciling the two viewpoints in a single model but, for the time being, we shall use 'individual' and 'household' almost interchangeably, and assume that the intended meaning is clear from the context. We assume that each individual has a need for shelter, subsistence goods (including services) and an associated income with which to purchase both.

Since most income is derived from employment, this at least links 'home' with 'workplace'. There is obviously also the physical linkage, which involves an assumed disutility of travel and, as part of this, an expenditure on the journey to work which reduces the disposable income available for shelter and subsistence goods. For these reasons, it is difficult to separate the study of residential and workplace location.

We can assume that a household makes some broad decision about th allocation of its income between housing, subsistence goods, journey t work, and possibly other items, such as 'savings'. (This follows the notio of a utility tree developed by Strotz (1957).) The amount of money availab for housing (and related services since it is assumed that a residential packag is being purchased) will be determined partly by available total incom partly by preferences and partly by what is on offer. It is simpler to think th analysis through for one-worker households, but real life is complicated b the existence of no-worker and multi-worker households.

Given these broad decisions, the individual or household can then carr out a search among available opportunities. This may be a joint search fo house and job, or for house alone (given a job) or for a job alone (given house). The pattern of available opportunities is, of course, continual changing through time. Conceptually at least, we can assume that the searc is structured in relation to type of house (size, age and condition, tenure an so on), location (and, in particular associated linkages to work, services an so on), environment (physical and social), and price (which will reflect a the preceding items in the list).

We can recall at this point that we are trying to be comprehensive. Indi viduals are competing in a complicated market process which involves othe individuals and the suppliers of housing. The market (or sub-markets i relation to different tenure categories) operates with a complex set c institutional rules.

In summary, then, our models must reflect and reproduce the individual' choice of housing in relation to his income and preferences (which mean that the models must distinguish person type), house type, location, environ ment and price within a complicated 'market' operation. In this analysis, fo the present, we are taking the supply side as given.

These hypotheses can now be sharpened (and sometimes simplified) s that we can build associated models. A number of examples are discusse below. The techniques used, in turn, are (i) spatial interaction modelling (ii) linear programming/economic theory/econometrics, (iii) simulation an (iv) ecological modelling.

10.5. SPATIAL INTERACTION MODELS OF RESIDENTIAL LOCATION

In the following discussion, we shall assume that we have a study are divided into zones of a suitable size and labelled by indices such as i and j Conventionally (and this is *merely* a convention) we shall associate i with th residence zone and j with the employment zone. We can now begin to discus spatial interaction models of residential and workplace location. We wi work from the simplest, rather unrealistic, models to much more complicated

ealistic, ones. In so doing, we are, more or less, giving a historical account
of the development of such models. The theoretical basis of the models can
be discussed rather briefly, partly because we are building on the theoretical
framework laid down in Chapter 6, and partly because a detailed account of
the entropy-maximizing basis is given in Chapter 4 of another book by the
author (Wilson, 1970-A).

The simplest spatial interaction model of residential location is that
developed by Lowry (1963, 1964) as part of a more general model. He
assumed a given distribution of jobs, that is, that E_j, the number of jobs in
each zone j, is given and that workers are allocated to residences around
their workplaces according to a simple spatial interaction hypothesis. If T_{ij}
is the number of people who live in zone i and work in zone j, he assumed,
in our notation

$$T_{ij} = gE_j f(c_{ij}) \tag{10.1}$$

where c_{ij} is the cost of travel from i to j, f a decreasing function, and g a
constant. Diligent readers of Chapter 6 will recognize this as an unconstrained
spatial interaction model, in which there is no residential (i-zone) mass term:
that is, the i-zone mass term is assumed to be 1.

The fact that the model is unconstrained means that its outputs (the T_{ij}s)
are inconsistent with the assumptions in that it is impossible to calculate a
value of g which will ensure that (assuming N zones)

$$\sum_{i=1}^{N} T_{ij} = E_j \tag{10.2}$$

is satisfied. We can also argue that there should be a residential mass term as
some residential zones are more attractive than others. Thus, however we
eventually decide to measure it, we should incorporate a mass term W_i to
represent the relative attractiveness of zone i.

Thus, we can transform the model of equation (10.1) into an attraction
constrained model, including a mass term, by writing

$$T_{ij} = B_j W_i E_j f(c_{ij}) \tag{10.3}$$

where

$$B_j = 1 \bigg/ \sum_{i=1}^{N} E_j f(c_{ij}) \tag{10.4}$$

B_j replaces g and its value, obtained from equation (10.4), ensures that the
constraint (10.2), which is one of our assumptions, is satisfied.

A very simple, implicit, assumption is being made in this model about the
supply side: that

$$\sum_{i=1}^{N} T_{ij}$$

houses are made available in zone i to meet demand. An alternative procedure is to assume that we are given the number of houses H_i available in each zone i. We now have an additional constraint

$$\sum_{j=1}^{N} T_{ij} = H_i \qquad (10.5)$$

to add to equation (10.2) and Chapter 6 tells us that we have a production-attraction constrained situation. The corresponding model is

$$T_{ij} = A_i B_j H_i E_j f(c_{ij}) \qquad (10.6)$$

where

$$A_i = 1 \bigg/ \sum_{j=1}^{N} B_j E_j f(c_{ij}) \qquad (10.7)$$

and

$$B_j = 1 \bigg/ \sum_{i=1}^{N} A_i H_i f(c_{ij}) \qquad (10.8)$$

The fact that A_i and B_j are calculated in this way ensures that equations (10.2) and (10.5) are satisfied. What sort of animal have we now got? If this is a location model, it appears to run counter to our earlier statement (in Section 10.2) that spatial interaction models used as location models are singly constrained, and that the unconstrained 'end' provides an estimate of the location variable. From equation (10.3), for example, we would take

$$\sum_{j=1}^{N} T_{ij}$$

as an estimate of the residential location pattern. However, in the doubly constrained model this quantity is given as H_i. In what sense is the equation (10.6)–(10.8) model a location model? It remains a location model for the *people* involved. It tells us which people live where. This reflects another part of an earlier discussion: that it is important to distinguish between people and stock. In the doubly constrained model we are taking the stock as given (for this model it may be estimated in another, supply-side, model) and we are locating people, jointly, to residences and workplaces.

It is also possible to develop hybrid models which are partly singly and partly doubly constrained (cf. Wilson, 1969). This would be appropriate, for example, if it were considered that for most zones, say the set Z_2, the simple supply-side mechanism of the singly constrained model operated, while for some zones, say in the set Z_1, there are population constraints, perhaps due to planning policy. This situation may apply in a situation of rapid suburban growth in a city where population in central areas is strictly controlled by redevelopment capacity. Let

$$Z = Z_1 \cup Z_2 \qquad (10.9)$$

be the total set of zones. Then the constraints are

$$\sum_{i=1}^{N} T_{ij} = E_j, \qquad j \in Z \qquad (10.10)$$

and

$$\sum_{j=1}^{N} T_{ij} = P_i, \qquad i \in Z_1 \text{ only} \qquad (10.11)$$

The hybrid model can then be written

$$T_{ij} = A_i B_j P_i E_j f(c_{ij}), \qquad i \in Z_1, \qquad j \in Z \qquad (10.12)$$

$$T_{ij} = B_j W_i E_j f(c_{ij}), \qquad i \in Z_2, \qquad j \in Z \qquad (10.13)$$

where

$$A_i = 1 \Big/ \sum_{j=1}^{N} B_j E_j f(c_{ij}), \qquad i \in Z_1 \text{ only} \qquad (10.14)$$

and

$$B_j = 1 \Big/ \left\{ \sum_{i \in Z_1} A_i O_i f(c_{ij}) + \sum_{i \in Z_2} W_i f(c_{ij}) \right\} \qquad (10.15)$$

One other kind of hybrid model can be usefully mentioned. We have already hinted at the beginning of this section that there may be different kinds of locational behaviour; this could be explicitly represented as different types of constraint. So far, we have not distinguished person type at all. Suppose now that n denotes type of locational behaviour, as follows:

$n = 1$: locationally unconstrained, seeking both house and job;

$n = 2$: production constrained, seeking job only;

$n = 3$: attraction constrained, seeking house only;

$n = 4$: production–attraction constrained, seeking neither house nor job.

Let T_{ij}^n be the number of persons of type n living in zone i and working in zone j. Then, from an assumption, we would expect to be given T_{**}^1, T_{i*}^2, T_{*j}^3 and T_{ij}^4. Alternatively, instead of T_{ij}^4, we may be given T_{i*}^4 and T_{*j}^4 and assume that T_{ij}^4 can be estimated from a production–attraction constrained model. Define

$$P_*^1 = T_{**}^1 = \sum_{i=1}^{N} \sum_{j=1}^{N} T_{ij}^1 \qquad (10.16)$$

$$H_i^2 = T_{i*}^2 = \sum_{j=1}^{N} T_{ij}^2 \tag{10.17}$$

$$E_j^3 = T_{*j}^3 = \sum_{i=1}^{N} T_{ij}^3 \tag{10.18}$$

$$H_i^4 = \sum_{j=1}^{N} T_{ij}^4 \tag{10.19}$$

and

$$E_j^4 = \sum_{i=1}^{N} T_{ij}^4 \tag{10.20}$$

and assume these are all given, so that equations (10.16)–(10.20) are constraints. Suppose we are also given (in the spirit of the model given by equations (10.6)–(10.8)) quantities which can be called H_i^* and E_j^* in other words, the total quantities of housing and jobs by zone, irrespective of the locational behaviour type of the occupants. Then we can define quantities H_i' and E_j' as follows:

$$H_i' = H_i^* - H_i^2 - H_i^4 \tag{10.21}$$

$$E_j' = E_j^* - E_j^3 - E_j^4 \tag{10.22}$$

H_i' is the quantity of housing in zone i being competed for by those seeking houses (in locational behaviour categories 1 and 3) and E_j' is the equivalent quantity for jobs in zone j. This means that we can impose additional constraints on the T_{ij}^ns as follows:

$$\sum_{j=1}^{N} T_{ij}^1 + \sum_{j=1}^{N} T_{ij}^3 = H_i' \tag{10.23}$$

and

$$\sum_{i=1}^{N} T_{ij}^1 + \sum_{i=1}^{N} T_{ij}^2 = E_j' \tag{10.24}$$

These constraints will now lead us to an interesting set of linked spatial interaction models. Let us consider the different categories in turn. Category 1 is constrained by equations (10.16), (10.23) and (10.24). The first of these would normally demand a proportionality factor K, the second A_is and B_js which we could call A_i^1 and B_j^1. Category 2 is constrained by equations (10.17), which needs an A_i^2, and (10.24) which needs a B_j^2. Category 3 is constrained by equations (10.18), which needs a B_j^3, and (10.23) which needs an A_i^3. Category 4 is independent: either T_{ij}^4 is given directly, or we use equations (10.19) and (10.20) as constraints to generate a journey-to-work model. Let us assume that we take the latter assumption. Note that A_i^1 and A_i^3 relate to he same constraint, (10.23), as do B_j^1 and B_j^2, (10.24). In practice, this means hat we can take

$$A_i^3 = A_i^1 \qquad (10.25)$$

nd

$$B_j^2 = B_j^1 \qquad (10.26)$$

hen, the models can be written as

$$T_{ij}^1 = K A_i^1 B_j^1 H_i' E_j' f_1(c_{ij}) \qquad (10.27)$$

$$T_{ij}^2 = A_i^2 B_j^1 H_i^2 E_j' f_2(c_{ij}) \qquad (10.28)$$

$$T_{ij}^3 = A_i^1 B_j^3 H_i' E_j^3 f_3(c_{ij}) \qquad (10.29)$$

$$T_{ij}^4 = A_i^4 B_j^4 H_i^4 E_j^4 f_4(c_{ij}) \qquad (10.30)$$

where

$$K = P_*^1 \bigg/ \sum_{i=1}^{N} \sum_{j=1}^{N} A_i^1 B_j^1 H_i' E_j' f_1(c_{ij}) \qquad (10.31)$$

$$A_i^1 = 1 \bigg/ \sum_{j=1}^{N} \left[K B_j^1 E_j' f_1(c_{ij}) + \sum_{j=1}^{N} B_j^3 E_j^3 f_3(c_{ij}) \right] \qquad (10.32)$$

$$B_j^1 = 1 \bigg/ \sum_{i=1}^{N} \left[K A_i^1 H_i' f_1(c_{ij}) + \sum_{i=1}^{N} A_i^2 H_i^2 f_2(c_{ij}) \right] \qquad (10.33)$$

$$A_i^2 = 1 \bigg/ \sum_{j=1}^{N} B_j^1 E_j' f_2(c_{ij}) \qquad (10.34)$$

$$B_j^3 = 1 \bigg/ \sum_{i=1}^{N} A_i^1 H_i' f_3(c_{ij}) \qquad (10.35)$$

$$A_i^4 = 1 \bigg/ \sum_{j=1}^{N} B_j^4 E_j^4 f_4(c_{ij}) \qquad (10.36)$$

$$B_j^4 = 1 \bigg/ \sum_{i=1}^{N} A_i^4 H_i^4 f_4(c_{ij}) \qquad (10.37)$$

These equations, (10.31)–(10.37), ensure that constraints (10.16), (10.23), (10.24), (10.17), (10.18), (10.19) and (10.20), respectively, are satisfied.

A digression on dynamics is appropriate at this point. Up to the model just developed, the elementary models discussed were incontravertably cross-sectional models. All people are involved, and the whole housing stock. It is implicitly assumed that, at any time, an equilibrium position is attained which is described by the model equations. In the latest model, however, a time period is at least implicitly referred to: that period which determines the locational behaviour categorization of the population. For example, the population of those seeking houses consists of new households and potential movers *in some time period*. If the time period is quite short, then the bulk of the population will be in category 4 (and the category 4 equations are, in effect, simply the journey-to-work equations of Chapter 9). Categories 1–3 are then concerned with marginal change. Provided that we can estimate the quantities which we have so far assumed to be given, $P_*^1, H_i^2, E_j^3, H_i^4, E_j^4, H_i^*$ and E_j^* for a time period, say t to $t + T$, then we have the basis of a dynamic model. However, it seems worthwhile to develop further the spatial interaction model before we proceed to build a dynamic one.

We stated in our hypotheses at the beginning of this section that it was important to build person type and house type into the model. So far, we have failed to do either. In the spatial interaction models presented so far, we have either implicitly assumed that all people are identical and all houses are identical or, more charitably, that the models have performed a lot of averaging around means in making their predictions. It is a relatively straightforward matter to remedy this situation by disaggregation by person type and house type, and we can also build in home price and the fact that it varies with type and location.

Suppose at this stage that the main person-type variable we wish to indicate is income, w; with house-type, we need not commit ourselves to a specific meaning, we simply specify type k. Our main variable is then T_{ij}^{kw}, the number of w-income people living in a type-k house in zone i, working in zone j. Suppose further that we are given H_i^k, the number of type-k houses in each zone i, E_j^w, the number of income w jobs in j, p_i^k, the price of a type-k house in zone i, and c_{ij}, the cost of travelling from i to j. Implicitly, for simplicity, we are assuming one worker per household, and that all income is derived from employment.

We can now consider building a spatial interaction model with H_i^k and E_j^w as mass terms, and c_{ij} as travel cost (cf. Wilson, 1970-B). This might lead us to suggest something of the form

$$T_{ij}^{kw} = A_i^k B_j^w H_i^k E_j^w f_w(c_{ij}) \qquad (10.38)$$

which is a doubly constrained model for each k, w combination. We have assumed a cost function which varies with w. However, this contains no reference to price p_i^k, and has no mechanisms to ensure that households live in houses (a) they can afford and (b) is sufficiently high-priced for their income. This can be achieved with the following device: Let q^w be the *average* amount which a w-income household spends on housing *after journey to work costs have been deducted*. Then consider a term of the form

$$e^{-\mu^w[p_i^k - q^w(w - c'_{ij})]^2} \qquad (10.39)$$

where c'_{ij} is the money part of c_{ij} and $q^w(w - c'_{ij})$ is the average amount vailable for housing for a w-income household living in i and working in j. f this differs significantly, in either direction, from p_i^k, then the expression in quare brackets in (10.39) rapidly becomes large, and the expression (10.39) tself becomes small. So we add this multiplicatively to the right-hand side of equation (10.38). This gives, as a revised form of model,

$$T_{ij}^{kw} = A_i^k B_j^w H_i^k E_j^w \, e^{-\beta^w c_{ij}} \times e^{-\mu^w [p_i^k - q^w (w - c_{ij}')]^2} \tag{10.40}$$

Now, a w-income household will only be assigned to a type-k home in zone i f p_i^k does not markedly differ from $q^w(w - c_{ij}')$. Just how markedly it differs s determined by the magnitude of μ^w. We thus now have a person-type, house-type, disaggregated version of the model presented as equations 10.6)–(10.8). A_i^k and B_j^w must be calculated to ensure

$$\sum_j \sum_w T_{ij}^{kw} = H_i^k \tag{10.41}$$

$$\sum_i \sum_k T_{ij}^{kw} = E_j^w \tag{10.42}$$

so that

$$A_i^k = 1 \Big/ \sum_j \sum_w B_j^w E_j^w \, e^{-\beta^w c_{ij}} \, e^{-\mu^w [p_i^k - q^w (w - c_{ij}')]^2} \tag{10.43}$$

and

$$B_j^w = 1 \Big/ \sum_i \sum_k A_i^k H_i^k \, e^{-\beta^w c_{ij}} \, e^{-\mu^w [p_i^k - q^w (w - c_{ij}')]^2} \tag{10.44}$$

The model given by equations (10.40), (10.43) and (10.44) now has an interesting mechanism, but it is still a cross-sectional model. Further, it has the unrealistic simplifying assumption of one worker per household. We must thus proceed in two steps: firstly, we must indicate how to remove the simplifying assumption and secondly, how to make the model dynamic. The first task is a relatively straightforward one provided that we assume that it is primarily the income of the head of the household which determines expenditure on housing. We then add a superscript m to T_{ij}^{kw}, making it T_{ij}^{kwm}, where $m = 1$ indicates a worker who is head of household, $m = 0$ a worker who is not. Non-workers would still have to be added in separately. Let r_1 be the average number of workers per household in zone i, so that there are H_i^k places in type-k houses for heads of households and $(r_i - 1)H_i^k$ for non-heads. We assume that both heads and non-heads compete for the same jobs. A similar method could be used for non-workers, heads or not! We then have to build models which satisfy the constraints

$$\sum_j \sum_w T_{ij}^{kw1} = H_i^k \tag{10.45}$$

$$\sum_j \sum_w T_{ij}^{kw0} = (r_i - 1)H_i^k \tag{10.46}$$

$$\sum_i \sum_k \sum_m T_{ij}^{kwm} = E_j^w \tag{10.47}$$

The reader can easily check that the appropriate model is

$$T_{ij}^{kw1} = A_i^{k1} B_j^w H_i^k E_j^w \, e^{-\beta^{w1}c_{ij}} \times e^{-\mu^w[p_i^k - q^w(w - c_{ij}')]^2} \tag{10.48}$$

$$T_{ij}^{kw0} = A_i^{k0} B_j^w (r_i - 1) H_i^k E_j^w \, e^{-\beta^{w0}c_{ij}} \tag{10.49}$$

where

$$A_i^{k1} = 1 \Big/ \sum_j \sum_w B_j^w E_j^w \, e^{-\beta^{w1}c_{ij}} \times e^{-\mu^w[p_i^k - q^w(w - c_{ij}')]^2} \tag{10.50}$$

$$A_i^{k0} = 1 \Big/ \sum_j \sum_w B_j^w E_j^w \, e^{-\beta^{w0}c_{ij}} \tag{10.51}$$

and

$$B_j^w = 1 \Big/ \bigg\{ \sum_i \sum_k A_i^{k1} H_i^k \, e^{-\beta^{w1}c_{ij}} \, e^{-\mu^w[p_i^k - q^w(w - c_{ij}')]^2}$$

$$+ \sum_i \sum_k A_i^{k0}(r_i - 1) H_i^k \, e^{-\beta^{w0}c_{ij}} \bigg\} \tag{10.52}$$

This is the model we now have to put into a dynamic framework by distinguishing the four types of locational behaviour which led to the aggregated model of equations (10.28)–(10.37). We can add a further superscript, n, with the same meanings as before. We can define P_*^{m1}, H_i^{kn}, E_j^{wn}, H_i^{k*}, E_j^{w*}, $H_i^{k'}$, $E_j^{w'}$ by analogy with P_1^*, H_i^n, E_j^n, H_i^*, E_j^*, H_i' and E_j'. The constraints to be satisfied by T_{ij}^{kwmn} are then

$$\sum_i \sum_j \sum_k \sum_w T_{ij}^{kwm1} = P_*^{m1} \tag{10.53}$$

$$\sum_j \sum_w T_{ij}^{kw11} + \sum_j \sum_w T_{ij}^{kw13} = H_i^{k'} \tag{10.54}$$

$$\sum_j \sum_w T_{ij}^{kw01} + \sum_j \sum_w T_{ij}^{kw03} = (r_i - 1)H_i^{k'} \tag{10.55}$$

$$\sum_i \sum_k \sum_m T_{ij}^{kwm1} + \sum_i \sum_k \sum_m T_{ij}^{kwm2} = E_j^{w'} \tag{10.56}$$

$$\sum_j \sum_w T_{ij}^{kw12} = H_i^{k2} \tag{10.57}$$

$$\sum_j \sum_w T_{ij}^{kw02} = (r_i - 1)H_i^{k2} \tag{10.58}$$

$$\sum_i \sum_k \sum_m T_{ij}^{kwm3} = E_j^{w3} \tag{10.59}$$

$$\sum_j \sum_w T_{ij}^{kw14} = H_i^{k4} \tag{10.60}$$

$$\sum_j \sum_w T_{ij}^{kw04} = (r_i - 1)H_i^{k4} \tag{10.61}$$

$$\sum_i \sum_k \sum_m T_{ij}^{kwm4} = E_j^{w4} \tag{10.62}$$

In the above,

$$H_i^{k'} = H_i^{k*} - H_i^{k2} - H_i^{k4} \tag{10.63}$$

and

$$E_j^{w'} = E_j^{w*} - E_j^{w3} - E_j^{w4} \tag{10.64}$$

The corresponding model equations are:

$$T_{ij}^{kw11} = K^1 A_i^{k11} B_j^{w1} H_i^{k'} E_j^{w'} e^{-\beta^{w11}c_{ij}} \times e^{-\mu^{w1}[p_i^k - q^w(w - c_{ij}')]^2} \tag{10.65}$$

$$T_{ij}^{kw01} = K^0 A_i^{k01} B_j^{w1} (r_i - 1)H_i^{k'} E_j^{w'} e^{-\beta^{w01}c_{ij}} \tag{10.66}$$

$$T_{ij}^{kw12} = A_i^{k12} B_j^{w1} H_i^{k2} E_j^{w'} e^{-\beta^{w12}c_{ij}} \tag{10.67}$$

$$T_{ij}^{kw02} = A_i^{k02} B_j^{w1} (r_i - 1)H_i^{k2} E_j^{w'} e^{-\beta^{w02}c_{ij}} \tag{10.68}$$

$$T_{ij}^{kw13} = A_i^{k11} B_j^{w3} H_i^{k'} E_j^{w3} e^{-\beta^{w13}c_{ij}} \times e^{-\mu^{w3}[p_i^k - q^w(w - c_{ij}')]^2} \tag{10.69}$$

$$T_{ij}^{kw03} = A_i^{k01} B_j^{w3} (r_i - 1)H_i^{k'} E_j^{w3} e^{-\beta^{w03}c_{ij}} \tag{10.70}$$

$$T_{ij}^{kw14} = A_i^{k14} B_j^{w4} H_i^{k4} E_j^{w4} e^{-\beta^{w14}c_{ij}} \tag{10.71}$$

$$T_{ij}^{kw04} = A_i^{k04} B_j^{w4} (r_i - 1)H_i^{k4} E_j^{w4} e^{-\beta^{w04}c_{ij}} \tag{10.72}$$

where

$$K^1 = P_*^{11} \Big/ \sum_i \sum_j \sum_k \sum_w A_i^{k11} B_j^{w1} H_i^{k'} E_j^{w'} e^{-\beta^{w11}c_{ij}} \times e^{-\mu^{w1}[p_i^k - q^{w1}(w - c_{ij}')]^2} \tag{10.73}$$

to ensure that (10.53) is satisfied with $m = 1$,

$$K^0 = P_*^{01} \Big/ \sum_i \sum_j \sum_k \sum_w A_i^{k01} B_j^{w1} (r_i - 1)H_i^{k'} E_j^{w'} e^{-\beta^{w01}c_{ij}} \tag{10.74}$$

to ensure that (10.53) is satisfied with $m = 0$,

$$A_i^{k11} = 1 \Bigg/ \Bigg\{ \sum_j \sum_w K^1 B_j^{w1} E_j^{w'} \, e^{-\beta^{w11}c_{ij}} \times e^{-\mu^{w1}[p_i^k - q^{w1}(w - c_{ij}')]^2}$$

$$+ \sum_j \sum_w B_j^{w3} E_j^{w3} \, e^{-\beta^{w13}c_{ij}} \times e^{-\mu^{w3}[p_i^k - q^{w3}(w - c_{ij}')]^2} \Bigg\} \quad (10.75)$$

to ensure that (10.54) is satisfied,

$$A_i^{k01} = 1 \Bigg/ \Bigg\{ \sum_j \sum_w K^0 B_j^{w1} E_j^{w'} \, e^{-\beta^{w01}c_{ij}} + \sum_j \sum_w B_j^{w3} E_j^3 \, e^{-\beta^{w03}c_{ij}} \Bigg\} \quad (10.76)$$

to ensure that (10.55) is satisfied

$$B_j^{w1} = 1 \Bigg/ \Bigg\{ \sum_i \sum_k K^1 A_i^{k11} H_i^{k'} \, e^{-\beta^{w11}c_{ij}} \times e^{-\mu^{w1}[p_i^k - q^{w1}(w - c_{ij}')]^2}$$

$$+ \sum_i \sum_k K^0 A_i^{k01} (r_i - 1) H_i^{k'} \, e^{-\beta^{w01}c_{ij}}$$

$$+ \sum_i \sum_k A_i^{k12} H_i^{k2} \, e^{-\beta^{w12}c_{ij}}$$

$$+ \sum_i \sum_k A_i^{k02} (r_i - 1) H_i^{k2} \, e^{-\beta^{w02}c_{ij}} \Bigg\} \quad (10.77)$$

to ensure that (10.56) is satisfied,

$$A_i^{k12} = 1 \Bigg/ \sum_j \sum_w B_j^{w1} E_j^{w'} \, e^{-\beta^{w12}c_{ij}} \quad (10.78)$$

to ensure that (10.57) is satisfied

$$A_i^{k02} = 1 \Bigg/ \sum_j \sum_w B_j^{w1} E_j^{w'} \, e^{-\beta^{w02}c_{ij}} \quad (10.79)$$

to ensure that (10.58) is satisfied,

$$B_j^{w3} = 1 \Bigg/ \Bigg\{ \sum_i \sum_k A_i^{k11} H_i^{k'} \, e^{-\beta^{w13}c_{ij}} \times e^{-\mu^{w3}[p_i^k - q^{w3}(w - c_{ij'}')]^2}$$

$$+ \sum_i \sum_k A_i^{k01} (r_i - 1) H_i^{k'} \, e^{-\beta^{w01}c_{ij}} \Bigg\} \quad (10.80)$$

to ensure that (10.59) is satisfied,

$$A_i^{k14} = 1 \Bigg/ \sum_j \sum_w B_j^{w4} E_j^{w4} \, e^{-\beta^{w14}c_{ij}} \quad (10.81)$$

o ensure that (10.60) is satisfied,

$$A_i^{k04} = 1 \bigg/ \sum_j \sum_w B_j^{w4} E_j^{w4} \, e^{-\beta^{w04} c_{ij}} \qquad (10.82)$$

o ensure that (10.61) is satisfied, and finally

$$B_j^{w4} = 1 \bigg/ \left\{ \sum_i \sum_k A_i^{k14} H_i^{k4} \, e^{-\beta^{w14} c_{ij}} + \sum_i \sum_k A_i^{k04} (r_i - 1) H_i^{k4} \, e^{-\beta^{w04} c_{ij}} \right\} \qquad (10.83)$$

o ensure that (10.62) is satisfied. Clearly, building this model even theoretically s a mammoth and complicated exercise. However, it is not conceptually overcomplicated. The reader who has been able to follow the building of the aggregated quasi-dynamic model given by equations (10.27)–(10.37) and of the disaggregated but comparative static model given by equations (10.40), (10.43) and (10.44) should be able to recognize the basis of the composite model which has just been derived.

We can now begin to see how we have the basis for a dynamic residential location model by putting time labels on the variables which are the exogenous variables for the spatial interaction part of the model: P_*^{11}, P_*^{01}, H_i^{k*}, E_j^{w*}, H_i^{k2}, H_i^{k4}, E_j^{w3} and E_j^{w4}. Suppose we are interested in a time period of t to $t + T$. At time t we will have a distribution of housing stock $H_i^{k*}(t)$ and jobs $E_j^{w*}(t)$. At time $t + T$, the overall distribution becomes $H_i^{k*}(t + T)$ (as the net result of demolitions, changes and new building) and $E_j^{w*}(t + T)$, (as a result of changes in the economy). The total population may change in such a way relative to the housing stock that we may anticipate a change in r_i, say from $r_i(t)$ to $r_i(t + T)$. Suppose the total population changes from $N(t)$ to $N(t + T)$, then our main task is to divide $N(t + T)$ into locational categories, 1–4. We might assume that we have the following kinds of information:

(1) initial population and distribution, $T_{ij}^{kwmn}(t)$;

(2) something on in-and-out migration from homes (including effects of births and deaths);

(3) something on in-and-out migration from jobs (including effects of births and deaths);

(4) something on household formation.

Clearly, we are now beginning to involve the other components of a general model. So that we are not taken too far out of our way, the remainder of this part of the discussion is postponed until the next chapter. However, there is one other important aspect of model closure which must be mentioned, relating to the set of house prices p_i^k. Once again, we can only raise the issue in a preliminary way and we return to it in Chapter 11.

Recall that, in Chapter 6, we defined accessibility to activities X_j, for residents of i. We can define

$$Q_i(X) = \sum_j X_j \, e^{-\beta^x c_{ij}} \qquad (10.84)$$

where β^x depends on the activity X. Following this principle, we could defin

$$Q_i^w(J) = \sum_j E_j^w\, e^{-\beta^w c_{ij}} \qquad (10.85)$$

as the access to w-income jobs for residents of i, and

$$Q_i^w(s) = \sum_j W_j^s\, e^{-\lambda^{sw} c_{ij}} \qquad (10.86)$$

as being the accessibility to services of type s for residents of i in income group w. It is also useful to define net residential density as

$$D_i = \sum_k H_i^k / L_i \qquad (10.87)$$

where L_i is residential land in zone i. We might then hypothesize a relationship of the form

$$p_i^k = \lambda^k a(1 - e^{-bD_i}) + \sum_w g^w Q_i^w(J) + \sum_s \sum_w h^{sw} Q_i^w(s) \qquad (10.88)$$

In other words, we hypothesize that type-k house prices in zone i are the product of a factor related to type of house, a factor which reflects increasing residential density (up to a limiting point) and the various accessibilities. Since the distribution of services, represented here as W_j^s, will be partly determined by the distribution of population (as discussed further below), then we see that population distribution, housing distribution and employment distribution all help determine p_i^k. This will clearly help us in formulating a general model. This particular formulation has been related explicitly to the comparative static form of the residential model. However, we can assume that the same hypotheses hold for the dynamic version. H_i^k in equation (10.87), for example, would simply be replaced by $H_i^{k*}(t)$.

It may now be useful to summarize the rather complicated argument of this section.

(1) We began with the simplest possible spatial interaction model as first used by Lowry. It was given by equation (10.1).

(2) We saw that this was inconsistent with respect to the assumptions which had been made about the distribution of employment E_j, and also that it did not contain a residential attractiveness term. These two considerations led to the model given in equations (10.3) and (10.4).

(3) It was then argued that a different assumption could be made about the workings of the supply side, and that a distribution of houses H_i, could be assumed as an alternative to the attractiveness factors W_i. This led to the doubly constrained model given in equations (10.6)–(10.8).

(4) We then saw how to develop a hybrid model, partly singly constrained using the mechanisms described in (2), and partly doubly constrained, using

he mechanisms described in (3), the latter so that planners' policy constraints an be reflected. This model was given by equations (10.12)–(10.15).

(5) Different types of locational behaviour were then introduced, and we aw that this led to the quasi-dynamic model presented in equations (10.27)–10.37).

(6) The next step was to introduce person type (especially income) and 1ouse type with price varying by type and location. A disaggregated version of the comparative static model described in (3) was built and presented in :quations (10.40), (10.43) and (10.44).

(7) We then showed how another type of hybrid model could be built: 1ne which removed the simplifying assumption of one worker per household. Linked models represented the residential location behaviour of heads of 1ouseholds and other workers. This model was presented in equations 10.48)–(10.52).

(8) Finally, we built a model which combined the features of (5), (6) and (7): a disaggregated quasi-dynamic model which distinguished heads of households and other workers. This was presented in equations (10.65)–(10.83).

(9) We then discussed what would be involved in incorporating the model thus developed in a general model of urban development, and how to close it with respect to the estimation of house prices. This discussion will be continued in Chapter 11.

10.6. MODELS OF RESIDENTIAL LOCATION USING ECONOMIC THEORY, ECONOMETRICS AND LINEAR PROGRAMMING

The economist brings a considerable number of tools of analysis to bear on the problem of building residential location models. First, and in some ways foremost, of these is the notion of land rent, which goes back to Ricardo or even Adam Smith. This is the notion that some plots of land are more productive than others, because of differences in fertility or location etc., and that the value of such differences can be collected by the landowner in the form of rent. In discussing rent, and associated concepts such as price, we shall follow Alonso (1964). He in turn follows Ratcliff (1949), quoting him as follows:

'It will be convenient to use the term "price" in its generic sense and to include under this term the market expression of contract rent, sales price and cost of ownership. These three values move together, though with un-evenness. Sales price, the price that a buyer is willing to pay after considering alternatives, represents the present or discounted value of future rental values. The cost of ownership is a function of both contract rent and sales price; the owner must recognize a cost of occupancy that is at least as great

as the rental income he might otherwise be receiving if he were to rent ou
his property, and no smaller than the total of interest on the investmen
taxes, maintenance and depreciation, which total, in the long run, is in balanc
with the rental value.' (Ratcliff, 1949, pp. 347–348). We will, therefore, usuall
use 'price' (and not 'rent') in this sense. Many economists have been primaril
concerned with the price of residential land, and have separated this from th
price of housing which goes with it. Generally speaking, we shall use 'hous
price' to refer to the appropriate bundle of housing services which are, o
can be, purchased, and which would, of course, include land price. Thus
having established the nature of the concept of price, one of the prim
interests of the economist is to predict it within a model.

In the typical economy, there are two kinds of animal: consumers (indi
viduals and households) and producers ('firms'). The economist brings tc
bear on this situation his theory of consumers' behaviour, and the theory o
the firm. They involve notions of demand and supply and market processe
which ensure that supply matches demand at an appropriate price.

In the very broadest terms, this works as follows. Suppose there are three
goods, 1, 2 and 3 (which might be housing, transport and 'all others', represented by 'money' possibly), and an individual r can buy quantities x_1^r, x_2^r
and x_3^r at prices p_1, p_2 and p_3, out of his total income I^r, all of which is
spent. We assume that the individual's *preferences* can be recorded in the
form of a utility function

$$U^r = U^r(x_1^r, x_2^r, x_3^r) \tag{10.89}$$

The individual then behaves so as to maximize this function, subject to his
budget constraint

$$\sum_k x_k^r p_k = I^r \tag{10.90}$$

This maximization problem can be solved to give the quantity of each good
purchased. Formally, we can write

$$x_k^r = x_k^r(p_1, p_2, p_3, I^r) \tag{10.91}$$

since the quantity purchased will depend on each of the prices and the
individual's income. This is the individual's *demand* for the kth good. Under
suitable circumstances, we can aggregate over individuals r, to obtain the
aggregate demand

$$x_k^* = \sum_r x_k^r \tag{10.92}$$

We can now consider a firm s. Its productive capability will be defined by its
production function. It will purchase factor inputs y_1^s, y_2^s and y_3^s, say (which

may be labour, land and capital) at prices p_1^f, p_2^f and p_3^f. If it produces good k, then its production function can be formally written as

$$x_k^s = x_k^s(y_1^s, y_2^s, y_3^s) \tag{10.93}$$

If it sells at price p_k, then its profit is

$$G = x_k^s p_k - \sum_e y_e^s p_e^f \tag{10.94}$$

It is ordinarily assumed that the firm behaves so as to maximize its profits, G in equation (10.94), subject to (10.93) as a constraint. We can solve for the y_e^ss in term of p_k (and the factor prices which we assume given) to give

$$x_k^s = x_k^s(p_k, p_1^f, p_2^f, p_3^f) \tag{10.95}$$

We can, under suitable conditions, aggregate to give

$$x_k^* = x_k^*(p_k, p_1^f, p_2^f, p_3^f) \tag{10.96}$$

and do this for each good k. Then, by setting supply equal to demand, (equations (10.92) and (10.96)), we can solve the resulting equation system for the prices p_k, for given factor prices, and then compute the quantities of the goods manufactured and consumed.

This presentation is perhaps grossly oversimplified. The reader who is dissatisfied with it can consult any standard economics text and find the discussion taken much further, more rigorously. However, it does provide a basis for explaining the difficulties confronting the urban economist, and the methods which have been suggested to date for solving these difficulties. Suppose, as suggested earlier, that in equation (10.89) for the individual consumer, x_1 represents 'housing', x_2 'transport' and x_3 'other'.

The first difficulty is concerned with making the institutional framework realistic, especially on the supply side. If we consider that a number of firms exist, in a perfectly competitive economy, to produce housing, then this is far from being realistic. The public sector is involved in a major way, and will be behaving according to mechanisms other than profit maximization. All parties will operate in a framework of complicated legal constraints.

A second difficulty concerns the nature of the housing good itself. The theories sketched earlier work best if goods can be produced in continuously varying amounts. In the case of housing, there are substantial indivisibilities, and the existence of a previously developed stock-housing is to some extent a capital good as well as a consumption good.

These difficulties, though great enough, are nothing compared to the most important of all: we saw in our earlier discussion in Section 10.4 that an important quality of housing as a good is its location, which determines connections to many other activities (and hence, in part, transport expenditure) and social and physical environment. It is this difficulty which has most troubled urban economic theorists: how to give the theories of economic behaviour a spatial dimension. For the housing consumer, the essence of the difficulty can be seen in terms of equations (10.89)–(10.91). These must now be made *location specific*. Thus, suppose L labels the location, then (10.89) becomes

$$U^{rL} = U^r(x_1^{rL}, x_2^{rL}, x_3^{rL}, I^r) \tag{10.97}$$

and equation (10.91) will become

$$x_k^{rL} = x_k^{rL}(p_1^L, p_2^L, p_3^L, I^r) \tag{10.98}$$

since the prices (at least for housing and transport) must now be considered to vary with location. *Formally the situation is even worse, as demand at a location will also be a function of prices at all other locations.* Alonso describes the ensuing difficulties very well:

'Consequently, the demand curves for the same individual will vary with his location. Since part of the problem of finding the market solution consists of finding individual locations, not knowing the locations of individuals we would not know which of their demand curves to use to build up our market demand curve.' In other words, it is no longer possible to aggregate to obtain equation (10.92). There is a corresponding difficulty on the supply side. It means that we can no longer model the market operation by setting supply equal to demand as we did in the earlier analysis.

Our first task therefore is to explore how economists have built a spatial dimension into their analysis and then we can see what this means for building models.

The basis of the current solution to the problem has its origins in the work of von Thunen (1826) on agricultural land use. This model has been formally developed by Dunn (1954) and Isard (1956). In the whole of this part of the argument, we are restating the work of Alonso (1964). We begin by explaining the structure of the argument in very broad terms, and then connecting back to our earlier discussion. Even the more detailed exposition will be a considerable simplification of Alonso's work and the interested reader should consult his 1964 book directly.

The essence of the argument connects to the notion of 'rent' and runs as follows. We have a land area which has a market at its centre and is otherwise used for agriculture. A farmer's profits result from the sale of his crop, less his factor costs, *less his transport costs.* The last named feature means that, for a given crop, land nearer the centre can command a rent relative to more distant land. The market would ensure that the farmer paid this rent to the landowner. In a competitive situation, any particular farmer would be able to offer a landlord at a location a rent, his *bid-rent*, for that location. The landlord then lets to the highest bidder. The actual land price surface is thus the upper envelope of the whole set of bid-rent surfaces.

Alonso has extended the bid-rent concept to be applicable to the urban firm and to the resident. In the case of the firm, land rent payable (henceforth called land price) is one of the cost terms subtracted from revenue in the estimation of profits. It is then possible to estimate a bid-price for a given location for a given level of profits. There is an equivalent procedure for the resident: land price now appears as one of the terms in the budget equation, and we can estimate a bid-price at a location for a given level of utility. Thus, there are now three competing users of land: farmers, firms and residents. Their bid-prices have been constructed in such a way as to be comparable. Landlords at each location now charge land prices which coincide with the highest bid made.

Once this conceptual breakthrough has been achieved, the rest of Alonso's analysis is concerned with showing how the market-clearing process works so that an appropriate equilibrium position is achieved.

Alonso has to make a number of simplifications in order to be able to complete his analysis. The most important is to assume that jobs are concentrated in the centre of the city, so that 'distance from the CBD' serves as an adequate measure of location, and commuting costs as a measure of transport costs. Also, he is primarily concerned with *land* rather than the whole *bundle* of housing services.

We can now indicate how these ideas work with the simplest equations which were introduced earlier. However, we make no distinction between farmer and firms. We also try to avoid the restrictive centrality assumption. Further, we distinguish between the land-rent component of housing price and the rest. Let $x_1^r(L)$ be the quantity of housing which could be purchased by individual r at location L, at price $p_1^H + p_1^R(L)$, where p_1^R is the rent component; let $x_2^r(L)$ be the corresponding expenditure on transport at price $p_2(L)$, and x_3^r at price p_3 (not assumed dependent on location), the rest. Then equations (10.89) to (10.91) (assuming for the moment that we need only consider prices at one location) become

$$U^r(L) = U^r(x_1^r(L), x_2^r(L), x_3^r, I^r) \tag{10.99}$$

$$x_1^r(L)(p_1^H + p_1^R(L)) + x_2^r(L)p_2(L) + x_3^r p_3 = I^r \tag{10.100}$$

and

$$x_1^r(L) = x_1^r(p_1^H, p_1^R(L), p_2(L), p_3, I^r) \tag{10.101}$$

$$x_2^r(L) = x_2^r(p_1^H, p_1^R(L), p_2(L), p_3, I^r) \tag{10.102}$$

$$x_3^r(L) = x_3^r(p_1^H, p_1^R(L), p_2(L), p_3, I^r) \tag{10.103}$$

The last equation shows that x_3^r will, of course, be a function of L. For a given value of U^r, say U_0^r, equation (10.99) determines an indifference surface in the variables x_1, x_2, x_3 and, perhaps one should say, for we are not yet sure what kind of animal it is, L. We can then use equation (10.100) to estimate a bid rent, $p_1^R(L)$, assuming other prices to be given, and x_1, x_2 and x_3 being determined when U_0^r is given. Thus, for each individual r, we have a bid-rent at each location for each level of utility U_0^r.

For the firm, land is a factor of production and so its price, $p_2^s(L)$ becomes a function of location, L. The price at which it can sell its product may also be location dependent, as may the cost of its labour, and so the equivalent of equations (10.93) to (10.95) is

$$x_k^s(L) = x_k^s(y_1^s(L), y_2^s(L), y_3^s) \tag{10.104}$$

is the production function, and the profit level is

$$G = x_k^s(L)p_k(L) - y_1^s(L)p_1^s(L) - y_2^s(L)(p_2^B + p_2^R(L)) - y_3^s p_3 \tag{10.105}$$

Note that, without loss of generality, we can use the same notation, $p_2^R(L)$ for the land rent : part of the buildings/land cost, as for residents. p_2^B is the buildings part of the cost. Then, a given level of profits G_0, determines a surface in $y_1^s(L)$, $y_2^s(L)$, y_3^s and $p_2^R(L)$. Thus, for a given $y_1^s(L)$, $y_2^s(L)$ and y_3^s, we can determine the bid-rent $p_2^R(L)$ which would give a level of profits G_0.

The market-clearing process now involves (i) for each L, the landlord at L searching bids in order to select the highest, and (ii) for each resident and each firm in turn, a search among their bids to find the available (acceptable) one which gives the highest utility or the highest profit. (This market clearing process in land rent takes place within an environment where other aggregate supply–demand relationships, for example on x_3^*, have been determined and satisfied.) One of Alonso's substantial achievements was to ensure that, under his restricted conditions, such a market-clearing aggregation could be defined and would operate in a unique way. The advantage of the more general formulation presented here is twofold: no assumption of centrality is needed and, in principle, we can consider L to label plots of given, finite size—though there is then a corresponding difficulty in giving $x_1^r(L)$ or $y_2^s(L)$ a meaning. (One solution is to make L a double label, L_1, L_2, where L_1 represents the total holding of a given landowner, and L_2 the whole set of sub-divisions within it. These sub-divisions will overlap, of course, and the final accepted sub-division will be determined by the bidding process.)

Perhaps the single main point of Alonso's work, no matter how it is formulated, is that the mechanism of the market-clearing process has to be made explicit before aggregation can be satisfactorily carried out. Other authors, who have started with more or less the same tools as Alonso, do not seem to have been as successful in this respect. Wingo (1961, p. 85) develops a demand function for individual consumption of residential land consumption, but then assumes that it can be aggregated in some simple way, more or less as equation (10.96) was derived from (10.93). Muth (1961, 1969) also begins with the same tools and develops a set of equations to describe the equilibium position of the individual in the housing market. However, he avoids he aggregation issue by simply discussing different kinds of behaviour for lifferent kinds of people (particularly by income and race). He also devotes a considerable amount of effort to a study of the equilibrium of housing producers. Yet another approach can be found in the work of Mills (1969). He avoids the aggregation problem by concentrating on an aggregate production function approach to the analysis problem.

The reader can pursue these various approaches in whatever detail he likes, beginning with the references cited above. There he can also find a guide to earlier work by urban economists, an account which will not be repeated here. Alonso's work seems to be the most fully developed at the present time, and it provides a micro-analytical framework against which many model-building attempts can be compared (including the spatial inter-action models which we will pursue in Section 10.8). There is, however, perhaps one major disappointment with all this work based on economic theory: with one possible exception (the Herbert–Stevens model to be dis-cussed further below), no very exciting operational models have developed from the work. Many insights and qualitative analyses have been obtained, but few effective models. One possible reason for this is that most economists in the field, having established their theoretical framework, then resort to essentially linear or log-linear econometric models for their empirical work. Alonso (1964, p. 126), for example, presents only one empirical equation, estimated for Philadelphia for the years 1950–1952, as follows:

$$pq = -222 \cdot 65 + 0 \cdot 4357(\pm 0 \cdot 1275)y - 90 \cdot 107(\pm 22 \cdot 703)t$$

$$R = 0 \cdot 69 \qquad S = 375 \cdot 67 \tag{10.106}$$

where

p = price per square foot, in dollars
q = number of square feet per family
y = family income in dollars
t = distance from centre of city in miles.

This equation is typical of the genre. Many more examples can be found in the book by Muth (1969) and some also in Mills (1969). The main point to make here is that these econometric models seem unduly simple relative to the theory which underpins them. For this reason, they will not be pursued any further here, though, of course, this is far from saying that they are without interest. The reader is referred to the original sources.

The possible exception referred to earlier was the Herbert–Stevens (1960) model of residential location. We examine this now, and it gives us the opportunity to explore linear programming as a technique for location modelling. The discussion fits appropriately into this section as the under-lying basis of the model is not very different from Alonso's, and indeed the work was carried out in the same stable in Philadelphia at about the same time.

The Herbert–Stevens model, in a notation as consistent as possible with other models in this book, can be written as follows. Maximize

$$Z = \sum_i \sum_k \sum_n T_{i*}^{kn}(b^{kn} - p_i^{kn}) \tag{10.107}$$

subject to

$$\sum_k \sum_n s_{kn} T_{i*}^{kn} \leqslant L_i \tag{10.108}$$

and

$$\sum_i \sum_k T_{i*}^{kn} = P^n \tag{10.109}$$

where

T_{i*}^{kn} = number of type n people locating in zone i in a house of type k;

b^{kn} = the residential budget allocated to the purchase of a residence of type k by a household of type n;

p_i^{kn} = cost to a household of group n of a type k house in i, *exclusive* of site cost;

s_{kn} = area utilized by a household of type n if it has a type k home;

L_i = area of land available for residential use in zone i,

and

P^n = population of type n to be allocated (in households).

No interaction, such as the journey to work, is represented explicitly in this model, but the cost of housing, p_i^{kn}, is to be interpreted as including the costs of all trips made by the household. Thus, the term $b^{kn} - p_i^{kn}$ in the maximand represents the bidding power for site rent, which is clearly equivalent to Alonso's bid-price, and so the model maximizes bid-prices subject to constraints on land availability and finding everyone a house. An analysis of the dual shows that, if bid-rent is maximized, actual rent paid is minimized. (Note that by adjusting L_i after a run of the model, zoning/policy type constraints could be built in, and thus carry out the same function as the hybrid spatial interaction model.) Relative to Alonso's micro-analysis, individual households have been grouped by type, and the market-clearing mechanism has been represented by the linear programming action. Thus, as the authors say in their original paper in relating their model to Alonso's: 'His method is difficult to apply directly, but we feel that our linear programming model provides an analogous approach that is both acceptable and workable'. The difficulties with the model in empirical terms are concerned with the estimation of the quantities b^{kn}, p_i^{kn} and s^{kn}. There are also theoretical problems which will be discussed below in Section 10.8. However, for the moment we acknowledge it as an elegant and relatively simple mathematical expression of Alonso's theory.

10.7. OTHER APPROACHES TO RESIDENTIAL LOCATION MODELLING

There are a number of techniques which we have not yet considered, in particular those based on ecological analysis and on the simulation concept. The first of these can be dealt with briefly. No fully formalized mathematical model has been developed by the ecological school. Perhaps the nearest approach to this was the model used to forecast land use in the Chicago Transportation Study (1960). All land uses were considered by the model; but the essence of the residential location mechanism was as follows. An assessment was made of the residential capacity of each zone in the study area. These assessments were then ranked according to distance from the centre and the existing percentage of capacity for each area was plotted, as shown in Figure 10.2. (Hamburg and Creighton, 1959; Wingo, 1961.)

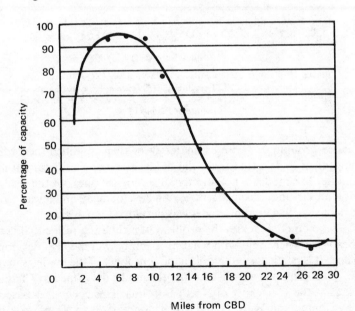

Figure 10.2   Residential capacities in Chicago. (Reproduced from J. R. Hamburg and R. L. Creighton, *AIP Journal*, **25**, Figure 3, p. 70, (1959). Reprinted by permission of the *Journal of the American Institute of Planners*.)

An estimate was then made of the shift in this curve caused by future residential development to give a result as depicted in Figure 10.3. (Hamburg and Creighton, 1959; Wingo, 1961.) This gives a proportion of new development in the forecast period which can be applied to each zone, (according to

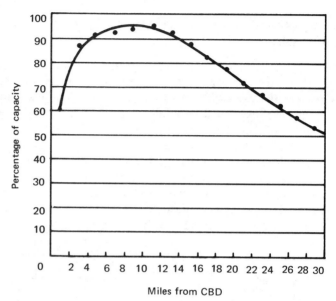

Figure 10.3   Shift of residential capacity curve. (Reproduced from J. R. Hamburg and R. L. Creighton, *AIP Journal*, **25**, Figure 5, p. 71 (1959). Reprinted by permission of the *Journal of the American Institute of Planners*)

its distance grouping). These estimates were then modified 'according to staff judgement and in that sense the model was not a fully formal mathematical one. The model is not strictly an ecological one, but the reader will see that it implies modified concentric ring development, and it was probably no accident that this kind of model was developed in Chicago!

A *simulation* model tackles the problem of estimating residential development head-on: where, and with what probability, will the next development take place? It is particularly suitable if the time focus of the model is marginal change. As an example, we will consider the model developed by Chapin and coworkers at the University of North Carolina. This account is based on a paper by Chapin and Weiss (1968) which summarizes six years work on the project.

The model-building exercise itself is preceded by an investigation of the factors which are most important in residential development. Seven strong ndependent variables emerged from this analysis, three of the 'first rank', our of the 'second'. They were:

First rank:
    marginal land not in use
    accessibility to work areas
    assessed value.

Second rank:
    travel distance to nearest major street
    distance to nearest available elementary school
    residential amenity
    availability of sewerage.

These factors were identified by a multiple regression analysis, presumably with 'new residential development' as the dependent variable. Particular attention was paid to the time sequence of development. In the complicated decision-making sequence which generates development, certain 'priming' operations were identified which were of particular significance.

For the operation of the model itself, the study area is divided into zones; in this case a square grid was used in which zone size was a mere 23 acres. For each zone, an attractiveness index was calculated using the factors described earlier. The total amount of development to be distributed is assumed given for each time period. Development is then allocated to zones (in fact to fractions of zones) using a random number generator biased so as to preserve the attractiveness distribution. The attractiveness indices are then recalculated for the next time period. Attractiveness is correspondingly increased if priming operations have been carried out. The prediction of the likely pattern of residential development in the study area is then made by taking the average of a large number of simulation runs.

10.8. COMPARISON OF THE DIFFERENT APPROACHES TO RESIDENTIAL LOCATION MODELLING: CONCLUDING COMMENTS AND SOME INTEGRATION

We have discussed a range of techniques for residential location modelling and it is now worthwhile to comment and to explore the relations between them.

The spatial interaction models have developed from a simple hypothesis that workers located in a gravity-like way around work-places, to something which incorporates a considerable degree of desirable detail. Indeed, in its most disaggregated form, as discussed above, it is almost misleading to call the model a spatial interaction model: what it actually does is to assign households by type to houses by type, taking into account, *among other things*, the house-workplace interaction. According to the parameter values, the 'other things' may be more important than the interaction; it is a matter of empirical test. It may be better, then, to call the model a *residential assignmen model*, though experience with the 'gravity model' shows that the historical name is usually preserved even when the model is perceived differently Perhaps the most important feature of the model is that it attempts to make the model's predictions maximally consistent with known or assumed information, and in this respect it is useful to acknowledge its entropy maximizing origins. This is one of its great strengths relative to the econo-metric models which typically follow analyses in economic theory. In this respect it is interesting to take the argument a stage further and ask whether the model in any sense contradicts the analyses of economic theorists. There is some indication that it does not. The estimates of the model can be viewed as statistical averages over the behaviour of individual households seeking locations. There seems to be no inherent reason why each one should not be maximizing a utility function. The assignment mechanism of the model can then be interpreted as the model's market-clearing mechanism. In the main model equations, supply-side variables H_i^k and the prices p_i^k appear explicitly. We indicated how the model could be closed by adding an equation which would estimate p_i^k. It would be possible to explore a variety of forms of this equation, including one which reflected measures of 'demand pressure'. We could also develop a supply-side model for the H_i^ks (total or incremental, preferably the latter of course). This all reinforces the interpretation of the model as an assignment model representing a market-clearing operation. It has one substantial advantage over the usual economist's model in this respect. Since we can choose whatever mechanism we like for estimating (or, for example, determining from a planning policy) H_i^k, and indeed p_i^k, ma-chinery other than perfect private market mechanisms can be investigated.

We should also remark that the spatial interaction model is easily extend-able. We have seen how the disaggregated model was developed from a very much simpler and less realistic one. With the same ease, effects of mechanisms which were considered important could be incorporated. For example, we might want to build in access to schools and shops, and to incorporate an index of their quality. (Or we might consider that these effects had already been incorporated through the p_i^ks.) Equally, if we can identify household behaviour which is predicted by micro-economic theory which *is* inconsistent with the model, then it should be possible to extend or amend it.

At this point, it is useful to compare the spatial interaction model with the economic linear programming model. The spatial interaction model estimates T_{ij}^{kw}, the linear programming model T_{i*}^{kn} (where n could conceivably be taken as w). The first point to note is that in the *LP* model there will only be as many non-zero T_{i*}^{kn}s as there are constraints. This is a fundamental theorem of linear programming and is presumably what Harris (1962) was referring to when he wrote: '... there is no cross-hauling, whereas this is prevalent in metropolitan interaction'. This means that, unless k and n (and possibly i)

present very finely defined groups, the LP model is unlikely to reflect the full variety of actual behaviour. In this sense, in particular, it is possible that the spatial interaction model is more satisfactory. This does lead to the interesting thought that it would be possible to develop an assignment model version (this time it would be misleading to call it a spatial interaction model) of the Herbert–Stevens model which would overcome this difficulty. Suppose we interpreted equations (10.107)–(10.109) as constraints and derived the appropriate entropy maximizing model. This would give (and note the expected sign of μ, as Z is being 'maximized')

$$T_{i*}^{kn} = A^n P^n \, e^{-\beta_i s^{kn}} \, e^{\mu(b^{kn} - p_i^{kn})} \tag{10.110}$$

and

$$A^n = 1 \Big/ \sum_i \sum_k e^{-\beta_i s^{kn}} \, e^{\mu(b^{kn} - p_i^{kn})} \tag{10.111}$$

to ensure that constraint (10.109) was satisfied, and β_i and μ would be calculated from

$$\sum_k \sum_n s^{kn} A^n P^n \, e^{-\beta_i s^{kn}} \, e^{\mu(b^{kn} - p_i^{kn})} = L_i \tag{10.112}$$

and

$$\sum_i \sum_k \sum_n A^n P^n \, e^{-\beta_i s^{kn}} \, e^{\mu(b^{kn} - p_i^{kn})} = Z \tag{10.113}$$

to ensure that constraints (10.108) and (10.107) respectively were satisfied. A^n, β_i and μ would have to be calculated iteratively, and sub-iterations would be needed to solve the equations for β_i and μ. Presumably Z could be increased until its upper limit was reached. As a conjecture, we could suppose that this is achieved by letting μ tend to some limit. Thus, the assignment model principle may provide an alternative to the Herbert–Stevens model which has an appropriately realistic 'blurring' (or Harris's 'cross-hauling') in its predictions. This discussion is taken several steps further in Senior and Wilson (1973).

The spatial interaction model also connects to the simulation principle. Essentially, in a simulation model, we need the probability, π_i say, of someone locating in zone i. In the simplest spatial interaction model, estimating T_{ij}, we could take

$$\pi_i = T_{i*}/T_{**} \tag{10.114}$$

where the asterisks as usual represent summation. The definition could be embellished in various ways by disaggregation. Note, however, that particular care must be taken to distinguish between the probabilities of households locating in a zone and of new housing stock being assigned to a zone. The simulation model example given earlier was concerned with the second and the use of the spatial interaction model in the manner suggested above would be most suitable for the first.

In general, then, we favour the spatial interaction model (perhaps more properly called a household assignment model) as the most flexible and general of the models presented, though clearly it should be connected as closely as possible to a basis in micro-analysis. The arguments of Senior and Wilson (1973), based on developments of the entropy-maximizing version of the Herbert–Stevens model, suggest that close links are possible. We should however, note one of its disadvantages (particularly relative to the econo metric model). It is often very difficult to estimate the parameters of the model, and even when methods can be found, they tend to use much computer time. Much work has been done in this field recently, though, and we shall return to the topic in Chapter 12.

10.9. UTILIZATION OF SERVICES: BASIC HYPOTHESES

In this section, we consider how people utilize a *given* distribution of services. That is, we are making an assumption analogous to that in an earlier discussion of residential location, that we can model what people do apart from the task of modelling housing supply, services and so on.

The term 'services' covers a wide variety of activities. We shall be concerned with five main categories: retail, personal, educational, health and recreational services. Broadly speaking, retail services are concerned with all shopping; personal services with such things as banks and solicitors; education mainly with schools, but also other establishments; health with doctors, health centres and hospitals; recreation with anything from cinemas and dance halls to open space. There are, of course, many points of detail which are being neglected: do we treat barbers and estate agents as shops or personal services, for example? But this need not concern us for the present and we assume that some suitable classification has been made.

Perhaps one of the main distinctions which can be drawn between different types of services is the regulation or otherwise of their use. The use of most shops, personal services and recreational services is not regulated: people are free to shop where they choose. However, access to schools and health centres is at least partly regulated. We shall be concerned mainly with un-regulated services (though, as we shall see, we may be constrained by a variety of price and access considerations). The problem of modelling people's behaviour in regulated systems is an important one—a problem to which a variety of operational research techniques is often appropriate—and we shall refer to it from time to time.

For unregulated services we may, then, assume that people are interested in satisfaction (or attractiveness) in relation to access and make their utilization decisions accordingly. For regulated services the same considerations apply, but the utilization decision is made by the regulating authority through its regulations. Clearly, in the case of unregulated services, we have a spatial interaction problem. We consider the spatial interaction model approach in the next section and then a number of alternatives in Section 10.11.

10.10. SPATIAL INTERACTION MODELS OF THE UTILIZATION OF SERVICES

The introduction to this section can be very brief since the reader will already be familiar with the spatial interaction model for shopping, which was used as a first example of a model in Chapter 4. This was a model of the form

$$S_{ij} = A_i(e_i P_i) W_j e^{-\beta c_{ij}} \tag{10.114}$$

where

$$A_i = 1 \Big/ \sum_j W_j e^{-\beta c_{ij}} \tag{10.115}$$

to ensure that

$$\sum_j S_{ij} = e_i P_i \tag{10.116}$$

In this model S_{ij} is the flow of retail expenditure from residential zone i to shopping zone j, e_i is mean expenditure per head in zone i, P_i is the population of zone i, W_j is the attractiveness of shops in j, c_{ij} is the cost of travel from i to j, and β is a parameter. We need not repeat the justification of this model here but, below, we will set it in its proper historical context and consider various ways of developing it further. We can note that, generally for unregulated services, we might expect the flows to satisfy a singly constrained spatial interaction model of the form

$$S_{ij} = A_i O_i W_j e^{-\beta c_{ij}} \tag{10.117}$$

where

$$A_i = 1 \Big/ \sum_j W_j e^{-\beta c_{ij}} \tag{10.118}$$

where O_i is the demand for the service generated by residents of zone i, and the other terms are the appropriate analogues of the shopping situation for the service under consideration.

We can now proceed as follows. We will begin with a discussion of the retail model, first setting it in its historical context, then considering some associated measurement problems, and some further developments.

A spatial interaction model was first used in the study of retailing by Reilly (1931). To be more precise, spatial interaction hypotheses were used by Reilly to delimit retail market areas. He assumed that a city i attracted people to its shops in relation to a factor P_i/d_i, where d_i was the distance between the person and the city, and P_i the city's population. Then, for a person faced with the choice of two cities (which might be two of our zones), if $P_i/d_i > P_j/d_j$, the person is in the market area of i. Clearly, this process delimits non-overlapping market areas and therefore Reilly's work does not represent a spatial interaction *model* in our sense. If Reilly had interpreted his hypothesis just slightly differently, that P_i/d_i represented the *probability* of the person going to i, then this would lead to a flow model of the form

$$S_i = K \frac{P_i P}{d_i} \qquad (10.119)$$

where P is the number of people at the location of the original population. More generally, we could write

$$S_{ij} = K \frac{P_i P_j}{d_{ij}} \qquad (10.120)$$

using an obvious notation, as an unconstrained spatial interaction model. So the idea of a spatial interaction model is implicit in Reilly's work, though he used the concepts to delimit non-overlapping market areas. (When there are more than two cities, other problems with Reilly's formula *do* give rise to some overlap in market areas, see Huff, 1964.) Reilly's work was further developed and refined by Converse (1949), though the basic limitations remained.

Although many people worked on spatial interaction models in the next two decades (and the early transport studies of the 1950s in the U.S.A. must have looked at shopping trips), no progress was made with retail models until the work of Huff (1962, 1964). In terms of our earlier notation, Huff proposed that

$$p_{ij} = \frac{W_j c_{ij}^{-n}}{\sum_j W_j c_{ij}^{-n}} \qquad (10.121)$$

represented the probability that a resident of i would shop in j, where W_j was measured as shopping centre size, in selling area for a class of goods (thus implying that the model was used separately for different types of good) and

j as travel time. Then

$$S_{ij} = C_i p_{ij} \tag{10.122}$$

where C_i is the number of consumers at i. Market areas were then expressed in terms of probability contours using (10.121).

Lakshmanan and Hansen (1965), working independently, used a traffic model modified to make it singly constrained, to produce the model which we have been using as an example and which was presented as equations (10.114) and (10.115) above. The reader can easily check that, with consistent definitions of the variables, the models of Huff and Lakshmanan and Hansen are equivalent. It is an interesting point in relation to the nature of scientific discovery that the same model could be derived from such different viewpoints.

Lowry (1964), again working independently, also used a spatial interaction model. As nearly as possible in our notation, it can be written

$$S_{ij}^k = g P_i c_{ij}^{-n_k} \tag{10.123}$$

$$S_j^k = \sum_i S_{ij}^k + h^k E_j \tag{10.124}$$

where S_{ij}^k is the flow for sector k, P_i is the population of i, E_j employment in j, S_j^k is total activity in j, g and h^k are constants and n_k is a parameter. As with Lowry's residential location model, the first equation represents a very primitive unconstrained spatial interaction model with no attractiveness factor. As Lowry was mainly interested in retail sector employment generated by some population distribution, P_i, his units were 'retail employment in sector k generated'. The important feature of Lowry's model for this discussion (other features will be noted in the section on the Lowry model in the next chapter) arises from the second equation and the term $h^k E_j$, which represents retail activity generated from employment. Since we can casually observe employed people shopping from work in lunch hours and so on, it seems sensible to incorporate such a term, and it is strange that no workers since Lowry have bothered to do so. Lowry assumed that only employees working in the same zone as the shopping centre shopped here. More generally, we would expect a spatial interaction term. We can also note that several authors have run the model separately for different types of good. Henceforth, we will assume that this should be done if possible, but we will not bother to carry the equivalent of Lowry's k subscript explicitly; any model written down is for some 'type of good'.

Although much work has been done on shopping models since the seminal work of the authors referred to above, no new conceptual breakthroughs have been achieved. Different measures have been used of distance and attractiveness, together with a variety of attenuation functions. However, a number of possible further developments can be briefly explored.

Our starting point should perhaps be a model represented by the followir equations (using the usual, or an obvious, notation):

$$S_{ij}^1 = A_i^1(e_i^1 P_i)W_j^1\, e^{-\beta^1 c_{ij}} \tag{10.12}$$

$$S_{ij}^2 = A_i^2(e_i^2 E_i)W_j^2\, e^{-\beta^2 c_{ij}} \tag{10.12}$$

$$A_i^1 = 1\Big/\sum_j W_j^1\, e^{-\beta^1 c_{ij}} \tag{10.12}$$

$$A_i^2 = 1\Big/\sum_j W_j^2\, e^{-\beta^2 c_{ij}} \tag{10.12}$$

and

$$S_{*j} = \sum_i S_{ij}^1 + \sum_i S_{ij}^2 \tag{10.12}$$

The superscript 1 denotes flow from 'home'; 2, flow from 'employment e_i^1 and e_i^2 now mean expenditure per head and per employee on the appro priate retail goods. It should not be difficult in principle to test such model though there may be data difficulties. Usually, we would expect to hav $\beta^2 > \beta^1$. β^2 may be so high that Lowry's original assumption could b considered sound, but that is a matter of empirical investigation. Empirica test would also show whether or not W_j^2 could be taken to be the same as W_j

The next obvious development arises from a consideration of behaviour i relation to the distance term. All the considerations of mode and mod availability of Chapter 9 for transport flows in general apply to shoppin trips. There are many ways in which we could disaggregate by mode. Th simplest is to add a modal superscript, k as in Chapter 9, to equations (10.125) (10.128) and include a k-summation in equations (10.129). However, thi causes a number of problems. We would have to estimate such quantities a e^{1k} and e^{2k}, and the model, like the transport model without a person-typ term, would not be able directly to take account of car availability. In directly, this would be taken into account through what would be, in effec a trip-end modal split model. So some kind of person-type superscript i needed also. This could simply be added. However, if we add this, togethe with the mode superscript, we are then obtaining turnover by aggregatin over a large number of modal runs. This may be all right in theory, but i practice there will rarely be the data to sustain it.

The principle to be used in applying spatial interaction model concepts t other services should by now be clear to the reader. A singly constraine spatial interaction model has been used by Morrill and Kelly (1970), fo example, to study the flow of patients to hospitals.

It is less likely that spatial interaction modelling methods will be applicabl to regulated service systems. For such a system, the mechanism represente

y the model will be the regulation mechanism. If a local authority builds its
rimary schools so that 'no child has to walk more than half a mile to school',
nd so that the 'market areas' do not overlap, then these rules represent the
nodel. Such cases can be tackled *ad hoc* in a straightforward manner. One
articular example of a regulated system is worth noting, however. Suppose
O_i is the demand for a service in i, and D_j is the 'supply'. Then T_{ij} may be
hosen (i.e. the regulations arranged so that this happens) so that

$$\sum_j T_{ij} = O_i \tag{10.130}$$

$$\sum_i T_{ij} = D_j \tag{10.131}$$

and some objective function is optimized. For example, travel cost

$$C = \sum_i \sum_j T_{ij} c_{ij} \tag{10.132}$$

nay be minimized. This is the 'transportation problem' of linear program-
ning. This may be considered a special case of a spatial interaction model—
loubly constrained and with parameter $\beta \to \infty$.

We should note that alternative principles of spatial interaction modelling,
nd especially those using 'intervening opportunities' concepts, could be and
ave been used for the service sector. Some interesting work has been done
along these lines, but no fundamentally new procedures have emerged (see
Harris, 1964, Cordey-Hayes and Wilson, 1970).

Finally, we should note that we have contented ourselves with writing
about total cross-section models and have not developed marginal dynamic
models equivalent to those in the corresponding residential location section.
This assumption seems to be justified: in effect, we are arguing that people
respond fairly quickly to changes in service sector supply, and therefore an
equilibrium approach is justified.

10.11. OTHER APPROACHES TO SERVICE UTILIZATION MODELLING

A number of other approaches to service-sector modelling are possible.
Many of them are conveniently reviewed in a National Economic Development Office publication (Distributive Trades E.D.C., 1970). As with residential location, some economists have studied the problem (for example, see
Bacon, 1970), but as yet no operational 'economic theory models' have been
developed. The main alternative approach to spatial interaction modelling
is based on the concept of market area, usually non-overlapping, and some
sub-set of the concepts associated with central place theory. The resulting

models are usually unsatisfactory simply because we know that market area do overlap and they will not be considered any further here. However, we should note that some of the concepts of central place theory, notably those associated with the idea of 'hierarchy', are obviously useful and have not yet been successfully incorporated into spatial interaction models, though there seems no reason why this should not be possible. It would be interesting to see central place theory rewritten, as it affects retailing and other service with spatial interaction model concepts replacing the non-overlapping market area concepts but the other main features being retained. It is tempting to se this as an exercise for the reader, but perhaps it is at least a Ph.D.-size prob lem! One final qualification must be added to these remarks: there may b some service sectors which would probably be regulated ones, where the market areas do *not* overlap, and some other techniques may then be appro priate, as noted in the previous section.

10.12. THE SUPPLY SIDE

In relation to the discussion of preceding sections on the location of person activities, we must now discuss the location of the buildings and associated facilities which provide the infrastructure of these activities. In particular, we are interested in the supply of housing, services and industry; the last two of which give the spatial distribution of jobs.

Different principles are involved in supply-side modelling. With population activity, both total cross-section and marginal models were appropriate in different circumstances. Much longer time periods are associated with build ings and generally it will only make sense to build marginal models. Further more, decisions about supply-side units are made by organizations. Typically there are far fewer organizations than individuals and therefore the style of model used for population activities, which is based on underlying statistical averaging assumptions, will not usually be appropriate. This is one reason why the relevant theory, for example of industrial location, is usually couched in micro-analytical terms based on the theory of the firm. This often mean that the only *comprehensive* models which we can set up from this sort of basis are econometric models which have properties consistent with micro analytical theory. A possible exception to this general rule is the housing sector, since relatively large numbers of new houses are built. In many cases however, the decisions involving a large proportion of these houses are made by a small number of organizations, for example, by local government authorities.

The obvious implication of the above discussion is that comprehensive supply-side models are difficult to build. There is often a saving grace, how- ever, when estimates of change in housing supply, services and jobs have to be made: these are precisely the variables which are to a greater or lesser

extent under the planners' potential control, either directly, as with the provision of public authority housing or services, or indirectly through planning
permission or zoning controls. Thus, on many occasions, a model as such is
not needed, only a specification of a range of alternative plans.

Given the implications of this introductory discussion, and particularly the
qualification of the preceding paragraph on the need for supply-side models,
we will content ourselves in the rest of this section simply by outlining briefly
some of the models which have been developed. The discussion of underlying
hypotheses will be postponed.

Firstly, we consider a very simple model of marginal housing supply, due
to Hansen (1959). He assumes that in the time period under consideration,
there is some given quantity of housing G to be allocated. The model predicts
H_i, the quantity allocated to zone i, as a function of vacant land in i, V_i, and
accessibility to, say, employment A_i, which we might take as

$$A_i = \sum_j E_j e^{-\beta c_{ij}} \tag{10.133}$$

using an obvious notation. Then

$$H_i = G \frac{V_i A_i^\alpha}{\sum_i V_i A_i^\alpha} \tag{10.134}$$

where α is a parameter to be estimated. This simple model has some useful
characteristics and in particular points out the dependence of the process on
land availability, as well as other desirable properties such as accessibility.
It has been discussed as a residential location model (Swerdloff and Stowers,
1966), but we see how useful it is to make the sharp distinction between the
location of people and the location of stock. This need not then be considered
as one of a number of alternative residential location models, but δH_i from
this model could be used as an input to a doubly constrained *person* dynamic
residential location model.

A completely different approach to modelling housing supply was
attempted by the Community Renewal Project in San Francisco (Robinson
et al., 1965). The essence of the model is a calculation of what different types
of people would pay for different types of housing, (including all existing
housing, which is 'aged' in the model), and then new housing supply is
generated which provides the highest yield for the developer. The main detail
of the model is reserved for the person-type and home-type dimensions and
there is relatively little spatial detail. However, it does represent an alternative
model-building principle for the housing supply side, though no work on
these lines seems to have been done since the San Francisco project.

In the case of services such as retailing, it is possible to argue that supply
adjusts rather elastically to meet demand, and that models of the form

described in Section 10.10 can thus also be considered to be supply-side models. This is, in effect, what Lowry (1964) assumed in his retail model. To seek alternative modelling approaches, we have to turn to econometric modelling. Since, as already argued, we have to do this for industrial location modelling, and since many modellers have anyway considered both sectors together, henceforth we shall do the same. Further, since some econometric model builders include equations for population or houses as part of their model system, we shall follow suit where appropriate and such equations can be considered as alternative residential or housing location models.

We shall consider three examples of econometric modelling which illustrate the problems of interest. Each piece of work was carried out by a firm of planning consultants in North America: Traffic Research Corporation in relation to Boston (Hill, 1965), Alan M. Voorhees and Associates in relation to Connecticut (Lakshmanan, 1968) and CONSAD in relation to Pittsburgh (Putman, 1967). The models are of the form

$$\delta x_i = \sum_j a_{ij} y_j + \sum_j b_{ij} \delta y_j \qquad (10.135)$$

where x_i represents some measure of activity in zone i, and δx_i is the change in some time period. y_is are 'explanatory' variables (which, as we shall see later, may include some of the x_is). The particular choice of variables depends on the hypotheses to be represented. These may be chosen so as to make the model maximally consistent with some micro-analytical theory, as noted earlier, or simply to reflect empirical relationships discovered through preliminary statistical analysis. In the three examples we are using, a wide variety of hypotheses is represented. We can attempt to put them together eclectically and we obtain the following summary.

Industrial employment locates independently of local consumer markets, but may depend on
  (i) access to labour market
  (ii) access to services
  (iii) access to other similar employment (because of inter-industry linkages)
  (iv) land capacity (which depends on land availability, value and development costs).

Service employment may depend on
  (i) access to consumers (households and organizations)
  (ii) access to related services
  (iii) access to the labour market
  (iv) land capacity

Population, or new housing, may depend on
  (i) access to jobs
  (ii) access to services
  (iii) housing quality and price

(iv) social structure represented by such things as affinities between income groups

(v) land capacity and associated density constraints.

The authors of the Empiric model (Hill, 1965) make a distinction between *located* variables, the measures of economic activity or location, and *locator* *variables*, the explanatory variables in addition to located variables which are sometimes used as such. Thus, for each located variable R_i, we have an equation of the form

$$\delta R_i = \sum_{j \neq i} a_{ij} \delta R_j + \sum_j b_{ij}(Z_j \text{ or } \delta Z_j) \qquad (10.136)$$

where the Z_js are locator variables, δZ_js the change in such variables, and the a_{ij}s and b_{ij}s are coefficients. In the original Toronto study, the variables chosen as located variables were

(i) white-collar population

(ii) blue-collar population

(iii) retail and wholesale employment

(iv) manufacturing employment

(v) other employment

and the locator variables were

(i) densities for land in different uses

(ii) zoning practices

(iii) car accessibility measures.

The other two models use a different concept of change, the so-called *differential shift*, and so a preliminary discussion of this concept is appropriate. It originates in the work of Fuchs (1962). We can proceed to a definition in terms of population change. Let $P_i(t)$ be the population of zone i at time t, and consider a period from 0 to T. Then, using an asterisk to denote summation, $P_*(t)$ is the population of the region, the study area, at time t. Then, define

$$\alpha(0, T) = \frac{P_*(T) - P_*(0)}{P_*(0)} \qquad (10.137)$$

as the regional rate of population change. We can use DS as an operator to represent differential shift, and

$$DSP_i(0, T) = P_i(T) - (1 + \alpha(0, T))P_i(0) \qquad (10.138)$$

Thus the differential shift in period 0 to T is the difference between the zonal population in time T and the population which would have been achieved if the zone had grown at the regional growth rate. Thus, differential shift emphasizes inter-zonal differences in the pattern of change. Note that, from the definition

$$\sum_i DSP_i(0, T) = 0 \qquad (10.139)$$

If the time period is clear from the context, the $(0, T)$ suffix will be dropped

Now, suppose we measure economic activity by employment, and let $E_i^k(t)$ be the employment in sector k in zone i at time t. Then the regional growth rate for sector k is defined as

$$\beta^k(0, T) = \frac{E_*^k(T) - E_*^k(0)}{E_*^k(0)} \qquad (10.140)$$

and the corresponding differential shift by

$$DSE_i^k(0, T) = E_i^k(T) - (1 + \beta^k(0, T))E_i^k(0) \qquad (10.141)$$

Model equations can now be formulated as before, with differential shift variables replacing the gross change variables. However, before we explore examples of such models, a digression is in order.

This digression aims to relate the differential variables defined above to alternate definitions. Although the alternative definitions will not be used again here, they may help the reader with the literature (see, for example, Smith, 1966).

The alternative referred to consists of definitions of *comparative, compositional* and *competitive* shifts. Essentially, comparative shift is the differential shift in total employment of a zone, relative to an expected regional growth of total employment; competitive shifts are shifts in total employment relative to expected growth calculated as though each sector grew at its regional rate; the compositional shift is the difference between the two and represents a changing sector-mix. Suppose

$$E_*^*(t) = \sum_k E_*^k(t) \qquad (10.142)$$

is total employment in the region at time t, and

$$E_i^*(t) = \sum_k E_i^k(t) \qquad (10.143)$$

is total employment in zone i at time t. Then

$$\gamma(0, T) = \frac{E_*^*(T) - E_*^*(0)}{E_*^*(0)} \qquad (10.144)$$

is the rate of change of total employment in the region. Let CPAR, CPOS and CPET be comparative, compositional and competitive shifts in zone i. Then, we can define

$$\text{CPAR } E_i^*(0, T) = E_i^*(T) - (1 + \gamma(0, T))E_i^*(0) \qquad (10.145)$$

$$\text{CPOS } E_i^*(0, T) = \sum_k \frac{E_i^k(0)E_*^k(T)}{E_*^k(0)} - \frac{E_i^*(0)E_*^*(T)}{E_*^*(0)} \qquad (10.146)$$

Using the definition of $\beta^k(0, T)$ from equation (10.140), CPOS $E_i^*(0, T)$ can be written

$$\text{CPOS } E_i^*(0, T) = \sum_k (1 + \beta^k(0, T))E_i^k(0) - (1 + \gamma(0, T))E_i^*(0) \quad (10.147)$$

Then, we can define

$$\text{CPET } E_i^*(0, T) = \text{CPAR } E_i^*(0, T) - \text{CPOS } E_i^*(0, T) \quad (10.148)$$

$$= E_i^*(T) - \sum_k (1 + \beta^k(0, T))E_i^k(0) \quad (10.149)$$

Note that using the earlier definition of differential shift in equation (10.141), if we sum over k we get

$$\sum_k DSE_i^k(T) = E_i^*(T) - \sum_k (1 + \beta^k(0, T))E_i^k(0) \quad (10.150)$$

$$= \text{CPET } E_i^*(0, T) \quad (10.151)$$

so competitive shift is the sum of individual differential shifts. This ends the digression and henceforth we shall use differential shift by sector, the definition of equation (10.141).

The Voorhees model was a set of equations each of the form

$$DSX_i^m(0, T) = \sum a_{mn}Y_i^n \quad (10.152)$$

for the shift in the variable X_i^m for zone i. The Y_i^ns are explanatory variables and the a_{mn}s are cofficients.

The independent variables, when the shift referred to an *industrial employment* sector, were:
  (i) sum of all service sector differential shifts
  (ii) total employment in the sector at time 0
  (iii) total service employment at time 0
  (iv) capacity for industrial employment
  (v) access to professional services.
The independent variables for service sector shifts were:
  (i) sum of all service sector differential shifts
  (ii) total differential shift in industrial employment
  (iii) total employment at time 0
  (iv) access to population.
The independent variables for population (by income group) shifts were:
  (i) differential shift in population in next highest income group
  (ii) total differential shift in industrial employment
  (iii) sum of all service sector differential shifts
  (iv) sum of population differential shifts
  (v) access to population in same income group
  (vi) capacity for additional population.

It is interesting to compare and contrast the EMPIRIC and Voorhees models in relation to our earlier eclectic list of hypotheses but this is left as an exercise for the reader. However, one important point should be noted at this stage: each model uses variables which are dependent in one equation as independent variables in others. This means that two-stage least-squares maximum-likelihood, or some other estimation technique must be used to estimate the coefficients rather than the simple regression analysis technique mentioned in Chapter 5 which would lead to biased estimates.

The third example, the CONSAD sub-model for the North East Corridor Transportation Project (NECPT) is mentioned because it shows how simpler models can be postulated which do not involve simultaneous equation estimation techniques (Putman, 1966). We use the notation developed above and, in addition, we introduce an accessibility variable as

$$A_i^E(t) = \sum_j E_j^*(t) f(c_{ij}) \tag{10.153}$$

as a measure of access to total employment. Then, the assumptions made, taking $k = 1$ as the basic/industrial sector, $k > 1$ as service sectors, were

$$DSE_i^1(0, T) = a_1 E_i^1(0) + a_2 E_i^*(0) + a_3 A_i(T) + a_4 \tag{10.154}$$

$$DSP_i(0, T) = b_1 P_i(0) + b_2 A_i(T) + b_3 E_i^*(T) + b_4 \tag{10.155}$$

where $a_1 - a_4$ and $b_1 - b_4$ are coefficients to be estimated. Service employment was not estimated through a shift mechanism, but in total (implying a strong equilibrium assumption) as

$$E_i^k(T) = c_1 E_i^k(0) + c_2 P_i(T) + c_3 E_i^*(T) + c_4 \tag{10.156}$$

The reader will recognize that this is a very crude retail model indeed, completely neglecting interaction outside the zone being estimated. Some difficulties were discovered in obtaining satisfactory empirical estimates in relation to these equations, and in a later paper Putman (1967), in developing a model for Pittsburgh, was using a different model altogether.

Many more examples of econometric models can be found in the literature (for two more recent pieces of work, see Moses and Williamson, 1963, and Seidman, 1969). Seidman's work, in particular, will be described in greater detail in Chapter 11.

10.13. REFERENCES

W. Alonso (1964) *Location and land use*, Harvard University Press, Cambridge, Mass.
R. Bacon (1970) An approach to the theory of consumer shopping behaviour, *Urban Studies*, **8**, pp. 55–64.
F. S. Chapin and S. F. Weiss (1968) A probabilistic model for residential growth, *Transportation Research*, **2**, pp. 375–390.

Chicago Area Transportation Study (1960) *Final Report*, Chicago.

P. Converse (1949) New laws of retail gravitation, *Journal of Marketing*, **14**, pp. 279–304.

* M. Cordey Hayes (1968) Retail location models, Working Paper 16, Centre for Environmental Studies, London.

M. Cordey Hayes and A. G. Wilson (1970) Spatial interaction, *Socio-economic planning sciences*, **5**, 73–96.

* E. L. Cripps and D. H. S. Foot (1969) The empirical development of an elementary residential location model for use in sub-regional planning, *Environment and Planning*, **1**, pp. 81–90.

* E. L. Cripps and D. H. S. Foot (1970) The urbanization effects of a third London airport, *Environment and Planning*, **2**, pp. 153–192.

Distributive Trades E.D.C. (1970) *Models for shopping studies*, National Economic Development Office, London.

E. S. Dunn (1954) *The location of agricultural production*, University of Florida Press, Gainsville.

* R. V. Eastin and P. Shapiro (1973) Design of a location experiment, *Transportation Research*, pp. 17–29.

* R. V. Eastin and P. Shapiro (1973) The design of a location experiment: a continuous formulation, *Transportation Research*, pp. 31–38.

J. W. Forrester (1968) *Principles of systems*, Wright–Allen Press, Cambridge, Mass.

J. W. Forrester (1969) *Urban dynamics*, M.I.T. Press, Cambridge, Mass.

V. R. Fuchs (1962) The determinants of the redistribution of manufacturing in the United States since 1929, *Review of Economics and Statistics*, **44**, pp. 167–177.

J. R. Hamburg and R. L. Creighton (1959) Predicting Chicago's land use pattern, *Journal of the American Institute of Planners*, **25**, pp. 67–72.

F. E. I. Hamilton (1967) Models of industrial location, in R. J. Chorley and P. Haggett (Eds.) *Models in geography*, Methuen, London, pp. 361–424.

W. G. Hansen (1959) How accessibility shapes land use, *Journal of American Institute of Planners*, **25**, pp. 73–76.

B. Harris (1962) Linear programming and the projection of land uses, Paper 20, Penn.–Jersey Transportation Study, Philadelphia.

B. Harris (1964) A model of location equilibrium for retail trade, mimeo, Institute for Urban Studies, University of Pennsylvania.

* B. Harris (1968) Quantitative models of urban development, in H. S. Perloff and L. Wingo (Eds.) *Issues in urban economics*, Johns Hopkins, Baltimore, pp. 363–412.

J. Herbert and B. H. Stevens (1960) A model for the distribution of residential activity in urban areas, *Journal of Regional Science*, **2**, pp. 21–36.

D. M. Hill (1965) A growth allocation model for the Boston region, *Journal of the American Institute of Planners*, **31**, pp. 111–120.

* A. G. Houghton (1971) The simulation and evaluation of housing location, *Environment and Planning*, **3**, pp. 383–394.

D. L. Huff (1962) A note on the limitations of intra-urban gravity models, *Land Economics*, **38**, pp. 64–66; **39**, pp. 81–89.

D. L. Huff (1964) Defining and estimating a trading area, *Journal of Marketing*, **28**, pp. 37–38; also reprinted in P. Ambrose (Ed.) (1970) *Analytical human geography*, Longman, London, pp. 161–171.

W. Isard (1956) *Location and space-economy*, M.I.T. Press, Cambridge, Mass.

T. R. Lakshmanan (1968) A model for allocating urban activities in a state, *Socio-economic planning sciences*, **1**, pp. 283–295.

T. R. Lakshmanan and W. G. Hansen (1965) A retail market potential model, *Journal of the American Institute of Planners*, **31**, pp. 134–143.

I. S. Lowry (1963) Location parameters in the Pittsburgh model, *Papers, Regional Science Association*, **2**, pp. 145–165.

I. S. Lowry (1964) *A model of metropolis*, RM-4035-RC, RAND Corporation, Santa Monica.

I. S. Lowry (1968) Seven models of urban development: a structural comparison, *Special Report* **97**, pp. 121–145, Highway Research Board, Washington, D.C.

* D. B. Massey (1969) Some simple models for distributing changes in employment within regions, Working Paper 24, Centre for Environmental Studies, London.

E. Mills (1969) The value of urban land, in H. S. Perloff (Ed.) *The quality of the urban development*, Resources for the Future, Washington, D.C., pp. 231–253.

R. L. Morrill and M. B. Kelley (1970) The simulation of hospital use and the estimation of location efficiency, *Geographical Analysis*, **2**, 283–300.

L. N. Moses and H. F. Williamson (1963) Value of time, choice of mode and the subsidy use in urban transportation, *Journal of Political Economy*, **71**, pp. 247–264; also reprinted in R. E. Quandt (Ed.) (1970) *The demand for travel: theory and measurement*, Heath Lexington Books, Lexington, Mass., pp. 197–220.

R. Muth (1961) The spatial structure of the housing market, *Papers, Regional Science Association*, **7**, pp. 207–220.

R. Muth (1969) *Cities and housing*, University of Chicago Press, Chicago.

S. H. Putman (1966) The analytical models for implementing the economic impact studies for the Northeast Corridor Transportation Project, paper presented to the Thirteenth National Meeting, Operations Research Society of America, Durham, N. Carolina.

S. H. Putman (1967) Intra-urban industrial location model design and implementation, *Papers, Regional Science Association*, **19**, pp. 199–214.

R. U. Ratcliff (1949) *Urban land economics*, McGraw-Hill, New York.

W. J. Reilly (1931) *The law of retail gravitation*, G. P. Putman and Sons, New York.

* T. Rhodes and R. Whitaker (1967) Forecasting shopping demand, *Journal of the Town Planning Institute*, **53**, pp. 188–192.

I. M. Robinson, H. B. Wolfe, and R. L. Barringer (1965) A simulation model for renewal programming, *Journal of the American Institute of Planners*, **31**, pp. 126–134.

D. Seidman (1969) *The construction of an urban growth model*, Plan Report No. 1, Technical Supplement, Volume A, Delaware Valley Regional Planning Commission, Philadelphia.

* M. L. Senior (1973) A review of urban economic, ecological and spatial interaction approaches to residential location modelling, *Environment and Planning*, **5**, pp. 165–197.

M. L. Senior and A. G. Wilson (1973) Disaggregated residential location models: some tests and further theoretical developments, in E. L. Cripps (Ed.), *Space–time concepts in regional science*, Pion, London, to be published.

D. M. Smith (1966) A theoretical framework for geographical studies of industrial location, *Economic Geography*, **42**, pp. 95–113.

R. H. Strotz (1957) The empirical implications of a utility tree, *Econometrica*, **25**, 269–280.

C. N. Swerdloff and J. N. Stowers (1966) A test of some first generation residential land-use models, *Highway Research Record*, **126**, pp. 38–59.

J. H. von Thunen (1826) *Der isolierte Staat*, Hamburg; translated as *The isolated state* by C. M. Wartenburg, with an introduction by P. Hall, Oxford University Press, Oxford, 1966.

A. G. Wilson (1968) Models in urban planning: a synoptic review of recent literature, *Urban Studies*, **5**, pp. 249–276; also reprinted in A. G. Wilson (1972) *Papers in urban and regional analysis*, Pion, London, pp. 3–30.

A. G. Wilson (1969) Developments of some elementary residential location models, *Journal of Regional Science*, **9**, pp. 377–385.

A. G. Wilson (1970-A) *Entropy in urban and regional modelling*, Pion, London.

* A. G. Wilson (1970-B) Disaggregating elementary residential location models, *Papers, Regional Science Association*, **24**, pp. 103–125.

A. G. Wilson (1972) Behavioural inputs to aggregative urban system models, pp. 71–90 in *Papers in urban and regional analysis*, Pion, London.

L. Wingo (1961) *Transportation and urban land*, Resources for the Future, Washington, D.C.

CHAPTER 11

Towards comprehensive models

11.1. INTRODUCTION

We have already seen that in urban and regional studies 'everything depends on everything else', and yet the preceding chapters have been concerned with partial models of particular sectors. A *comprehensive* model, or a *general* model, is one in which as many interdependencies as possible are incorporated. In this chapter, then, we begin to attempt to put the pieces of earlier chapters together and to explore the task of building a comprehensive model.

Since locational behaviour must be at the core of any general model, the issues which were discussed at the beginning of Chapter 10 are again relevant here. Although the answers to the questions raised are the same, it is convenient to remind ourselves both of issues and of responses. We will be concerned mainly with *population activity* rather than *physical stock*. In modelling terms (and this also reflects the preceding sentence) we will be more concerned with *demand* than *supply*. We shall mostly be *aggregative* rather than very *micro*. We would prefer to be more *marginal* than cross-sectional, though in describing examples of general models we shall often be concerned with cross-sectional approaches.

In seeking the components for a general model, we can fairly directly utilize the previous four chapters: Chapter 7 for demographic models, Chapter 8 for economic models, Chapter 9 for transport models and Chapter 10 for locational models. We would expect them to be linked together according to a scheme such as that described in Chapter 3, and particularly in Figures 3.1 and 3.2. However, that was only an outline scheme, and in this chapter we must be much more specific. Considerable 'fitting together' problems then arise. For example, how do we fit a Chapter 9-like transport model into a general model in which most of the transport flows have already been predicted (differently!) by the residential location and service utilization models? Such questions will be resolved as they arise.

This introduction, then, relates this chapter to the rest of the book. There is a sense in which it is a microcosm of the whole book, and so we give it the same kind of structure. Rather than begin (as might be possible in some kind of ideal world) with a complete, but rather abstract, overall discussion, we present a number of examples of general models which have been built in the past. These examples are chosen to illustrate the use of different techniques:

models based on spatial interaction concepts (Sections 11.2 and 11.3) econometrics (Section 11.4) and two kinds of simulation method (Section 11.5). These examples should provide a feel for the task of building a comprehensive model and at the same time offer an historical account of development. We then proceed to a more general discussion. In Section 11.6 we outline a set of principles which forms a basis for building a general model and in Section 11.7 we look at the abstract structure of a model developed along these lines. A specific example of such a model is presented in Section 11.8 and some concluding comments are made in Section 11.9.

11.2. SPATIAL INTERACTION MODELS: THE LOWRY MODEL

It is convenient that the structure of this chapter is such that the first general model to be presented as an example is that of Lowry (1964). Enough is known from Chapter 3, and from the study of the partial models in Chapters 7–10, to make the problem clear: the parts must be synthesized with a rich interdependence of components. Lowry's model achieves this in the most elegant and (somewhat deceptively) simple way. The core of the model consists of two spatial interaction models and so it serves as a suitable illustration for this section. Thus, the best introduction to the task of building a general model is to display the Lowry model in action as we shall now do.

In the following account, we mostly use Lowry's original notation, though it is modified slightly to bring it into accord with the notation in the rest of this book. For this section only, we follow Lowry in allowing identical main variable letters with different numbers (or types) of subscripts or superscripts to represent different variables. If an index is dropped, then this implies summation and our usual asterisk notation will not be used here.

Variables can be constructed from the following definitions:

$$A = \text{area of land}$$
$$E = \text{employment}$$
$$P = \text{population}$$
$$c = \text{trip cost}$$
$$z = \text{constraints}$$

The subscripts and superscripts which are used in conjunction with these definitions are:

$$U = \text{unusable land}$$
$$B = \text{basic sector}$$
$$R = \text{retail sector (meaning the whole service sector)}$$
$$H = \text{household sector}$$
$$k = \text{class of establishment within retail sector}$$
$$m = \text{number of classes of retail establishments}$$
$$i, j = \text{zones}$$
$$n = \text{number of zones}$$

Lowry notes: 'The logical structure of the model can be expressed in nine simultaneous equations and three inequalities.' These follow: they are as Lowry presented them, but in a different order which facilitates the discussion of their solution.

E_j^B, employment in the basic sector, is assumed given.

Land use

$$A_j^H = A_j - A_j^u - A_j^B - A_j^R \tag{11.1}$$

This land is considered to be available for residential use.

Household sector

$$P = f \sum_{j=1}^{n} E_j \tag{11.2}$$

where f is an inverse activity rate.

$$P_j = g \sum_{i=1}^{n} E_i f_{res}(c_{ij}) \tag{11.3}$$

where f_{res} is a decreasing function of travel cost, c_{ij} and equation (11.3), as explained in Section 10.4, is, in effect, a simple spatial interaction model.

g can be calculated to ensure that

$$P = \sum_{j=1}^{n} P_j \tag{11.4}$$

and the estimates of P_j are modified to ensure that a maximum density constraint is not infringed:

$$P_j \leqslant z^H A_j^H \tag{11.5}$$

Retail sector

Total employment in the kth retail sector is assumed to be proportional to population:

$$E^{Rk} = a^k P \tag{11.6}$$

for a set of constants a^k. Then, this is allocated spatially according to another simple spatial interaction model (cf. Section 10.10)

$$E_j^{Rk} = b^k \left[c^k \sum_{i=1}^{n} P_i f_k(c_{ij}) + d^k E_j \right] \tag{11.7}$$

where c^k and d^k give the relative weights of home-based and job-based service utilization and b^k is calculated to ensure that

$$E^k = \sum_{j=1}^{n} E_j^k \tag{11.8}$$

The E_j^ks are adjusted to ensure that

$$E_j^k > z^{Rk} \tag{11.9}$$

where z^{Rk} is some minimum. If this is infringed, E_j^k is set to zero. At this stage, retail land use can be calculated from

$$A_j^R = \sum_k e^k E_j^{Rk} \tag{11.10}$$

where e^ks are constants. It is adjusted to ensure that

$$A_j^R \leqslant A_j - A_j^U - A_j^B \tag{11.11}$$

since the right-hand side is maximum available land.

Finally we can obtain total employment:

$$E_j = E_j^B + \sum_k E_j^{Rk} \tag{11.12}$$

Initially, the constants f, a^k, c^k, d^k, e^k, z^H and z^{Rk} are given, together with the functions f_{res} and f_k. That is to say, these quantities are obtained from some estimation, or calibration, procedure exogenous to the model as described here. The quantities A_j, A_j^U, A_j^B, E_j^B and c_{ij} are all given at the outset.

The equations can then be solved iteratively, progressing from equation (11.1) to equation (11.12) in sequence in the order presented above (which is why this order differs from Lowry's). Initially, A_j^R is set to zero and E_j to E_j^B.

The mechanism of the model is almost self-evident. In equation (11.1) the amount of land available for housing is calculated. In equation (11.2) the total population is estimated by applying an inverse activity rate f to total employment. This is spatially distributed to give P_j in equation (11.3); g is a normalizing factor calculated to ensure that equation (11.4) is satisfied, and the estimate of P_j is modified, if necessary, to ensure that the maximum density constraints expressed by the inequalities (11.5) hold. Retail employment generated in the different sectors is estimated in equation (11.6) by applying retail employment generating coefficients to the population. This is spatially distributed as E_j^{Rk} by equation (11.7), with b^k as a normalizing factor to ensure that (11.8) holds, and again adjustments are made to ensure that constraints are satisfied, this time the minimum size constraints of (11.9). Retail land use is calculated from (11.10) and the estimate is adjusted to ensure that this does not exceed total land available, as expressed by (11.11). Total employment can then be calculated, by zone, as in equation (11.12). This mechanism is summarized in Figure 11.1.

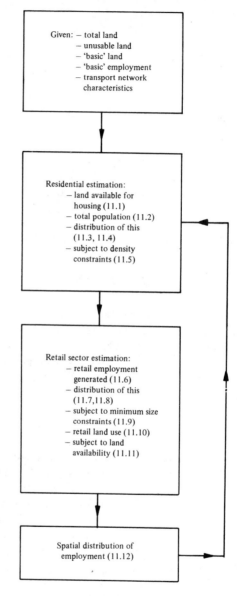

Figure 11.1   Structure of the Lowry model

The iteration proceeds until the estimates of residential population and retail employment do not change beyond some limit. This iterative procedure is essentially only a method of solving the equations and at this stage, it should not be given any further significance. The behaviour of the model is sometimes exhibited slightly differently in that, in each iteration, an *increment* of population and retail employment is supposed to be added. Equations (11.2), (11.3), (11.4), (11.6), (11.7), (11.8), (11.10) and (11.12) then all apply to increments. However, the constraints (11.5), (11.9) and (11.11) must all be applied to total quantities and therefore a full account of the latest population and employment quantities must obviously be retained. This picture of the model is not important to the presentation of the model as mainly used in this chapter, but it does throw light on the way that other people have perceived Lowry's model and has conditioned some of the interpretations of, and modifications made to, it.

A short digression is appropriate at this point to explain the structure of Lowry's model as a general model in the context of this book. The presentation so far rather masks the assumptions which are made about total population and total employment (in effect, our Chapter 7 and Chapter 8 models). In fact, although these quantities are estimated in the iterative procedure, they can be estimated once and for all outside it. If E is total population, then equation (11.2) can be written

$$P = fE \tag{11.13}$$

and we can sum equation (11.12) over zones j to give

$$E = E^B + \sum_k E^{Rk} \tag{11.14}$$

E^B, of course, is given. We also have equation (11.6) which is repeated here for convenience:

$$E^{Rk} = a^k P \tag{11.6}$$

We can solve the above three sets of equations for P, E^{Rk} and E in terms of the given quantity E^B. Substitute for P from equation (11.13) into (11.6), and for E^{Rk} from (11.6) into (11.14):

$$E = E^B + \sum_k a^k f E \tag{11.15}$$

which can be re-arranged to give

$$E = \frac{E^B}{1 - f\sum_k a^k} \tag{11.16}$$

Then, from (11.14),

$$P = \frac{fE^B}{1 - f\sum_k a^k} \tag{11.17}$$

and from (11.16),

$$E^{Rk} = \frac{fa^kE^B}{1 - f\sum_k a^k} \tag{11.18}$$

These quantities can be calculated at the outset and fixed in the model iteration to speed convergence, as noted and practised by Lowry himself. Equation (11.2) could be replaced by (11.17) and taken outside the iterative cycle. E_i in equation (11.3) still has to be set initially as E_i^B. Equation (11.6) can be replaced by (11.18) and removed from the iterative cycle. Further, we can also observe that, implicitly, equation (11.3) estimates journey to work as

$$T_{ij} = gE_if_{res}(c_{ij}) \tag{11.19}$$

and equation (11.7) service utilization as

$$S_{ij}^{Hk} = b^kc^kP_if_k(c_{ij}) \tag{11.20}$$

and

$$S_{jj}^{Wk} = b^kd^kE_j \tag{11.21}$$

for respective home-based and work-based trips to services. Thus, without changing the model at all, Figure 11.1 can be re-arranged as Figure 11.2. This account of the Lowry model makes explicit the extremely simple assumptions which are being made in some aspects of the model (and we shall return to a detailed discussion of these later) but, none-the-less, it is complete.

The account of the Lowry model above is intended to give an overall understanding of the model and it reflects most published descriptions of it. It has also been modified and developed using equations (11.1)–(11.12), or sub-sets of these, as a basis. However, this presentation underates the full richness of Lowry's model and it also fails to display the full mechanism of, for example, the constraint adjustment procedures. Lowry himself gives a full verbal description of the details, but it is now most useful to develop the notation a stage further and to present a full mathematical description. This only appears to have been attempted once before, by Batty (1971). The presentation here differs slightly in notation and equation presentation from that of Batty, but the reader can check that his interpretation of the detailed Lowry model agrees in all respects with ours.

Additional indices are introduced to make the iterative manipulations clear: p is used for the outer iterative loop and q is used for inner loops, once

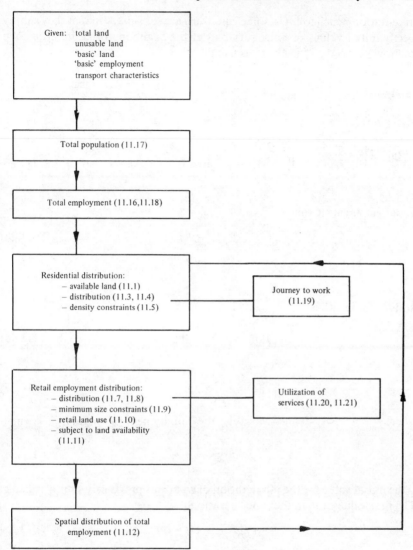

Figure 11.2 Structure of the Lowry model: alternative representation

for the residential constraint adjustment and once for the retail constraint adjustment. The quantities which are being estimated in inner loops are P_i and E_j^k. Their values in the pth outer iteration will be written as $P_i(p)$ and $E_j^k(p)$. In the inner loop, P_i will have the value $P_i(p, q)$ on the qth, though this q, of course, now refers to a quite different inner iteration. The rest of the notation of the earlier presentation is extended in a self-evident way. In the presentation which follows, some equations are subsidiary in that they simply specify initial values of some variables at the beginning of an iteration. We can now proceed; E_j^B is given, as usual.

Land use

$$A_j^R(1) = 0 \tag{11.22}$$

$$A_j^H(p) = \begin{cases} A_j - A_j^U - A_j^B - A_j^R(p) & \text{if } A_j - A_j^U - A_j^B - A_j^R(p) \geqslant 0 \\ 0 & \text{if } A_j - A_j^U - A_j^B - A_j^R(p) < 0 \end{cases} \tag{11.23}$$

Initial employment values

$$E_j(1) = E_j^B \tag{11.24}$$

$$E_j^{Rk}(1) = 0 \tag{11.25}$$

Residential location

$$P(p) = f \sum_{j=1}^n E_j(p) \tag{11.26}$$

$$r_j(p) = \sum_{i=1}^n E_i(p) f_{\text{res}}(c_{ij}) \tag{11.27}$$

where r_j is a newly defined variable: the employment potential at j. Then,

$$g'(p) = \frac{P}{\sum_{j=1}^n r_j} \tag{11.28}$$

is the initial value for the pth iteration of what was previously simply called g. The first value of P_j in the inner iteration is

$$P_j(p, 1) = g'(p) r_j(p) \tag{11.29}$$

Define sets $Z_1(p, q)$ and $Z_2(p,q)$ such that

$$j \in Z_1(p, q) \quad \text{if } P_j(p, q) \geqslant z_j^H A_j^H(p) \tag{11.30}$$

and

$$Z_1(p, q) \cup Z_2(p, q) = Z \tag{11.31}$$

where Z is the set of all zones. Thus, $Z_1(p, q)$ is the set of all zones which infringe the maximum density constraints at the qth inner iteration of the pth outer iteration. Then, the surplus population from Z_1 zones is re-allocated by recalculating g such that

$$g(p, q) = \frac{N - \sum_{j \in Z_1(p,q)} z_j^H A_j^H(p)}{\sum_{j \in Z_2(p,q)} r_j(p)} \tag{11.32}$$

Then,

$$P_j(p, q + 1) = \begin{cases} z_j^H A_j^H(p), & j \in Z_1(p, q) \\ g(p, q) r_j, & j \in Z_2(p, q) \end{cases} \tag{11.33}$$

Thus, for zones in $Z_1(p, q)$, their populations have been set to the maximum possible; these have been subtracted from the total (in the numerator of the expression for $g(p, q)$) and $g(p, q)$ calculated so that when the remaining population (now including the surplus) is allocated in proportion to r_j,

$$\sum_{j=1}^{n} P_j(p) = P(p)$$

is satisfied. Equations (11.31)–(11.33) are solved iteratively from $q = 1$ to some final value, q_{fin} say, which is achieved when $Z_1(p, q_{\text{fin}})$ is the null set. The iteration is necessary since when the first surplus is re-allocated by the above procedure, new zones may infringe the constraints for the first time. At the end of this inner iteration, we set

$$P_j(p) = P_j(p, q_{\text{fin}}) \tag{11.34}$$

Retail location

$$E^{Rk}(p) = a^k P(p) \tag{11.35}$$

Then

$$s_j^k(p) = c^k \sum_{i=1}^{n} P_i(p) f_k(c_{ij}) + d^k E_j(p) \tag{11.36}$$

is the retail potential for sector k at j, made up of a population potential and a local employment retail service generating term. Then,

$$b^{k1}(p) = \frac{E^{Rk}(p)}{\sum_{j=1}^{n} s_j^k(p)} \tag{11.37}$$

is the initial value of the old b^k and

$$E_j^{Rk}(p, 1) = b^{k1}(p) s_j^k(p) \tag{11.38}$$

the first estimate of E_j^{Rk} in the inner iteration. We can now define a second inner iteration in relation to the retail minimum size constraints which, in procedure, is analogous to the earlier residential one, but with the additional complication that 'infringing' zones can only be added to the set of such zones one at a time, beginning with the worst, in case the allocation of the surplus pushes remaining infringers over the minimum size limit. Thus, we define sets $Z_3^k(p, q)$ and $Z_4^k(p, q)$ such that

$$j \in Z_3^k(p, q) \quad \text{if } E_j^{Rk}(p, q) \leqslant z^{k\min}$$

and

$$E_j^{Rk}(p, q) \leqslant q_j^{\min}\{E_j^{Rk}(p, q)\} \tag{11.39}$$

where $q^{\min}$ means the qth from minimum over j in the set $\{E_j^{Rk}(p, q)\}$. (Some appropriate rule will have to be formulated in the case of one or more E_j^{Rk}s being equal, but the precise form of this is unimportant.)

$$Z_3^k(p, q) \cup Z_4^k(p, q) = Z \tag{11.40}$$

Then,

$$b^k(p, q) = \frac{E^{Rk}(p)}{\sum_{j \in Z_4^k(p, q)} s_j^k(p)} \tag{11.41}$$

and

$$E_j^{Rk}(p, q + 1) = \begin{cases} 0 & \text{if } j \in Z_3^k(p, q) \\ b^k(p, q)s_j^k(p) & \text{if } j \in Z_4^k(p, q) \end{cases} \tag{11.42}$$

Equations (11.39)–(11.42) are solved iteratively, for each k, from $q = 1$ to $q = q_{\text{fin}}$ (when $Z_3^k(p, q_{\text{fin}})$ is the empty set) and then

$$E_j^{Rk}(p) = E_j^{Rk}(p, q_{\text{fin}}) \tag{11.43}$$

Retail land use is then calculated from

$$A_j^R(p + 1) = \begin{cases} \sum_{k=1}^{m} e^k E_j^{Rk}(p) & \text{if } \sum_k e^k E_j^{Rk}(p) \leqslant A_j - A_j^u - A_j^B \\ A_j - A_j^u - A_j^B & \text{if } \sum_k e^k E_j^{Rk}(p) > A_j - A_j^u - A_j^B \end{cases} \tag{11.44}$$

The second possibility permits what Lowry called 'overcrowding' or, in effect, high-rise building, for the retail sector, and this equation is so written that the land use constraint is satisfied. Finally

$$E_j(p + 1) = E_j^B + \sum_{k=1}^{m} E_j^{Rk}(p) \tag{11.45}$$

Equations (11.23)–(11.45) are then solved iteratively from $p = 1$ to $p = p_{\text{fin}}$. The iteration ends when $P_j(p_{\text{fin}} - 1)$ and $P_j(p_{\text{fin}})$, and $E_j^{Rk}(p_{\text{fin}} - 1)$ and $E_j^{Rk}(p_{\text{fin}})$ differ only by some preset small amount.

1.3. VARIANTS AND FURTHER DEVELOPMENTS OF THE LOWRY MODEL

There are many variants of the Lowry model, each representing some kind of possible development. We shall consider a number of these in turn, mainly reporting, with specific comment on the modification under discussion, but with no general comments until all have been described.

It is convenient to begin with an account of improvements to the two location sub-models. In fact, this task has already been carried out, in Section 10.5 for the residential model, and Section 10.10 for the retail model, and we need only report the results here. The Lowry residential model was given in spatial interaction format in equation (10.1). We showed how it could be modified to ensure consistency with its own internal assumptions, and we introduced an attractiveness factor, W_i. If we drop the attractiveness factor in the first instance, we can write equations (10.3) and (10.4) together as

$$T_{ij} = \frac{E_j f_{\text{res}}(c_{ij})}{\sum_{i=1}^{n} f_{\text{res}}(c_{ij})} \qquad (11.46)$$

Then,

$$P_i = f \sum_{j=1}^{n} T_{ij} = \sum_{j=1}^{n} \frac{f E_j f_{\text{res}}(c_{ij})}{\sum_{i=1}^{n} f_{\text{res}}(c_{ij})} \qquad (11.47)$$

If we add the attractiveness factor back in, this becomes

$$P_i = \sum_{j=1}^{n} \frac{f W_i E_j f_{\text{res}}(c_{ij})}{\sum_{i=1}^{n} W_i f_{\text{res}}(c_{ij})} \qquad (11.48)$$

It is also possible to assume that the inverse activity rate f varies by zone, in which case equation (11.47) could be rewritten

$$P_i = \sum_{j=1}^{n} \frac{f_j E_j f_{\text{res}}(c_{ij})}{\sum_{i=1}^{n} f_{\text{res}}(c_{ij})} \qquad (11.49)$$

The retail model can be modified in a parallel way, except that, additionally, we must decide what to do about the employment term. The discussion in Chapter 10 goes from equation (10.123) to equation (10.129). For present Lowry model purposes, if we first neglect the employment term (i.e. set $c^k = 1$, $d^k = 0$) and attractiveness factors, but put in a service employment generating factor which varies by zone (and note the use of *employment* units for e_i^k rather than *cash* as in Chapters 4 and 10), then the retail equivalent of equation (11.49) is

$$E_j^{Rk} = \sum_{i=1}^{n} \frac{e_i^k P_i f_k(c_{ij})}{\sum_{j=1}^{n} f_k(c_{ij})} \qquad (11.50)$$

In general terms, retail employment generated by total employment could be represented in a similar model. Suppose we put a superscript H on equation (11.50) variables, to represent 'generated from home', and write it

$$E_j^{HRk} = \sum_{i=1}^{n} \frac{e_i^{Hk} P_i f_k^H(c_{ij})}{\sum_{j=1}^{n} f_k^H(c_{ij})} \tag{11.51}$$

then employment generated from work, using an obvious notation, is

$$E_j^{WRk} = \sum_{i=1}^{n} \frac{e_i^{Wk} E_i f_k^W(c_{ij})}{\sum_{j=1}^{n} f_k^W(c_{ij})} \tag{11.52}$$

Then

$$E_j^{Rk} = E_j^{HRk} + E_j^{WRk} \tag{11.53}$$

If we also add attractiveness factors W_j^H and W_j^W then equations (11.51)–(11.53) give

$$E_j^{HRk} = \sum_{i=1}^{n} \frac{e_i^{Hk} P_i W_j^H f_k^H(c_{ij})}{\sum_{j=1}^{n} W_j^H f_k^H(c_{ij})} \tag{11.54}$$

$$E_j^{WRk} = \sum_{i=1}^{n} \frac{e_i^{Wk} E_i W_j^W f_k^W(c_{ij})}{\sum_{j=1}^{n} W_j^W f_k^W(c_{ij})} \tag{11.55}$$

and

$$E_j^{Rk} = E_j^{HRk} + E_j^{WRk} \tag{11.56}$$

Equations (11.54)–(11.56) are equivalent to equations (10.125)–(10.129) of Chapter 10. Many modifications have been made to the Lowry model using either one or a combination of the sub-model improvements outlined above.

Next, it is convenient to discuss Garin's (1966) matrix formulation of the Lowry model, which leads to some interesting insights. The formulation is essentially incremental and we modify our notation accordingly. Let $\Delta P_i(p)$ and $\Delta E_j^{Rk}(p)$, for example, be the increments to P_i and E_j^{Rk} in the pth iteration. As usual, we are given basic employment, as a vector

$$\mathbf{E}^B = \begin{pmatrix} E_1^B \\ E_2^B \\ \cdot \\ \cdot \\ E_n^B \end{pmatrix} \tag{11.57}$$

Garin used the equation (11.49) version of the residential model, and defined a matrix $\mathbf{A}^1$ such that

$$A_{ij}^1 = \frac{f_{\text{res}}(c_{ij})}{\sum_{i=1}^{n} f_{\text{res}}(c_{ij})} \tag{11.58}$$

He also defines the diagonal matrix

$$\hat{\mathbf{F}} = \begin{pmatrix} f_1 & 0 \dots \\ 0 & f_2 \dots \end{pmatrix} \tag{11.59}$$

so that the first iteration version of equation (11.49) can be written

$$\Delta \mathbf{P}(1) = \mathbf{A}^1 \hat{\mathbf{F}} \mathbf{E}^B \tag{11.60}$$

(Garin in fact defines $\mathbf{E}^B$ as the *transpose* of a vector, and then matrices which operate from the right. This author prefers operators to operate from the left!) or

$$\Delta \mathbf{P}(1) = \mathbf{A}\mathbf{E}^B \tag{11.61}$$

where

$$\mathbf{A} = \mathbf{A}^1 \hat{\mathbf{F}} \tag{11.62}$$

Garin then used the equation (11.50) version of the service model, but with only one sector, so that the k superscript can be dropped. He then defines the matrix $\mathbf{B}^1$ so that

$$B^1_{ij} = \frac{f_k(c_{ij})}{\sum_{j=1}^{n} f_k(c_{ij})} \tag{11.63}$$

and a matrix of service employment generating coefficients so that

$$\hat{\mathbf{e}} = \begin{pmatrix} e_1 & 0 \dots \\ 0 & e_2 \dots \end{pmatrix} \tag{11.64}$$

Then the first iteration form of (11.50) is

$$\Delta \mathbf{E}^R(1) = \mathbf{B}^1 \hat{\mathbf{e}} \mathbf{P} \tag{11.65}$$

$$= \mathbf{B}\Delta \mathbf{P}(1) \tag{11.66}$$

where

$$\mathbf{B} = \mathbf{B}^1 \hat{\mathbf{e}} \tag{11.67}$$

We can substitute from equation (11.61) into (11.66) to give

$$\Delta \mathbf{E}^R(1) = \mathbf{BAE}^B \tag{11.68}$$

The second iteration can then be carried out in an obvious way to give

$$\Delta \mathbf{P}(2) = \mathbf{A}\Delta \mathbf{E}^R(1) = \mathbf{ABAE}^B \tag{11.69}$$

and

$$\Delta \mathbf{E}^R(2) = \mathbf{B}\Delta \mathbf{P}(2) = \mathbf{BABAE}^B \tag{11.69a}$$

In general,

$$\Delta \mathbf{P}(n) = \mathbf{A}(\mathbf{BA})^{n-1} \mathbf{E}^B \tag{11.69b}$$

and

$$\Delta E^R(n) = (BA)^n E^B \qquad (11.69c)$$

The iteration continues until all the elements of $\Delta P(n)$ and $\Delta E^R(n)$ are less than some given small number. Then

$$P = \sum_{p=1}^{pfin} \Delta P(p) \qquad (11.69d)$$

and (adding E^B to give total employment)

$$E = E^B + \sum_{p=1}^{pfin} \Delta E^R(p) \qquad (11.70)$$

where p_{fin} is the last iteration.

The insights from Garin's formulation are obtained from noting that since $(BA)^p \to 0$ as $p \to \infty$, the series in (11.70), with $p_{fin} = \infty$, converges as follows:

$$E = \sum_{p=0}^{\infty} (BA)^p E^B \qquad (11.71)$$

$$= (I - BA)^{-1} E^B \qquad (11.72)$$

where I is the identity matrix. Then from (11.73),

$$P = A(I - BA)^{-1} E^B \qquad (11.73)$$

Thus, instead of carrying through the usual iteration, it is possible to invert the matrix $I - BA$, and to use equations (11.72) and (11.73).

This analysis also gives an indication as to why the incremental procedure is equivalent to Lowry's non-incremental procedure. Using the matrices defined above, the equivalent non-incremental procedure would be, starting with

$$E^R(0) = E^B \qquad (11.74)$$

$$P(p) = A(E^B + E^R(p - 1)) \qquad (11.75)$$

$$E^R(p) = BP(p) = BA(E^B + E^R(p - 1)) \qquad (11.76)$$

Equation (11.76) can be extended as

$$E^R(p) = BA(E^B + BA(E^B + E^R(p - 2))) \qquad (11.77)$$

$$= BA(E^B + BA(E^B + BA(E^B + E^R(p - 3))) \qquad (11.78)$$

and so on to give

$$E^R(p) = BA(E^B + BAE^B + (BA)^2 E^B + \ldots) \qquad (11.79)$$

and this is equivalent to equation (11.71) if E^B is added to give total employment. The Garin model as originally presented, and as described above,

learly omits many important features of the Lowry model. There is only one
ervice sector, there are no trips to services from workplaces, and there is no
onstraint checking procedure. We next explore whether such simplifying
ssumptions are necessary to a matrix formulation. We show that they can
>e relaxed almost completely, although to achieve this for the constraints
>rocedure involves a mechanism which differs from Lowry's, possibly for
he better. Thus we proceed as follows: first, we introduce several service
ectors into the Garin version of the model; second, we introduce work-based
ervice trips, but with only one service sector; third, we have work-based
ervice trips and several service sectors; fourth, we add a constraint procedure.

Define $\mathbf{B}^{k1}$ such that

$$B_{ij}^{k1} = \frac{f_k(c_{ij})}{\sum_{j=1}^{n} f_k(c_{ij})} \tag{11.80}$$

Define $\hat{\mathbf{e}}^k$ such that

$$e_{ij}^k = \delta_{ij} e_i^k \tag{11.81}$$

where δ_{ij} is a Kronecker delta. Then equation (11.50) could be written

$$\mathbf{E}^{Rk} = \mathbf{B}^{k1} \hat{\mathbf{e}}^k \mathbf{P} \tag{11.82}$$

$$= \mathbf{B}^k \mathbf{P} \tag{11.83}$$

where

$$\mathbf{B}^k = \mathbf{B}^{k1} \hat{\mathbf{e}}^k \tag{11.84}$$

The equations equivalent to (11.61)–(11.72) are now:

$$\Delta \mathbf{P}(1) = \mathbf{A} \mathbf{E}^B \tag{11.85}$$

as before

$$\Delta \mathbf{E}^{Rk}(1) = \mathbf{B}^k \Delta \mathbf{P}(1) \tag{11.86}$$

Then,

$$\Delta \mathbf{P}(2) = \mathbf{A} \Delta \mathbf{E}^R(1) = \mathbf{A} \sum_{k=1}^{m} \Delta \mathbf{E}^{Rk}(1) \tag{11.87}$$

so

$$\Delta \mathbf{P}(2) = \mathbf{A} \sum_{k=1}^{m} \mathbf{B}^k \mathbf{A} \mathbf{E}^B \tag{11.88}$$

using (11.85), and

$$\Delta \mathbf{P}(2) = \mathbf{A} \mathbf{B} \mathbf{A} \mathbf{E}^B \tag{11.89}$$

defining

$$B = \sum_{k=1}^{m} B^k \qquad (11.90)$$

Then

$$\Delta E^{Rk}(2) = B^k \Delta P(2) = B^k ABAE^B \qquad (11.91)$$

and

$$\Delta P(3) = A \sum_{k=1}^{m} \Delta E^{Rk}(2) = ABABAE^B \qquad (11.92)$$

In general, we can now see

$$\Delta P(p) = A(BA)^{p-1}E^B \qquad (11.93)$$

$$\Delta E^{Rk}(p) = B^k A(BA)^{p-1}E^B \qquad (11.94)$$

$$\Delta E^R(p) = (BA)^p E^B \qquad (11.95)$$

We now sum and let $p \to \infty$, obtaining

$$P = A \sum_{p=1}^{\infty} (BA)^{p-1}E^B \qquad (11.96)$$

$$E^{Rk} = B^k A \sum_{p=1}^{\infty} (BA)^{p-1}E^B \qquad (11.97)$$

$$E^R = \sum_{p=1}^{\infty} (BA)^p E^B \qquad (11.98)$$

and

$$E = E^B + E^R = \sum_{p=1}^{\infty} (BA)^{p-1}E^B \qquad (11.99)$$

So, since

$$\sum_{p=1}^{\infty} (BA)^{p-1} = (I - BA)^{-1} \qquad (11.100)$$

equations (11.96)–(11.99) can be written

$$P = A(I - BA)^{-1}E^B \qquad (11.101)$$

$$E^{Rk} = B^k A(I - BA)^{-1}E^B \qquad (11.102)$$

$$E^R = (I - BA)^{-1}E^B - E^B \qquad (11.103)$$

$$E = (I - BA)^{-1}E^B \qquad (11.104)$$

So, with a suitable definition of **B**, the results are the same in aggregate as before, with equation (11.102) giving the sectoral disaggregation.

We now introduce a work-based service interaction on the lines of equations (11.51) and (11.52), but firstly with only a single k. We can define matrices $\mathbf{B}^1$, $\hat{\mathbf{e}}$ and $\mathbf{B}$ as in equations (11.63)–(11.67) above, but distinguishing home-based and work-based. Thus, we define a $\mathbf{B}^H$ and a $\mathbf{B}^W$. Then, equation (11.51) can be written

$$\mathbf{E}^{HR} = \mathbf{B}^H\mathbf{P} \tag{11.105}$$

and (11.52)

$$\mathbf{E}^{WR} = \mathbf{B}^W\mathbf{E} \tag{11.106}$$

In the usual iterative procedure, we would have

$$\Delta\mathbf{P}(1) = \mathbf{A}\mathbf{E}^B \tag{11.107}$$

in the usual way, and

$$\Delta\mathbf{E}^{HR}(1) = \mathbf{B}^H\Delta\mathbf{P}(1) = \mathbf{B}^H\mathbf{A}\mathbf{E}^B \tag{11.108}$$

$$\Delta\mathbf{E}^{WR}(1) = \mathbf{B}^W\mathbf{E}^B \tag{11.109}$$

Then,

$$\Delta\mathbf{P}(2) = \mathbf{A}(\mathbf{B}^H\mathbf{A} + \mathbf{B}^W)\mathbf{E}^B \tag{11.110}$$

$$\Delta\mathbf{E}^{HR}(2) = \mathbf{B}^H\mathbf{A}(\mathbf{B}^H\mathbf{A} + \mathbf{B}^W)\mathbf{E}^B \tag{11.111}$$

$$\Delta\mathbf{E}^{WR}(2) = \mathbf{B}^W(\mathbf{B}^H\mathbf{A} + \mathbf{B}^W)\mathbf{E}^B \tag{11.112}$$

$$\Delta\mathbf{P}(3) = \mathbf{A}((\mathbf{B}^H\mathbf{A})^2 + \mathbf{B}^H\mathbf{A}\mathbf{B}^W + \mathbf{B}^W\mathbf{B}^H\mathbf{A} + \mathbf{B}^{W2})\mathbf{E}^B \tag{11.113}$$

$$\Delta\mathbf{E}^{HR}(3) = \mathbf{B}^H\mathbf{A}[(\mathbf{B}^H\mathbf{A})^2 + \mathbf{B}^H\mathbf{A}\mathbf{B}^W + \mathbf{B}^W\mathbf{B}^H\mathbf{A} + \mathbf{B}^{W2}]\mathbf{E}^B \tag{11.114}$$

$$\Delta\mathbf{E}^{WR}(3) = \mathbf{B}^W[(\mathbf{B}^H\mathbf{A})^2 + \mathbf{B}^H\mathbf{A}\mathbf{B}^W + \mathbf{B}^W\mathbf{B}^H\mathbf{A} + \mathbf{B}^{W2}]\mathbf{E}^B \tag{11.115}$$

We can now see that, in general,

$$\Delta\mathbf{P}(p) = \mathbf{A}(\mathbf{B}^H\mathbf{A} + \mathbf{B}^W)^{p-1} \tag{11.116}$$

$$\Delta\mathbf{E}^{HR}(p) = \mathbf{B}^H\mathbf{A}(\mathbf{B}^H\mathbf{A} + \mathbf{B}^W)^{p-1} \tag{11.117}$$

$$\Delta\mathbf{E}^{WR}(p) = \mathbf{B}^W(\mathbf{B}^H\mathbf{A} + \mathbf{B}^W)^{p-1} \tag{11.118}$$

Now,

$$\sum_{p=0}^{\infty} (\mathbf{B}^H\mathbf{A} + \mathbf{B}^W)^p = (\mathbf{I} - \mathbf{B}^H\mathbf{A} - \mathbf{B}^W)^{-1} \tag{11.119}$$

We can obtain, on summing,

$$\mathbf{P} = \mathbf{A}(\mathbf{I} - \mathbf{B}^H\mathbf{A} - \mathbf{B}^W)^{-1}\mathbf{E}^B \tag{11.120}$$

$$\mathbf{E}^{HR} = \mathbf{B}^H\mathbf{A}(\mathbf{I} - \mathbf{B}^H\mathbf{A} - \mathbf{B}^W)^{-1}\mathbf{E}^B \tag{11.121}$$

$$\mathbf{E}^{WR} = \mathbf{B}^W(\mathbf{I} - \mathbf{B}^H\mathbf{A} - \mathbf{B}^W)^{-1}\mathbf{E}^B \tag{11.122}$$

and

$$\mathbf{E} = \mathbf{E}^B + \mathbf{E}^{HR} + \mathbf{E}^{WR} \tag{11.123}$$

$$= [\mathbf{I} + (\mathbf{B}^H\mathbf{A} + \mathbf{B}^W)(\mathbf{I} - \mathbf{B}^H\mathbf{A} - \mathbf{B}^W)^{-1}]\mathbf{E}^B \tag{11.124}$$

Note that

$$[\mathbf{I} + (\mathbf{B}^H\mathbf{A} + \mathbf{B}^W)(\mathbf{I} - \mathbf{B}^H\mathbf{A} - \mathbf{B}^W)^{-1}]$$

$$= [\mathbf{I} + (\mathbf{B}^H\mathbf{A} + \mathbf{B}^W)(\mathbf{I} - \mathbf{B}^H\mathbf{A} - \mathbf{B}^W)^{-1}](\mathbf{I} - \mathbf{B}^H\mathbf{A} - \mathbf{B}^W)(\mathbf{I} - \mathbf{B}^H\mathbf{A} - \mathbf{B}^W)^-$$

$$\tag{11.125}$$

$$= (\mathbf{I} - \mathbf{B}^H\mathbf{A} - \mathbf{B}^W)^{-1} \tag{11.126}$$

so that $\mathbf{E}$ in equation (11.124) can be written

$$\mathbf{E} = (\mathbf{I} - \mathbf{B}^H\mathbf{A} - \mathbf{B}^W)^{-1}\mathbf{E}^B \tag{11.127}$$

(This could have been proved directly, of course, if the increments of $\mathbf{E}$ had been calculated in the earlier calculation.)

It remains to present a matrix version of the model for the case when work based service interaction is allowed *and* the service sectors are disaggregated. We can define matrices B^{Hk1}, B^{Wk1}, $\hat{e}^{Hk}$, $\hat{e}^{Wk}$ by analogy with the previous two cases, and then $\mathbf{B}^{Hk}$ and $\mathbf{B}^{Wk}$. If we then define

$$\mathbf{B}^H = \sum_{k=1}^{m} \mathbf{B}^{Hk} \tag{11.128}$$

$$\mathbf{B}^W = \sum_{k=1}^{m} \mathbf{B}^{Wk} \tag{11.129}$$

and that, with these definitions, equations (11.120)–(11.122), and (11.127) still hold with, in addition

$$\mathbf{E}^{HRk} = \mathbf{B}^{Hk}\mathbf{A}(\mathbf{I} - \mathbf{B}^H\mathbf{A} - \mathbf{B}^W)^{-1}\mathbf{E}^B \tag{11.130}$$

$$\mathbf{E}^{WRk} = \mathbf{B}^{Wk}(\mathbf{I} - \mathbf{B}^H\mathbf{A} - \mathbf{B}^W)^{-1}\mathbf{E}^B \tag{11.131}$$

A final remark can be made about all these matrix models. The location sub-models can all be amended on the lines of equation (11.48) or (11.54) or (11.55) by having attractiveness factors incorporated. This is done by changing the definitions of A_{ij}^1 or B_{ij}^1 (suitably disaggregated). For example, in relation to (11.48), A_{ij}^1 from equation (11.58) would be amended to

$$A_{ij}^1 = \frac{W_i f_{res}(c_{ij})}{\sum_{i=1}^{n} W_i f_{res}(c_{ij})} \tag{11.132}$$

Thus, all the 'disaggregation' problems of Garin's version of the Lowry model can be rectified. We must now tackle the constraints.

Batty (1971) has shown how both population density and minimum size constraints can be incorporated into a Garin matrix version of the Lowry model using a method of this author (Wilson, 1969-A) which was explained in Chapter 10. The procedure is that described in relation to an elementary residential location model in equations (10.9)–(10.15). Let us first investigate the problem of incorporating this constraint procedure into the fully specified Lowry model given by equations (11.22)–(11.45). This obviously does not make sense unless the location sub-models are replaced by improved spatial interaction models, and therefore we do this as well. We first investigate the modification.

Land use

Equations (11.22) and (11.23) are unchanged.

Initial employment values

Equations (11.24) and (11.25) are unchanged.

Residential location

No inner iteration will be needed this time. Initially,

$$T_{ij}(1) = B_j W_i E_j(1) f_{res}(c_{ij}) \tag{11.133}$$

where

$$B_j = 1 \bigg/ \sum_i W_i f_{res}(c_{ij}) \tag{11.134}$$

$$P_i(1) = \sum_j f_j T_{ij} \tag{11.135}$$

On subsequent iterations, we form a set $Z_1(p)$ such that

$$i \in Z_1(p) \quad \text{if } P_i(p-1) \geqslant z_i^H A_i^H(p) \tag{11.135}$$

and $Z_2(p)$ in the set of zones which remain. For each $p > 1$, we set the population of any zone, i, in the set $Z_1(p)$ to its maximum value, $z_i^H A_i^H(p)$, and we have two spatial interaction models as follows:

$$T_{ij}(p) = A_i(p) B_j(p) z_i^H A_i^H(p) E_j(p) f_{res}(c_{ij}), \quad i \in Z_1(p) \tag{11.136}$$

$$T_{ij}(p) = B_j(p) W_i E_j(p) f_{res}(c_{ij}), \quad i \in Z_2(p) \tag{11.137}$$

The balancing factors are $A_i(p)$ (which should be carefully distinguished from $A_i^H(p)$) and $B_j(p)$ and are given by

$$A_i(p) = 1 \bigg/ \sum_{j=1}^n B_j E_j(p) f_{res}(c_{ij}), \quad i \in Z_1(p) \tag{11.138}$$

$$B_j(p) = 1 \bigg/ \left[\sum_{i \in Z_1(p)} A_i(p) z_i^H A_i^H(p) f_{\text{res}}(c_{ij}) + \sum_{i \in Z_2(p)} W_i f_{\text{res}}(c_{ij}) \right] \quad (11.139)$$

Equations (11.138) and (11.139) have to be solved iteratively. Batty (197 1972) gives an alternative procedure for this where, in effect, this iteration incorporated into the outer loop, which may explain why the convergence 'i very slow'. (We perhaps need to emphasize that W_i is assumed to be a constan If it is chosen to vary within the p-iteration as is possible, then it would b necessary to reintroduce an inner iteration and to form the set $Z_i(p, q)$ fo each q.) Finally we can form $P_i(p)$ as

$$P_i(p) = \sum_j f_j T_{ij}(p) \quad (11.140)$$

Retail location

We will use models like those in equations (11.51) and (11.52), but using al interaction notation. We do have an inner iteration on this occasion. So w define interaction variables $S_{ij}^{HRk}(p, q)$ and $S_{ij}^{WRk}(p, q)$, using an obviou notation. Then, from equations (11.51) and (11.52) we get, for the first inne iteration

$$S_{ij}^{HRk}(p, 1) = A_i^{HRk}(p, 1) e_i^{Hk} P_i(p) W_j^{HRk} f_1^H(c_{ij}) \quad (11.141)$$

where

$$A_i^{HRk}(p, 1) = 1 \bigg/ \sum_{j=1}^n W_j^{HRk} f_1^H(c_{ij}) \quad (11.142)$$

Similarly

$$S_{ij}^{WRk}(p, 1) = A_i^{WRk}(p, 1) e_i^{Wk} E_i(p) W_j^{WRk} f_1^W(c_{ij}) \quad (11.143)$$

where

$$A_i^{WRk}(p, 1) = 1 \bigg/ \sum_{j=1}^n W_j^{WRk} f_1^W(c_{ij}) \quad (11.144)$$

Total retail activity, on which the constraints are judged, is then obtained from

$$E_j^{Rk}(p, 1) = \sum_i \{ S_{ij}^{HRk}(p, 1) + S_{ij}^{WRk}(p, 1) \} \quad (11.145)$$

We then define sets $Z_3^k(p, q)$ and $Z_4^k(p, q)$ as before such that

$$j \in Z_3^k(p, q) \quad \text{if } E_j^{Rk}(p, q) \leqslant z^{k\min}$$

$$\text{and } E_j^{Rk}(p, q) \leqslant q \min \{ E_j^{Rk}(p, q) \} \quad (11.146)$$

Using the same definition as in relation to equation (11.39), and

$$Z_3^k(p, q) \cup Z_4^k(p, q) = Z \tag{11.147}$$

Then

$$S_{ij}^{HRk}(p, q) = 0, \qquad j \in Z_3^k(p, q) \tag{11.148}$$

$$S_{ij}^{HRk}(p, q) = A_i^{HRk}(p, q) e_i^{Hk} P_i(p) W_j^{HRk} f_k^H(c_{ij}) \qquad j \in Z_4^k(p, q) \tag{11.149}$$

where

$$A_i^{HRk}(p, q) = 1 \bigg/ \sum_{j \in Z_4^k(p, q)} W_j^{HRk} f_k^H(c_{ij}) \tag{11.150}$$

Similarly,

$$S_{ij}^{WRk}(p, q) = 0, \qquad j \in Z_3^k(p, q) \tag{11.151}$$

$$S_{ij}^{WRk}(p, q) = A_i^{WRk}(p, q) e_i^{Wk} E_i(p) W_j^{WRk} f_k^W(c_{ij}), \qquad j \in Z_4^k(p, q) \tag{11.152}$$

where

$$A_i^{WRk}(p, q) = 1 \bigg/ \sum_{j \in Z_4^k(p, q)} W_j^{WRk} f_k^W(c_{ij}) \tag{11.153}$$

$$E_j^{Rk}(p, q + 1) = \sum_i \{ S_{ij}^{HRk}(p, q) + S_{ij}^{WRk}(p, q) \} \tag{11.154}$$

Equations (11.146) to (11.154) are solved iteratively until $q = q_{\text{fin}}$, which is reached when $Z_3^k(p, q_{\text{fin}})$ is the null set. Then equations (11.43) to (11.45) are as before.

The modified Lowry model just described is, arguably, the best modification available in that it contains the best available (possibly with the addition of an inner iteration in the residential sub-model, as indicated earlier) sub-models and constraint procedures, but retains all the main features of Lowry's original model. As mentioned earlier, Batty (1971, 1972-A) has shown that the constraint procedures can be incorporated in a matrix version of the model, though he uses a much simpler land-use accounting mechanism than Lowry himself. Essentially, the procedure involves incorporating balancing factors as needed to meet constraints into the A and B matrices. However, the constraints can only be checked in an outer loop *after* each inversion of the main matrix; the full land-use accounting equations could also easily be incorporated at this stage. Batty at each outer iteration adjusts the balancing factors, as mentioned earlier, but does not put them into a full inner iteration procedure. This means that the balancing factor convergence is part of the overall outer convergence, as noted. An alternative to this would be to invert the matrix and calculate the new distributions, to check the constraints and then to find the balancing factors in an inner iteration before recycling through the outer loop. Since one of the effects of using the matrix procedure would be at least to generate *all* population and employment in the first cycle through the outer loop, such a procedure may be quite efficient. However, unless the matrix inversion method is particularly quick, it may be just as efficient to use the non-matrix modified model described above. Mathematically, both procedures should produce equivalent answers.

This is an appropriate point to introduce another variant of the Lowry model; appropriate because it offers an alternative constraining procedure and in so doing, also offers a supply-side mechanism. The discussion of supply in relation to the location models of Chapter 10 applies again here, and so we need not repeat it. Essentially, supply is represented by the attraction factor in the two location sub-models. The developers of the Cambridge model (Echenique, Crowther and Lindsay, 1969) choose floorspace as a means of attraction. They find from empirical evidence that floorspace can be estimated in a separate supply-side spatial interaction model which distributes it around basic employment; implicitly, they estimate total available floorspace from the given amount of basic employment. The quantity actually used by the basic employment sector is then subtracted, to give a distribution of available floorspace for residential and retail use. The residential and retail location submodels are then spatial interaction models in which available floorspace is the measure of attraction. There is an iterative procedure very similar to Lowry's original, but with different constraint checking and related action procedures. This works as follows: after the residential location sub-model is run, floorspace needed (obtained by applying a standard factor) is estimated and checked against available space. Any population overflow is noted. The retail model is then run and the floorspace constraint again checked. Retail use outbids residential use, so that if there is a shortfall, an appropriate number of people allocated to the zone are also counted as overflow. The two overflows are then added and a subsidiary spatial interaction model allocates this back to employment centres to be re-allocated with newly generated employment on the next iteration. (Clearly, an incremental procedure is used). On the next iteration, available floorspace excludes any already taken up. The iteration proceeds until convergence is achieved in the usual way.

Lowry model modifications of a different kind are reported by Cordey Hayes, Broadbent and Massey (1971) and Barras *et al.* (1971) in relation to a model developed at the Centre for Environmental Studies. This model again utilizes 'best available' spatial interaction models as location models, and some useful work is carried out on the nature of basic and service employment in relation to the overall employment sectors. The main innovation, however, is the introduction of a hierarchical model structure which is particularly useful when the study area decomposes into a number of fairly self-contained ub-regions. Another feature of this presentation is the unusually explicit treatment of external zones.

The material presented in this section should form a 'principles of Lowry model building' in the sense that the depths of the model and some of its important variants have been explored. For alternative summarizing views of developments of the Lowry model, the reader is referred to the papers by Goldner (1971) and Batty (1972-A). The discussion could be taken a good deal further. A number of relatively untouched issues will be mentioned in the rest of this section, but serious discussion is postponed until later in the chapter as the related issues are applicable to most general models. However, at this stage a shopping list may be useful.

We can see from Chapters 7 and 8 that the aggregative models associated with the Lowry model could be improved. A proper demographic model could be used instead of the simple assumption relating total population to basic employment. On the economic side, an input–output model could be used. It is often stated that the Lowry model builds on an economic base model, but this criticism is misleading and unfair to Lowry's model. It arises because of Lowry's use of the term 'basic employment', but he clearly intended the definition to be based on the *locational* behaviours of sectors (though this is obviously correlated with 'export' notions). If, in fact, an input–output model were used to predict employment by sector, the Lowry model form need not change, showing its real independence of economic base concepts. What would happen is that the a_ks in equation (11.6), at present assumed given, would be related in a manner determined by the input–output model (Wilson, 1971, p. 125).

The iterative procedure used in the Lowry model makes it tempting to re-interpret the model as an incremental *dynamic* model and, in any case, it is useful to explore the question in this context. Again, however, the detailed discussion will be postponed until later. Dynamic versions of the model have been produced by Crecine (1964, 1968) and Batty (1972-B).

It is evident that the Lowry model has been one of the richest sources of stimulation in urban and regional model building. Some of the further developments to be discussed in the rest of this chapter have their historical roots there. However, as the causal structure, for example, is loosened, so that less depends on basic employment as a full dynamic structure is assembled, the resulting models look less and less like Lowry's original, and we can begin to consider that something new is developing.

11.4. ECONOMETRIC MODELS: THE PENN–JERSEY MODEL

We have, of course, already seen one econometric general model: that of the Traffic Research Corporation (Hill, 1965), which we discussed in Chapter

10, in the context of industrial location. It had a rather simple overall struc ture, though it was complicated in that it involved simultaneous equation and correspondingly tricky estimation procedures. The reader can refer bac to it in the context of this section. However, our principal econometric cas study is the Penn–Jersey model. Inevitably, of course, in the way that th Lowry model was much more than two spatial interaction sub-models, th Penn–Jersey is more than just a set of equations to be estimated by econc metric methods.

The very mention of 'Penn–Jersey' stirs both the heart and the nervou system of anyone involved with model building in the early 1960s. It repre sented much the most ambitious attempt of the period to build a genera model and a good deal of research was carried out under its umbrella. Fo example, the Herbert–Stevens' model described in Chapter 10 was develope in this way, and only replaced by an econometric model in the light o operational difficulties. Much of this work was reported in Penn–Jersey technical papers and some of these, again as with the Herbert–Stevens model in the journal literature. But most of this reported work was exploratory an until recently it has been difficult to obtain information on the fina operational general model. The situation has now been rectified by th publication of a substantial report by Seidman (1969) which has the un usual feature that it describes in detail the many practical problem associated with model building and is essential reading for any seriou research worker. Our task in this section, however, is to describe th Penn–Jersey model (or at least the principle of it) in such a way that reasonable understanding is achieved, and so that it can be compare with other approaches. For this reason, the notation used in Seidman' report is modified here to be more in accord with the rest of the book Further, details, particularly whole series of fine adjustments, are omitte in this presentation, and the reader requiring these is referred to the origina document. However, it is hoped that no features essential to understanding the workings of the model are omitted.

In relation to the basic Chapter 10 questions, which were raised again in Section 11.1, we are again more concerned with activity rather than stock, though in this case economic activity (measured as employment and including basic employment) as well as population activity (so that, in passing, we describe a new industrial location model). Housing and other physical stock are not explicit, though land use is. That is, subject to land use constraints, there is an implicit assumption that supply of physical stock meets demand, rather as in the Lowry model. The approach used is aggregative, rather than micro, in the usual way. However, two of the major sub-models, concerned with residential and manufacturing employment location, are *marginal* rather than cross-sectional, and so again this case study illustrates something new for us in this respect.

The overall structure of the model as a general model is not entirely clear from Seidman's report, but an attempt is made in Figure 11.3 to summarize it in a form to make it comparable with other models.

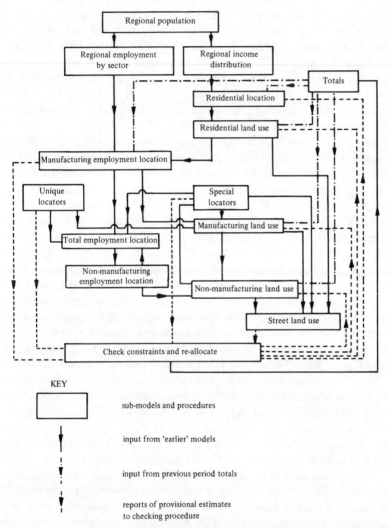

Figure 11.3 Structure of the Penn–Jersey model.

There is a definite sequence for working through the sub-models. This has some implications in relation to assumptions about causal structure, but these are not very strong. It should also be stressed that the sequence presented here is to some extent this author's own interpretation and does not always correspond with the sequence in which the sub-models are discussed in Seidman's report.

The model operates sequentially in time through a series of 5-year periods. We shall take one of these periods to be from t to $t + T$ in our usual way. The first sub-model is concerned with regional demographic analysis. This utilizes a cohort survival model similar in principle to that described in Chapter 7 except that it has a category for 'race' as well as for age and sex. A rather simple assumption is made about *net* migration which seems to perpetuate whatever happens to be the base-year pattern. However, the model is sufficiently similar to our Chapter 7 model that we shall say no more about it here. For details, the reader is referred to Chapter IX of Seidman's (1969) report and a paper by Chevan (1965).

Figure 11.3 shows that the next two sub-models are directly connected to the demographic model. This is most important for the regional employment model since it means that the simple and rather unusual assumption is being made that employment is just related to population via age–sex specific economic activity rates. The unemployment rate is held constant at 6%. This procedure is in conflict with that implied by Chapters 7 and 8 which suggest implicitly that there should be separate regional demographic and economic models and that the relative balance of labour force and jobs should imply something about migration and activity rates. However, in this case, such a simple procedure produces an estimate of the total labour force and a simple linear regression model is used to allocate this to different employment sectors. The other model directly connected to the demographic model is the income distribution model. Historical evidence is presented to show that the percentages of population in different income quintiles have remained quite constant over time. This distribution is then used in the income projection model, the main task of which now becomes the prediction of future median income and the estimation of the new income-class boundaries. Clearly, some assumption has to be made about the median, and this is done. In the model, four income classes are used, and the projection task is to adjust the boundaries of the classes for future periods. This procedure is important, and will feature in the first sub-model to be discussed in detail below.

The unique locators and special locators are handled at the outset, outside the main model. Unique locators are those for which employment distribution and land use are handled in this way: either because they have unique locational characteristics or simply because there is not the expertise available to handle them. Special locators have employment handled in this way, but land use determined within the model. Unique locators were such things as agriculture, mining, passenger stations, universities and most utilities, and special locators included hospitals and government. A full list is given in Seidman (1969), p. 210, but clearly the actual list would vary from study area to study area.

Figure 11.3 then shows that the seven principal sub-models of the Penn–Jersey model are executed in sequence: residential location, residential land use, manufacturing employment location, manufacturing land use, non-manufacturing employment (henceforth called 'service' for brevity, even if not exactly correct), service land use and street land use. One box shows the estimation of the total employment distribution since, as we shall see, this is determined rather as in the Lowry model in an inner iterative procedure involving the service sub-model. The dashed lines then show that all the outputs of the various sub-models are input to a constraint checking and re-allocation procedure before new totals are formed for the distributions at the end of the period. We shall now describe each of these sub-models and procedures in turn.

Although we do not discuss the regional population and employment models any further, we should define the variables which represent their outputs. The output of the demographic model which forms the input to the income distribution model is simply total households in the region. We shall use the symbol P for this, although it refers to households rather than population, to make the notation more easily comparable with that used for the Lowry model. Again, as with the Lowry model, an omitted index will imply summation. The regional economic model gives us employment by sector, for which we shall write E^{Mk} as the kth manufacturing sector and E^{Sk} as the kth service sector.

Since this model is recursive, it is useful to attach time labels to our variables. We shall use t for the beginning of the period and $t + T$ for the end, and $(t, t + T)$ to represent the period itself.

Income distribution at the regional level

The task of this model is to allocate the total population $P(t + T)$ to income groups $P^w(t + T)$, where w is an index which identifies discrete income groups. The distribution of households around median income has been shown by historical analysis to be remarkably constant. Suppose this distribution is given as $f(I/\bar{I})$: the proportion of households with income I when the median income is $\bar{I}$. Thus, if $\bar{I}(t + T)$ can be forecast, then

$$P^I(t + T) = P(t + T)f(I|\bar{I}) \qquad (11.155)$$

can be obtained as population with income I or more precisely as a population distribution, since I is a continuous variable. The main problem is then to identify future income *classes*: that is, the definition of the boundaries of each w class for future time periods. The essence of this task is: the classes w are used to represent types of locational behaviour and therefore it is necessay to estimate classes such that locational behaviour is equivalent in different time periods. The mechanism for doing this is as follows: let $a_w(t)$ be the upper boundary of income class w at time t. $a_0(t)$ is zero, of course, for all t. Then,

$$a_w(t + T) = \left[1 + \pi_1 \frac{(\bar{I}(t + T) - \bar{I}(t))}{\bar{I}(t)}\right]a_w(t) \tag{11.156}$$

π_1 is a parameter which could be anything between 0 and 1. At the lower extreme, the boundaries do not change; at the upper end, the boundaries move in proportion to the median income. (As many parameters are involved in this model, we shall denote them by π with a subscript, as otherwise we shall run out of letters. Usually, parameters will be period specific, but we shall not show $(t, t + T)$ specifically to avoid too much messiness.)

Finally,

$$P^w(t + T) = \int_{a_{w-1}(t+T)}^{a_w(t+T)} P^I(t + T)\,\mathrm{d}I \tag{11.157}$$

Residential location

$P^w(t + T)$ now has to be allocated among zones j. In these models the first estimates are provisional and may be amended following later constraint checks. So we estimate $P_j^w(t + T)$ as follows

$$P_j^w(t + T) = P_j^w(t) + T \cdot \frac{\mathrm{d}P_j^w}{\mathrm{d}t} \tag{11.158}$$

$$\frac{\mathrm{d}P_j^w}{\mathrm{d}t} = \frac{\sum_i [M_{ij}^w(t, t + T) - M_{ji}^w(t, t + T)] + p^w P_j^w(t)}{T} \tag{11.159}$$

where p^w allocates a share of the change from $P^w(t)$ to $P^w(t + T)$ to zone j; p^w is calculated as follows:

$$p^w \sum_j P_j^w(t) = \sum_j [P_j^w(t + T) - P_j^w(t)] \tag{11.160}$$

$$M_{ij}^w(t, t + T) = \pi_2^w P_i^w(t) A_j^E(t, t + T). \text{Max } [0, (U_j^w(t, t + T) - U_i^w(t, t + T))] \tag{11.161}$$

$$A_j^E(t, t + T) = \text{Min } [2A_j^R(t), A_j^R(t) + A_j(t) - A_j^u(t) - A_j^R(t) - A_j^M(t) - A_j^S(t)] \tag{11.162}$$

$$U_i^w(t, t + T) = \sum_l a_l^w X_{li}^R \tag{11.163}$$

The notation used is an obvious one ($A_j(t)$ is currently useable land, $A_j^u(t)$ is 'utility' land, for streets, and the others are as in the Lowry model, but with R for H, M for B and S for R) and the sequence of equations presented above tells their own story. The mechanism involved is quite different to Lowry's and different to the Herbert–Steven's model, but it has its own elegance.

Equation (11.158) is simply an accounting equation, which says that the main task in this dynamic model is to estimate the rate of change which has been formally written as dP_j^w/dt. In equation (11.159), this is estimated as net migration—since $M_{ij}^w(t, t + T)$ is migration of w-households from i to j in the period—plus the zone's share of growth, $p^w P_j^w(t)$. The associated migration model is presented in equation (11.161). Movement only takes place from i to j if $U_j^w > U_i^w$, where U_j^w is a linear sum of independent variables, given in equation (11.163), which express the residential desirability of an area. Migration from i is assumed proportional to $P_i^w(t)$, and to j, to A_j^E, which is called the 'effective area'. The equation for this is (11.162), and this says that effective area is the minimum of residential land plus available land, twice residential land at the beginning of the period. This prevents large 'empty' zones from becoming too attractive, and represents the fact that no zone is likely to more than double its residential land use in one period. With this minimum of explanation, the reader should himself further digest the workings of the model. Further comments will be made on it in a later section.

The actual independent variables used in equation (11.163) are as follows:

$$X_{1j}^R(t, t + T) = \frac{P_j^3(t) + P_j^4(t)}{\sum_w P_j^w(t)} \qquad (11.164)$$

Since four income groups were used, this variable is 'proportion of population of j in the two highest income groups at the beginning of the time period'.

$$X_{2j}^R(t, t + T) = \frac{\sum_w P_j^w(t)}{A_j^R(t)} \qquad (11.165)$$

and this is net residential density at the beginning of the period.

$$X_{3j}^R(t, t + T) = Y_j(t) \qquad (11.166)$$

where $Y_j(t)$ is a weighted sum of different accessibilities at the beginning of the time period, in fact, it is usually taken as inaccessibility. This concept utilizes intervening opportunities concepts (cf. Appendix 2).

$$X_{4j}^R(t, t + T) = \text{Min} \left[\frac{A_j(t) - A_j^u(t) - A_j^R(t) - A_j^M(t) - A_j^S(t)}{A_j(t)}, 0 \cdot 6 \right] \qquad (11.167)$$

which is the proportion of land available for residential use at the beginning of the period, with a maximum of $0 \cdot 6$.

$$X_{5j}^R(t, t + T) = \frac{A_j^M(t) + A_j^S(t)}{A_j(t)} \qquad (11.168)$$

is the proportion of land in 'economic' use.

It is appropriate at this stage to explain how such a model is an econometric model and how the coefficients are estimated. This is done in outline only, and the reader is referred to Seidman's (1969) report for more details. The coefficients to be estimated are the a_i^w's of equation (11.163). Of course, they cannot be estimated directly from this equation because the U_i^ws are not directly measurable. What happens is that the intermediate variables in equations (11.159)–(11.163) are eliminated and an expression is obtained for zonal population change as a function of these coefficients. The resulting formulation is non-linear because of the step function introduced in the migration equation (11.161). Then, in principle, the coefficients can be estimated using non-linear multiple regression analysis. Steepest-descent methods are used, and the problem is made harder by the fact that many of the variables involved are collinear. An attempt to alleviate this problem was made by rotating the variables using component analysis, using the transformed variables for the regression analysis, and then transforming back again. In other words, the practical complexities must be added to the above presentation which emphasizes only the conceptual aspects.

So far, the units employed have always been households. When the residential location model has been run in this way, zonal populations are calculated by multiplying households by average household size for the zone. This is taken as the base-year household size for the zone, multiplied by the ratio of regional household size at the end of the period to regional household size at the beginning. The two factors in this ratio are obtained from the demographic model.

Residential land use

The outputs of the residential location model complete the set of inputs needed for the residential land use models. We have already introduced residential land use in j as the variable $A_j^R(t)$. At the end of the period, we have

$$A_j^R(t + T) = a_j^R(t + T) \sum_w P_j^w(t + T) \qquad (11.169)$$

where $a_j^R(t)$ is the amount of residential land consumed per household in j. This is the quantity which is estimated in an econometric equation:

$$a_j^R(t + T) = \pi_3 (\bar{I}_j(t + T) - \bar{C}_j(t + T))^{\pi_4} \times \exp \left[\sum_l b_l X_{lj}^{RL}(t + T) \right] \quad (11.170)$$

where π_3, π_4 and the b_ls are sets of parameters to be determined. $\bar{I}_j(t + T)$ is the median income in zone j and this can be calculated from the $P_j^w(t + T)$s. $\bar{C}_j(t + T)$ is the expenditure on transport for an equivalent time period to that in which income is measured. Presumably it can be taken as proportional to accessibility. The independent variables $X_{lj}^{RL}(t + T)$ are relative accessibilities to opportunities of type l which will be defined shortly. Thus the theory underlying this model has some connections (and was designed to have) with

.lonso's (1964) approach: residential land consumption is a function of
vailable income after transport costs have been deducted, the position of the
rban margin (as will be seen shortly) and accessibilities. The urban margin
lays a role through the definition of relative accessibility. Previously, we
itroduced a weighted accessibility, Y_j; we now employ $Y_j^l(t)$, accessibility to
pportunities of type l in zone j, and $Y_m^l(t)$ (which is obtained by averaging
.ver zones at the margin), the accessibility at the margin. Then

$$X_{lj}^{RL}(t + T) = Y_m^l(t) - Y_j^l(t) \tag{11.171}$$

'he same principle is used to estimate the price of a household plot of land as

$$\,_j^R(t + T) = \pi_5(\bar{I}_j(t + T) - \bar{C}_j(t + T))^{\pi_6} \times \exp\left[\sum_l b_l^p X_{lj}^{RL}(t + T)\right] \tag{11.172}$$

vhere π_5, π_6 and the b_l^ps are again coefficients to be estimated. Once more,
.on-linear multiple regression analysis is used.

Manufacturing employment location

This sub-model uses the same mathematical framework as the residential
ocation model, and so we can first define the variables and then present the
equations with relatively little explanation. Let $E_j^{Mk}(t)$ and $E_j^{Sk}(t)$ be the
.mounts of employment in zone j at time t in the kth manufacturing sector
and the kth retail sector respectively. Let $M_{ij}^{Mk}(t, t + T)$ be the 'migration' of
,obs from i to j in period t to $t + T$ for the kth manufacturing sector; similarly,
we can define $M_{ij}^{Sk}(t, t + T)$. U_i^{Mk} and U_i^{Sk} are the terms equivalent to U_i in
the residential model, and X_{li}^{Mk} and X_{li}^{Sk} are the sets of independent variables.
The model equations for the manufacturing sector are then:

$$E_j^{Mk}(t + T) = E_j^{Mk}(t) + T\frac{dE_j^{Mk}}{dt} \tag{11.173}$$

$$\frac{dE_j^{Mk}}{dt} = \sum_i \{N_{ji}^{Mk}(t, t + T) - M_{ij}^{Mk}(t, t + T)\} + p^{Mk}E_j^{Mk}(t) \tag{11.174}$$

where

$$p^{Mk}\sum_j E_j^{Mk}(t) = E^{Mk}(t + T) - E^{Mk}(t) \tag{11.175}$$

$$M_{ij}^{Mk}(t, t + T) = \pi_6^{Bk}E_i^{Mk}(t)A_j^{EMk}(t, t + T) \text{ Max } [0, (U_j^{Mk} - U_i^{Mk})] \tag{11.175}$$

A^{EMk} is the effective area for this sector. It is not clear whether this should be
all manufacturing-sector land or a proportion, and so we include a parameter

which can be adjusted if necessary:

$$A_j^{EMk}(t, t + T)$$
$$= \pi_7^{Mk} \text{Min} [2A^M(t), A^M(t) + A(t) - A^u(t) - A^R(t) - A^M(t) - A^S(t)] \quad (11.176)$$

$$U_i^{Mk} = \sum_l a_l^{Mk} X_{li}^{Mk}(t + T) \quad (11.177)$$

The same comments on estimation, component analysis and 'reduced form' made at the end of the section on the residential location model apply here.

The independent variables used in the Penn–Jersey study for this purpose were:

$$X_{1j}^{Bk}(t + T) = \frac{A_j^R(t + T)}{\sum_w p_j^w(t + T)} \quad (11.178)$$

that is, net residential density at time $t + T$.

$$X_{2j}^{Bk}(t + T) = \text{miles of navigable waterfront} \quad (11.179)$$

$$X_{3j}^{Bk}(t + T) = \frac{P_j^3(t + T) + P_j^4(t + T)}{\sum_w p_j^w(t + T)} \quad (11.180)$$

$$X_{4j}^{Mk}(t + T) = \frac{\sum_k E_j^{Mk}(t)}{A_j(t)} \quad (11.181)$$

that is, gross manufacturing employment density at time t.

$$X_{5j}^{Mk}(t + T) = \text{Min} \left[\frac{A_j(t) - A_j^M(t) - A_j^R(t) - A_j^M(t) - A_j^S(t)}{A_j(t)}, \quad 0 \cdot 6 \right] \quad (11.182)$$

which is proportion of land available, with a maximum of 0·6.

$$X_{6j}^{Bk}(t + T) = Y_j(t) \quad (11.183)$$

which is the weighted accessibility term used previously.

Manufacturing land use

We can next proceed to estimate manufacturing land use at time $t + T$. Simple trend-projection formulae are used in this case, as it proved too difficult to identify good econometric relationships, but parameters are included which allow the past trends to be adjusted. Slightly different procedures are used according to whether the zone has an increasing or declining amount of manufacturing employment.

For zones j in which manufacturing employment is decreasing,

$$A_j^M(t + T) = A_j^M(t) \left[1 + \pi_8 \frac{\sum_k [E_j^{Mk}(t + T) - E_j^{Mk}(t)]}{\sum_k E_j^{EM}(t)} \right] \quad (11.184)$$

where π_8 is a parameter which is less than one if land is given up less than proportionately to employment decline, as would be expected.

For zones j in which manufacturing employment is increasing, it is convenient first to define a number of sets. All zones are divided into five concentric rings, and the rate of increase in manufacturing land use is taken as proportional to the change in employment in all zones in the ring of which a particular zone is a member. Thus, let $Z^M(j)$ be the set of zones in the ring of which j is a member. Then

$$A_j^M(t + T) = A_j^M(t) + \pi_9 \sum_{j^1 \in Z^M(j)} A_{j^1}^M(t) \cdot \frac{\sum_k [E_j^{Mk}(t + T) - E_j^{Mk}(t)]}{\sum_{j^1 \in Z^M(j)} \sum_k E_{j^1}^{Mk}(t)} \quad (11.185)$$

π_9 is a parameter which is less than one if new firms are locating at a higher density than at time t, and is greater than one for the opposite situation.

Service employment location

As indicated earlier, this sub-model is a total cross-section model. Essentially, it is a spatial interaction model of the type with which the reader of this book will by now be very familiar. However, in detail, it employs an unusual mixture of intervening opportunities and gravity model concepts. The model evidently has its origins in a paper by Harris (1964).

The main variables are $S_{ij}^{HSk}(t)$ and $S_{ij}^{WSk}(t)$; the first of these is the amount of service activity generated in zone j in sector k from households in zone i, and the second is a similar variable for service activity generated from workplaces. Then, if π_{10} and π_{11} are factors which convert from activity measures, such as turnover, to employment, then

$$E_j^{Sk}(t + T) = \sum_i (\pi_{10} S_{ij}^{HSk}(t + T) + \pi_{11} S_{ij}^{WSk}(t + T)) \quad (11.186)$$

The spatial interaction model for retail activity generated from households is obtained as follows:

$$S_{ij}^{HSk}(t + T) = O_i^{Hk}(t + T)[R_{ij_{\mu-1}}^{HSk}(t + T) - R_{ij_\mu}^{HSk}(t + T)] \quad (11.187)$$

where $O_i^{Hk}(t + T)$ is the total amount of retail activity in sector k generated by residents of i, and $R_{ij}^{HSk}(t + T)$ is the probability that a unit of activity will pass beyond the μth zone, written, j_μ, away from i. This 'ordering' of zones is crucial to the intervening opportunities model. The notation used here was first presented in a paper by the author (Wilson, 1967). Strictly, j_μ should be $j_\mu(i)$, of course, but the i is left as 'understood' (see Appendix 2). Then

$$R_{ij_\mu}^{HSk}(t + T) = K_i^{Hk}[1 + \pi_{12}^{Hk} W_{ij}^{Hk}(t + T)]^{-\pi_{13}^{Hk}} \times e^{-\pi_{14}^{Hk} W_{ij}^{Hk}(t + T)} \quad (11.188)$$

[In a conventional intervening opportunities model, this expression would be simply

$$R_{ij}^{HSk}(t + T) = K\, e^{-\pi^{Hk} W_{ij}^{Hk}(t + T)} \qquad (11.189)]$$

K_i^{Hk} is a normalizing factor for each zone i to ensure that

$$\sum_{\mu} R_{ij_\mu}^{HSk}(t + T) = 1 \qquad (11.190)$$

and so

$$K_i^{Hk} = [(1 + \pi_{12}^{Hk} W_{ij_0}^{Hk}(t + T))^{-\pi_{13}^{Hk}}\, e^{-\pi_{14}^{Hk} W_{ij0}^{Hk}(t + T)}$$
$$- (1 + \pi_{12}^{Hk} W_{ij_n}^{Hk}(t + T))^{-\pi_{13}^{Hk}}\, e^{-\pi_{14}^{Hk} W_{ij_n}^{Hk}(t + T)}]^{-1} \qquad (11.191)$$

Conventionally, W_{ij} is the number of intervening opportunities between i and j, but in this case it is a weighted sum of intervening opportunities and distance:

$$W_{ij}^{Hk}(t + T) = \pi_{15}^{Hk} V_{ij}^{Hk}(t + T) + (1 - \pi_{15}^{Hk}) c_{ij} \qquad (11.192)$$

where $V_{ij}^{Hk}(t + T)$ is the number of intervening opportunities at $t + T$ scaled by a zone-size factor, and c_{ij} is the usual generalized cost of travel. π_{15}^{Hk} is a parameter which measures the relative importance of intervening opportunities and distance.

$$V_{ij}^{Hk}(t + T) = \sum_{\substack{s.t. \\ c_{i\mu} \leqslant c_{ij}}} v_{1\mu}(t + T) s_j^{\pi_{16}^{Hk}} \qquad (11.193)$$

where $v_j(t + T)$ is the number of opportunities at $t + T$ in j, and sj is a scale factor relating to zone size. This equation has been modified from that given in Seidman (1969), as the verbal and mathematical description of the equations differ. We have followed the verbal description.

A formally similar set of equations to (11.187)–(11.193) could be presented for $S_{ij}^{WSk}(t + T)$.

The service model is thus an extremely ambitious one and the successful development, calibration and use of this model in the Penn–Jersey study was a substantial achievement in itself. Five parameters have to be estimated for each sector, for each of the two sources of demand for service activity. Seidman (1969) presents results for only four parameters using a notation in a table which is inconsistent with the text, and so there was scope for misinterpretation here. Steepest-descent methods were used for this.

The main purpose of this model, of course, is to estimate service employment, but to estimate O_i^W for the S_{ij}^{WSk} model, total employment in zone i is needed. This is initially guessed, and there is an iterative procedure for this part of the overall model as indicated in Figure 11.3. There is another possible reason for having this sub-iteration: the opportunities measure, v_j^k, may itself be taken as employment and a similar problem would arise.

Service land use

We can now proceed to estimate service land use, $A_j^S(t + T)$. Once again it proved impossible to establish good econometric relationships, and therefore a method was used which is identical to that for manufacturing land use. Thus, we can repeat the equivalents of equations (11.184) and (11.185) without further explanation: for zones in which service employment is decreasing

$$A_j^S(t + T) = A_j^S(t)\left[1 + \pi_{17} \frac{\sum_k [E_j^{Sk}(t + T) - E_j^{Sk}(t)]}{\sum_k E_j^{Sk}(t)} \right] \qquad (11.194)$$

and for zones in which service employment is increasing

$$A_j^S(t + T) = A_j^S(t) + \pi_{18} \sum_{j' \in Z^S(j)} A_{j'}^S(t) \sum_{j' \in Z^S(j)} \frac{\sum_k [E_{j'}^{Sk}(t + T) - E_{j'}^{Sk}(t)]}{\sum_{j' \in Z^S(j)}\sum_1 E_{j'}^{Sk}(t)} \qquad (11.195)$$

Street land use

A simple linear model was used to estimate the change in street land use. For any land use l, let

$$A_j^l(t, t + T) = A_j^l(t + T) - A_j^l(t) \qquad (11.196)$$

These quantities have now been obtained for all land uses except streets (denoted by the superscript u). Then the model is

$$A_j^u(t + T) = A_j^u(t) + A_j^u(t, t + T) \qquad (11.197)$$

where

$$A_j^u(t, t + T) = \pi_{19} A_j^R(t, t + T) + \pi_{20} A_j^M(t, t + T) + \pi_{21} A_j^S(t, t + T) \qquad (11.198)$$

where π_{19}, π_{20} and π_{21} are coefficients estimated by regression analysis. Seidman (1969) actually divides $A_j^S(t, t + T)$ into retail and office uses, but we have not done so here in order not to introduce new variables at this stage.

This completes our account of the main sub-models of the Penn–Jersey general model, apart from two final points. First, as indicated on Figure 11.3, all sub-model estimates are provisional and therefore subjected to a number of feasibility checks. These range from simple matters, such as avoiding negative values of obviously positive quantities (the sort of thing which can turn up in econometric models), to maximum values of rates of growth or decline in individual districts or groups of districts. Excess is then re-allocated. Complex procedures are used which will not be described in detail here. Seidman notes that the procedures did generate problems and ends by recommending that simple procedures be used where possible: 'Considerable time might have been saved if we had (1) set simple limits to maximum rates of growth and decline for each dependent variable and (2) prorated all excesses or deficits to other districts in proportion to the totals in the districts, rather than to projected rates of growth of the districts.' However, as was clear from our discussion of the Lowry model, constraint procedures *are* important, and are probably most significant in adding a realistic 'richness' to the model. This is especially true of an econometric model which is more likely to turn up odd results, such as negative population, than a model which is internally constrained on many matters.

The second point to note in conclusion is the absence of a transport model. However, it should be emphasized that the Penn–Jersey model as described here was intended to produce land use and activity distribution *inputs* for a transport model, and a Chapter 9-type model was subsequently used in this way.

11.5. OTHER APPROACHES TO BUILDING GENERAL MODELS

So far in this chapter we have outlined in some detail two general models, the ones whose 'style' is most closely in accord with the rest of the book. This very brief section simply records the fact that other approaches are possible and outlines some of them in the barest detail.

An important class of general models is that of those based on a particular method of analysis developed in the context of control engineering (Forrester, 1961, 1968). This mode of analysis has been built into a special computer language called DYNAMO by workers at M.I.T. The essence of the method is simple: model variables are defined which fall into three categories: level, rate or auxiliary variables. In diagrammatic terms, they are represented by the symbols shown in Figure 11.4.

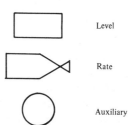

Figure 11.4 Forrester's symbols for level, rate and auxiliary variables

The level variables describe the state of the system at some time t and the rate variables the changes in level variables in some period, say t to $t + T$. The auxiliary variables are functions of any other available level, rate or auxiliary variables. A simple feedback loop is shown in Figure 11.5.

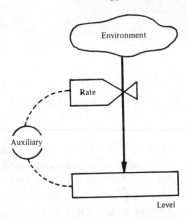

Figure 11.5   Simple feedback loop

A level variable is changed by an inflow from the environment 'controlled' by a rate variable. The rate variable is a function of an auxiliary variable which is itself connected to the level variable—hence the feedback. The system of feedback loops employed in a model can be much more complicated, and such an example will be shown later. In the DYNAMO language, a typical equation for a level variable is:

$$U.K. = U.J + (DT)(UA.JK + UB.JK + LTU.JK - UD.JK - UTL.JK) \quad (11.199)$$

U is some level variable, J and K represent times (the equivalent of our t and $t + T$), DT the time interval, UA.JK is a rate, UA for the period J to K, and similarly for the other rates. A typical equation for the rate variable is:

$$UA.JK = (U.J + L.J)(UAN)(AMMP.J) \quad (11.200)$$

where UAN and AMMP.J are auxiliary variables. These may be specified as numbers or in further equations. It is now easy to see how structural flow diagrams such as that of Figure 11.5 can be turned into equations in the DYNAMO language.

The first general model to be produced using this language was that for the Susquehanna River Basin, (Hamilton *et al.*, 1969). The river basin is a large region, divided into eight sub-regions for modelling purposes. Thus the spatial level of resolution is a coarse one. Further, the demographic and economic sub-models are applied to each sub-region more or less separately. Thus the model has the simple structure shown in Figure 11.6.

A separate water model was built as this represented one of the main foci of interest of the particular study. Thus, in terms of the structure of this book, a Chapter 7-type demographic model is to be used with a Chapter 8-like

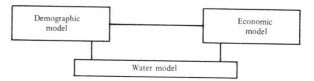

Figure 11.6   Structure of the Susquehanna River Basin model

economic model. The demographic model was of the Chapter 7-cohort-survival type, but looks rather different, expressed in the DYNAMO language. Somewhat simpler assumptions were made about migration. The economic model was an economic-base model using employment units. The two models interacted through the estimation of unemployment which follows from the separate use of the two sub-models. This in turn affected the migration rate in the demographic model and so there was a feedback loop between the two sub-models. In many ways, the model contains a lot of interesting detail: for example, jobs by wage are estimated. The locational analysis features are, however, very crude.

The next model to use the DYNAMO language was that of Forrester (1969). His model contains three types of component: enterprises, measured in 'productive units', houses and workers. There are three classes within each: new, mature and declining enterprises; premium, worker and underemployed housing; managerial–professional, labour and underemployed workers. These nine level variables define the state of the system and are shown related to the 22 rate variables which determine them in Figure 11.7.

The three kinds of level variable are not shown as connected on this figure but they are in fact interconnected through auxiliary variables. Figure 11.8 shows the way in which one flow rate is determined.

The equations (11.199) and (11.200) presented earlier are examples of the equations used by Forrester. The model is thus very simple in structure: the new value of a level variable is determined by the old value plus the 'rate' changes, which are themselves determined in other equations. The crucial task is then to get a good set of equations for the rate variables. Forrester makes a lot of extremely simple assumptions together with a number of more complicated ones. Neither type of assumption is justified in relation to the literature in general. Forrester's argument is that he is primarily interested in reproducing the structure of urban problems.

Neither of the two models outlined above has been empirically tested to any significant extent, and this is one of their principal weaknesses. However, in principle, this *could* be done and the sub-models and assumptions *could* be improved in relation to other work in the field. A possibly more fundamental criticism relates to the poor level of spatial resolution. Hamilton *et al.* have only eight sub-regions, while Forrester has only one together with an

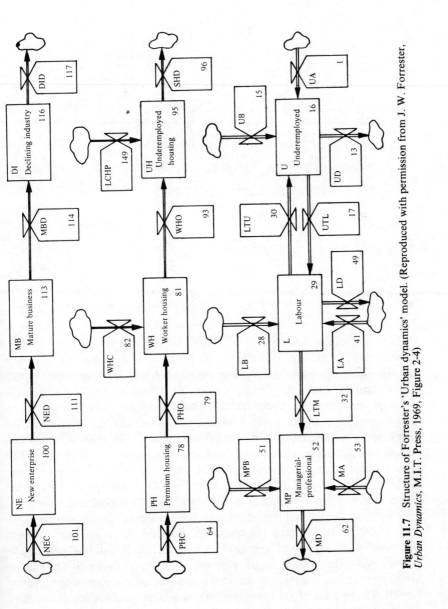

Figure 11.7 Structure of Forrester's 'Urban dynamics' model. (Reproduced with permission from J. W. Forrester, *Urban Dynamics*, M.I.T. Press, 1969, Figure 2-4)

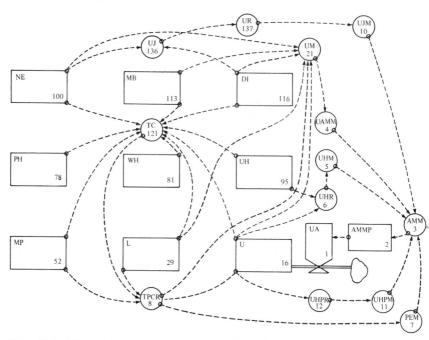

Figure 11.8 Diagram for one rate variable. (Reproduced with permission from J. W. Forrester, *Urban Dynamics*, M.I.T. Press, 1969, Figure 2.5.)

'environment' which is, of course, not modelled. It is easy to see, from equations (11.199) and (11.200) that the DYNAMO language does not at present readily lend itself to improving this situation. The only available subscripts are for time labels, which means that a new variable has to be defined and, more importantly, a separate equation written down for it, for each zonal characteristic or interzonal interaction. The tedium of this can easily be avoided by using spatial labels on subscripts (several of them) and using loops, in a language such as FORTRAN.

Three quite different approaches can be mentioned very briefly, and the reader is referred to the references cited for details. It is possible in principle to associate a model-building effort with the associated design problem and, if an appropriate objective function can be defined, to use optimization methods. Such an approach generated Schlager's (1965) 'land-use plan design model'. Next, there are a number of simulation models which use human participation, on a quasi-decision-taking basis, which are called gaming models. The essence of such games is, of course, the specification of the rules. One of the best-known games (Duke, 1967) uses a version of the Lowry model for this purpose, and the whole field is reviewed by Taylor (1972). Finally, a different approach altogether has been developed by the author (Wilson,

973-B), partly in an attempt to incorporate more realistic behavioural mechanisms into our models (including in particular, *learning* procedures) and partly to try a fresh approach to the aggregation problem.

1.6. PRINCIPLES FOR BUILDING A GENERAL MODEL

Now that we have studied examples of general models, it is appropriate to stand back for a while, and to examine their structure in a more abstract way. Then, we can identify model-building principles for general models. The argument can be summarized in five steps, as follows.

(1) The components of the system of interest, and their characteristics, should be identified.

(2) They can be grouped into sub-systems.

(3) Variables should be precisely defined in relation to spatial, temporal and sectoral aggregation questions.

(4) The mechanisms of change or causal structure of the model should then be identified.

(5) Formal model equations in terms of the variables defined under (3) can then be constructed to represent the mechanisms of (4).

We now proceed with the argument in more detail, illustrating it as we go. The 'system of interest' is simply 'that which we are interested in', and it is given an ostensive definition as the object of our analysis. The system of interest related to this book should be clear by now, at least in broad terms. More specific definitions can be constructed, as appropriate, for more specific purposes. We can suppose that the system consists of a number of components, and its state is described by the characteristics of these components. There are three main types of component in urban and regional analysis: people, organizations and physical infrastructure. The *activities* of people and organizations can be seen as characteristics of basic components; the products of activities, goods by a firm, wages for a person and so on, can be seen as characteristics of activities and hence also of the basic components. We can consider that people form a social system, and organizations an economic one. Physical infrastructure is part of the economic system, but is separately distinguished here because of its importance in urban and regional analysis. The next step is to explore the sub-system structure in more detail.

A sub-system may be defined as a sub-set of the basic components of the whole system, or a sub-set of characteristics of all components, or a sub-set of characteristics of a sub-set of components. 'Overlap' will be permitted. It should be emphasized from the outset that sub-system definition is entirely for the convenience of the analyst and it plays no fundamental role. The intention is to attempt to reduce an analytical problem of high dimensionality to a set of problems each of lower dimensionality. Steps will be taken, of course, to ensure as far as possible that the overall original dimensionality is not lost.

For urban and regional analysis, we first defined sub-systems of interest in Chapter 3. We now amend these definitions slightly for convenience in general model building. What follows is, of course, one example only since there are many possible ways of proceeding. We are interested, as before, in overall population and overall economic activity. We can anticipate the aggregation discussion and call these the spatially aggregated (SA) population and economic activity sub-systems. As we saw in Chapters 7, 8 and 10 we are interested in the spatial distribution of population and economic activity, and, for reasons which will become clear later, we shall define sub systems which describe this in two ways. First, we shall use the same component characteristic definitions as in the SA-sub-systems and call the resulting systems the spatial demographic and spatial economic sub-systems. Second, we shall identify spatial population sub-systems which relate to the major population activities and spatial economic sub-systems which relate to the spatial economy as perceived by the population. Thus, for population activities, we define sub-systems concerned with residence, workplace, utilization of services and utilization of transport facilities, and economic sub-systems associated with housing, jobs, services and transport facilities. This housing sub-system is concerned with physical infrastructure, as is the transport facilities sub-system. We shall consider that physical infrastructure associated with other economic activities is dealt with internally in the activity sub-systems. We do, however, define a sub-system for land use, which we show in broad terms as a function of the spatial economy. These definitions are shown diagrammatically in Figure 11.9. The reader will quickly recognize most of these components as sub-models which have been discussed in earlier chapters of the book.

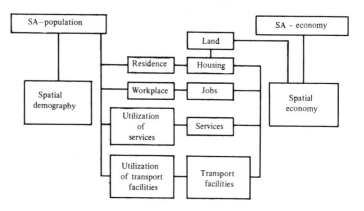

Figure 11.9   Outline of static structure of a general model

The third step of the argument is concerned with variable definitions. Variables describe components, either by giving the measured value of characteristics of a component (or each of a group of components) or by giving the number of components with certain characteristics (i.e. of a type). Both these methods of variable description, and a mixture of them, will be used. It is important to define variables which are as simply and closely associated as possible with components and their measurable characteristics. Much bad analysis results when this is not done. The main steps for variable definition are as follows:

(1) Identify the basic components.

(2) Identify the characteristics of interest associated with these components, and an aggregation decision may be involved in deciding how many characteristics to have (e.g. 'recreation' or a list of separate recreational activities).

(3) Decide how to measure characteristics: scales, intervals, groupings and so on.

(4) Decide if it is necessary to aggregate components, and how many of the original set of component characteristics to associate with the aggregate variable.

We discuss each of these points in turn. If is particularly important, as we have seen, to associate variables as closely as possible with basic components. This principle is related to accounting techniques: it is important to be able, if at all possible, to trace the life history of each component.

Then, in all the other variable definition issues, aggregation problems are involved as usual. The main problem in identifying characteristics of interest is that we nearly always identify more than we can conveniently handle. This means that, out of all the characteristics of interest, it is often necessary for practical reasons to choose a sub-set. However, we may choose a different sub-set to construct variables which relate to different sub-systems. At this point, we may conveniently introduce the idea of the *subscript list*. If, each time we define a set of characteristics for one variable, we have to use a separate subscript letter for each, then we soon run out of letters. We shall use a single letter, a subscript list, to denote a set of characteristics. This has the additional advantage of strengthening the connection between variables which are defined and the basic components to which they refer. For example, we may wish to define a variable which is the number of houses by type (size, age, tenure, etc.) by location. We write them, as in Chapter 10, as H_i^k, but k can now be considered to be a subscript list which may have more than one component.

Next, we must consider how to measure characteristics, and this is closely involved with aggregation decisions. For spatial aggregation we shall adopt our usual convention of defining location by zone, labelled $i, j, \ldots$ and so on. The level of resolution is then determined by the size of zones. Temporal aggregation refers to the time period within which an 'event', a change in value of a variable is recorded. Usually, we shall refer to events taking place within the period t to $t + T$ without specifying the exact time. The level of resolution is determined by the magnitude of T. In the limit, of course, it can be infinitesimally small. Sector aggregation decisions are determined partly by an ability to measure accurately, and partly by the amount of information we can practically carry. For either reason, we may prefer to say that a person has an income in the range of £20–25 per week, rather than that his income is £23·50. If we do this, we have to define intervals and boundary points.

So far the discussion has proceeded as though we could individually identify components. In practice, we almost always have to group them, and this is where the greatest loss of information takes place. (It would make useful study to quantify the amount of information lost in different kinds of aggregation.) Components can be grouped as follows: for any given set of characteristics we can aggregate components with similar characteristic values. For example, if $C_k(i, j, M)$ denotes that person k lives in zone i, works in zone j and is in income group M, then we can aggregate over k for fixed i, j, M and say that $C(i, j, M)$ is the number of people who live in zone i, work in zone j and are in income group M.

Typically, there will be a long list of characteristics associated with each component, each potentially useful for some purpose or other, but this kind of aggregation would usually only use a sub-set, aggregating differently to construct variables for different sub-systems (and different analytical purposes). For example, a person k may be characterized by $C_k(i, j, M, x_1, x_2, \ldots)$ and may aggregate to $C(i, j, M, x_1, x_2, \ldots)$, $C(i, j, M)$, $C(i, M)$ or $C(j, M)$ for different purposes. The problem here is that whereas $C_k(i, j, M, x_1, x_2, \ldots)$ can be specified as a set of values of $i, j, M, \ldots$ for $k = 1, 2, \ldots N$ where N is total population, and so involves $N \times k$ numbers where k is the number of characteristics, $C(i, j, M, x_1, x_2, \ldots)$ is a matrix involving

$$\prod_{n=1}^{K} c_n$$

where c_n is the number of cells associated with the nth characteristic. This number increases very rapidly with K.

We noted earlier that there is another kind of variable associated with component aggregation. This arises when a component characteristic is detached and aggregated on its own. The aggregation may relate to a sub-set of the component population defined by further characteristics. Thus, in relation to an earlier example, M_k^{ij} may be the income of the kth person (who lives in i and works in j). Then, keeping i, j fixed,

$$\sum_{k \in (i, j)} M_k^{ij}$$

s the total income of people who live in i and work in j. It is more usual to construct an average from such an aggregated variable. A more familiar example is p_i^k as the average price of a type k have in zone i.

Finally, we define two special types of variable. For any variable, $y(t)$, which takes some value at time t, we define $\Delta y(t, t + T)$ to be the change in that variable from t to $t + T$. In some cases we shall formulate main model equations in terms of $y(t)$, total cross-section, and sometimes in terms of $\Delta y(t, t + T)$, marginal. Secondly, it is useful to introduce variables which are *external* to the system, but which affect system variables. They will usually be denoted as $x_1, x_2, \ldots$. This means that they can appear as independent variables in the system model equations, but do not appear as dependent variables. Their role will become clearer later. This concludes the rather lengthy discussion on variable construction, which will be illustrated in the next section. Meanwhile, we must proceed to the remaining two items: mechanisms of change (causal structure) and the structure of the model equations.

This discussion is, of course, a reworking of the model-builder's 'check list' discussion of Chapter 4 in relation to the particular context of building a general model. Roughly speaking, we have reached the stage where we should be dealing with 'treatment of time' and 'theory', which we have here called the mechanisms of change. In this case some sub-models will be marginal, others cross-sectional. In the general model context, as distinct from the single partial model case, we also have to decide the nature of inter-model linkages, which may be called causal structure though 'mechanisms of change' is preferable. As ever, the decisions are partly conditioned by practicality and data availability, and the principles involved can only really be illustrated by example. Therefore, using the sub-models and modes of analysis which have been developed thus far in the book, the argument may run as follows. SA-Population and SA-economic models, by definition, apply to the whole study area. They should provide totals to which variables of other models should aggregate. The same techniques could be applied at the zonal level; in either case, there are then likely to be substantial stochastic fluctuations which the models would not handle adequately. However, at least on the demographic side, this may be worth doing to obtain indices of 'pressure' which can be used to estimate intra-urban migration or to play some other role in the residential location model. For the spatial economy, a different sub-model would be used and, at this stage, changes in land use could be calculated. All models mentioned so far would be marginal, though the SA-economic model in a slightly different sense from the others. Thus, the models defined so far are those in the outermost four boxes of Figure 11.9.

The models developed in Chapter 10 suggest that changes in residential and workplace location, and housing and job supply, can only be handled simultaneously, and then on a marginal basis. This would then give changes in demand for services and transport by origin, while the spatial economic model will have already provided estimates of changes in the provision of service and transport facilities.

Thus, at this stage, service and transport utilization can be estimated in total cross-section models. Hence, when we try to reconstruct Figure 11.9 to represent the mechanisms of change, it emerges as in Figure 11.10 (Totals at

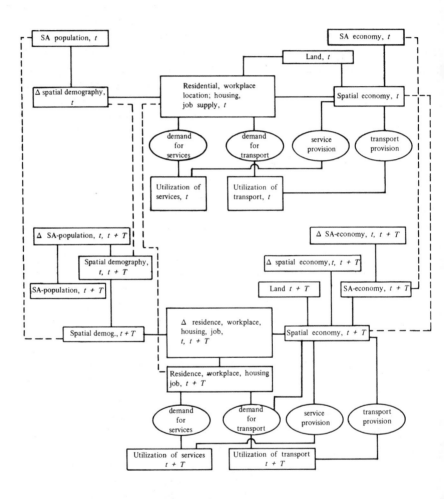

Figure 11.10 Outline of dynamic structure of a general model

t and $t + T$ are shown). The argument can now be repeated and stated more simply in relation to Figure 11.10. The top half of the diagram records the state of the system at time t. Then, changes in the population and the economy,

patially aggregated and disaggregated, are calculated (and since these boxes
at present have no inputs, obviously we shall eventually be seeking more
detail here). Then, in one simultaneous operation, changes in residential and
workplace location are calculated. The $t + T$ values are obtained for these
five sub-models by adding in the t values (the five dotted lines). Then, the new
spatial demand for services and transport and the provision of facilities can
be calculated and noted respectively, and the two $t + T$ cross-sections
obtained for service and transport included. It should be emphasized again,
before we leave the 'mechanisms of change' topic, that this particular presentation is *one* example only. The general point to note is that this exercise, or
something similar, has to be undertaken at this stage.

Finally, in this introductory discussion, we must discuss the nature of the
model equations. Roughly speaking, we expect the equations to turn up in
blocks which accord with the boxes of Figure 11.10 or its equivalent, with
earlier blocks appearing before later blocks. In other words, the *order* of
equations reflects the mechanisms of change, as well as the context of the
equation. Usually, there will be some difficulty in that, almost always, there
will be some variables in 'early' equations which are only properly available
after 'later' ones have been solved. These situations can usually only be
resolved mathematically by iteration. Such an iteration is partly a mathematical device for solving the equation, but it partly reflects (though need not
accurately represent except in its final outcome) various bargaining and
adjustment processes which actually take place during the period within
which change is being modelled. The main equations in each block will be
those which have the main sub-system variables as dependent variables.
There may be more equations for 'intermediate' variables in the calculations.
A variable should appear as a dependent variable only once, but it will be
recalled, however, that there will usually be 'external' variables which appear
only as independent variables.

Formally, equations may be written as

$$y_i(t + T) = y_i(y_1(t), y_2(t + T), \Delta y_3(t, t + T), \ldots) \qquad (11.201)$$

or

$$\Delta y_i(t, t + T) = \Delta y_i(y_1(t), y_2(t + T), \Delta y_3(t, t + T), \ldots) \qquad (11.202)$$

according to whether a total cross-section or marginal change is being
modelled. The variables on the right-hand side are the independent variables
in this particular case. They themselves will either appear as dependent
variables in an earlier equation (or occasionally a later equation if iterative
methods are used) or will be external. In the examples shown, the independent
variables can be either cross-sectional or marginal, and refer to t or $t + T$
in the first case, or the period t to $t + T$ in the second. This will be the typical
situation; however, there is no reason why earlier times, $t - T, t - 2T$ etc.

should not appear in principle. If T tends to zero, then question (11.202)
would become a first-order differential equation. This reminds us that
(although it would be unusual in relation to the present state of the art) the
sequence of equations (11.201)–(11.202) could be extended to second- and
higher-order difference or differential equations.

To summarize: the main equations will be those with main sub-system
variables as dependent variables. These, together with any associated
equations in intermediate variables, represent the mechanism of change for
the main variable or block, and the position of the block in the overall scheme
is another aspect of this. To illustrate this simply, note the following: we may
have a main equation

$$y_i = (y_1^2 + y_2^2 + y_3^2)^{\frac{1}{3}} + (y_1 + y_2)^2$$

and we may feel it more convenient to define intermediate variables

$$y_4 = y_1^2 + y_2^2 + y_3^2$$

$$y_5 = y_1 + y_2$$

so that

$$y_i = y_4^{\frac{1}{3}} + y_5^2$$

There are also other types of equation which play an important role, the most
important being two types of accounting equation. If a model is marginal,
with a main equation such as (11.202) then there will be another equation of
the form

$$y_i(t + T) = y_i(t) + \Delta y_i(t, t + T) \qquad (11.203)$$

Such equations express the conservation laws of the system. The second
type of accounting relation arises when a variable is used at two different
levels in the model, say $C(i, M)$ and $C'(j, M)$, and then we must ensure that

$$\sum_i C(i, M) = \sum_j C'(j, M)$$

This kind of equation ensures the internal consistency of the model, which is
of the greatest importance.

* 11.7. A GENERAL URBAN AND REGIONAL MODEL: VARIABLES, STRUCTURE AND FORMAL EQUATIONS

In the previous section, we discussed principles for building a general
model in relation to five issues: components, sub-systems, variables, structure
or mechanisms of change and the equation system. In illustrating the argument, we outlined the basic components of an urban and regional system and
presented the basic sub-system structure in Figure 11.9. We discussed how to

construct variables using the concept of a subscript list, proceeded some way with an elaboration of causal structure and produced Figure 11.10. We must now complete the discussion, beginning by defining variables which we will relate to sub-systems and the causal structure, and then we can proceed to writing down a full equation system in formal terms.

Two levels of spatial aggregation will be distinguished: I is used for the whole study area, and J for any other similar region; i and j are used as zone labels within I in the usual way. We work with a discrete time period, t to $t + T$ as before. Usually, we will use different letters for variables referring to the same components, but which have been aggregated in different ways. For population, we shall use w at the study area scale, and P, $\hat{P}$ or $\hat{\hat{P}}$, at the finer scale. We shall use different letters again for population variables which relate to the main population activities: N for residential–workplace location, S for service utilization, and T for transport utilization. The various subscript lists needed for the population variables are:

a—for the population sub-systems (SA and spatial), usually age and sex;
b—for the residential–workplace sub-system, usually income, occupation or social class, family size, or household structure index;
f—for the utilization of services sub-system, usually income and social class;
n—for the utilization of transport sub-system, usually trip purpose, income and car ownership.

Thus, the main variables relating to population are (time indices omitted):

w_I^a—study area population type a;

P_i^b—type b population resident in i;

$\hat{P}_i^f$—type f population resident in i;

$\hat{\hat{P}}_i^n$—type n population resident in i.

Just occasionally, we will use $\hat{w}_i^a$ as the type a population in *zone* i. The population activity variables will be defined in relation to supply-side variables, so we construct these first. The subscript list characterizing economic activity is g, and so we have:

q_I^g—study area economic activity of type g;

Q_i^g—type g activity in zone i.

Then, particular sections are identified as population-perceived economic activity. The appropriate subscript lists are defined as:

k—house type, usually size, price, age, condition, tenure;
w—job type, usually wage, skill;
s—service type, usually type of activity, possibly quality and price;
m—transport-facility type, usually mode.

The variables which represent the population-perceived outputs of the spatial economy are then:

H_i^k—type k houses in i;

E_j^w—type w jobs in j;

W_j^s—provision (or attractiveness) of services of type s in j;

c_{ij}^m—cost of travel from i to j by facility m.

At this stage, we can conveniently introduce land use. Let u be the subscript list which characterizes land use, and then

L_i^u—amount of land in use in i.

Finally, we can define the population activity variables, noting both demand and supply characteristics, and dealing with residential and workplace location jointly. We define

N_{ij}^{kwb}—type-b population living in a type-k house in i and working in type-w job in zone j. (Later, we shall find that for the specific choice of the subscript list b which is made, there are b-categories for people who do not work. The j and w are then irrelevant for these categories and the notation is amended accordingly);

S_{ij}^{sf}—type-f population in zone i utilizing type-s services in j;

T_{ij}^{mn}—trips made from i to j by facility type m by people of type n.

We shall also sometimes find it convenient to define variables which measure total demand for services and transport in a zone. This can be done with one variable for the former and two for the latter:

e_i^{sf}—per type-f person demand for services of type-s in zone i, so that total demand is: $e_i^{sf} \hat{P}_i^f$, and

Ω_i^n—number of trips per head by type-n people in zone i;

Γ_i^n—the unit expenditure on these trips.

Then total trips of this type generated in zone i is $\Omega_i^n \hat{\hat{P}}_i^n$ (usually written O_i^n) and total expenditure is $\Gamma_i^n \hat{\hat{P}}_i^n$ (usually written C_i^n).

Time indices are added and 'change' variables are constructed, in the usual way, for example as $w_l^q(t)$ or $\Delta w_l^q(t, t + T)$. The main sub-system variables can now be depicted in a figure with the same structure as Figure 11.9.

The next step is to elaborate our notions of the mechanisms of change which are so far represented in Figure 11.10. A number of 'change' boxes were left unconnected. This is because our full understanding of the mechanism of change fails us at this point: we are simply not capable of offering an explanation for things like changing birth rates in formal model terms. We overcome these difficulties, and keep the model comprehensive, in a purely

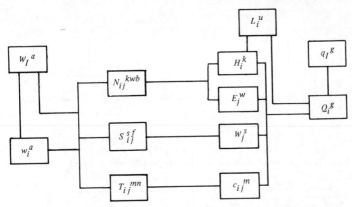

Figure 11.11   Static general model structure, showing variables

formal sense, of course, but nevertheless useful, by using the concept introduced earlier of external variables. Change in our system of interest comes
about mainly through decisions of people and organizations made in response
to the previous system state, and possibly other external factors. Thus, we
define two kinds of external variable which are concerned with public
response, x^P, and organizational response, x^O. It is also useful to define
external variables concerned with demographic change, x^D, and with technological change, x^T. Thus, we can now add slightly to Figure 11.10, and it is
in any case useful to construct it again with relevant variables in the boxes.
This we do in Figure 11.12. The 'response' variables are shown as functions
of the time t state variables. Given the time t state, this diagram expresses a
sequence of calculation for obtaining the $t + T$ state which can be expressed
as follows.

Spatially aggregated population (Either this or the next operation could be
first)

Calculate $\Delta w_I^a(t, t + T)$ as a function of existing population, $x_1^D(t, t + T)$,
$x_2^D(t, t + T), \ldots$, and add this to $w_I^a(t)$ to obtain $w_I^a(t + T)$.

Spatially aggregated economy

Calculate $\Delta q_I^g(t, t + T)$ as a function of previous production levels, $q_I^g(t)$,
and $x_1^P(t, t + T), \ldots x_1^O(t, t + T), \ldots x_1^T(t, t + T), \ldots$. Add this to $q_I^g(t)$ to
obtain $q_I^g(t + T)$. We shall see later, that in relation to the Chapter 8 model,
we shall re-interpret this as meaning 'calculate new technical coefficients and
final demand terms as a function of ...' and use these in an input–output
model to obtain $q_I^g(t + T)$.

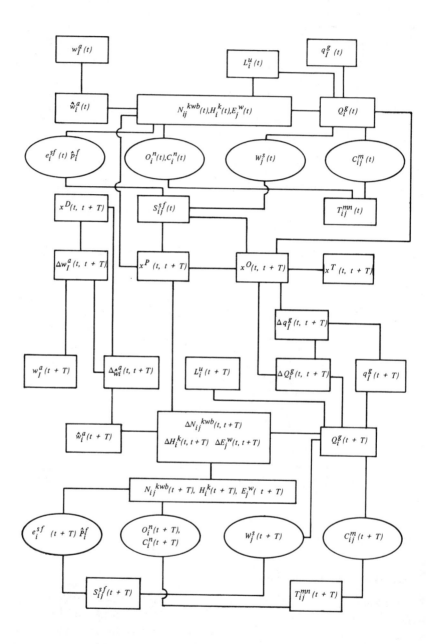

Figure 11.12   Dynamic general model structure, showing variables

spatial demographic subsystem (This and the next operation can be carried out in parallel or in either order).

Calculate $\Delta \hat{w}_i^a(t, t + T)$ as a function of external variables, and possibly of $w_i^a(t, t + T)$, and add to $\hat{w}_i^a(t, t + T)$ to obtain $w_i^a(t + T)$. This step will be very difficult to carry out in practice in this form because of the difficulty of estimating intra-urban migration between small zones. We might therefore content ourselves with estimating 'natural increase', defined as $\Delta \hat{\hat{w}}_i^a(t, t + T)$.

Spatial economy

Calculate $\Delta Q_i^g(t, t + T)$ as a function of external variables, and possibly $\Delta q_i^g(t, t + T)$. Add to $Q_i^g(t)$ to obtain $Q_i^g(t + T)$.

Population-perceived economic activity

We can then obtain, from $\Delta Q_i^g(t, t + T)$ or $Q_i^g(t, t + T)$ as appropriate, change in *housing*, $\Delta H_i^k(t, t + T)$, change in *employment*, $\Delta E_j^w(t, t + T)$, service facilities, $W_j^s(t + T)$, and transport facilities measured as $c_{ij}^m(t + T)$. We shall see as we proceed that the first two are required in marginal form, the second two in total form, though they could be obtained in either form at this stage.

Land use

At this stage, land-use changes consequent on changes in the spatial economy can be calculated, eventually to give $L_i^u(t + T)$. It is quite likely that because of land-use constraints, an inner iteration between this step and the preceding steps will be necessary. It may only be possible to satisfy some constraints through an outer iteration.

Residential and workplace location

This calculation is at the heart of the model. It is necessary to proceed in a number of steps and to add to our notation. We have to clarify the nature of the demand for housing and for jobs, and the supply of these quantities, and the inter-relationship of demand and supply in an accounting sense.

Demand is made up of people who decide to move house or job, or enter the market for the first time. For brevity, we shall refer to all of them as movers. We then split $\Delta N_{ij}^{kwb}(t, t + T)$ into three categories, $\Delta^l N_{ij}^{kwb}(t, t + T)$, for $l = 1, 2$ and 3 corresponding to people who change jobs only (or require one for the first time), change houses only, or change both. It is also useful to define $\Delta^4 N_{ij}^{kwb}(t, t + T)$ as the non-movers in the period. We now consider the accounting relationship of movers to supply. Some of the people who

move house and some of these who move job will free houses and jobs fo
the supply pool. Thus the supply of houses and jobs is not simply $\Delta H_i^k(t, t + T$
and $\Delta E_j^w(t, t + T)$, but should have released houses and jobs added. We defin
total supply as $\Delta^T H_i^k(t, t + T)$ and $\Delta^T E_j^w(t, t + T)$ and 'released' houses and
jobs as $\Delta^R H_i^k(t, t + T)$ and $\Delta^R E_j^w(t, t + T)$ so that

$$\Delta^T H_i^k(t, t + T) = \Delta H_i^k(t, t + T) + \Delta^R H_i^k(t, t + T) \qquad (11.204$$

and

$$\Delta^T E_j^w(t, t + T) = \Delta E_j^w(t, t + T) + \Delta^R E_j^w(t, t + T) \qquad (11.205$$

$\Delta H_i^k(t, t + T)$ and $\Delta E_j^w(t, t + T)$ are themselves made up of additions and
subtraction, and, using an obvious notation, it is sometimes useful to identify
these explicitly as

$$\Delta H_i^k(t, t + T) = \Delta^A H_i^k(t, t + T) - \Delta^S H_i^k(t, t + T) \qquad (11.206$$

and

$$\Delta E_j^w(t, t + T) = \Delta^A E_j^w(t, t + T) - \Delta^S E_j^w(t, t + T) \qquad (11.207$$

The main steps in this part of the calculation are now evident and can be
summarized as follows:

(1) Calculate the various kinds of movers, which is $\Delta^l N_{ij}^{kwb}(t, t + T$
aggregated over the spatial indices involved in the change.

(2) Calculate homes and jobs released, $\Delta^R H_i^k(t, t + T)$ and $\Delta^R E_j^w(t, t + T)$

(3) Calculate total supply using equations (11.204) and (11.205).

(4) Allocate demand to supply to obtain $\Delta^l N_{ij}^{kwb}(t, t + T)$, $1 = 1, 2, 3$.
$N_{ij}^{kwb}(t, t + T)$ can then be obtained using accounting equations.

Demand for services (This step and the next can be carried out in parallel or
in either order)

We can next assume that the *per capita* demand for services at time $t + T$,
$e_i^{sf}(t + T)$ is a simple function of the distribution of population by type, and
perhaps some economic variables, and can be estimated at this stage.

Demand for transport

Similarly, we assume that $O_i^n(t + T)$ and $C_i^n(t + T)$ can be estimated at
this stage.

Utilization of Services (This step and the next can be carried out in parallel
or in either order)

The variable which represents utilization of services at time $t + T$,
$S_{ij}^{sf}(t + T)$, can be estimated in a cross-sectional equilibrium model as a

unction of $e_i^{sf}(t + T)$, $\hat{P}_i^f(t + T)W_j^s(t + T)$ and $c_{ij}^m(t + T)$, all of which are ow available.

Utilization of transport facilities

$T_{ij}^{mn}(t + T)$ can be estimated in a cross-sectional equilibrium model as a unction of $O_i^n(t + T)$, $C_i^n(t + T)$, $c_{ij}^m(t + T)$ and measures of destination ttractiveness which can be constructed from both population and economic ctivity distribution, and could be written $W_j^{Tn}(t + T)$ for destinations j. It is unlikely to be directly a function of the type of transport facility used for etting there. There may also be capacity constraints on some destinations of the form

$$\sum_i \sum_m T_{ij}^{mn}(t + T) \leqslant D_j^n(t + T) \tag{11.208}$$

and the $D_j^n(t + T)$s would be functions mainly of external variables.

We can now proceed to the next major step of the argument and write down formal model equations to represent the mechanisms whose structures have been elaborated above. We use the same headings again and in view of the earlier explanation, the presentation is brief unless further development is called for. As a preliminary, we summarize, in Figure 11.13, the sequence of calculation just outlined. This is, in essence, a 'linearized' version of Figure 11.12. We show 'parallel' calculations as such, but indicate the order adopted here by position on the vertical axis. A final step has been added for constraint checks'. The formal equations for each step can now be written as follows:

Step 1. SA-population

$$\Delta w_I^a(t, t + T) = \Delta w_I^a(w_I^a(t), w_j^a(t), \ldots x_1^D(t, t + T)) \tag{11.209}$$

Note that the change in population is a function of initial population in regions other than I as well as I itself. Then

$$w_I^a(t + T) = w_I^a(t) + \Delta w_I^a(t, t + T) \tag{11.210}$$

Step 2. SA-economy

$$\Delta q_I^g(t, t + T) = \Delta q_I^g(q_I^g(t), q_j^g(t), \ldots x_1^P(t, t + T), \ldots x_1^0(t, t + T), \ldots) \tag{11.211}$$

and

$$q_I^g(t + T) = q_I^g(t) + \Delta q_I^g(t, t + T) \tag{11.212}$$

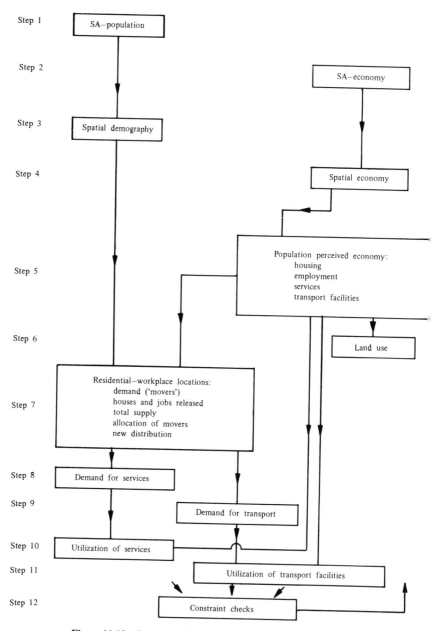

Figure 11.13   Sequence of sub-models in dynamic general model

Step 3. Spatial demographic sub-system

Because of the difficulties of estimating $\Delta\hat{w}_i(t, t + T)$, we shall concentrate on natural increase only:

$$\Delta\hat{w}_i^a(t, t + T) = \Delta\hat{w}_i^a(\hat{w}_i^a(t), x_1^D(t, t + T), \ldots) \qquad (11.213)$$

Step 4. Spatial economy

$$\Delta Q_i^q(t, t + T) = \Delta Q_i^q(Q_i^q(t), q_1^q(t + T), \Delta q_1^q(t, t + T), x_1^P(t, t + T), \ldots,$$
$$x_1^0(t, t + T), \ldots) \qquad (11.214)$$

$$Q_i^q(t + T) = Q_i^q(t) + \Delta Q_i^q(t, t + T) \qquad (11.215)$$

Step 5. Population-perceived economic activity (In the following equations, here and in Step 6, $Q_i^g(t, t + T)$ stands for the list of such variables over all g)

$$\Delta H_i^k(t, t + T) = \Delta H_i^k(\Delta Q_i^q(t, t + T), \ldots) \qquad (11.216)$$

$$H_i^k(t + T) = H_i^k(t) + \Delta H_i^k(t, t + T) \qquad (11.217)$$

$$\Delta E_j^w(t, t + T) = \Delta E_j^w(\Delta Q_i^q(t, t + T), \ldots) \qquad (11.218)$$

$$E_j^w(t + T) = E_j^w(t) + \Delta E_j^w(t, t + T) \qquad (11.219)$$

$$\Delta W_j^s(t, t + T) = \Delta W_j^s(\Delta Q_i^q(t, t + T), \ldots) \qquad (11.220)$$

$$W_j^s(t + T) = W_j^s(t) + \Delta W_j^s(t, t + T) \qquad (11.221)$$

$$\Delta c_{ij}^m(t, t + T) = \Delta c_{ij}^m(\Delta Q_i^q(t, t + T), \ldots) \qquad (11.222)$$

$$c_{ij}^m(t + T) = c_{ij}^m(t) + \Delta c_{ij}^m(t, t + T) \qquad (11.223)$$

Step 6. Land use

$$\Delta L_i^u(t, t + T) = \Delta L_i^u(\Delta Q_i^q(t, t + T), \ldots) \qquad (11.224)$$

$$L_i^u(t + T) = L_i^u(t) + \Delta L_i^u(t, t + T) \qquad (11.225)$$

Step 7. Residential and workplace location

Step 7a. Demand estimates

The demand for jobs from those fixed in houses is

$$\Delta^1 N_{i*}^{k*b}(t, t + T) = \Delta^1 N_{i*}^{k*b}(N_{ij}^{kwb}(t), \ldots \Delta E_j^w(t, t + T), \ldots$$
$$\Delta\hat{w}_i^a(t, t + T), \ldots x_1^P(t, t + T), \ldots) \qquad (11.226)$$

The demand for housing from those fixed in jobs is

$$\Delta^2 N_{*j}^{*wb}(t, t + T) = \Delta^2 N_{*j}^{*wb}(N_{ij}^{kwb}(t), \ldots \Delta H_i^k(t, t + T), \ldots$$
$$\Delta \hat{w}_i^a(t, t + T), \ldots x_1^P(t, t + T), \ldots) \qquad (11.227)$$

The demand for housing and jobs for those changing both simultaneously is

$$\Delta^3 N_{**}^{**b}(t, t + T) = \Delta^3 N_{**}^{**b}(N_{ij}^{kwb}(t), \ldots \Delta H_i^k(t, t + T), \ldots$$
$$\Delta E_j^w(t, t + T), \ldots \Delta \hat{w}_i^a(t, t + T), \ldots \qquad (11.228)$$
$$x_1^P(t, t + T), \ldots)$$

Step 7b. Houses and jobs released

Groups 1 and 2 release some jobs:

$$\Delta^R E_j^w(t, t + T) = \Delta^R E_j^w(\Delta^1 N_{i*}^{k*b}(t, t + T), \ldots \Delta^3 N_{**}^{**b}(t, t + T, \ldots) \qquad (11.229)$$

and groups 2 and 3 release some houses:

$$\Delta^R H_i^k(t, t + T) = \Delta^R H_i^k(\Delta^2 N_{*j}^{*wb}(t, t + T), \ldots \Delta^3 N_{**}^{**b}(t, t + T), \ldots) \qquad (11.230)$$

Step 7c. Total supply of houses and jobs

$$\Delta^T H_i^k(t, t + T) = \Delta H_i^k(t, t + T) + \Delta^R H_i^k(t, t + T) \qquad (11.231)$$

$$\Delta^T E_j^w(t, t + T) = \Delta E_j^w(t, t + T) + \Delta^R E_j^w(t, t + T) \qquad (11.232)$$

Step 7d. Allocation of movers

$$\Delta^1 N_{ij}^{kwb}(t, t + T) = \Delta^1 N_{ij}^{kwb}(\Delta^1 N_{i*}^{k*b}(t, t + T), \Delta^T E_j^w(t, t + T), c_{ij}^m(t + T), \ldots) \qquad (11.233)$$

$$\Delta^2 N_{ij}^{kwb}(t, t + T) = \Delta^2 N_{ij}^{kwb}(\Delta^2 N_{*j}^{*wb}(t, t + T), \Delta^T H_i^k(t, t + T), \ldots$$
$$c_{ij}^m(t + T), \ldots) \qquad (11.234)$$

$$\Delta^3 N_{ij}^{kwb}(t, t + T) = \Delta^3 N_{ij}^{kwb}(\Delta^3 N_{**}^{**b}(t, t + T), \Delta^T H_i^k(t, t + T), \ldots$$
$$\Delta^T E_j^w(t, t + T), \ldots c_{ij}^m(t + T), \ldots) \qquad (11.235)$$

Such formal equations show the bare bones of these extremely complicated relationships. More detail was given earlier in Chapter 10, of course, and we shall return again to this level of detail in the general model context later in this Chapter.

Step 7e. New residential–workplace distribution

$$N_{ij}^{kwb}(t + T) = \sum_{l=1}^{4} \Delta^l N_{ij}^{kwb}(t, t + T) \qquad (11.236)$$

Step 8. Demand for services

$$e_i^{sf}(t + T) = e_i^{sf}(N_{i*}^{kwb}(t + T), \ldots W_j^s(t + T), \ldots c_{ij}^m(t + T), \ldots) \quad (11.237)$$

Step 9. Demand for transport

$$O_i^n(t + T) = O_i^n(N_{i*}^{kwb}(t + T), \ldots Q_i^g(t + T), \ldots, c_{ij}^m(t + T), \ldots) \quad (11.238)$$

$$C_i^n(t + T) = C_i^n(N_{i*}^{kwb}(t + T), \ldots Q_i^g(t + T), \ldots, c_{ij}^m(t + T), \ldots) \quad (11.239)$$

Step 10. Utilization of services

$$S_{ij}^{sf}(t + T) = S_{ij}^{sf}(e_i^{sf}(t + T), \hat{P}_i^f(t + T), W_j^s(t + T), \ldots, c_{ij}^m(t + T) \ldots)$$
$$(11.240)$$

Step 11. Utilization of transport facilities

$$T_{ij}^{mn}(t + T) = T_{ij}^{mn}(O_i^n(t + T), C_i^n(t + T), W_j^s(t + T), Q_i^g(t + T), \ldots$$
$$D_j^n(t + T) \ldots c_{ij}^m(t + T), \ldots) \quad (11.241)$$

We have proceeded in this sub-section at a high level of abstraction in order to show clearly the structure of the overall analytical problem. However, there are many other problems associated with the task of building a general model which only become evident in the context of an attempt to be more specific. We have already seen examples of such problems in earlier sections of this chapter on other people's general models. In the next sub-section, therefore, we shall be as specific as possible, and present an example of a general model using the principles just elaborated.

* 11.8. AN EXAMPLE OF A GENERAL MODEL

We can present a specific example of a general model which is in broad accord with the structure of the model outlined in the previous sub-section by doing two things: making the subscript lists explicit and making the formal equations specific and explicit. When the second task is undertaken, it will often be convenient to introduce intermediate variables which will lead to an increase in the number of equations. In presenting an explicit example, we must deal with one particular difficulty: the state of the art is such that sub-models for some steps are much more effectively developed than others. In this presentation, an attempt will be made to keep a balance: simpler than usual versions (by comparison, for example, with sub-models presented in earlier chapters of this book) of the more developed models will sometimes be used, and what might be called 'speculative' versions of some of the less developed ones.

A second major difficulty concerns possible ways of linking models through constraint procedures. Inter-sub-model linkages arising from the hypo thesized mechanism of change have been built-in through the structur outlined in the last section. However, the sub-model variable estimates coul be unreasonable in various ways, for example, more than the availabl amount of land could be utilized; we have seen many other examples of situations where constraints are needed. Constraints are difficult to handl because any calculated excess has to be redistributed. For example, if to many people are allocated to residences in a zone, the excess must be re distributed to other zones. There are two alternatives: first, an *ad hoc* pro cedure could be used at the time the excess is identified, but this then mean that, in effect, the resulting sub-model mechanism is different to that originall intended; or second, the sub-model mechanisms should have capacity constraints built into them. However, in the second case, the capacity con straints usually involve information which only becomes available when a later sub-model has been run, and this means adjustments can only be made in an outer iterative loop, as indicated in Figure 11.13. We saw an example of such a loop in a version of the Lowry model in Section 11.3. We shall adopt the second of these methods as being theoretically preferable, though we should recall Seidman's (1969) opinion that such procedures hardly seemed worth the effort in the Penn–Jersey case and that something simpler would have sufficed. Therefore we shall note points where such constraint pro cedures might operate. The next step, then, is to specify subscript lists. We discuss each in turn.

The subscript list a, for population sub-systems, will be taken as age r and sex X, so that a variable such as $w_I^a(t)$ can be written as $w_I^{rX}(t)$. In this case, it is necessary to specify both indices explicitly in formulating specific equations, since there are different kinds of equations for different values of r, and sex has to be distinguished since births are to females only. This is not always necessary: sometimes, even when the subscript list has been specified, the single letter can be retained as a shorthand, and we will do this where possible.

The subscript list b relates to the residential–workplace sub-system, and in this example we wish to identify a person's income and household type. Here we can take advantage of a commonality in subscript lists: the subscript list w relates to job type and in this example will be taken simply as income. Since most income is derived from employment, we shall not separately include 'income' in the list b. Thus we can take b as a single household type index, and we shall use the following conventions:

$b = 1$ denotes a working head of household,
$b = 2$ denotes a working non-head of household,
$b = 3$ denotes a non-working head of household,
$b = 4$ denotes a non-working non-head of household.

The subscript list f, used in relation to service activity, we will also take as income w. The subscript list n is concerned with transport activity, and here we wish to identify trip type p, then using n as a single letter with the following conventions:

$n = 1$ denotes a car owner (strictly, this should be 'denotes having a car available', but this is a more difficult concept to deal with, as we saw in Chapter 9).

$n = 2$ denotes a non-car owner.

That is, the subscript list n is represented by (p, n), with n now as a single subscript and, as with a, we shall show both explicitly.

The economic activity subscript list g can be taken as a reasonably fine version of the *Standard Industrial Classification* (S.I.C.) or something similar.

The definitions of subscript lists associated with variables representing population-perceived economic activity can then be taken as follows: k is home type, which will be tenure coupled with a size/age/condition index. Average home price for a type-k home in i will be separately identified as p_i^k. We have already defined w as income; s is service type and will usually be an aggregation of a number of gs; m is transport-facility type and will be taken as mode; u refers to land use and will be taken as an aggregation of gs.

With these definitions, the main variables are w_I^{rX}, P_i^b, $\hat{P}_i^w$, $\hat{\hat{P}}_i^n$, q_I^g, H_i^k (and p_i^k), E_j^w, W_j^s, c_{ij}^m, L_i^u, N_{ij}^{kwb}, S_{ij}^{sw} (and e_i^{sw}) and T_{ij}^{pmn} (and O_i^{pn} and C_i^{pn}). There are slight amendments of the earlier definitions in that in two cases, a and n, explicit lists have been shown, as (rX) and (pn). In most other cases, the 'list' can be considered as a single index as indicated for the purposes of this example. The formal model equations of the previous section more or less still hold, but we have to be careful in imposing certain restrictions. For example, an equation in $\Delta^1 N_{ij}^{kwb}(t, t + T)$ only has meaning for $b = 1$ and $b = 3$ since only these categories of people work. For $b = 2$ and $b = 4$, j and w subscripts will be replaced by an asterisk, for example as in $N_{i*}^{k*2}(t)$. This shows up the main disadvantage of not associating an income variable with the list b as we have now 'lost' the income of non-workers. This is particularly important for non-working heads of households, the $b = 3$ category, and we shall re-introduce this income with a special notation later.

We are now in a position to present the specific equations for this example. We shall proceed in turn through each of the steps identified in the previous section.

Step 1. SA-population

We begin by introducing the three basic demographic rates concerned with birth, death (or rather, survival) and migration as functions of external variables. Since we use survival rates rather than death rates, we shall estimate

$w_I^{rX}(t + T)$ directly rather than use $\Delta w_I^{rX}(t, t + T)$ as in the formal equations. Thus, using an obvious notation and Rogers' assumptions (cf. Chapter 7) we have

$$b_k^{IX}(t, t + T) = b_k^{IX}(x_1^D(t, t + T), \ldots) \qquad (11.242)$$

as the birth rate in I of sex X to mothers in age group k in the period t to $t + T$,

$$s_{rr-1}^{IX}(t, t + T) = s_{rr-1}^{IX}(x_1^D(t, t + T), \ldots) \qquad (11.243)$$

as the survival rate from age groups $r - 1$ to age group r in region I for sex X, and

$$m_{rr-1}^{IJX}(t, t + T) = m_{rr-1}^{IJX}(x_1^D(t, t + T), \ldots) \qquad (11.244)$$

as the rate of migration (and survival from $r - 1$ to r) from J to I for sex X in t to $t + T$. Then, for $r = 1$,

$$W_I^{1X}(t + T) = \sum_{k=\alpha_{cB}}^{\beta_{cB}} b_k^{IX}(t, t + T)W_I^{kF}(t) \qquad (11.245)$$

where α_{cB} and β_{cB} are the limits of the child-bearing age groups, and for $r > 1$,

$$w_I^{rX}(t + T) = s_{rr-1}^{IX}(t, t + T)w_I^{r-1X}(t) + \sum_{J \neq I} m_{rr-1}^{IJX}(t, t + T)w_J^{r-1X}(t) \qquad (11.246)$$

Step 2. SA-economy

We will assume that the SA-economy can be represented by an input–output model which uses employment units as the basic measure of activity. Then, in period t to $t + T$, we assume that the technical coefficients change as functions of external variables:

$$\Delta a_I^{gh}(t, t + T) = \Delta a_I^{gh}(x_1^T(t, t + T), \ldots) \qquad (11.247)$$

where $a_I^{gh}(t)$ is the input–output coefficient, in employment units, relating sector g (as input) to sector L (as output). So

$$a_I^{gh}(t + T) = a_I^{gh}(t) + \Delta a_I^{gh}(t, t + T) \qquad (11.248)$$

Similarly, if $y_I^g(t)$ is the final demand for g in I at time t, we suppose

$$\Delta y_I^g(t, t + T) = \Delta y_I^g(x_1^P(t, t + T), \ldots) \qquad (11.249)$$

and

$$y_I^g(t + T) = y_I^g(t) + \Delta y_I^g(t, t + T) \qquad (11.250)$$

As long as employment units are used, there is no need to represent factor inputs, and changes in these, explicitly, though any changes will be implicit in changes in the technical coefficients. Then, if the vector of outputs, q_i^q is written $\mathbf{q}_I$, the matrix of technical coefficients $\mathbf{a}_I$ and the final demand vector $\mathbf{y}_I$, then the model estimate for $\mathbf{q}_I(t + T)$ is

$$\mathbf{q}_I(t + T) = (\mathbf{I} - \mathbf{a}_I)^{-1}\mathbf{y}_I \qquad (11.251)$$

Step 3. The spatial demographic sub-system

As with the SA-population model, we can set up the basic rates, but this time they are defined for small areas. We use a $\hat{}$ to distinguish these. Migration rates are not needed, as only natural growth is being calculated at this point. Thus,

$$\hat{b}_k^{iX}(t, t + T) = \hat{b}_k^{iX}(x_1^D(t, t + T), \ldots) \qquad (11.252)$$

and

$$\hat{s}_{rr-1}^{iX}(t, t + T) = \hat{s}_{rr-1}^{iX}(x_1^D(t, t + T), \ldots) \qquad (11.253)$$

As time t population, we use

$$\hat{w}_i^{rX}(t) = \pi_1^{ir}(t) \cdot N_{i*}^{***}(t) \qquad (11.254)$$

Here π_1^{ir} is a coefficient which tells us the proportion of the time t population in i in age group r. (In general, when 'common-usage' symbols are available for coefficients and rates, such as b, s and m above, they will be used, but otherwise π with a numerical subscript.) Asterisks, as usual, denote summation. Then, for $r = 1$

$$\hat{\hat{w}}_i^{1X}(t + T) = \sum_{k=\alpha_{cB}}^{\beta_{cB}} \hat{b}_k^{iX}(t, t + T)\hat{w}_i^{kF}(t) \qquad (11.255)$$

and for $r > 1$

$$\hat{\hat{w}}_i^{rX}(t, t + T) = \hat{s}_{rr-1}^{iX}(t, t + T)w_i^{r-1X}(t) \qquad (11.256)$$

provide estimates of natural increase.

Step 4. Spatial economy

Suppose we select a sub-set of available variables (and designate them as Z_i^k—the kth variable, and its value for zone i) which can be used to explain changes in the spatial economy. These variables can be used as $Z_i^k(t)$, $Z_i^k(t + T)$ or $\Delta Z_i^k(t, t + T)$. Note however, that $(t + T)$, or $(t, t + T)$ variables can only be used if they have been calculated before they are required in a particular equation, or if they are Q variables themselves, if simultaneous equation estimation techniques are used. This means that, typically, variables used will refer to time t, or will be economic activity variables which have already been calculated in an earlier equation. Then, the model can be expressed in the form

$$\Delta Q_i^g(t, t + T) = \pi_5^g(t, t + T)\pi_6^{ig}(t, t + T)\left\{\sum_k \pi_2^k(t, t + T)Z_i^k(t)\right.$$

$$+ \sum_k \pi_3^k(t, t + T)Z_i^k(t + T) \qquad (11.257)$$

$$\left. + \sum_k \pi_4^k(t, t + T)\Delta Z_i^k(t, t + T)\right\}$$

where the πs are coefficients as usual. In practice, of course, many of these would be fixed as zero. $\pi_5^g(t, t + T)$ is a normalizing coefficient calculated to ensure that

$$\sum_{i \in I} Q_i^g(t + T) = q_i^g(t + T) \qquad (11.258)$$

where

$$Q_i^g(t + T) = Q_i^g(t) + \Delta Q_i^g(t, t + T) \qquad (11.259)$$

$\pi_6^{ig}(t, t + T)$ is a coefficient which is set as 1 unless adjustments need to be made because of land-use constraints being infringed. We will show how it could be calculated later.

Step 5. Population-perceived economic activity

We can consider that one of the g-sectors is housing, and that this also forms a single land-use sector for step 6. Thus, the immediate task is to determine $\Delta^A H_i^k(t, t + T)$ and $\Delta^s H_i^k(t, t + T)$. Again, a whole spectrum of models is available, ranging as in the land-use case from wholly endogenous to wholly exogenous. In this case, a trend projection seems less suitable because of the 'lumpiness' of some kinds of residential development. For the purpose of this example, we shall use a version of Hansen's simple model (see Chapter 10) for additional private housing, and assume that public housing and all demolitions are determined exogenously by the local authority. We can show how such a scheme might work by first elaborating the equations for the SA and spatial economic sector concerned with housing. Suppose this is g_h. It is also useful, temporarily, to distinguish tenure (as private or public) within the subscript list k; for these purposes, we shall write k as $k\tau$, where τ is tenure: $\tau = 1$ for private, $\tau = 2$ for public. Then, $\pi_7^\tau(t, t + T) \times \Delta q^{gh}(t, t + T)$ is the total number of additional dwellings in tenure group τ. π_7 is a coefficient which converts from employment units to dwelling units, and determines the proportion just mentioned. Thus, $\pi_7^1(t, t + T)\Delta q^{g_h}(t, t + T)$ is the number of private dwellings. To construct a Hansen-type model, we need an accessibility term and a vacant land term. We assume that accessibility to employment at the beginning of the period will suffice, and so define

$$X_i(t) = \sum_j E_j^*(t)\, e^{-\beta c_{ij}(t)} \qquad (11.260)$$

as the accessibility, using an obvious notation. Land available for residential use is

$$L_i^{vR}(t + T) = \pi_8^i(t, t + T)L_i^v(t) \qquad (11.261)$$

where $L_i^v(t)$ is total vacant land at t in i, and $\pi_8^i(t, t + T)$ is a coefficient (obviously less than or equal to 1) which is the proportion of this available for private development. Then

$$\Delta^A H_i^{k1}(t, t + T) = \pi_9^{ik}(t, t + T)\,[\pi_7^1(t, t + T)\Delta q^{g_h}(t, t + T)]$$

$$\times \frac{L_i^{vR}(t + T)X_i(t)}{\sum_{i \in I} L_i^{vR}(t + T)X_i(t)} \qquad (11.262)$$

and

$$\Delta^A H_i^{k2}(t, t + T) = \Delta^A H_i^{k2}(x_1^0(t, t + T), \ldots) \qquad (11.263)$$

for the public sector and

$$\Delta^s H_i^{k\tau}(t, t + T) = \Delta^s H_i^{k\tau}(x_1^0(t, t + T), \ldots), \qquad \tau = 1, 2 \qquad (11.264)$$

for demolitions. This procedure completely determines $\Delta H_i^k(t, t + T)$ (where we can now revert to k as the original subscript list). In equation (11.264) $\pi_9^{ik}(t, t + T)$ is a coefficient which is included to allow for the possibility of adjustment because of constraint procedures. Employment generated by this construction activity could then be estimated from

$$Q_i^{g_h}(t + T) = \sum_k [\pi_{10}^k(t, t + T)\Delta^A H_i^k(t, t + T) + \pi_{11}^k(t, t + T)\Delta^s H_i^k(t, t + T)]$$

$$\qquad (11.265)$$

where π_{10}^k and π_{11}^k are coefficients which give the amount of employment associated with building and demolition. This replaces the equations of the set (11.257–11.259) for $g = g_h$.

The other population-perceived economic activity variables can be obtained more simply. Employment could be calculated from

$$E_j^w(t + T) = \sum_g \pi_{12}^{gw}(t + T)Q_j^g(t + T) \qquad (11.266)$$

(within which we assume $\Delta^s E_j^w(t, t + T)$ job losses in the period) and

$W_j^s(t + T)$ as a simple function of service-sector variables:

$$W_j^s(t + T) = \sum_g \pi_{13}^{gs}(t + T)Q_j^g(t + T) \qquad (11.267)$$

where π_{12}^{gw} and π_{13}^{gs} are conversion coefficients; $c_{ij}^m(t + T)$ can be taken as specified exogenously. Formally,

$$c_{ij}^m(t + T) = c_{ij}^m(x_1^0(t, t + T), \ldots) \qquad (11.268)$$

Step 6. Land use

To present a simple model for the purposes of this example, we borrow the basic idea of the Penn–Jersey land-use model in the following form:

$$\Delta L_i^u(t, t + T) = \pi_{14}^{iul(Q)}(t, t + T) L_i^u(t) \times \frac{\sum_{g \in u} \Delta Q_i^g(t, t + T)}{\sum_{g \in u} Q_i^g(t)} \qquad (11.269)$$

We have assumed that the gs aggregate exactly into land-use classes u, and so $\sum_{g \in u}$ has an obvious meaning. The equation then assumes that the change in land use is proportional to the relative change in employment in u-activities and the amount of land in use u at the beginning of the period. The coefficient $\pi_{14}^{iul(Q)}$ then, of course, implicitly contains most of a host of difficult modelling problems. $l(Q)$ is defined as follows:

$$\begin{aligned} l(Q) &= 1 \quad \text{if } \Delta Q_i^g(t, t + T) > 0 \\ &\quad 2 \quad \text{if } \Delta Q_i^g(t, t + T) < 0 \end{aligned} \qquad (11.270)$$

and enables the coefficient to have different values for growth and decline. π_8 is greater than or less than 1 according to whether new activity is locating at lower or higher densities than existing activity. Finally,

$$L_i^u(t + T) = L_i^u(t) + \Delta L_i^u(t, t + T) \qquad (11.271)$$

At this point, a number of constraints can be checked. The most fundamental is that total land use predicted by the model should not exceed land available. If v is the category among the us which represents vacant land, then we require

$$L_i^v(t + T) = L_i^*(t + T) - \sum_{u \neq v} L_i^u(t + T) \geqslant 0 \qquad (11.272)$$

If this constraint is infringed, then two kinds of adjustment are possible. Firstly, the coefficients π_{14} could be changed to generate higher densities, or the coefficients π_6 or π_9 in steps 4 and 5 could be changed to amend the spatial distribution of economic activity. If the latter course is adopted, there could then be an iteration around steps 4, 5 and 6 until the constraints are satisfied. More typically, a mixture of the two methods could be used. There are many possible 'models' for such adjustment processes, ranging from wholly endogenous to wholly exogenous. The latter case would arise in a situation where land use planning controls were very strong. Thus, the purpose of the model-building exercise, and the nature of the situation in the particular study area, are crucial to the decision on the type of adjustment procedure to use here. And, of course, we should also remark that many other constraints could be usefully incorporated, as in the Penn–Jersey case. However, we shall not be any more explicit about this at present.

Step 7. Residential and workplace location

We now have to work through steps 7a to 7e as listed under step 7 in Section 11.7. A lengthy preliminary discussion is necessary, however. As we attempt to become more specific, we recognize the problem of handling residential and workplace location, and in particular making the demand and supply estimates, as being perhaps the hardest task in building a general model. With the variable and subscript list definitions which have been made for this example, we shall see that demand and supply can arise from demographic and household structure changes as well as from desires to change house or job. Thus, what was earlier called the mover pool has now become something wider and in step 7a we shall refer to housing and job demand pools, and in step 7b to housing and job supply pools. Our task is to estimate the transitions which have a bearing on these.

The state of this sub-system at time t is characterized by the following variables (for this particular set of definitions of subscript lists): $N_{ij}^{kw1}(t)$, working heads of households; $N_{ij}^{kw2}(t)$, working non-heads of households; $N_{i*}^{k3}(t)$, non-working heads of households j; $N_{i*}^{k*4}(t)$, non-working non-heads of households. The overall demand pools are represented by variables like those on the left-hand sides of equations (11.226)–(11.228) in the previous section, but we must now specify them more precisely for each b-value, and indeed, for clarity, we shall refer to specific b-values for the rest of the section. The set of demand variables are listed in Table 11.1. Note that, while everyone lives somewhere, we assign *houses* to heads of households, while we refer to *residential places* for non-heads of households.

People can move into these demand pools as a result of a great variety of transitions: any (i, k) can go to (i', k'), any (j, w) to (j', w'), and any b to b'. These could be double or triple transitions when two or three of (i, k), (j, w) or b change for an individual. It would be helpful at some stage to build a full accounting-based model (c.f. Rees and Wilson, 1973) which identified all the transitions explicitly, estimated 'at risk' populations and calculated and predicted an appropriate set of transition rates. However, we shall not proceed with the full development here. We shall group together some of the

Table 11.1.   Demand variables

$\Delta^1 N_{i*}^{k*1}(t, t + T)$	Working heads of households, fixed in (i, k) houses, but seeking jobs
$\Delta^1 N_{i*}^{k*2}(t, t + T)$	Working non-heads of households, fixed in (i, k) residential places, but seeking jobs
$\Delta^2 N_{*j}^{*w1}(t, t + T)$	Working heads of households, fixed in (j, w) jobs, but seeking houses
$\Delta^2 N_{*j}^{*w2}(t, t + T)$	Working non-heads of households, fixed in (j, w) jobs, but seeking residential places
$\Delta^2 N_{**}^{**3}(t, t + T)$	Non-working heads of households seeking houses
$\Delta^2 N_{**}^{**4}(t, t + T)$	Non-working non-heads of households seek residential places
$\Delta^3 N_{**}^{**1}(t, t + T)$	Working heads of households seeking houses and jobs simultaneously
$\Delta^3 N_{**}^{**2}(t, t + T)$	Working non-heads of households seeking residential places and jobs simultaneously

different kinds of transitions and define rates on an *ad hoc* basis. We wish to identify rates associated with the following group of transitions.

(1) People changing house or residential place, including out-migration from the area.

(2) Non-heads of households becoming heads.

(3) Heads of households becoming non-heads.

(4) Workers changing jobs.

(5) Non-workers becoming workers.

(6) Workers becoming non-workers.

(7) Deaths.

(8) Births.

(9) In-migration.

We shall define rates to be associated with the major transitions associated with each group, and then subsidiary rates where appropriate which will allow us to deal with double and triple transitions. We discuss each group of transitions in turn.

(1) *People changing house or residential place, including out-migration from the area*

Let $\pi_{15}^{ikb}(t, t + T)$, $b = 1,2,3,4$ be the rates at which individuals move house (or residential place as appropriate). We can consider this to be the *unforced* transition rate. It is also useful to define $\pi_{16}^{ikjwb}(t, t + T)$, $b = 1,2$ and π_{16}^{ik**b} $(t, t + T)$, $b = 3,4$ to be the rates at which individuals move from (i, k) houses which are demolished: the *forced* rate. Let $\pi_{17}^{ikb}(t, t + T)$ be the rate at which people move out of the study area altogether, and let $\pi_{18}^{ikb}(t, t + T)$, $b = 1,2$ be the proportion of house or residential place movers who are also seeking jobs.

(2) Non-heads of households becoming heads

Let $\pi_{19}^{bb'}(t, t + T), b = 2,4, b' = 1,3$ be the ratio at which non-heads become heads, and hence seekers of houses. Let $\pi_{20}^{2;1}(t, t + T)$ be the proportion of those making the $b = 2$ to $b = 1$ transition who also decide to seek a new job.

(3) Heads of households becoming non-heads

Let $\pi_{21}^{ikbb'}(t, t + T), b = 1,3, b' = 2,4$ be the rate at which heads of households living in (i, k) houses, become non-heads. Let $\pi_{22}^{1;2}(t, t + T)$ be the rate at which those moving from $b = 1$ to $b = 2$ also decide to change jobs.

(4) Workers changing jobs

Let $\pi_{23}^{jwb}(t, t + T), b = 1,2$ be the rate at which b-workers make *unforced* moves from (j, w) jobs; let $\pi_{24}^{ikjwb}(t, t + T), b = 1,2$ be the proportion of b-workers (i, k) houses making *forced* moves because (j, w) jobs are lost in the time period. Let a proportion $\pi_{25}^{jwb}(t, t + T), b = 1,2$ move out of the study area altogether. Let $\pi_{26}^{jwb}(t, t + T), b = 1,2$ be the proportion of job-movers who also decide to seek new houses or residential places.

(5) Non-workers becoming workers

Let $\pi_{27}^{bb'}(t, t + T), b = 3,4, b' = 1,2$ be the rate at which non-workers become workers. Of these four transitions, $b = 3$ to $b = 2$ has been dealt with under (3) and $b = 4$ to $b = 2$ under (2) above, and they will not be considered any further here. Let $\pi_{28}^{3;1}(t, t + T)$ be the proportion of those moving from $b = 3$ to $b = 2$ who decide to seek a new home (as well as a job) in the process, and $\pi_{28}^{4;2}(t, t + T)$ be the proportion of those moving from $b = 4$ to $b = 2$ who decide to seek a new residential place in the process.

(6) Workers becoming non-workers

Let $\pi_{29}^{jwbb'}(t, t + T), b = 1,2, b' = 3,4$ be the rate at which workers become non-workers. Of these four transitions, $b = 1$ to $b = 4$ is dealt with under (3) above, and $b = 2$ to $b = 3$ is dealt with under (2) above. We shall continue to deal with 1 to 4 under (3), but we shall deal with 2 to 3 under this heading, rather than (2), as $\pi_{29}^{jwbb'}$ contains more information than $\pi_{19}^{bb'}$ because of the (j, w) subscripts. Let $\pi_{30}^{1;3}(t, t + T)$ be the proportion of those moving from $b = 1$ to $b = 3$ who decide also to seek a new home, and $\pi_{30}^{2;4}(t, t + T)$ the proportion of those moving from $b = 2$ to $b = 4$ who decide also to seek a new residential place.

(7) Deaths

Let $\pi_{31}^{ikb}(t, t + T), b = 1,3,4$ be the rate of deaths of people in $b = 1,3,4$ categories resident in (i, k) houses; let $\pi_{32}^{jwb}(t, t + T), b = 1,2$ be the rate of deaths of workers in (j, w) jobs. We assume that the estimates of $\pi_{31}^{ik1}(t, t + T)$ and $\pi_{32}^{jw1}(t, t + T)$ are consistent.

(8) *Births*

We will assume that T is sufficiently small that all births are into the $b = 4$ category. We assume these as a number rather than a rate, and let $B^4(t, t + T)$ be the number of births.

(9) *In-migration*

We also represent in-migrants by absolute numbers: let $M^b(t, t + T)$ be the number of type-b in-migrants in the time period. Note that in our definition of out-migration in (1) and (6) above, and in-migration here, we have made the simplifying assumption that it is *not* possible to live in the study area and work outside, or vice versa. Little is lost conceptually in making this assumption. The study area could be designed with quasi-external zones so that the assumption is reasonable, or if necessary, the real-life complications could be added in later.

It can easily be checked that this list contains all the major transitions. Formally, the rates which have been defined can be considered for the present example to be functions of external variables. In many cases, it is easy to see how they relate to other known sub-models, for example, in relation to demographic change and household formation. However, one of the important features of this example is that it identifies and highlights a number of important transition rates which are not usually studied. An important research task is to obtain more empirical information on these rates, and to build models of them as functions of other variables. This would also reveal a number of strong interdependencies between rates which have here been defined to be independent: for example, between heads of households' and dependents' movement rates in (1) above.

It remains a relatively complicated task to collect together the flows as different components of the demand variables (defined in Table 11.1) for step 7a. As a preliminary, we first identify all the flows explicitly for each group of transitions and in doing this, we also note the relevant flow for the important 'non-mover' calculation, and houses and jobs released to facilitate our calculations of supply in step 7b. Thus, for each group of transitions, we identify the flows associated with

- (a) housing demand
- (b) job demand
- (c) simultaneous housing–job demand
- (d) residential-place demand
- (e) simultaneous residential-place–job demand
- (f) the non-mover calculation
- (g) houses released
- (h) jobs released.

We again proceed through each group of transitions in turn identifying the ~~ows~~ flows generated under the headings (a)–(h) listed above. If there is no flow ~~ontribution~~ contribution for a particular heading, the heading is omitted. Although this ~~rocedure~~ procedure is rather laborious, it is the best way to ensure that no contribution ~~inadvertently~~ is inadvertently omitted, and also to avoid any double counting. We list ~~eparately~~ separately the flows for each b-value, or pair of b-values, in each group.

(1) *People changing house or residential place, including out-migration from the area*

$$b = 1$$

(a) *Housing demand.* There is a contribution

$$F_1^{jw}(t, t + T) = \sum_i \sum_k (1 - \pi_{18}^{ik1}(t, t + T))(1 - \pi_{17}^{ik1}(t, t + T)) \qquad (11.273)$$

$$\times [\pi_{15}^{ik1}(t, t + T)N_{ij}^{kw1}(t) + \pi_{16}^{ik1}(t, t + T)\Delta^s H_i^k(t, t + T)]$$

~~o~~ to $\Delta^2 N_{*j}^{*w1}(t, t + T)$.

(c) *Simultaneous housing–job demand.* There is a contribution

$$F_2(t, t + T) = \sum_i \sum_k \pi_{18}^{ik1}(t, t + T)(1 - \pi_{17}^{ik1}(t, t + T))$$

$$\times \sum_j \sum_w \left[\pi_{15}^{ik1}(t, t + T)N_{ij}^{kw1}(t) \qquad (11.274) \right.$$

$$\left. + \pi_{16}^{ikjw1}(t, t + T)\Delta^s H_i^k(t, t + T) \right]$$

to $\Delta^3 N_{**}^{**1}(t, t + T)$.

(f) *Non-mover calculation.*

$$F_3^{ijkw}(t, t + T) = \pi_{15}^{ik1}(t, t + T)N_{ij}^{kw1}(t) + \pi_{16}^{ikjw1}(t, t + T)\Delta^s H_i^k(t, t + T)$$
$$(11.275)$$

is to be subtracted from $N_{ij}^{kw1}(t)$.

(g) *Houses released.*

$$F_4^{ik}(t, t + T) = \pi_{15}^{ik1}(t, t + T)\sum_j \sum_w N_{ij}^{kw1}(t) \qquad (11.276)$$

is the number of (i, k) houses released.

(h) *Jobs released.*

$$F_5^{jw}(t, t + T) = \sum_i \sum_k \pi_{18}^{ik1}(t, t + T)$$
$$(11.277)$$
$$\times [\pi_{15}^{ik1}(t, t + T)N_{ij}^{kw1}(t) + \pi_{16}^{ikjw1}(t, t + T)\Delta^s H_i^k(t, t + T)]$$

(j, w) jobs are released.

$$b = 2$$

(d) *Residential places demand.* There is a contribution

$$F_6^{jw}(t, t + T) = \sum_i \sum_k (1 - \pi_{18}^{ik2}(t, t + T))(1 - \pi_{17}^{ik2}(t, t + T))$$

$$\times [\pi_{15}^{ik2}(t, t + T)N_{ij}^{kw2}(t) + \pi_{16}^{ikjw2}(t, t + T)\Delta^s H_i^k(t)] \tag{11.278}$$

to $\Delta^2 N_{*j}^{*w2}(t, t + T)$.

(e) *Simultaneous residential-place–job demand.* There is a contribution

$$F_7(t, t + T) = \sum_i \sum_k \pi_{18}^{ik2}(t, t + T)(1 - \pi_{17}^{ik2}(t, t + T))$$

$$\times \sum_j \sum_w [\pi_{15}^{ik2}(t, t + T)N_{ij}^{kw2}(t) + \pi_{16}^{ikjw2}(t, t + T)\Delta^s H_i^k(t)] \tag{11.279}$$

to $\Delta^3 N_{**}^{**2}(t, t + T)$.

(f) *Non-mover calculation.*

$$F_8^{ikjw2}(t, t + T) = \pi_{15}^{ik2}(t, t + T)N_{ij}^{kw2}(t) + \pi_{16}^{ikjw2}(t, t + T)\Delta^s H_i^k(t, t + T) \tag{11.280}$$

is to be subtracted from $N_{ij}^{kw2}(t)$.

(h) *Jobs released.*

$$F_9^{jw}(t, t + T) = \sum_i \sum_k [\pi_{18}^{ik2}(t, t + T)\pi_{15}^{ik2}(t, t + T)N_{ij}^{kw2}(t)$$

$$+ \pi_{16}^{ikjw2}(t, t + T)\Delta^s H_i^k(t, t + T)] \tag{11.281}$$

(j, w) jobs are released.

$$b = 3$$

(a) *Housing demand.* There is a contribution

$$F_{10}(t, t + T) = \sum_i \sum_k [(1 - \pi_{17}^{ik3}(t, t + T)) \times \pi_{15}^{ik3}(t, t + T)N_{l*}^{k*3}(t)$$

$$+ \pi_{16}^{ik**3}(t, t + T)\Delta^s H_i^k(t, t + T)] \tag{11.282}$$

to $\Delta^2 N_{**}^{**3}(t, t + T)$.

(f) *Non-mover calculation.*

$$F_{11}^{ik}(t, t + T) = \pi_{15}^{ik3}(t, t + T)N_{i*}^{k*3}(t) + \pi_{16}^{ik**3}(t, t + T)\Delta^s H_i^k(t) \quad (11.283)$$

is to be subtracted from $N_{i*}^{k*3}(t)$.

(g) *Houses released.*

$$F_{12}^{ik}(t, t + T) = \pi_{15}^{ik3}(t, t + T)N_{i*}^{k*3}(t) \quad (11.284)$$

is the number of (i, k) houses released.

$$\underline{b = 4}$$

(d) *Residential-place demand.* There is a contribution of

$$F_{13}(t, t + T) = \sum_i \sum_k [(1 - \pi_{17}^{ik4}(t, t + T)\pi_{15}^{ik4}(t, t + T)N_{i*}^{k*4}(t)$$

$$+ \pi_{16}^{ik**4}(t, t + T)\Delta^s H_i^k(t, t + T)] \quad (11.285)$$

to $\Delta^2 N_{**}^{***4}(t, t + T)$.

(f) *Non-mover calculation*

$$F_{14}^{ik}(t, t + T) = \pi_{15}^{ik4}(t, t + T)N_{i*}^{k*4}(t) + \pi_{16}^{ik**4}(t, t + T)\Delta^s H_i^k(t, t + T) \quad (11.286)$$

should be subtracted from $N_{i*}^{k*4}(t)$.

(2) *Non-heads of households becoming heads*

$$\underline{b = 2 \text{ to } b = 1}$$

(a) *Housing demand.* There is a contribution

$$F_{15}^{jw}(t, t + T) = (1 - \pi_{20}^{2;1}(t, t + T))\pi_{19}^{2;1}(t, t + T)\sum_i \sum_k N_{ij}^{kw2}(t) \quad (11.287)$$

to $\Delta^2 N_{*j}^{*w1}(t, t + T)$.

(c) *Simultaneous housing–job demand.* There is a contribution

$$F_{16}(t, t + T) = \pi_{20}^{2;1}(t, t + T)\pi_{19}^{2;1}(t, t + T)\sum_i \sum_k \sum_j \sum_w N_{ij}^{kw2} \quad (11.288)$$

to $\Delta^3 N_{**}^{***1}(t, t + T)$.

(f) *Non-mover calculation.*

$$F_{17}^{ikjw}(t, t + T) = \pi_{19}^{2;1}(t, t + T)N_{ij}^{kw2}(t) \quad (11.289)$$

is to be subtracted from $N_{ij}^{kw2}(t)$.

(h) *Jobs released.*

$$F_{18}^{jw}(t, t + T) = \pi_{19}^{2,1}(t, t + T) \sum_i \sum_k N_{ij}^{kw2}(t) \qquad (11.290)$$

(j, w) jobs are released.

$$b = 2 \text{ to } b = 3$$

This will be dealt with under (6) below

$$b = 4 \text{ to } b = 1$$

(c) *Simultaneous housing–job demand.* There is a contribution

$$F_{19}(t, t + T) = \pi_{19}^{4,1}(t, t + T) \sum_i \sum_k N_{i*}^{k*4}(t) \qquad (11.291)$$

to $\Delta^3 N_{**}^{**1}(t, t + T)$.

(f) *Non-mover calculation.*

$$F_{20}^{ik}(t, t + T) = \pi_{19}^{4,1}(t, t + T) N_{i*}^{k*4}(t) \qquad (11.292)$$

is to be subtracted from $N_{i*}^{k*4}(t)$.

$$b = 4 \text{ to } b = 3$$

(a) *Housing demand.* There is a contribution

$$F_{21}(t, t + T) = \pi_{19}^{4,3}(t, t + T) \sum_i \sum_k N_{i*}^{k*4}(t) \qquad (11.293)$$

to $\Delta^2 N_{**}^{**3}(t, t + T)$.

(f) *Non-mover calculation.*

$$F_{22}^{ik}(t, t + T) = \pi_{19}^{4,3}(t, t + T) N_{i*}^{k*4}(t) \qquad (11.294)$$

is to be subtracted from $N_{i*}^{k*4}(t)$.

(3) *Heads of households becoming non-heads*

$$b = 1 \text{ to } b = 2$$

(d) *Residential-place demand.* There is a contribution

$$F_{23}^{jw}(t, t + T) = (1 - \pi_{22}^{1,2}(t, t + T)) \sum_i \sum_k \pi_{21}^{ik1,2}(t, t + T) N_{ij}^{kw1}(t) \quad (11.295)$$

to $\Delta^2 N_{*j}^{*w2}(t, t + T)$.

(e) *Simultaneous residential-place–job demand.* There is a contribution

$$F_{24}(t, t + T) = \pi_{22}^{1,2}(t, t + T) \sum_i \sum_k \pi_{21}^{ik1,2}(t, t + T) \sum_j \sum_w N_{ij}^{kw1}(t) \quad (11.296)$$

to $\Delta^3 N_{**}^{**2}(t)$.

(f) *Non-mover calculation.*

$$F_{25}^{ikjw}(t, t + T) = \pi_{21}^{ik1,2}(t, t + T)N_{ij}^{kw1}(t) \qquad (11.297)$$

hould be subtracted from $N_{ij}^{kw1}(t)$.

(g) *Houses released.*

$$F_{26}^{ik}(t, t + T) = \pi_{21}^{ik1,2}(t, t + T)\sum_{j}\sum_{w} N_{ij}^{kw1}(t) \qquad (11.298)$$

$i, k)$ houses are released.

(h) *Jobs released.*

$$F_{27}^{jw}(t, t + T) = \pi_{22}^{1,2}(t, t + T)\sum_{i}\sum_{k} \pi_{21}^{ik1,2}(t, t + T)N_{ij}^{kw1}(t) \quad (11.299)$$

$j, w)$ jobs are released.

$$\underline{b = 1 \text{ to } b = 4}$$

(d) *Residential-place demand.* There is a contribution

$$F_{28}(t, t + T) = \sum_{i}\sum_{k} \pi_{21}^{ik1,4}(t, t + T)N_{ij}^{kw1}(t) \qquad (11.300)$$

to $\Delta^2 N_{**}^{**4}(t, t + T)$.

(f) *Non-mover calculation.*

$$F_{29}^{ikjw}(t, t + T) = \pi_{21}^{ik1,4}(t, t + T)N_{ij}^{kw1}(t) \qquad (11.301)$$

is to be subtracted from $N_{ij}^{kw1}(t)$.

(g) *Houses released.*

$$F_{30}^{ik}(t, t + T) = \pi_{21}^{ik1,4}(t, t + T)\sum_{j}\sum_{w} W_{ij}^{kw1}(t) \qquad (11.302)$$

(i, k) houses are released.

(h) *Jobs released.*

$$F_{31}^{jw}(t, t + T) = \sum_{i}\sum_{k} \pi_{21}^{ik1,4}(t, t + T)N_{ij}^{kw1}(t) \qquad (11.303)$$

(j, w) jobs are released.

$$\underline{b = 3 \text{ to } b = 2}$$

(e) *Simultaneous residential-place–job demand.* There is a contribution

$$F_{32}(t, t + T) = \sum_{i}\sum_{k} \pi_{21}^{ik3,2}(t, t + T)N_{i*}^{k*3}(t) \qquad (11.304)$$

to $\Delta^3 N_{**}^{**2}(t, t + T)$.

(f) *Non-mover calculation.*

$$F_{33}^{ik}(t, t + T) = \pi_{21}^{ik3,2}(t, t + T)N_{i*}^{k*3}(t) \tag{11.305}$$

is to be subtracted from $N_{i*}^{k*3}(t)$.

(g) *Houses released.*
$F_{33}^{ik}(t, t + T)$ in equation (11.305) also gives the number of (i, k) houses released.

$$\underline{b = 3 \text{ to } b = 4}$$

(a) *Residential-place demand.* There is a contribution

$$F_{34}(t, t + T) = \sum_i \sum_k \pi_{21}^{ik3,4}(t, t + T)N_{i*}^{k*3}(t) \tag{11.306}$$

to $\Delta^2 N_{**}^{***4}(t, t + T)$.

(f) *Non-mover contribution.*

$$F_{35}^{ik}(t, t + T) = \pi_{21}^{ik3,4}(t, t + T)N_{i*}^{k*3}(t) \tag{11.307}$$

is to be subtracted from $N_{i*}^{k*3}(t)$.

(g) *Houses released.*
$F_{35}^{ik}(t, t + T)$ in equation (11.307) also gives the number of (i, k) houses released.

(4) *Workers changing jobs*

$$\underline{b = 1}$$

(b) *Job demand.* There is a contribution

$$F_{36}^{ik}(t, t + T) = \sum_j \sum_w (1 - \pi_{26}^{jw1}(t, t + T))(1 - \pi_{25}^{jw1}(t, t + T))$$
$$\times [\pi_{23}^{jw1}(t, t + T)N_{ij}^{kw1}(t) + \pi_{24}^{ikjw1}(t, t + T)\Delta^s E_j^w(t, t + T)] \tag{11.308}$$

to $\Delta^1 N_{i*}^{k*1}(t, t + T)$.

(c) *Simultaneous housing–job demand.* There is a contribution which can be estimated in terms of these rates, but an alternative estimate has been obtained as $F_2(t, t + T)$ under (1) above. We shall assume that the two estimates are consistent, and, to discourage double counting, shall not explicitly write down the second one.

(f) *Non-mover calculation.* Some of the non-mover (from (c) above) have already been calculated under (1). Thus

$$F_{37}^{ikjw}(t, t + T) = (1 - \pi_{26}^{jw1}(t, t + T))[\pi_{23}^{jw1}(t, t + T)N_{ij}^{kw1}$$
$$+ \pi_{24}^{ikjw1}(t, t + T)\Delta^S E_j^w(t, t + T)] \tag{11.309}$$

are to be subtracted from $N_{ij}^{kw1}(t)$.

(g) *Houses released.* These have already been calculated, in effect, under (1) above.

(h) *Jobs released.* Some of these have already been calculated under (1) above. There remains a contribution

$$F_{38}^{jw}(t, t + T) = (1 - \pi_{26}^{jw1}(t, t + T))\sum_i \sum_k [\pi_{23}^{jw1}(t, t + T)N_{ij}^{kw1}(t)$$
$$+ \pi_{24}^{ikjw1}(t, t + T)\Delta^S E_j^w(t, t + T)] \tag{11.310}$$

to the total of (j, w) jobs released.

$$\underline{b = 2}$$

(b) *Job demand.* There is a contribution

$$F_{39}^{ik}(t, t + T) = (1 - \pi_{26}^{jw2}(t, t + T))(1 - \pi_{25}^{jw2}(t, t + T))$$
$$\times [\pi_{23}^{jw2}(t, t + T)N_{ij}^{kw2}(t, t + T) + \pi_{24}^{ikjw2}(t, t + T)\Delta^S E_j^w(t, t + T)] \tag{11.311}$$

to $\Delta^1 N_{i*}^{k*2}(t, t + T)$.

(e) *Simultaneous residential-place–job demand.* There is a contribution

$$F_{40}(t, t + T) = \sum_j \sum_w \pi_{26}^{jw2}(t, t + T)(1 - \pi_{25}^{jw2}(t, t + T))$$

$$\times \sum_i \sum_k [\pi_{23}^{jw2}(t, t + T)N_{ij}^{jw2}(t) \tag{11.312}$$

$$+ \pi_{24}^{ikjw2}(t, t + T)\Delta^S E_j^w(t, t + T)]$$

to $\Delta^3 N_{**}^{**2}(t, t + T)$.

(f) *Non-mover calculation.*

$$F_{41}^{ikjw}(t, t + T) = \pi_{23}^{jw2}(t, t + T)N_{ij}^{kw2}(t) + \pi_{24}^{ikjw2}(t, t + T)\Delta^S E_j^w(t, t + T) \tag{11.313}$$

should be subtracted from $N_{ij}^{kw2}(t)$.

(h) *Jobs released.*

$$F_{42}^{jw}(t, t + T) = \pi_{26}^{jw2}(t, t + T) \sum_i \sum_k [\pi_{23}^{jw2}(t, t + T)N_{ij}^{kw2}(t, t + T)$$

$$+ \pi_{24}^{ikjw2}(t, t + T)\Delta^S E_j^w(t, t + T)] \tag{11.314}$$

(j, w) jobs are released.

(5) *Non-workers becoming workers*

$$b = 3 \text{ to } b = 1$$

(b) *Job demand.* There is a contribution

$$F_{43}^{ik}(t, t + T) = (1 - \pi_{28}^{3;1}(t, t + T))\pi_{27}^{3;1}(t, t + T)N_{i*}^{k*3}(t) \tag{11.315}$$

to $\Delta^1 N_{i*}^{k*1}(t, t + T)$.

(c) *Simultaneous housing–job demand.* There is a contribution

$$F_{44}(t, t + T) = \pi_{28}^{3;1}(t, t + T)\pi_{27}^{3;1}(t, t + T) \sum_i \sum_k N_{i*}^{k*3}(t) \tag{11.316}$$

to $\Delta^3 N_{**}^{**1}(t, t + T)$.

(f) *Non-mover calculation.*

$$F_{45}^{ik}(t, t + T) = \pi_{27}^{3;1}(t, t + T)N_{i*}^{k*3}(t, t + T) \tag{11.317}$$

should be subtracted from $N_{i*}^{k*3}(t, t + T)$.

(g) *Houses released.*

$$F_{46}^{ik}(t, t + T) = \pi_{28}^{3;1}(t, t + T)\pi_{27}^{3;1}(t, t + T)N_{i*}^{k*3}(t) \tag{11.318}$$

(i, k) houses are released.

$$b = 3 \text{ to } b = 2$$

These transitions have been handled under (3) above.

$$b = 4 \text{ to } b = 1$$

These transitions have been handled under (2) above.

$$b = 4 \text{ to } b = 2$$

(b) *Job demand.* There is a contribution

$$F_{47}^{ik}(t, t + T) = (1 - \pi_{28}^{4;2}(t, t + T))\pi_{27}^{4;2}(t, t + T)N_{i*}^{k*4}(t) \tag{11.319}$$

to $\Delta^1 N_{i*}^{k*2}(t, t + T)$.

(e) *Simultaneous residential-place–job demand.* There is a contribution

$$F_{48}(t, t + T) = \pi_{28}^{4;2}(t, t + T)\pi_{27}^{4;2}(t, t + T)N_{i*}^{k*4}(t) \qquad (11.320)$$

to $\Delta^3 N_{**}^{**2}(t, t + T)$.

(f) *Non-mover calculation.*

$$F_{49}^{ik}(t, t + T) = \pi_{27}^{4;2}(t, t + T)N_{i*}^{k*4}(t) \qquad (11.321)$$

should be subtracted from $N_{i*}^{k*4}(t)$.

(6) *Workers becoming non-workers*

$$b = 1 \text{ to } b = 3$$

(a) *Housing demand.* There is a contribution

$$F_{50}(t, t + T) = \pi_{30}^{1;3}(t, t + T)\sum_j \sum_w \pi_{29}^{jw1,3}(t, t + T)\sum_i \sum_k N_{ij}^{kw1}(t) \quad (11.322)$$

to $\Delta^2 N_{**}^{**3}(t, t + T)$.

(f) *Non-mover calculation.*

$$F_{51}^{ijkw}(t, t + T) = \pi_{29}^{jw1,3}(t, t + T)N_{ij}^{kw1}(t) \qquad (11.323)$$

should be subtracted from $N_{ij}^{kw1}(t)$. We can also note that

$$F_{52}^{ik}(t, t + T) = (1 - \pi_{30}^{1;3}(t, t + T))\sum_j \sum_w \pi_{29}^{jw1,3}(t, t + T)N_{ij}^{kw1}(t) \quad (11.324)$$

remain fixed in i, k houses. No allocation procedure is needed for this group.

(g) *Houses released.*

$$F_{52}^{ik}(t, t + T) = \pi_{30}^{1;3}(t, t + T)\sum_j \sum_w \pi_{29}^{jw1,3}(t, t + T)N_{ij}^{kw1}(t) \quad (11.325)$$

(i, k) houses are released.

(h) *Jobs released.*

$$F_{53}^{jw}(t, t + T) = \pi_{29}^{jw1,3}(t, t + T)\sum_i \sum_k N_{ij}^{kw1}(t) \qquad (11.326)$$

(j, w) jobs are released.

$$b = 1 \text{ to } b = 4$$

This transition has already been dealt with under (3) above.

$$b = 2 \text{ to } b = 3$$

Although this arises under (2) above, we deal with it here for reasons explained earlier.

(a) *Housing demand*. There is a contribution

$$F_{54}(t, t + T) = \sum_j \sum_w \pi_{29}^{jw2,3}(t, t + T) \sum_i \sum_k N_{ij}^{kw2}(t) \qquad (11.327)$$

to $\Delta^2 N_{**}^{**3}(t, t + T)$.

(f) *Non-mover calculation*.

$$F_{55}^{ikjw}(t, t + T) = \pi_{29}^{jw2,3}(t, t + T)N_{ij}^{kw2}(t) \qquad (11.328)$$

must be subtracted from $N_{ij}^{kw2}(t)$.

(h) *Jobs released*.

$$F_{56}^{jw}(t, t + T) = \pi_{29}^{jw2,3}(t, t + T) \sum_i \sum_k N_{ij}^{kw1}(t) \qquad (11.329)$$

(j, w) jobs are released.

$$b = 2 \text{ to } b = 4$$

(d) *Residential-place demand*. There is a contribution

$$F_{57}(t, t + T) = \pi_{30}^{2,4}(t, t + T) \sum_j \sum_w \pi_{29}^{jw2,4}(t, t + T) \sum_i \sum_k N_{ij}^{kw2}(t) \quad (11.330)$$

to $\Delta^2 N_{**}^{**4}(t, t + T)$.

(f) *Non-mover calculation*.

$$F_{58}^{ikjw}(t, t + T) = \pi_{29}^{jw2,4}(t, t + T)N_{ij}^{kw2}(t) \qquad (11.331)$$

is to be subtracted from $N_{ij}^{kw2}(t)$. We should also note the flow

$$F_{59}^{ik}(t, t + T) = (1 - \pi_{30}^{2,4}(t, t + T)) \sum_j \sum_w \pi_{29}^{jw2,4}(t, t + T)N_{ij}^{kw2}(t) \quad (11.332)$$

of individuals who remain resident in the same (i, k) residential places.

(h) *Jobs released*.

$$F_{60}^{jw}(t, t + T) = \pi_{29}^{jw2,4}(t, t + T) \sum_i \sum_k N_{ij}^{kw2}(t) \qquad (11.333)$$

(j, w) jobs are released.

7) *Deaths*

$$b = 1$$

(f) *Non-mover calculation.*

$$F_{61}^{ikjw}(t, t + T) = \pi_{31}^{ik1}(t, t + T)N_{ij}^{kw1}(t) \tag{11.334}$$

$$= \pi_{32}^{jw1}(t, t + T)N_{ij}^{kw1}(t) \tag{11.335}$$

is to be subtracted from $N_{ij}^{kw1}(t)$. We assume the two alternative estimates are consistent.

(g) *Houses released.*

$$F_{62}^{ik}(t, t + T) = \pi_{31}^{ik1}(t, t + T)\sum_j \sum_w N_{ij}^{kw1}(t) \tag{11.336}$$

is the number of (i, k) houses released.

(h) *Jobs released.*

$$F_{63}^{jw}(t, t + T) = \pi_{32}^{jw1}(t, t + T)\sum_i \sum_k N_{ij}^{kw1}(t) \tag{11.337}$$

is the number of (j, w) jobs released.

$$b = 2$$

(f) *Non-mover calculations.*

$$F_{64}^{ikjw}(t, t + T) = \pi_{32}^{jw2}(t, t + T)N_{ij}^{kw2}(t) \tag{11.338}$$

is to be subtracted from $N_{ij}^{kw2}(t)$.

(h) *Jobs released.*

$$F_{65}^{jw}(t, t + T) = \pi_{32}^{jw2}(t, t + T)\sum_i \sum_k N_{ij}^{kw2}(t) \tag{11.339}$$

is the number of (j,w) jobs released.

$$b = 3$$

(f) *Non-mover calculations.*

$$F_{66}^{ik}(t, t + T) = \pi_{31}^{ik3}(t, t + T)N_{i*}^{k*3}(t) \tag{11.340}$$

is to be subtracted from $N_{i*}^{k*3}(t)$.

(g) *Houses released.* $F_{66}^{ik}(t, t + T)$ in equation (11.340) also gives the number of (i, k) houses released.

$$b = 4$$

(f) *Non-mover calculations.*

$$F_{67}^{ik}(t, t + T) = \pi_{31}^{ik4}(t, t + T)N_{i*}^{k*4}(t) \tag{11.341}$$

is to be subtracted from $N_{i*}^{k*4}(t)$.

(8) *Births*

$$b = 4$$

(d) *Residential-place demand.* There is a contribution

$$F_{68}(t, t + T) = B^4(t, t + T) \tag{11.342}$$

to $\Delta^2 N_{**}^{***4}(t, t + T)$.

(9) *In-migration*

$$b = 1$$

(c) *Simultaneous housing–job demand.* There is a contribution

$$F_{69}(t, t + T) = M^1(t, t + T) \tag{11.343}$$

to $\Delta^3 N_{**}^{***1}(t, t + T)$.

$$b = 2$$

(e) *Simultaneous residential-place–job demand.* There is a contribution

$$F_{70}(t, t + T) = M^2(t, t + T) \tag{11.344}$$

to $\Delta^3 N_{**}^{***2}(t, t + T)$.

$$b = 3$$

(a) *Housing demand.* There is a contribution

$$F_{71}(t, t + T) = M^3(t, t + T) \tag{11.345}$$

to $\Delta^2 N_{**}^{***3}(t, t + T)$.

$$b = 4$$

(d) *Residential-place demand.* There is a contribution

$$F_{72}(t, t + T) = M^4(t, t + T) \tag{11.346}$$

to $\Delta^2 N_{**}^{***4}(t, t + T)$.

Step 7a. Demand for houses, residential places and jobs

The variables representing the different types of demand categories were listed in Table 11.1. In the preceding introductory discussion, we identified the flows resulting from the various transitions which contribute directly to each variable. Thus:

$$\Delta^1 N_{i*}^{k*1}(t, t + T) = F_{36}^{ik}(t, t + T) + F_{43}^{ik}(t, t + T) \tag{11.347}$$

$$\Delta^1 N_{i*}^{k*2}(t, t + T) = F_{39}^{ik}(t, t + T) + F_{47}^{ik}(t, t + T) \tag{11.348}$$

$$\Delta^2 N_{*j}^{*w1}(t, t + T) = F_1^{jw}(t, t + T) + F_{15}^{jw}(t, t + T) \tag{11.349}$$

$$\Delta^2 N_{*j}^{*w2}(t, t + T) = F_6^{jw}(t, t + T) + F_{23}^{jw}(t, t + T) \tag{11.350}$$

$$\Delta^2 N_{**}^{**3}(t, t + T) = F_{10}(t, t + T) + F_{21}(t, t + T) + F_{50}(t, t + T) \\ + F_{54}(t, t + T) + F_{71}(t, t + T) \tag{11.351}$$

$$\Delta^2 N_{**}^{**4}(t, t + T) = F_{13}(t, t + T) + F_{28}(t, t + T) + F_{34}(t, t + T) \\ + F_{57}(t, t + T) + F_{68}(t, t + T) + F_{72}(t, t + T) \tag{11.352}$$

$$\Delta^3 N_{**}^{**1}(t, t + T) = F_2(t, t + T) + F_{16}(t, t + T) + F_{19}(t, t + T) \\ + F_{44}(t, t + T) + F_{69}(t, t + T) \tag{11.353}$$

$$\Delta^3 N_{**}^{**2}(t, t + T) = F_7(t, t + T) + F_{24}(t, t + T) + F_{32}(t, t + T) \\ + F_{40}(t, t + T) + F_{48}(t, t + T) + F_{70}(t, t + T) \tag{11.354}$$

It is also useful at this stage to have explicit equations for the non-movers, and again our task is easy using the (f) headings in the preliminary discussion:

$$\Delta^4 N_{ij}^{jw1}(t, t + T) = N_{ij}^{kw1}(t) - F_3^{ijkw}(t, t + T) - F_{25}^{ijkw}(t, t + T) \\ - F_{29}^{ijkw}(t, t + T) - F_{37}^{ikjw}(t, t + T) \\ - F_{51}^{ikjw}(t, t + T) - F_{61}^{ikjw}(t, t + T) \tag{11.355}$$

$$\Delta^4 N_{ij}^{kw2}(t, t + T) = N_{ij}^{kw2}(t) - F_8^{ijkw}(t, t + T) - F_{17}^{ijkw}(t, t + T) \\ - F_{41}^{ijkw}(t, t + T) - F_{55}^{ikjw}(t, t + T) - \\ - F_{58}^{ikjw}(t, t + T) - F_{64}^{ikjw}(t, t + T) \tag{11.356}$$

$$\Delta^4 N_{i*}^{k*3}(t, t + T) = N_{i*}^{k*3}(t) - F_{11}^{ik}(t, t + T) - F_{33}^{ik}(t, t + T) \\ - F_{35}^{ik}(t, t + T) - F_{45}^{ik}(t, t + T) \\ - F_{66}^{ik}(t, t + T) \tag{11.357}$$

$$\Delta^4 N_{i*}^{k*4}(t, t + T) = N_{i*}^{k*4}(t) - F_{14}^{ik}(t, t + T) - F_{20}^{ik}(t, t + T)$$
$$- F_{22}^{ik}(t, t + T) - F_{49}^{ik}(t, t + T) \tag{11.358}$$
$$- F_{67}^{ik}(t, t + T)$$

We can also recall at this stage the two groups of quasi-non-movers, those who change from $b = 1$ to $b = 3$ but do not move house ($F_{52}^{ik}(t, t + T)$ in equation (11.324)), and those who change from $b = 2$ to $b = 4$ ($F_{59}^{ik}(t, t + T)$ in equation (11.332)) but do not change residential place. These individuals will not appear explicitly in the allocation models in step 7e.

Step 7b. Houses and jobs released

We can now estimate $\Delta^R H_i^k(t, t + T)$ and $\Delta^R E_j^w(t, t + T)$ for the specific example, and produce the equivalents of equations (11.229) and (11.230) by using headings (g) and (h) of the preliminary discussion:

$$\Delta^R H_i^k(t, t + T) = F_4^{ik}(t, t + T) + F_{12}^{ik}(t, t + T) + F_{26}^{ik}(t, t + T)$$
$$+ F_{30}^{ik}(t, t + T) + F_{33}^{ik}(t, t + T) + F_{35}^{ik}(t, t + T)$$
$$+ F_{46}^{ik}(t, t + T) + F_{52}^{ik}(t, t + T) + F_{62}^{ik}(t, t + T) \tag{11.359}$$
$$+ F_{65}^{ik}(t, t + T)$$

$$\Delta^R E_j^w(t, t + T) = F_5^{jw}(t, t + T) + F_9^{jw}(t, t + T) + F_{18}^{jw}(t, t + T)$$
$$+ F_{27}^{jw}(t, t + T) + F_{31}^{jw}(t, t + T) + F_{38}^{jw}(t, t + T)$$
$$+ F_{42}^{jw}(t, t + T) + F_{53}^{jw}(t, t + T) + F_{56}^{jw}(t, t + T) \tag{11.360}$$
$$+ F_{60}^{jw}(t, t + T) + F_{63}^{jw}(t, t + T) + F_{65}^{jw}(t, t + T)$$

Step 7c. Total supply of housing and jobs

The total supply of houses and jobs is now given by

$$\Delta^T H_i^k(t, t + T) = \Delta H_i^k(t, t + T) + \Delta^R H_i^k(t, t + T) \tag{11.361}$$

$$\Delta^T E_j^w(t, t + T) = \Delta E_j^w(t, t + T) + \Delta^R E_j^w(t, t + T) \tag{11.362}$$

At this point we can also conveniently deal with the supply of residential places for dependents. We know from equations (11.350) and (11.354) that the overall demand for residential places for working dependents is

$$D^{R2}(t, t + T) = \sum_j \sum_w \Delta^2 N_{*j}^{*w2}(t, t + T) + \Delta^3 N_{**}^{**2}(t, t + T) \tag{11.363}$$

and from equation (11.352), the overall demand for places for non-working dependents is

$$D^{R4}(t, t + T) = \Delta^2 N_{**}^{***4}(t, t + T) \tag{11.364}$$

We also know from equations (11.356) and (11.358) that $\Delta^4 N_{ij}^{kw2}(t, t + T)$ and $\Delta^4 N_{i*}^{k*4}(t, t + T)$ dependents do not move, and from equations (11.332) that $N_{59}^{ik}(t, t + T)$ working dependents cease to work in the time period but keep the same residential place. At time t, for $b = 2,4$ we can define the quantities

$$r_i^{k2}(t) = \frac{\sum_j \sum_w N_{ij}^{kw2}(t)}{H_i^k(t)} \tag{11.365}$$

$$r_i^{k4}(t) = \frac{N_{i*}^{k*4}(t)}{H_i^k(t)} \tag{11.366}$$

as the number of type-b places available per (i, k) house. We now define quantities $R_i^{kb}(t, t + T)$ for the *period* t to $t + T$, assumed a function of external variables, such that $R_i^{kb}(t, t + T)\Delta^T H_i^k(t, t + T)$ is the number of residential places for type-b dependents in (i, k) houses. We assume that the quantities $R_i^{kb}(t, t + T)$ are normalized so that the overall supply of residential places meets overall demand. That is, so that

$$\sum_i \sum_k R_i^{kb}(t, t + T)\Delta^T H_i^k(t, t + T) = D^{Rb}(t, t + T), \qquad b = 2,4 \tag{11.367}$$

It is then possible, of course, that when the quantities $r_i^{kb}(t + T)$ are calculated when the $t + T$ allocations become known, they will differ from $r_i^{kb}(t)$. Although we have assume that $R_i^{kb}(t, t + T)$ is a function of external variables for the present, it is easy to see how a good hypothesis may be that it is proportional to $\Delta^T H_i^k(t, t + T)$ with a normalizing factor proportional to $D^{Rb}(t, t + T)$. If such a sub-model can be built, this means, in effect, that $r_i^{kb}(t + T)$, which are closely related to occupancy rates, have been predicted as functions of the initial populations and the transition rates defined earlier.

Before we proceed to step 7d, we now embark on another preliminary discussion about the comparison of overall demand and supply. There is no reason, of course, why overall demand and supply in the model as at present formulated should coincide, and in the real world, typically, they do not. We can handle this situation in the model as follows: let the last value of i, which we call i_F, and an associated single value of k, k_F, be a dummy housing category, which will register either a housing surplus or the amount of homelessness. Let $(j_F w_F)$ be a corresponding category for jobs. Then, the amount of homelessness for heads of households is

$$H_{i_F}^{k_F}(t, t + T) = \sum_j \sum_w [\Delta^2 N_{*j}^{*w1}(t, t + T)] + \Delta^2 N_{**}^{***3}(t, t + T)$$

$$+ \Delta^3 N_{**}^{**1}(t, t + T) - \sum_{i \neq i_F} \sum_{k \neq k_F} \Delta^T H_i^k(t, t + T) \tag{11.368}$$

(with a negative value being interpreted as a surplus), and the amount of unemployment is

$$E_{j_F}^{W_F}(t, t + T) = \sum_i \sum_k [\Delta^1 N_{i*}^{k*1}(t, t + T) + \Delta^1 N_{i*}^{k*2}(t, t + T)]$$

$$+ \Delta^3 N_{**}^{**1}(t, t + T) + \Delta^3 N_{**}^{**2}(t, t + T) \quad (11.369)$$

$$- \sum_{j \neq j_F} \sum_{w \neq w_F} \Delta^T E_j^w(t, t + T)$$

These measures should be interpreted carefully since, unless T is very small, they relate to the period t to $t + T$ and are not the usual cross-section measures.

The various transition rates involving (i, k) and/or (j, w) can then be interpreted as transition into the homeless or unemployed pool, and these *particular rates should all be normalized so that total demand is equal to total supply plus homelessness or unemployment.* We shall assume that inbalance can be handled in this way and henceforth we shall not distinguish (i_F, k_F) and (j_F, w_F) explicitly. We can now proceed to step 7d.

Step 7d. Allocation of housing and job demand

We now proceed to build an entropy-maximizing model along the lines of the final Chapter 10 model, though this one will be somewhat more elaborate. Our task is to estimate the variables $\Delta^1 N_{ij}^{kw1}(t, t + T)$, $\Delta^2 N_{ij}^{kw1}(t, t + T)$, $\Delta^3 N_{ij}^{kw1}(t, t + T)$, $\Delta^1 N_{ij}^{kw2}(t, t + T)$, $\Delta^2 N_{ij}^{kw2}(t, t + T)$, $\Delta^3 N_{ij}^{kw2}(t, t + T)$, $\Delta^2 N_{i*}^{k*3}(t, t + T)$, $\Delta^2 N_{i*}^{k*4}(t, t + T)$. The demand and supply totals which constrain these variables have been estimated in the preceding discussion and we now utilize these. In addition, as appropriate, we specify the usual transport cost and housing budget constraint equations. We proceed, for each b-value in turn, though occasionally variables involving 'other' b-values appear in particular constraint sets. The demand constraint for working heads seeking jobs only is

$$\sum_j \sum_w \Delta^1 N_{ij}^{kw1}(t, t + T) = \Delta^1 N_{i*}^{k*1}(t, t + T) \quad (11.370)$$

This group competes for jobs with other groups, and so the supply constraint is

$$\sum_i \sum_k \Delta^1 N_{ij}^{kw1}(t, t + T) + \sum_i \sum_k \Delta^1 N_{ij}^{kw2}(t, t + T) + \sum_i \sum_k \Delta^3 N_{ij}^{kw1}(t, t + T)$$

$$+ \sum_i \sum_k \Delta^3 N_{ij}^{kw2}(t, t + T) = \Delta^T E_j^w(t, t + T) \quad (11.371)$$

We assume that all $b = 1$ people within a w-group have the same transport and housing budget constraint parameters, and so these constraints can be written

$$\sum_i \sum_k \sum_j [\Delta^1 N_{ij}^{kw1}(t, t + T) + \Delta^2 N_{ij}^{kw1}(t, t + T) + \Delta^3 N_{ij}^{kw1}(t, t + T)]c_{ij}$$

$$= C^{1w}(t, t + T) \tag{11.372}$$

and

$$\sum_i \sum_k \sum_j [\Delta^2 N_{ij}^{kw1}(t, t + T) + \Delta^3 N_{ij}^{kw1}(t, t + T)][p_i^k - q^w(w - c_{ij}')]^2$$

$$= \sigma^{1w2}(t, t + T) \tag{11.373}$$

The demand constraint for $b = 1$ people seeking houses only is

$$\sum_i \sum_k \Delta^2 N_{ij}^{kw1}(t, t + T) = \Delta^2 N_{*j}^{*w1}(t, t + T) \tag{11.374}$$

and for those seeking houses and jobs simultaneously:

$$\sum_i \sum_k \sum_j \sum_w \Delta^3 N_{ij}^{kw1}(t, t + T) = \Delta^3 N_{**}^{**1}(t, t + T) \tag{11.375}$$

The supply side constraint for $b = 1$ people seeking housing also involves $b = 3$ people, and is

$$\sum_i \sum_k \Delta^2 N_{ij}^{kw1}(t, t + T) + \sum_j \sum_w \Delta^3 N_{ij}^{kw1}(t, t + T) + \Delta^2 N_{i*}^{k*3}(t, t + T)$$

$$= \Delta^T H_i^k(t, t + T) \tag{11.376}$$

This completes the specification of constraints for working heads of households.

For working dependents, the demand constraint for those seeking jobs only is

$$\sum_j \sum_w \Delta^1 N_{ij}^{kw2}(t, t + T) = \Delta^1 N_{i*}^{k*2}(t, t + T) \tag{11.377}$$

The corresponding supply constraint has already been specified as equation (11.371). We shall assume that dependents locate independently of any housing budget term, and so we only have a transport constraint for $b = 2$ people:

$$\sum_i \sum_k \sum_j [\Delta^1 N_{ij}^{kw2}(t, t + T) + \Delta^2 N_{ij}^{kw2}(t, t + T) + \Delta^3 N_{ij}^{kw2}(t, t + T)]c_{ij} = C^{2w}$$

$$\tag{11.378}$$

The demand constraint for working dependents seeking residential places only is

$$\sum_i \sum_k \Delta^2 N_{ij}^{kw2}(t, t + T) = \Delta^2 N_{*j}^{*w2} \qquad (11.379)$$

The corresponding supply constraint also involves working dependents who are also seeking jobs and is

$$\sum_j \sum_w [\Delta^2 N_{ij}^{kw2}(t, t + T) + \Delta^3 N_{ij}^{kw2}(t, t + T)]$$
$$= R_i^{k2}(t, t + T) \times \Delta^T H_i^k(t, t + T) \quad (11.380)$$

The demand constraint for working dependents seeking residential places and jobs simultaneously is

$$\sum_i \sum_k \sum_j \sum_w \Delta^3 N_{ij}^{kw2}(t, t + T) = \Delta^3 N_{**}^{**2}(t, t + T) \qquad (11.381)$$

Equation (11.380) is the corresponding supply constraint for residential places and equation (11.371) that for jobs.

The demand constraint for non-heads of households seeking houses is

$$\sum_i \sum_k \Delta^2 N_{i*}^{k*3}(t, t + T) = \Delta^2 N_{**}^{**3}(t, t + T) \qquad (11.382)$$

The corresponding supply constraint is equation (11.376). The cost constraint is

$$\sum \sum \Delta^2 N_{i*}^{k*3}(t, t + T)[p_i^k - q^w(w - c_{ij})]^2 = \sigma^{3w^2}(t, t + T) \quad (11.383)$$

The demand constraint for non-working dependents seeking residential places is

$$\sum_i \sum_k \Delta^2 N_{i*}^{k*4}(t, t + T) = \Delta^2 N_{**}^{**4}(t, t + T) \qquad (11.384)$$

The supply constraint is

$$\Delta^2 N_{i*}^{k*4}(t, t + T) = R_i^{k4}(t, t + T)\Delta^T H_i^k(t, t + T) \qquad (11.385)$$

In this case, the constraint actually directly gives the required quantity.

This completes the specification of the constraint set. The binding constraints for each variable being estimated are summarized in Table 11.2. The demand and supply terms which appear on the right-hand side of these constraint equations have all been estimated in earlier steps, while the remaining right-hand side terms, $C^{1w}(t, t + T)$, $\sigma^{1w^2}(t, t + T)$, $C^{2w}(t, t + T)$ and $\sigma^{3w^2}(t, t + T)$ can be considered to be functions of external variables.

Table 11.2

Variable	Constraints
$\Delta^1 N_{ij}^{kw1}(t, t + T)$	(11.370), (11.371), (11.372)
$\Delta^2 N_{ij}^{kw1}(t, t + T)$	(11.372), (11.373), (11.374), (11.376)
$\Delta^3 N_{ij}^{kw1}(t, t + T)$	(11.371), (11.372), (11.373), (11.375), (11.376)
$\Delta^1 N_{ij}^{kw2}(t, t + T)$	(11.377), (11.379), (11.371)
$\Delta^2 N_{ij}^{kw2}(t, t + T)$	(11.378), (11.379), (11.380)
$\Delta^3 N_{ij}^{kw2}(t, t + T)$	(11.371), (11.378), (11.380), (11.381)
$\Delta^2 N_{i*}^{k*3}(t, t + T)$	(11.376), (11.382), (11.383)
$\Delta^2 N_{i*}^{k*4}(t, t + T)$	(11.384), (11.385)

The entropy-maximizing models which result from this set of constraints are:

$$\Delta^1 N_{ij}^{kw1}(t, t + T) = A_i^{1/1k}(t, t + T)B_j^w(t, t + T)\Delta^1 N_{i*}^{k*1}(t, t + T)$$
$$\times \, \Delta^T E_j^w(t, t + T)\,e^{-\beta^{1w}(t, t+T)c_{ij}} \tag{11.386}$$

$$\Delta^2 N_{ij}^{kw1}(t, t + T) = A_i^k(t, t + T)B_j^{2/1w}(t, t + T)\Delta^T H_i^k(t, t + T)$$
$$\times \, \Delta^2 N_{*j}^{*w1}(t, t + T)\,e^{-\beta^{1w}(t, t+T)c_{ij}}$$
$$\times \, e^{-\mu^{1w}(t, t+T)[p_i^k - q^w(w - c'_{ij})]^2} \tag{11.387}$$

$$\Delta^3 N_{ij}^{kw1}(t, t + T) = K^{3/1}(t, t + T)A_i^k(t, t + T)B_j^w(t, t + T)\Delta^3 N_{**}^{**1}(t, t + T)$$
$$\times \, \Delta^T H_i^k(t, t + T) \times \Delta^T E_j^w(t, t + T)\,e^{-\beta^{1w}(t, t+T)c_{ij}}$$
$$\times \, e^{-\mu^{1w}(t, t+T)[p_i^k - q^w(w - c'_{ij})]^2} \tag{11.388}$$

$$\Delta^1 N_{ij}^{kw2}(t, t + T) = A_i^{1/2k}(t, t + T)B_j^w(t, t + T)\Delta^1 N_{i*}^{k*2}(t, t + T)$$
$$\Delta^T E_j^w(t, t + T)\,e^{-\beta^{2w}(t, t+T)c_{ij}} \tag{11.389}$$

$$\Delta^2 N_{ij}^{kw2}(t, t + T) = A_i^{2,3/2k}(t, t + T)B_j^{2/2w}(t, t + T)R_i^{k2}(t, t + T)$$
$$\Delta^T H_i^k(t, t + T) \times \Delta^2 N_{*j}^{*w2}(t, t + T)\,e^{-\beta^{2w}(t,t+T)c_{ij}} \tag{11.390}$$

$$\Delta^3 N_{ij}^{kw2}(t, t + T) = K^{3/2}(t, t + T)A_i^{2,3/2k}(t, t + T)B_j^w(t, t + T)$$
$$\Delta^3 N_{**}^{**2}(t, t + T)R_i^{k2}(t, t + T)\Delta^T H_i^k(t, t + T)$$
$$\times \, \Delta^T E_j^w(t, t + T)\,e^{-\beta^{2w}(t, t+T)c_{ij}} \tag{11.391}$$

$$\Delta^2 N_{i*}^{k*3}(t, t + T) = K^{2/3}(t, t + T)A_i^k(t, t + T)\Delta^2 N_{**}^{**3}(t, t + T)$$
$$\times \, \Delta^T H_i^k(t, t + T) \times e^{-\mu^{3w}(t, t+T)[p_i^k - q^w(w - c'_{ij})]^2} \tag{11.392}$$

and finally

$$\Delta^2 N_{i*}^{k*4}(t, t + T) = R_i^{k4}(t, t + T)\Delta^T H_i^k(t, t + T) \qquad (11.393)$$

Equation (11.393), of course, is simply a repeat of equation (11.385). We assume that $R_i^{k4}(t, t + T)$ has been so calculated that equation (11.384) is also satisfied.

The terms $A_i^{1/1k}(t, t + T)$, $B_j^w(t, t + T)$, $A_i^k(t, t + T)$, $B_j^{2/1w}(t, t + T)$, $K^{3/1}(t, t + T), A_i^{1/2k}(t, t + T), A_i^{2,3/2k}(t, t + T), B_j^{2/2w}(t, t + T), K^{3/2}(t, t + T)$, $K^{2/3}(t, t + T)$, in the model equations are related in the usual way to the Lagrangian multipliers associated with the constraint equations, in this case equations (11.370), (11.371), (11.376), (11.374), (11.375), (11.377), (11.380), (11.379), (11.381) and (11.382) respectively. Equations for these terms can be obtained in the usual way by substituting from the appropriate model equations into the constraint equations and solving. This will produce a large set of non-linear simultaneous equations which would have to be solved iteratively. They will be similar in character to the equations (10.73)–(10.83) in the final residential–workplace location model discussion in Chapter 10. The equations for the above terms will not be spelled out explicitly here as this is a straightforward algebraic task.

Step 7e. New distribution of individuals to residences and workplaces

We can now calculate $N_{ij}^{kw1}(t + T)$, $N_{ij}^{kw2}(t + T)$, $N_{i*}^{k*3}(t + T)$ and $N_{i*}^{k*4}(t + T)$.

$$N_{ij}^{kw1}(t + T) = \sum_{l=1}^{4} \Delta^1 N_{ij}^{kw1}(t, t + T) \qquad (11.394)$$

$$N_{ij}^{kw2}(t + T) = \sum_{l=1}^{4} \Delta^l N_{ij}^{kw2}(t + T) \qquad (11.395)$$

$$N_{i*}^{k*3}(t + T) = \Delta^2 N_{i*}^{k*3}(t, t + T) + \Delta^4 N_{i*}^{k*3}(t, t + T) + F_{52}^{ik}(t, t + T) \qquad (11.396)$$

$$N_{i*}^{k*4}(t + T) = \Delta^2 N_{i*}^{k*4}(t, t + T) + \Delta^4 N_{i*}^{k*4}(t, t + T) + F_{59}^{ik}(t, t + T) \quad (11.397)$$

The rather odd final terms in the last two equations are the two flows, $b = 1$ to $b = 3$ but no change of house and $b = 2$ to $b = 4$ and no change of residential place, which are not picked up either in the allocation model or the non-mover calculation.

Step 8. Demand for services

The subscript list f is taken as w for this example. Let $\pi_{33}^{sw}(t + T)$ be the per capita expenditure, for a household whose head has wage w, for s-type rvices. Then, we can estimate the whole demand, $e_i^{sw}(t + T)\hat{P}_i^w(t + T)$, as

$$e_i^{sw}(t + T)\hat{P}_i^w(t + T) = \pi_{33}^{sw}(t + T)\sum_j \sum_k N_{ij}^{kw1}(t + T) \qquad (11.398)$$

tep 9. Demand for transport

We have to produce specific versions of equations (11.238) and (11.239) with the subscript list n replaced by $(p.n)$, where p stands for trip purpose and for car-availability status. We might hypothesize relationships of the form:

$$O_i^{pn}(t + T) = \sum_b \pi_{34}^{ipnb}(t + T)\sum_k N_{i*}^{k*b}(t + T)$$

$$\times \left[\sum_j E_j^*(t + T)e^{-\beta^{pn}(t+T)c_{ij}}\right]^{\alpha_1^{pn}(t+T)} \qquad (11.399)$$

where $\pi_{34}^{ipnb}(t + T)$ is a set of trip rates, and $\alpha_1^{pn}(t + T)$ is an elasticity with espect to accessibility provision, and

$$C_i^{pn}(t + T) = \sum_b \pi_{35}^{ipnb}(t + T)\sum_k N_{i*}^{k*b}(t + T)$$

$$\times \left[\sum_j E_j^*(t + T)e^{-\beta^{pn}(t+T)c_{ij}}\right]^{\alpha_2^{pn}(t+T)} \qquad (11.400)$$

with similar definitions of coefficients. At this stage, although it is a supply quantity rather than a demand quantity, we can also assume that $D_j^{pn}(t + T)$ s given. This is either (a) a capacity constraint for trip attractions or (b) a measure of zonal attractiveness. We shall assume for simplicity in this example that it is always a *constraint*. (For the model when such assumptions are relaxed, see Wilson, 1973-A.)

Step 10. Utilization of services

The term $S_{ij}^{sw}(t + T)$ must satisfy the production constraint

$$\sum_j S_{ij}^{sw}(t + T) = e_i^{sw}(t + T) \qquad (11.401)$$

and a transport constraint which has the form of equation (11.400). For these subscript lists, it can be written

$$\sum_s \sum_i \sum_j S_{ij}^{sw}(t + T)c_{ij}(t + T) = C^w(t + T) \qquad (11.402)$$

This generates the entropy-maximizing model

$$S_{ij}^{sw}(t + T) = A_i^{sw}(t + T)e_i^{sw}(t + T)W_j^s(t + T)e^{-\beta^w(t+T)c_{ij}(t+T)} \qquad (11.403)$$

where $A_i^{sw}(t + T)$ is the usual factor related to the Lagrangian multiplier associated with equation (11.401).

Step 11. Utilization of transport services

The trip variable, for our specific subscript lists, can be written $T_{ij}^{pmn}(t + T)$. It is constrained by

$$\sum_j \sum_m T_{ij}^{pmn}(t + T) = O_i^{pn}(t + T) \qquad (11.404)$$

$$\sum_i \sum_m T_{ij}^{pmn}(t + T) = D_j^{pn}(t + T) \qquad (11.405)$$

and

$$\sum_i \sum_j \sum_m T_{ij}^{pmn}(t + T)c_{ij}^m(t + T) = C^{pn}(t + T) \qquad (11.406)$$

This leads to the entropy-maximizing model

$$T_{ij}^{pmn}(t + T) = A_i^{pn}(t + T)B_j^{pn}(t + T)O_i^{pn}(t + T)D_j^{pn}(t + T)$$
$$\times\ e^{-\beta^{pn}(t + T)c_{ij}^m(t + T)} \qquad (11.407)$$

where $A_i^{pn}(t + T)$ and $B_j^{pn}(t + T)$ are the usual balancing factors.

11.9. CONCLUDING COMMENTS

We end this chapter with some comments on the position which has been reached. In Chapters 7–10, we discussed particular sub-models in depth. In Sections 11.2–11.5 of this chapter, we have discussed various approaches which have been employed to build a general model, and interesting features of the overall task are illustrated in each case. Often an author whose main interest is the development of a general model does not use the 'latest' sub-model in each part of his model system, and we saw that some of the sub-models can be improved using the results of Chapters 7–10 with little difficulty. We then went on to discuss principles for building a general model, given the above thoughts as a background. We explored the account structures of a general model: how to make the pieces fit together in an internally consistent way; and we began the extremely difficult task of exploring the mechanisms of change in urban and regional systems. This led us to a formal statement of a general model in Section 11.7 and a specific example in Section 11.8. In this example, we had to tackle another question of balance: the fact that we have a deeper knowledge of some sub-models than others, and we tried to develop some sub-models further (if such developments were necessary to the overall framework) and, in other cases, we presented examples of sub-models of which more detailed versions were available from earlier chapters. For example, the residential–workplace location model outlined in Section 11.8 is a further development of that of Chapter 10, with the new features being 'forced' on us by the accounting procedure underpinning the general model. The transport model, on the other hand, presented in steps 9 and 11 of Section 11.8, is a simpler version of some of the models presented in Chapter 9.

All this means that the reader who wishes to build his own general model using the methods of this book has a number of choices available to him. His model design decisions will be made according to his purposes, model-building abilities, data availability and tastes. He could decide to use an 'off-the-shelf' model from Sections 11.2–11.5, but possibly improving some of the sub-models using material from Chapters 7–10. Or, he could attempt to live up to the more advanced principles of Sections 11.6–11.8, but again possibly redesigning some of the sub-models for his own purposes. It is hoped that enough material has been presented in Chapters 7–11 to teach model-building *methods* in depth, so that models can be built for any specific purpose: very simple models for teaching purposes, models to match data availability for practical planning purposes or more advanced, and probably more complicated, models for a host of research purposes.

11.10. REFERENCES

W. Alonso (1964) *Location and land use*, Harvard University Press, Cambridge, Mass.

R. Barras, T. A. Broadbent, M. Cordey Hayes, D. B. Massey and K. Robinson (1971) An operational urban development model of Cheshire, *Environment and Planning*, 3, pp. 115–234.

M. Batty (1971) Design and construction of a sub-regional land use model, *Socio-economic planning sciences*, 5, pp. 97–124.

M. Batty (1972-A) Recent developments in land use modelling: a review of British research, *Urban Studies*, 9, pp. 151–177.

M. Batty (1972-B) Dynamic simulation of an urban system, in A. G. Wilson (Ed.) *Patterns and processes in urban and regional systems*, Pion, London, pp. 44–82.

A. Chevan (1965) Population projection systems, Technical Paper No. 3., Penn.–Jersey Transportation Study, Philadelphia.

M. Cordey Hayes, T. A. Broadbent and D. B. Massey (1971) Towards operational urban development models, in M. Chisholm, A. E. Frey and P. Haggett (Eds.) *Regional forecasting*, Butterworths, London, pp. 221–254.

J. P. Crecine (1964) TOMM: time-oriented metropolitan model, CRP Technical Bulletin, 6, CONSAD Research Corporation, Pittsburgh.

J. P. Crecine (1968) A dynamic model of urban structure, P-3803, RAND Corporation, Santa Monica.

R. D. Duke (1967) Planning research at Michigan State University: an interview with John L. Taylor, *Journal of the Town Planning Institute*, 53, pp. 239–241.

M. Echenique, D. Crowther and W. Lindsay (1969) A spatial model of urban stock and activity, *Regional Studies*, 3, pp. 281–312.

J. W. Forrester (1961) *Industrial dynamics*, John Wiley, New York.

J. W. Forrester (1968) *Principles of systems*, Wright–Allen Press, Cambridge, Mass.

J. W. Forrester (1969) *Urban Dynamics*, M.I.T. Press, Cambridge, Mass.

R. A. Garin (1966) A matrix formulation of the Lowry model for intra-metropolitan activity location, *Journal of the American Institute of Planners*, **32**, pp. 361–364.

W. Goldner (1971) The Lowry model heritage, *Journal of the American Institute of Planners*, **37**, pp. 100–110.

H. R. Hamilton *et al.* (1969) *Systems simulation for regional analysis*, M.I.T. Press, Cambridge, Mass.

B. Harris (1964) A note on the probability of interaction at a distance, *Journal of Regional Science*, **15**, pp. 31–35.

D. M. Hill (1965) A growth allocation model for the Boston Region, *Journal of the American Institute of Planners*, **31**, pp. 111–120.

I. S. Lowry (1964) *A model of metropolis*, RM-4035-RC, RAND Corporation, Santa Monica.

* I. S. Lowry (1968) Seven models of urban development: a structural comparison, *Special Report 97*, Highway Research Board, Washington, D.C., pp. 121–145.

P. H. Rees and A. G. Wilson (1973) Accounts and models for spatial demographic analysis I: aggregate populations, *Environment and Planning*, **5**, 61–90.

K. Schlager (1965) A land use plan design model, *Journal of the American Institute of Planners*, **31**, pp. 103–111.

D. R. Seidman (1969) *The construction of an urban growth model*, Plan Report No. 1, Technical Supplement, Volume A, Delaware Valley Regional Planning Commission, Philadelphia.

J. L. Taylor (1972) *Instructional planning systems*, Cambridge University Press, London.

A. G. Wilson (1967) A statistical theory of spatial distribution models, *Transportation Research*, **1**, pp. 253–269.

A. G. Wilson (1969-A) Developments of some elementary residential location models, *Journal of Regional Sciences*, **9**, pp. 377–385.

* A. G. Wilson (1969-B) The integration of accounting and location theory in urban modelling, in A. J. Scott (Ed.) *Studies in regional science*, Pion, London, pp. 89–104; also reprinted in A. G. Wilson (1972) *Papers in urban and regional analysis*, Pion, London, pp. 154–169.

A. G. Wilson (1971) Generalizing the Lowry model, in A. G. Wilson (Ed.) *Urban and regional planning*, Pion, London, pp. 121–133; also reprinted in A. G. Wilson (1972) *Papers in urban and regional analysis*, Pion, London, pp. 58–70.

A. G. Wilson (1973-A) Further developments of entropy maximizing transport models, *Transportation planning and technology*, **1**, 183–193.

A. G. Wilson (1973-B) Learning and control mechanisms for urban modelling, Working Paper 35, Department of Geography, University of Leeds.

CHAPTER 12

Practical considerations: data, calibration and testing

2.1. THE NATURE OF THE CALIBRATION AND TESTING TASK

We had one example of calibration in Chapter 4, when the parameter n in the model given by equation (4.18) was estimated by maximizing the sum of squares of differences between predicted and observed terms in equation (4.21). Since then, we have concentrated on model-building principles and have neglected the topic of calibration and testing. The principle of calibration of a model is to choose the parameters of the model to optimize one or more goodness-of-fit statistics. In this chapter we outline methods for doing this for a wide range of examples and firstly we detail the range of the calibration problem in relation to the models of Chapters 7–11. Following this, we concentrate on method: in Section 12.2 we discuss the task of defining goodness-of-fit statistics and in Section 12.3 we show how to find parameters which optimize these in different examples. In Section 12.4 we add a note on the task of estimating entire unsmoothed empirical curves. Then in Sections 12.5–12.9 we review the calibration and testing problems for the models of Chapters 7–11, in each case paying special attention to likely data availability. In Section 12.10, some special procedures and short cuts are described.

We note at the outset that we concentrate more on calibration than on testing, though since calibration almost always involves the calculation of goodness-of-fit statistics which can then be evaluated for the best fit, this is little restriction.

There are three main types of calibration. The models of Chapters 7 and 8, the demographic and economic models, and the category analysis trip-generation model of Chapter 9 all involve the calculation of rates or coefficients for particular sub-groups of the population. This process is a kind of model calibration. The art is to group sub-sets of the total population into categories in such a way that the rates for each sub-set are stable, and the actual distribution of values for each sub-set about the 'mean' rate is a 'narrow' one. This kind of analysis is what Winsten (1967) calls regression analysis without prior hypothesis about the nature of the response surface; more typically a linear assumption is made about this surface, leading to *linear* regression analysis.

Next, indeed, we consider parameter estimation in linear models of the form

$$y = a_0 + a_1 x_1 + a_2 x_2 + \ldots \tag{12.1}$$

or log linear models

$$\log y = a_0 + a_1 x_1 + a_2 x_2 + \ldots \tag{12.2}$$

in situations where observations are available of $(y, x_1, x_2, \ldots)$ and $a_0, a_1,$ $a_2, \ldots$ are parameters to be estimated. This estimation task is standard and well-known: a sum of squares will be minimized, and some statistic such as R^2 used to measure goodness-of-fit. This technique can only be used when rather strong assumptions are satisfied: the independent variables should not be correlated with each other, they should be normally distributed, and the unwritten error term should also be normally distributed and should have mean zero. Needless to say, this method of parameter estimation is often used in circumstances where these conditions are not satisfied, and biased estimates of the parameters may then be obtained. Examples of the use of linear equations within one of the models discussed in this book are the trip generation equations (9.1) and (9.2) in Chapter 9.

We should note that some models which do not at first sight appear to be linear can be transformed to take a linear form. For example

$$y = a_0 x_1^{a_1} x_2^{a_2} \ldots \tag{12.3}$$

or

$$y = a_0 \, e^{a_1 x_1} \, e^{a_2 x_2} \ldots \tag{12.4}$$

become

$$\log y = a_0 + a_1 \log x_1 + a_2 \log x_2 + \ldots \tag{12.5}$$

or

$$\log_e y = \log_e a_0 + a_1 x_1 + a_2 x_2 + \ldots \tag{12.6}$$

(which is equivalent to equation (12.2)) after taking logs. Most of the models which appear in Chapters 9–11 are intrinsically non-linear (a concept which, according to Batty (1971) was first introduced by Draper and Smith (1966)) in that they cannot be transformed this way. A simple example is the shopping model given in equation (4.18) in Chapter 4.

Non-linear models may have one or more parameters and, unsurprisingly, the complexity of the calibration procedure increases rapidly as the number of parameters increases. Where several parameters are involved, an issue may arise as to whether they should be estimated sequentially or simultaneously.

In the following sub-sections, we shall assume that methods of estimating rates and parameters in linear models are, on the whole, familiar and we shall concentrate almost entirely on parameter estimation in non-linear models.

12.2. GOODNESS-OF-FIT STATISTICS

Suppose we have a set of observations, x_i^{obs}, and a set of model predictions, x_i, how do we compare the two? The simplest measure is the sum of squares (which we used for this purpose in Chapter 4):

$$S = \sum_i (x_i - x_i^{obs})^2 \tag{12.7}$$

This will take a minimum value for the 'best' fit, though it will be difficult to assess how good the fit is as the value of S depends on the dimensions of the variables and the units chosen.

Perhaps a better procedure of direct comparison is to plot x_i against x_i^{obs}, and to fit a straight line between them, say using the model

$$x_i = a_0 + a_1 x_i^{obs} \tag{12.8}$$

For an exact fit, a_0 should be zero and a_1 should be 1. Deviation from these values shows a worsening fit, and the actual values (together with an inspection of the plots) may give an indication of any systematic bias in the model.

The next step is to find measures of association between x_i and x_i^{obs} which are dimensionless. Any standard statistical programme which estimated a_0 and a_1 in equation (12.8) would also estimate the correlation R between the sets of variables and R^2, the amount of variance explained by the model:

$$R^2 = 1 - \frac{\sum_i (x_i - x_i^{obs})^2}{\sum_i [x_i^{obs} - (1/n)\sum_i x_i^{obs}]^2} \tag{12.9}$$

where n is the number of variables R^2 varies between 1, for an exact correspondence and 0.

The other obvious alternative is to use χ^2 defined as

$$\chi^2 = \sum_i \frac{(x_i^{obs} - x_i)^2}{x_i} \tag{12.10}$$

The use of these (and other measures) are discussed in the urban modelling context by Batty (1970, 1971) and Evans (1971). In calibration, we would find model parameter values to maximize R^2 and to minimize χ^2.

The variables x_i used to construct these variables may be any model outputs. In a spatial interaction model, they should usually be the interaction matrices, though it such a model is singly constrained and is being used as a location model, then spatial distribution of some interaction-end totals, a distribution of some activity, may be appropriate.

The problem which often arises when goodness-of-fit statistics such as those defined above are used in urban and regional modelling for calibration purposes is that they vary rather slowly as the parameters of the model vary. That is, they are often relatively insensitive to parameter estimation. This problem can be avoided in many cases of parameter estimation in non-linear models by the use of maximum-likelihood procedures (or, in this case analogously, by entropy-maximizing procedures). Such methods for this field are discussed as maximum-likelihood methods by Blackburn (1970), Evans (1971) and Batty and Mackie (1972), and as entropy-maximizing methods by this author (Wilson, 1970). Another equivalent procedure can be derived from Bayesian methods, as in Hyman (1969). The method will be explained here only in the broadest outline, and the reader is referred to the previously cited works for the details. Assume that the model can be written so that p_i is the probability of a member of the population being in the i-state, so

$$p_i = \frac{x_i}{x} \qquad (12.11)$$

for total population x, and x_i^{obs} is the number observed in state i as before. Then the likelihood function is

$$L = \prod_i p_i^{x_i^{obs}} \qquad (12.12)$$

and it can be shown that the best estimates of the model's parameters can be obtained by choosing those which maximize L, or more usually, and equivalently, log L.

This procedure is equivalent to the entropy-maximizing procedure (see Appendix 1 and Wilson, 1970) in the following sense. For each parameter of the model, the procedure produces an equation to be solved for that parameter. This equation turns out to be the constraint equation which would be used to generate the same model as an entropy-maximizing model, and the equivalent parameter is then the Lagrangian multiplier associated with the constraint. Either way, the parameter is obtained by solving the appropriate equation. It is really a matter of taste and convenience as to whether maximum-likelihood methods or entropy-maximizing methods are used to produce the equation which is to be solved for each parameter. The important point is that, for each parameter, there *is* such an equation, and the statistic associated with it is the *best* goodness-of-fit statistic for that parameter.

The method is best illustrated by an example. Consider a one-parameter version of the shopping model given in equation (4.18):

$$S_{ij} = A_i e_i P_i W_j c_{ij}^{-\beta} \qquad (12.13)$$

The maximum-likelihood equation for β is

$$\sum_i \sum_j S_{ij} \log c_{ij} = \sum_i \sum_j S_{ij}^{obs} \log c_{ij} \qquad (12.14)$$

using an obvious notation. That is, S_{ij} is to be substituted from equation (12.13) into (12.14) and (12.14) solved for β. The entropy-maximizing constraint which gives rise to the β term in the entropy-maximizing derivation of equation (12.13) is

$$\sum_i \sum_j S_{ij} \log c_{ij} = C \qquad (12.15)$$

where C is a constant which in this case turns out to be the same as the right-hand side of equation (12.14) and so the resulting estimation procedures are the same. (Note also that if *mean* trip expenditure is known, this implies that the right-hand side quantities are known.)

If an exponential function was used, so that the model was

$$S_{ij} = A_i e_i P_i W_j \, e^{-\beta c_{ij}} \qquad (12.16)$$

then the maximum-likelihood equation would be

$$\sum_i \sum_j S_{ij} c_{ij} = \sum_i \sum_j S_{ij}^{obs} c_{ij} \qquad (12.17)$$

and the entropy-maximizing equation

$$\sum_i \sum_j S_{ij} c_{ij} = C \qquad (12.18)$$

which are identical, and which can be solved for β. This does remind us, of course, that we still have to choose between alternative forms of function in such models.

If a second parameter is now introduced, as in the equation (4.18) models, a new estimating equation must be found for that parameter (see Batty and Mackie, 1972). For α in the equation (4.18) model the maximum-likelihood equation is

$$\sum_i \sum_j S_{ij} \log W_j = \sum_i \sum_j S_{ij}^{obs} \log W_j \qquad (12.19)$$

and the equivalent entropy-maximizing constraint would be

$$\sum_i \sum_j S_{ij} \log W_j = \log W \qquad (12.20)$$

where $\log W$ is in fact given by the right-hand side of (12.19) and is to be interpreted as the total benefit obtained by people choosing centre j where they can obtain benefit log W_j relative to other centres. (In the original derivation of this term, another method was used (Wilson, 1967, 1970) and this argument now suggests that where a new parameter is involved, it is better to introduce a new constraint explicitly.)

It is interesting to reflect that the above discussion records the theoretical respectability of a result which had been known in practice for a long time, at least for the main parameter of a spatial interaction model; that the most sensitive fitting statistic for the parameter in the cost function was something like mean-trip length. The newer results, however, have not only given us theoretical justification, but also more precision: we now know that mean-trip length is appropriate if the trip cost function is $e^{-\beta c_{ij}}$, but for a general function, $f(c_{ij})$, it should be written in the form $e^{-\beta h(c_{ij})}$ and then the mean value of $h(c_{ij})$ will be the appropriate statistic. Thus, for the power function, as we have seen, $c_{ij}^{-\beta}$ can be written $e^{-\beta \log c_{ij}}$ and so the mean value of $\log c_{ij}$ is the best statistic.

We can summarize the overall discussion as follows. For each parameter in a model, ideally the maximum-likelihood estimating equation (or entropy-maximizing constraint equation) should be obtained, and this provides the appropriate goodness-of-fit statistic. However, we still need to know something about the goodness-of-fit of the model as a whole, and for this we will still need something like R^2 or χ^2 tests applied to the model's main variables. This will not only give us the overall indication we need, but may help us to choose between different forms of function: for example, for travel impedance.

12.3. THE MECHANICS OF PARAMETER ESTIMATION

Again, we concentrate mainly on estimation procedures for parameters with non-linear models. In the first instance, to illustrate the methods available for parameter computation, we will consider only single parameter models. The model predictions x_i can then, for these purposes, be considered functions of the parameter, say β, only, and similarly the goodness-of-fit statistics. Thus, our task is to maximize $R^2(\beta)$, or to minimize $\chi^2(\beta)$ or to solve

$$C(\beta) = C^{\text{obs}} \qquad (12.21)$$

where C is the 'function' which turns up in the maximum-likelihood equation. (For the single parameter shopping model, equation (12.17) would be the specific form of (12.21) for example.) Figure 12.1 shows diagrammatically what is involved in the three cases mentioned. Almost always, the procedure used to find β when the model is non-linear will be a numerical one within a computer. In each case, the problem is to identify the value of β indicated by the point P on the figure.

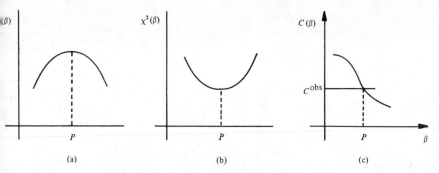

Figure 12.1 Maximum, minimum and equation solving problems in calibration

For the minimization and maximization problems, some sort of search procedure is usually used. The simplest possible procedure is to run the model for a range of values of β, and choose the β which optimizes the statistic, if necessary repeating with a smaller increment connecting the different β-values. However, this is relatively inefficient. Batty (1971) illustrates the use of Fibbonaci and 'golden-section' search routines in this context. Suppose, for definiteness, that we are trying to maximize $R^2(\beta)$ in Figure 12.1(a). At the kth step of the procedure to be described, it has been established that β lies between β_1^k and β_2^k (as in Figure 12.2) and β_3^k and β_4^k are chosen such that

$$\beta_1^k < \beta_3^k < \beta_4^k < \beta_2^k \tag{12.22}$$

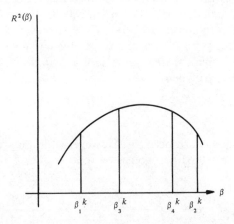

Figure 12.2 Fibbonaci search. (Based, with permission, on M. Batty in *Environment and Planning*, Vol. 3, Pion, 1971, Figure 2, p. 420.)

β_3^k and β_4^k are chosen such that

$$\beta_3^k = \frac{F_{N-1-k}}{F_{N+1-k}}(\beta_2^k - \beta_1^k) + \beta_1^k \tag{12.23}$$

$$\beta_4^k = \frac{F_{N-k}}{F_{N+1-k}}(\beta_2^k - \beta_1^k) + \beta_1^k \tag{12.24}$$

where the Fs are the Fibbonaci numbers defined by

$$\left. \begin{array}{l} F_0 = F_1 = 1 \\ F_n = F_{n-1} + F_{n-2}, \qquad n \geqslant 2 \end{array} \right\} \tag{12.25}$$

If $R^2(\beta_3^k) > R^2(\beta_4^k)$ then β lies in the interval (β_1^k/β_4^k) and if $R^2(\beta_3^k) < R^2(\beta_4^k)$, β lies in the interval (β_3^k/β_2^k). This gives two bounds for the next stage. Batty shows that after N steps, the remaining interval, δ^N, is at most

$$\delta^N = \frac{1}{F_N}(\beta_2^1 - \beta_1^1) + \varepsilon \tag{12.26}$$

for some small number ε, and so F_N, and hence N, can be determined from equation (12.26) for any desired value of δ^N.

Golden-section search replaces F_{N-1-k}/F_{N+1-k} in equation (12.23) by the number $0 \cdot 382$ (to which it is approximately equal for large N) and F_{N-k}/F_{N+1-k} in equation (12.24) by $0 \cdot 618$ for similar reasons. Batty (1971) notes that golden-section search is approximately 13% slower than Fibbonaci search, though it is easier to programme for the computer.

These procedures can also be used for the equation-solving problem of Figure 12.1(c) and equation (12.21). An equivalent problem (and again we follow Batty, 1971) is to minimize $|C(\beta) - C^{\text{obs}}|$. However, other methods are also available for equation solving and it is to these that we now turn.

The simplest possible iterative procedure is as follows. Suppose after k steps, our estimate is β^k. Then

$$\beta^{k+1} = \beta^k \frac{C(\beta^k)}{C^{\text{obs}}} \tag{12.27}$$

is a suitable adjustment procedure. However, this may converge rather slowly, and Hyman (1969) has suggested that for $k > 1$, the second-order formula

$$\beta^{k+1} = \frac{(C^{\text{obs}} - C(\beta^{k-1}))\beta^k - (C^{\text{obs}} - C(\beta^k))\beta^{k-1}}{C(\beta^k) - C(\beta^{k-1})} \tag{12.28}$$

should produce more rapid convergence, and several workers have since used this result.

Another possibility is to use a Newton–Raphson procedure. Let

$$\beta^{k+1} = \beta^k + \varepsilon^k \tag{12.29}$$

Then

$$C(\beta^{k+1}) = C(\beta^k + \varepsilon^k)$$

$$= C(\beta^k) + \varepsilon^k \left.\frac{\partial C}{\partial \beta}\right|_{\beta^k} \tag{12.30}$$

to the first-order in ε^k. Since we wish $C(\beta^{k+1})$ to be C^{obs}, ε^k can be obtained from equation (12.30) as

$$\varepsilon^k = \frac{C^{\mathrm{obs}} - C(\beta^k)}{(\partial C/\partial \beta)|_{\beta^k}} \tag{12.31}$$

and equations (12.29) and (12.31) define a suitable iterative procedure. The derivative can be evaluated numerically.

These methods can be extended to the case where two or more parameters are to be estimated. Where many parameters are involved, the model system can usually be decomposed in some obvious way, and the calibration problem correspondingly. Firstly then, let us consider a two-parameter problem: our model is a function of parameters α and β; our general goodness-of-fit statistics are $R^2(\alpha, \beta)$, $\chi^2(\alpha, \beta)$; the maximum-likelihood equation for α is, say

$$W(\alpha, \beta) = W^{\mathrm{obs}} \tag{12.32}$$

and for β, say,

$$C(\alpha, \beta) = C^{\mathrm{obs}} \tag{12.33}$$

The important point to note at the outset is that all the statistics are functions of both parameters. This means that, in principle, the parameters have to be estimated simultaneously. We should also note that Batty (1971) found that, with a two-parameter spatial interaction model, the response surfaces of the goodness-of-fit statistics were such that no *one* of them could be used to determine both parameters simultaneously. However, if, as recommended, maximum-likelihood equations are used, there is one such equation for each parameter, and the difficulty disappears. This was demonstrated for the same model by Batty and Mackie (1972).

This is also a convenient point to include a warning about 'accidental' optimal values of some goodness-of-fit statistics for some two-parameter models and, in particular, the shopping model shown in equation (4.18). The reader can easily check that if $\alpha = 1$ and $\beta = 0$ in the case where W_j is taken as S_{*j}^{obs}, then $S_{ij} = S_{ij}^{\mathrm{obs}}$ exactly. R^2, for example, is then 1. The response surface of $R^2(\alpha, \beta)$ is then peaked towards the maximum at $\alpha = 1$, $\beta = 0$, and this makes R^2 virtually useless for calibration purposes with this kind of model. This is another good reason for using the maximum-likelihood equations for parameter estimation. The 'bogus calibration' problem was first discussed in a Government Paper on the flows of goods to ports (Ministry of Transport, 1966).

Before discussing how the univariate methods can be extended, it is useful to comment on the separability of the calibration problem. The likely result (which is being stated at the level of conjecture, with some empirical backing, but not as a general *proved* theoretical result) is that the maximum-likelihood statistic for a parameter is likely to be maximally independent of variation of other parameters (though unlikely to be completely independent), but mutual *dependence* is likely to be the order of the day with other statistics.

The simplest calculation scheme for a two-parameter model involves the computation of goodness-of-fit statistics for a 'grid' of parameters of α and β. The values of α and β which optimize the statistics can be chosen, and the computation repeated if necessary for a finer grid around this value. This method, although rarely the most efficient, is simple and robust and has been much used in practice.

The obvious way in which to attempt to improve this method is by using Fibbonaci or golden-section search algorithms. This can be done within an iterative scheme as follows: for given α, calculate β using an efficient search procedure; iterate as necessary.

When the maximum-likelihood equations are being solved, two variable versions of the adjustment schemes given by (12.27) and (12.28) could easily be developed. A two-variable Newton–Raphson scheme to solve equations (12.32) and (12.33) can be developed as follows. Suppose

$$\alpha^{k+1} = \alpha^k + \varepsilon_1^k \tag{12.34}$$

and

$$\beta^{k+1} = \beta^k + \varepsilon_2^k \tag{12.35}$$

From equation (12.32)

$$W(\alpha^k + \varepsilon_1^k, \beta^k + \varepsilon_2^k) = W^{\text{obs}}$$

$$= W(\alpha^k, \beta^k) + \varepsilon_1^k \left.\frac{\partial W}{\partial \alpha}\right|_{\alpha^k, \beta^k} + \varepsilon_2^k \left.\frac{\partial W}{\partial \beta}\right|_{\alpha^k, \beta^k} \tag{12.36}$$

and from equation (12.33)

$$C(\alpha^k + \varepsilon_1^k, \beta^k + \varepsilon_2^k) = C^{\text{obs}}$$

$$= C(\alpha^k, \beta^k) + \varepsilon_1^k \left.\frac{\partial C}{\partial \alpha}\right|_{\alpha^k, \beta^k} + \varepsilon_2^k \left.\frac{\partial C}{\partial \beta}\right|_{\alpha^k, \beta^k} \tag{12.37}$$

These are simultaneous equations which can be solved for ε_1^k and ε_2^k, so that equations (12.34)–(12.37) form a suitable iterative scheme.

12.4. A NOTE ON ESTIMATING 'UNSMOOTHED' CURVES

Suppose we had a model of the form

$$T_{ij} = KO_iD_jf(c_{ij}) \tag{12.38}$$

in the usual notation and where K is a constant. Then the *form* of $f(c_{ij})$ can be examined by plotting observed values of T_{ij}/O_iD_j against c_{ij}. This is a plot of $f(c_{ij})$ up to the constant, K. More typically, K would be replaced by one or more balancing factors, say

$$T_{ij} = A_iB_jO_iD_jf(c_{ij}) \tag{12.39}$$

again in the usual notation. A plot of T_{ij}/O_iD_j against c_{ij} now gives a possibly biased picture of $f(c_{ij})$ because the A_is and B_js are themselves functions of $f(c_{ij})$ and are not constants. How, in this situation, can we get a reasonable empirical picture of what we might expect to be the function $f(c_{ij})$? The original calibration procedure of the Bureau of Public Roads (1965) for gravity models helps answer this question. We are not recommending this as a *calibration* procedure as such, but only in this context as a way of answering the question raised above. We illustrate the method with the model given in equation (12.39). The aim is to calculate the 'mean' value of $f(c)$ for a range of points 'c'. Suppose c varies, as a label, over such a range, and we use the notation $c_{ij} \in c$ to denote that c_{ij} falls in a certain range, say $a(c) \leqslant c_{ij} \leqslant b(c)$, where $a(c)$ and $b(c)$ are defined for each label c. As a convention, c itself may be taken as the mid-point of the range. Suppose the ranges are exclusive and exhaustive: each c_{ij} is in one and only one. The function $f(c_{ij})$ is then defined either as

$$f(c_{ij}) = f(c), \qquad c_{ij} \in c \tag{12.40}$$

or is obtained by interpolation between function values for adjacent cs; $f(c)$ is obtained as follows. After k iterations, suppose

$$T_{ij}^k = A_i^kB_j^kO_iD_jf^k(c_{ij}) \tag{12.41}$$

where

$$\sum_j T_{ij}^k = O_i \tag{12.42}$$

determines A_i and

$$\sum_i T_{ij}^k = D_j \tag{12.43}$$

determines B_j^k. We adjust $f^k(c_{ij})$ to ensure that the number of trips in the range 'c' reproduce observations. That is, so that

$$\sum_{c_{ij} \in c} T_{ij}^k = \sum_{c_{ij} \in c} T_{ij}^{obs} \tag{12.44}$$

for each c. This can be achieved by setting

$$f^{(k+1)}(c) = f^{(k)}(c) \frac{\sum_{c_{ij} \in c} T_{ij}^{obs}}{\sum_{c_{ij} \in c} T_{ij}^k} \qquad (12.45)$$

In this way, we obtain an unsmoothed function $f(c)$. This procedure is analogous to that of equation (12.27), and there is presumably a second-order improved version analogous to equation (12.28).

We may then wish to decide whether the resulting function is 'most like' a negative exponential function, or a power function or whatever, and to estimate parameters for a smoothed function by maximum-likelihood methods. In the same way as it is unwise to carry out linear regression analysis without looking at a plot of the observations, it may be argued that it is unwise to estimate the parameters for some smooth function without looking at the unsmoothed function $f(c)$ as calculated above. We shall note another application of this method in relation to housing expenditure in Section 12.8.

12.5. DEMOGRAPHIC MODELS

Unlike many other model sectors, the demographic modelling sector has a wealth of data available to it from census and birth and death registration returns. We emphasized in our discussion in Section 7.7 that the data have to be manipulated very carefully to get them into the form needed for calculating model rates and an accounting framework is essential for this purpose. There is no need to repeat that discussion here. This rate-estimation task is the main calibration task for this set of models. There may, however, be additional tasks, arising from possible sub-models for birth and death rates, and from the use of a spatial interaction model of migration. If a migration model of the form of that given in equations (7.35) and (7.36) is developed, then the standard procedures described above should be used to estimate β^r. There may also be sub-models for migration outflow and inflow (or attractiveness), the O_i^r and W_j^r terms in (7.35), and this may involve either regression analysis or category analysis and a procedure analogous to that used for trip generation. Interested readers should pursue the discussion of simultaneous or sequential estimation in this context in Section 12.7, which could also be applied in principle to these migration models.

12.6. ECONOMIC MODELS

The calibration problems with economic models are similar in principle to those of demographic models, mostly involving rate calculations for the input–output tables which can then give the technical coefficients needed for the model, but the data problems are much worse. It is difficult to assemble the data to build input–output models at the national scale in the U.K., for example, let alone at the urban and regional scale. Almost always, an urban or regional model can only be built if a special survey is carried out, as was the case with Artle's (1959) work on Stockholm and Morrison's (1972) work on Peterborough to cite but two examples. Faced with this situation, others have attempted to devise methods for estimating rates for local models by 'adjusting' in some way rates obtained from national models (see Hewings, 1971, Round, 1972).

Separate econometric sub-models may be built and estimated to provide final-demand variables in the input–output models: for example, see Stone (1967). These can be calibrated using standard regression techniques.

Unsurprisingly, multi-regional input–output models are even more rare than single-region ones. When, ultimately, they are developed, then there will be spatial interaction model calibration problems. The nearest point to this being reached in the U.K. is perhaps Chisholm's (1971) and O'Sullivan's (1971) work on freight flows.

12.7. TRANSPORT MODELS

There are two main sources of transport data for model calibration: special surveys, which have been common in large cities in the last 10–15 years and, for particular trip purposes, notably the journey to work, census data. In the U.K., census work-trip data are available from the 1961, 1966 and 1971 censuses, and for some areas in 1966 and 1971 they are available on a reasonably fine-zone system. The special surveys are usually available for one point in time only, but in some cities, such as London, second surveys are now being carried out—the second in 1972 following the first in 1962. In general, then, we can start from the assumption that some reasonably good data will be available, in the case of the special surveys collected specifically for model calibration, and so we can proceed to discuss their use.

We first illustrate the calibration problem using the model described in Section 9.4. For convenience we repeat the main equations of the model here. In equation (9.7), we refer to household category h, and later we define this to be the triple (I, n, p), where I is income group, n is car-ownership (in the associated household) and p is the family-structure index. Thus, using this explicitly, and assuming that 'n' in O_i^n refers to non-car-owning ($n = 1$, say) and car-owning ($n = 2$, say), equation (9.7) can be written

$$O_i^n = \sum_{I=1}^{6} \sum_{n' \in H(n)} \sum_{p=1}^{6} a_i(I, n', p) T(I, n', p) \qquad (12.46)$$

where $n' \in H(n)$ means that the summation is for $n' = 0$ only for $n = 1$, and $n' = 1,2$ or more, for $n = 2$. Equation (9.27), coupled with the number of households, if i, in zone, gives $a_i(I, n, p)$ as

$$a_i(I, n, p) = H_i f(p) \int_{a_I}^{a_{I+1}} P(n|x)\phi(x)\,\mathrm{d}x \tag{12.47}$$

The trip attractions were given in equation (9.15) which is repeated directly here:

$$D_j = \sum_l b_j(l)t(l) \tag{12.48}$$

The trip-distribution and modal-choice equations are (9.40)–(9.44) and are also repeated directly:

$$e^{-\beta^n C_{ij}^n} = \sum_{k\in\gamma(n)} e^{-\beta^n c_{ij}^k} \tag{12.49}$$

$$T_{ij}^{*n} = A_i^n B_j O_i^n D_j e^{-\beta^n C_{ij}^n} \tag{12.50}$$

$$A_i^n = 1 \bigg/ \sum_j B_j D_j e^{-\beta^n C_{ij}^n} \tag{12.51}$$

$$B_j = 1 \bigg/ \sum_i \sum_n A_i^n O_i^n e^{-\beta^n C_{ij}^n} \tag{12.52}$$

$$T_{ij}^{kn} = T_{ij}^{*n} \frac{e^{-\lambda^n c_{ij}^k}}{\sum_{k\in\gamma(n)} e^{-\lambda^n c_{ij}^k}} \tag{12.53}$$

Equations (12.46)–(12.53) are cycled through separately for each trip purpose and these trips are then added together, combined with commercial vehicle trips (Section 9.5) and bus trips, and are then input as vehicle trips to the assignment procedure.

With the assignment procedure described in Section 9.6 no calibration is involved, except adjustment of network representation and link speed flow characteristics to obtain the best possible fit to write flow data. But this is to adjust the components of the model as simplification of the real world to best fit the real world; it is not *parameter* adjustment, and hence is not calibration in the usual sense. Suppose then, that our task is to estimate the parameters in equations (12.46)–(12.53) (for each trip purpose, except in equation (12.47) which is common to all purposes).

In the trip-generation equations, the rates $T(I, n', p)$ in (12.46) and $t(l)$ in (12.48) have to be obtained. The distributions of households, H_i and economic activities, $b_j(l)$ can be obtained from location models or as planning inputs. The distributions $f(p)$, $P(n|x)$ and $\phi(x)$ each have parameters which have to be estimated by comparing predicted distribution of these quantities with observed distributions. (The only possible complication in this process arises when $\phi(x)$ has to be estimated from zonal car-ownership data, and this procedure is described in Chapter 9.)

β^n in equation (12.50) can be estimated by the methods described in the previous two sub-sections, with mean-trip length as goodness-of-fit statistic. That is, β^n is chosen to ensure that

$$\sum_i \sum_j T_{ij}^{*n} C_{ij}^n = \sum_i \sum_j T_{ij}^{*nobs} C_{ij}^n \tag{12.54}$$

There is one unusual feature of this particular model: C_{ij}^n is constructed from the modal costs, c_{ij}^k, by equation (12.49) and is itself a function of β^n. So, if the right-hand side of equation (12.54) is considered as the 'observed' value, then this also varies with the parameter. However, the right-hand side varies much more slowly with β^n than the left-hand side, and no difficulties arise in practice.

We now proceed to the modal split equation (12.53). Define, for convenience,

$$M_{ij}^{kn} = \frac{T_{ij}^{kn}}{T_{ij}^{*n}} \tag{12.55}$$

Then the maximizing-likelihood equation, or entropy-maximizing constraint equation, (cf. Wilson, 1973) is

$$\sum_i \sum_j \sum_{k \in \gamma(n)} M_{ij}^{kn} c_{ij}^k = \sum_i \sum_j \sum_{k \in \gamma(n)} M_{ij}^{knobs} c_{ij}^k \tag{12.56}$$

and so λ^n can be found by solving this equation using the methods of section 12.3.

This completes our discussion of the main structure of the transport model calibration process, but a number of other points must now be noted. First, we have assumed above that in both equations (12.50) and (12.53), the negative exponential function is best. Other forms of function should also be tested, and the methods of Section 12.4 should be used to produce unsmoothed, but correctly normalized, empirical functions for inspection. Thus, we could rewrite equation (12.50) as

$$T_{ij}^{*n} = A_i^n B_j O_i^n D_j f^{nD}(C_{ij}^n) \tag{12.57}$$

and obtain $f^{nD}(C_{ij}^n)$ as follows. Let $f^{nD(m)}(C)$ be the estimate of f^{nD} after m steps in some iterative procedure. Then

$$f^{nD(m+1)}(C) = f^{nD(m)}(C) \frac{\sum_{C_{ij}^n \in C} T_{ij}^{*nobs}}{\sum_{C_{ij}^n \in C} T_{ij}^{*n(m)}} \tag{12.58}$$

where $T_{ij}^{*n(m)}$ is the model estimate after m steps.

In such a procedure, the equation for C_{ij}^n, (12.49) would have to be replaced by one which was independent of the travel function chosen, for example

$$C_{ij}^n = \min_k (c_{ij}^k) \tag{12.59}$$

or the obvious generalization of equation (12.49), which would be

$$f^{nD}(C_{ij}^n) = \sum_{k \in \gamma(n)} f^{nD}(c_{ij}^k) \tag{12.60}$$

After n steps, we would have

$$f^{nD(m)}(C_{ij}^{n(m)}) = \sum_{k \in \gamma(n)} f^{nD(m)}(c_{ij}^k) \tag{12.61}$$

and C_{ij}^n in equation (12.58) would have to be replaced by $C_{ij}^{n(m)}$.

When a function has been chosen by this procedure, then in order to estimate the parameters of the corresponding smoothed function, the maximum-likelihood equation is

$$\sum_i \sum_j T_{ij}^{*n} h^n(C_{ij}^n) = \sum_i \sum_j T_{ij}^{*nobs} h^n(C_{ij}^n) \tag{12.62}$$

where h is defined by

$$e^{h^n(C_{ij}^n)} = f^{nD}(C_{ij}^n) \tag{12.63}$$

A similar procedure could be developed for the modal split function. In the distribution model above, we choose $f^{nD}(C)$ to ensure that trips for which $C_{ij}^n \in C$ equalled observed trips in the same class. The equivalent modal split criteria, based on the maximum-likelihood equation (12.56) would be: estimate $f^{nM}(c)$ such that

$$M_{ij}^{kn} = \frac{f^{nM}(c_{ij}^k)}{\sum_{k \in \gamma(n)} f^{nM}(c_{ij}^k)} \tag{12.64}$$

with observed modal share equal to model modal share for each cost group $c_{ij}^k \in c$. That is, at the mth step of an iterative procedure

$$f^{nM(m+1)}(c) = f^{nM(m)}(c) \frac{\sum_{c_{ij}^k \in c} M_{ij}^{knobs}}{\sum_{c_{ij}^k \in c} M_{ij}^{kn(m)}} \tag{12.65}$$

using an obvious notation.

This procedure emphasizes the role of $f^{nM}(c_{ij}^k)$ in the modal split model; or $e^{-\lambda^n c_{ij}^k}$ in equation (12.53). It is more customary, as in the discussions of equation (9.38) and (9.39), to divide numerator and denominator by $e^{-\lambda^n c_{ij}^k}$ or $f^{nM}(c_{ij}^k)$ and to see modal split as a function of cost differences, in the case of the negative exponential function, or whatever combination of costs from several modes, in the case of the general function. This creates a feeling that the model, and the resulting maximum-likelihood fitting procedure, should perhaps be stated directly in terms of such differences. However, it seems probable that an equation of the form (12.62) is in any case the only way in which this can be done and all the modes treated equally symmetrically, so perhaps in terms of model *form* we are being sufficiently general. This does, however, suggest an alternative to the fitting procedure. We might emphasize modal choice between each pair of modes, so that we write (12.62) as

$$N_{ij}^{kk'n} = \frac{T_{ij}^{kn}}{T_{ij}^{k'n}} = \frac{M_{ij}^{kn}}{M_{ij}^{k'n}} = \frac{f^{nM}(c_{ij}^k)}{f^{nM}(c_{ij}^{k'})} \tag{12.66}$$

and choose $f^{nM}(c)$ so that relative modal shares are equal in the model and the survey. This only produces a neat result if the form of f is such that (12.66) can be rewritten in terms of cost differences or cost ratios. Suppose, either

$$\frac{f^{nM}(c_{ij}^k)}{f^{nM}(c_{ij}^{k'})} = F^{nM}(c_{ij}^k - c_{ij}^{k'}) \tag{12.67}$$

or

$$\frac{f^{nM}(c_{ij}^k)}{f^{nM}(c_{ij}^{k'})} = F^{nM}(c_{ij}^k/c_{ij}^{k'}) \tag{12.68}$$

The first case arises when f is an exponential function, and the second when f is a power function. The reader can easily check that, apart from replacing e by another constant, or changing the base of logarithms when C_{ij} is replaced by log C_{ij} to get the power function, these are the only functions of cost differences or cost ratios respectively for which relationships (12.66) and (12.67) hold in conjunction with the modal split equations (12.62) and (12.66). Other forms of function could be used in (12.62), but this would not lead to a function of cost differences or ratios in equation (12.66). The converse result is slightly different: a wide range of functions of cost differences or ratios could be used, but unless it was an exponential or power function, separability in the form (12.66) would not be possible.

This suggests that we could also investigate the other kind of separability: we could seek functional forms such that

$$N_{ij}^{kk'n} = f^{nM}(c_{ij}^k) - f^{nM}(c_{ij}^{k'}) \tag{12.69}$$

and

$$N_{ij}^{kk'n} = F^{nM}(c_{ij}^k - c_{ij}^{k'}) \tag{12.70}$$

or

$$N_{ij}^{kk'n} = F^{nM}(c_{ij}^k/c_{ij}^{k'}) \tag{12.71}$$

Equations (12.69) and (12.70) could only be compatible if

$$N_{ij}^{kk'n} = a(c_{ij}^k - c_{ij}^{k'}) \tag{12.72}$$

for some constant a, and equation (12.69) and (12.70) only if

$$N_{ij}^{kk'n} = a(\log c_{ij}^k - \log c_{ij}^{k'}) \tag{12.73}$$

neither of which we shall consider further.

Returning to the main line of the argument, the converse case is to hypothesize that

$$N_{ij}^{kk'n} = F^{kk'nM}(c_{ij}^k - c_{ij}^{k'}) \tag{12.74}$$

for the cost difference case (which is the only one we will consider): the reader can repeat the argument which follows for the power function case without difficulty. Notice that labels kk' have been added, since in principle a different function could be chosen for each k, k' pair. The function need only be defined for $k \neq k'$ and $k > k'$ (say). In fact, it is useful to assume that for $k = k'$

$$F^{kknM}(0) = 1 \tag{12.75}$$

and that

$$F^{kk'nM}(c_{ij}^k - c_{ij}^{k'}) = \frac{1}{F^{k'knM}(c_{ij}^{k'} - c_{ij}^k)} \tag{12.76}$$

to extend the definition to all (k, k') combinations.

If we sum the first equation in (12.64) over k, we get

$$\sum_{k \in \gamma(n)} N_{ij}^{kk'n} = \frac{1}{M_{ij}^{k'n}} \tag{12.77}$$

so (replacing k' by k and k by k'),

$$M_{ij}^{kn} = \frac{1}{\sum_{k' \in \gamma(n)} N_{ij}^{k'kn}} \tag{12.78}$$

So that, in terms of the arbitrary function $F^{kk'nM}(c_{ij}^k - c_{ij}^{k'})$,

$$M_{ij}^{kn} = \frac{1}{\sum_{k' \in \gamma(n)} F^{k'knM}(c_{ij}^{k'} - c_{ij}^k)} \tag{12.79}$$

Thus, for any F, there is always a simple formula for M_{ij}^{kn}. Recalling equation (12.75), it can also be written

$$M_{ij}^{kn} = \frac{1}{1 + \sum_{k' \in \gamma(n), \neq k} F^{k'knM}(c_{ij}^{k'} - c_{ij}^k)} \tag{12.80}$$

The earlier result was that this can only be translated into the separable form (12.64) if F is the exponential function.

From the calibration viewpoint, we can now take (12.74) as the model. The procedure for estimating an unsmoothed function would be, using a by now obvious argument,

$$F^{kk'nM(m+1)}(\Delta c) = F^{kk'nM(m)}(\Delta c)\frac{\sum_{c_{ij}^k - c_{ij}^{k'} \in \Delta c} N_{ij}^{kk'nobs}}{\sum_{c_{ij}^k - c_{ij}^{k'} \in \Delta c} N_{ij}^{kk'n(m)}} \quad (12.81)$$

in order to get $N_{ij}^{kk'n}$ right within each cost differential bracket, Δc.

We can now summarize the position reached on modal split calibration as follows. For the Chapter 9 model, restated as equation (12.53) we gave the maximum-likelihood equation to be solved as (12.56). We have since shown how to use the Section 12.4 method to investigate alternative forms of function. If we choose to work with the model given in equation (12.64), we use the procedure given in (12.65). If we chose a function $f^{nM}(c)$ on this basis and then wished to estimate the parameters of the corresponding smoothed function, the maximum-likelihood equation to solve for the parameters would be

$$\sum_i \sum_j \sum_{k \in \gamma(n)} M_{ij}^{kn} h^n(c_{ij}^k) = \sum_i \sum_j \sum_{k \in \gamma(n)} N_{ij}^{knobs} h^n(c_{ij}^k) \quad (12.82)$$

where

$$e^{h^n(c_{ij}^k)} = f^{nM}(c_{ij}^k) \quad (12.83)$$

If, however, we choose to work in terms of cost differences, then the model equation is (12.74) (with modal split being given by (12.78) and we estimate an unsmoothed function $F^{kk'nM}(\Delta c)$ by the procedure (12.81). To estimate the parameters of the corresponding smoothed function, the maximum-likelihood equation is

$$\sum_i \sum_j N_{ij}^{kk'n} h^{kk'n}(c_{ij}^k - c_{ij}^{k'}) = \sum_i \sum_j N_{ij}^{kk'nobs} h^{kk'n}(c_{ij}^k - c_{ij}^{k'}) \quad (12.84)$$

where

$$e^{h^{kk'n}(c_{ij}^k - c_{ij}^{k'})} = F^{kk'nM}(c_{ij}^k - c_{ij}^{k'}) \quad (12.85)$$

If we additionally decided that $F^{kk'nM} = F^{nM}$, that is, the functional form was independent of k and k', the summations in equations (12.82) and (12.84) would be extended to cover k and k'.

This concludes our discussion of how to apply the methods of Section 12.4 to the distribution and modal split models to explore the construction of alternative functions for these models.

The second major point to discuss concerns the relationship of C_{ij}^n to the c_{ij}^ks. The exponential form given in equation (12.49) is a natural and convenient form for the model as described in Chapter 9. We have already indicated in the discussion of equation (12.61) that if the distribution model function is changed, there is a case for replacing equation (12.49) with (12.61). It is however, made clear in an earlier book, (Wilson, 1970, p. 34) that any form of function could be explored for this task. In general, then, we might assume that

$$C_{ij}^n = \phi^n(c_{ij}^1, c_{ij}^2, \ldots) \tag{12.86}$$

In the absence of further knowledge, we might replace equation (12.49) by (12.61), but there is no reason why we should not try to investigate the form of ϕ^n by other means. However, the only available way to do this is to run the model for a range of ϕ^ns and see which one gives the best overall goodness-of-fit statistics for the model. If the goodness-of-fit statistics are relatively insensitive to the choice of ϕ^n, then there would be a case for retaining either equation (12.49) or equation (12.61) for convenience.

A third major point to be taken up concerns other parameters which are implicit in the model as stated so far, and in particular the weights internal to the generalized costs c_{ij}^k. We show in equation (9.20), that

$$c_{ij}^k = a_1 t_{ij}^k + a_2 e_{ij}^k + a_3^k d_{ij}^k + p_j^k + \delta_j^k \tag{12.87}$$

where the terms on the right-hand side relate to travel time, excess time, operating costs, parking costs and a modal penalty respectively. Detailed definitions are given in Chapter 9 following equation (9.30); a_1, a_2 and a_3^k are coefficients to be estimated. Several questions arise at more or less fundamental levels. For example, other functional forms could be tested in which different independent variables were used. The essential calibration question, though, is: should the parameters a_1, a_2 and a_3^k be estimated simultaneously with other parameters in the distribution and modal split models, or outside the model? It seems reasonable to obtain at least the relative weights in this way, even though the overall sensitivity of cost is trip length and modal split is determined within the model by other parameters.

Quarmby (1967) has shown how the weights a_1, a_2 and a_3^k can be estimated using discriminant analysis. The terms a_1 and a_2, which value different kinds of time, were expressed as a percentage of income, and in this form have been utilized (as relative weights, λ^n still being determined by calibration within the model) in other studies (cf. the SELNEC Study, Wilson, Hawkins, Hill and Wagon, 1969). In the SELNEC Study, *ad hoc* adjustments were made to improve the fit in the distribution and modal split models. It was found, for example, that for the c_{ij}^ks in the distribution model, the terms $p_j^k + \delta^k$ were best omitted, but they were retained in the modal split model. In effect, then, slightly different generalized costs were used in two of the sub-models.

In the case where there are only two modes, we should note that the modal split model, and hence the weights in the generalized cost expression, can be estimated by logit regression analysis (Theil, 1965, pp. 77–87). The model, or persons of type n, can be written

$$p_{ij}^{kn} = \frac{1}{1 + e^{-\lambda^n(c_{ij}^k - c_{ij}^{k'})}} \qquad (12.88)$$

where p_{ij}^{kn} is the probability that a person will travel from i to j by mode k (the other mode being k'). Algebraic manipulation gives

$$\frac{p_{ij}^{kn}}{1 - p_{ij}^{kn}} = e^{\lambda^n(c_{ij}^{k'} - c_{ij}^k)} \qquad (12.89)$$

so that, using equation (12.86)

$$\log \frac{p_{ij}^{kn}}{1 - p_{ij}^{kn}} = \lambda^n a_1(t_{ij}^{k'} - t_{ij}^k) + \lambda^n a_2(e_{ij}^{k'} - e_{ij}^k) + \lambda^n a_3^k d_{ij}^k - \lambda^n a_3^{k'} d_{ij}^{k'} + a_0 \qquad (12.90)$$

where

$$a_0 = p_j^k - p_j^{k'} + \delta^k - \delta^{k'} \qquad (12.91)$$

The coefficients in this equation can now be obtained by regression analysis.

It remains only to discuss briefly the calibration issues which arise from other kinds of transport models, such as those outlined in the 'further developments' section of Chapter 9. Perhaps the dominant feature of the American models discussed around equations (9.81) to (9.96) in Chapter 9— the Quandt–Baumol abstract mode model, the Charles Rivers Associates sequential disaggregate model and Ben-Akiva's simultaneous disaggregate model—is that they are all designed so that their parameters can be estimated by standard econometric techniques. In the case of the three examples cited, this can be achieved simply by taking logs in the main model equations. It is almost as though the desire to use such estimation procedures forms a major component of model design criteria. In other words, these models arise from a much more inductive (as opposed to deductive style) than has been the policy in most of this book. If a more deductive style is adopted, this throws more onus on the model builder to *understand* his parameters, and eventually to develop sub-models which predict parameter values as part of his overall theory. One of the benefits of the maximum-likelihood or entropy-maximizing approaches, for example, is that the parameter p^n which turns up in equation (12.50) is obtained by solving the maximum-likelihood equation (12.54), and its behaviour can be predicted if the future value of

$$C^n = \sum_i \sum_j T_{ij} C_{ij}^n \qquad (12.92)$$

can be predicted. This emphasizes a new model-building problem rather than a parameter-estimation problem.

Apart from these observations, there is nothing to be added to the remarks on the calibration of these models which were made in Chapter 9. There *are* real issues of sequential versus simultaneous estimation, but we would argue, as in the discussion on the generalized cost weights above, that some separability is not a bad thing. Some authors associate sequential estimation with the hypothesis that travellers make sequential choices, and simultaneous estimation with the hypothesis that travellers make simultaneous multiple choices (cf. Brand, 1972, Ruiter, 1972, for example), but it can be argued that such an identification of behavioural hypotheses with methods for estimating more aggregative models cannot be made.

We should perhaps note finally, in relation to the three examples under discussion, that two of the models are disaggregate models and would be estimated by using household rather than zone-aggregated data. Then, if the various probabilities on the left-hand side of these equations are interpreted as frequencies, they will usually be (0 1) variables.

It only remains to comment on the calibration issues raised by the suggested modifications to the 'mainstream' Chapter 9 model in equations (9.108) through to (9.128). The main issue raised in equation (9.109), for example, which is

$$T_{ij}^{pn} = A_i^{pn} O_i^{pn} X_j^p \, e^{-\beta_i^{pn} c_{ij}^{pn}} \tag{12.93}$$

is that the parameter is now a function of i. The maximum-likelihood equation would be

$$\sum_j T_{ij}^{pn} c_{ij}^{pn} = \sum_j T_{ij}^{pnobs} c_{ij}^{pn} \tag{12.94}$$

On the face of it, a large problem has been created because each equation contains all the β_i^{pn}s. However, this should not be too serious. We could devise an iterative scheme as follows: take some set of starting values for the β_i^{pn}s (say $\beta_i^{pn} = \beta^{pn}$ obtained in the usual way without i-dependence). Then solve each equation (12.94) for β_i^{pn} keeping the others fixed. Then repeat with the new estimates and so on. Convergence should be fairly rapid. An analogous problem and solution would arise with λ_i^{pn} in equation (9.11) if it was decided to keep the i on the λ_i^{pn}.

The disaggregate model given by equation (9.124)–(9.128) presents no special problems. However, if h still referred to an individual, then it would be customary to drop h from β_i^{pn} and λ_{ij}^{pn} and to estimate β_i^p, λ_{ij}^p by something like logit regression analysis on household data, possibly carrying out the analysis separately for a number of groups.

12.8. LOCATION MODELS

We now turn to the location models of Chapter 10, beginning with residential-location models. The data requirements for calibrating the simpler

atial interaction models are very similar to those of journey-to-work
ansport models, for obvious reasons, and are usually easily met. Data is a
ore difficult problem for the disaggregated models whether of the spatial
teraction/assignment type or the economic theory type. It then becomes
cessary to have data on houses by location by type, and price, and jobs by
cation and wage as independent variables. Since the dependent variable is
$_j^{kw}$, observations of this are also needed for calibration purposes. These
rts of data are not readily available and, ideally, special surveys are needed.
his is often not possible, and more makeshift methods have to be used;
stimating' observed values of T_{ij}^{kw} by making conditional probability
ssumptions, for instance (and for an example of this, see Senior and Wilson,
973).

When the data is available, the calibration problems are relatively straight-
orward. For the simpler models, the procedures outlined in Sections 12.2–
2.3 for one- and two-parameter spatial interaction models can be used.
Methods analogous to those of Section 12.7 for transport models could be
sed to investigate the possibilities of using alternative functional forms for
ttractiveness factors and cost functions. There is also scope here for in-
estigating a variety of possible measures of attractiveness as well as
unctional transformations of whatever measure is used.

In the case of the disaggregated spatial interaction model, the principles
re similar though now, of course, there are more parameters. The simplest
xample of such a model was that given in equation (10.40):

$$T_{ij}^{kw} = A_i^k B_j^w H_i^k E_j^w \, e^{-\beta^w c_{ij}} \, e^{-\mu^w [p_i^k - q^w(w - c_{ij}')]^2} \qquad (12.95)$$

The maximum-likelihood equation for β^w is

$$\sum_i \sum_j \sum_k T_{ij}^{kw} c_{ij} = \sum_i \sum_j \sum_k T_{ij}^{kw\,\text{obs}} c_{ij} = C^w \qquad (12.96)$$

n the usual way, and for μ^w is

$$\sum_i \sum_j \sum_k T_{ij}^{kw}[p_i^k - q^w(w - c_{ij}')]^2 = \sum_i \sum_j \sum_k T_{ij}^{kw\,\text{obs}}[p_i^k - q^w(w - c_{ij}')]^2 = \sigma_w^2$$
$$(12.97)$$

The usual calibration procedure is to take a set of starting values for all the
β^w and μ^w, and then, given these, to find β^w and λ^w for each w in turn using the
two-variable Newton–Raphson procedure of equations (12.34)–(12.37), and
then to repeat the cycle with the new values until a suitable convergence is
achieved. (For an example, see Cripps and Cater (1972).)

Again, alternative cost functions could be estimated using the methods of
Section 12.4, and in this case, an alternative functional form for the budget-
price term, $e^{-\mu^w[p_i^k - q^w(w - c_{ij}')]^2}$ could be investigated.

Define

$$v_i^{kw} = p_i^k - q^w(w - c'_{ij})$$ (12.9?)

We could then replace $e^{-\mu^w v_i^{kw^2}}$ in equation (12.95) by $f^w(v_i^{kw})$ where $f^w($ was determined by an iterative process in which, after the mth iteration

$$f^{w(m+1)}(v) = f^{w(m)}(v) \frac{\sum_{v_i^{kw} \in v} T_{ij}^{kwobs}}{\sum_{v_i^{kw} \in v} T_{ij}^{kw(m)}}$$ (12.9?)

The econometric models of residential location mentioned in Section 10. have parameters which, by definition, can be estimated by standard pro cedures. In the case of the economic theory approach, as represented by th Herbert–Stevens' model in equations (10.107)–(10.109), there are no visibl parameters in the model, but some are implicit in the definition of the bi rents b_i^{kn}. It is common, for example, to assume a linear form for b_i^{kn} and the to estimate the coefficients by regression analysis using actual rent data. Suc a procedure would also have to be used to estimate b_i^{kn} in the integrated mode presented in equations (10.110)–(10.113). But also the parameter μ woul have to be estimated, with

$$\sum_i \sum_k \sum_n T_{i*}^{kn} b_i^{kn} = \sum_i \sum_k \sum_n T_{i*}^{knobs} b_i^{kn} = Z^{obs}$$ (12.100

as maximum-likelihood equation (cf. equation (10.113)).

We can now turn to models of the utilization of services. The mos commonly-used model in this field is the shopping model and, even fo shopping, the data are often poor. The only systematic data in the U.K. ar provided by the Census of Distribution, which takes place spasmodically and in such a way that successive censuses are rarely comparable. Informa tion on housing expenditure or shopping goods is available from the Famil Expenditure Survey. Information on shopping trips is only available from special surveys, and usually in person-trip units rather than shopping expenditure units. Some interaction data is vital to shopping-mode calibration as, without it, the only goodness-of-fit statistics which can be used are those which suffer from the $\alpha = 1$, $\beta = 0$ 'bogus calibration' problem. Interaction and other necessary data probably could be obtained for a range of public services, libraries, health services, welfare services and so on, from tickets and records of various kinds, but there is little experience of modelling in these fields. Data are even more difficult to come by for other private services: banking, legal services and so on.

If data can be assembled, and a spatial interaction model is to be built, the calibration task is straightforward and has, in fact, been discussed as the basic example in Sections 12.2 and 12.3.

It only remains to mention the models of the location of economic activity n Section 10.7. Since these are all econometric models, they can be estimated by standard procedures.

2.9. A NOTE ON GENERAL MODELS

Most general models are likely to be assemblies of partial models whose calibration problems we have been discussing above. If the models are linked, however, as are the residential-location model and the service-sector model within Lowry's general model, then in theory there is a degree of inter-dependence of the parameters in the different models. This is no different in principle to the interdependence of parameters in a multi-parameter partial model and can be handled in the same way, using an iterative procedure. This has been done for the Lowry model by Batty (1970), who found that although there was some relationship between the parameters of the two main models, this was not particularly strong, and the calibration task was straightforward.

2.10. SOME SPECIAL PROCEDURES

There are many special and alternative procedures which can be adopted for model calibration and testing within the general framework presented in this section. Many of the procedures outlined above involve nests of iterative cycles, both in calibration, and within the model itself (for example calculating A_is and B_js). These iterations can be very time-consuming on the computer, and there is much scope for investigating alternative ways of structuring the iteration in an attempt to save time. Two examples are presented here: first, an approximation used in the calibration of the distribution model in the SELNEC study, and second, a non-iterative calculation for solving the maximum-likelihood equation for β in a distribution model. These methods will only be outlined here, and the reader is referred to the original papers for the details by Wilson, Hawkins, Hill and Wagon (1969), and Evans (1971) respectively.

In the SELNEC case, the problem was the time taken up during the iterative calculation for A_i^n and B_j in a model of the form of equation (12.50) with two-person types, so that there were two parameters to be estimated, β^1 and β^2. The essence of the procedure adopted to relieve the situation was to calibrate (that is, to run the model for a range of β^1 and β^2) using a singly constrained model, with B_js fixed at 1, but with D_j replaced by $\hat{B}_j D_j$, where $\hat{B}_j$ was obtained from one doubly constrained run. The hope is that the B_js are relatively insensitive to variations in β^1 and β^2. Then, of course, final values of β^1 and β^2 can be checked and corrected with more doubly constrained runs. This turned out to be a useful time-saving procedure.

Evans (1971) is concerned with a maximum-likelihood equation of the form of (12.54), but stated as follows for one-person type:

$$C(\beta) = \sum_i \sum_j T_{ij} c_{ij} = y \tag{12.101}$$

where y is the observed value and the equation is to be solved for β. The essence of the method is that $C(\beta)$ can be calculated from $C(O)$ and the derivatives of C evaluated at $\beta = 0$ in a Taylor expansion:

$$C(\beta) = C(0) + \beta \frac{dC(0)}{d\beta} + \frac{\beta^2}{2!} \frac{d^2C(0)}{d\beta^2} + \ldots \tag{12.102}$$

His paper contains explicit formulae for the derivatives up to the tenth order. If $C(\beta)$ in equation (12.102) is replaced by the observed value y from equation (12.101), then this gives a polynominal equation in β which can be solved by any of the standard methods. The number of terms needed in the Taylor expansion can be estimated by looking at the first-order approximation for β.

12.11. REFERENCES

* W. Alonso (1968) Predicting best with imperfect data, *Journal of the Institute of American Institute of Planners*, **34**, pp. 248–255.

R. Artle (1959) *The structure of the Stockholm economy*, Business Research Institute of the Stockholm School of Economics; republished in 1965 by the Cornell University Press, Ithaca, New York.

M. Batty (1970) Some problems of calibrating the Lowry model, *Environment and Planning*, **2**, pp. 95–114.

M. Batty (1971) Exploratory calibration of a retail location model using search by golden section, *Environment and Planning*, **3**, pp. 411–432.

M. Batty and S. Mackie (1972) The calibration of gravity, entropy and related models of spatial interaction, *Environment and Planning*, **4**, pp. 131–250.

A. J. Blackburn (1970) A non-linear model of the demand for travel and An alternative approach to aggregation and estimation in the non-linear model, in R. E. Quandt (Ed.) (1970) *The demand for travel: theory and measurement*, Heath Lexington Books, Lexington, Mass., pp. 163–196.

D. Brand (1972) The state of the art of travel demand forecasting; a critical review, mimeo, Harvard University, Cambridge, Mass.

Bureau of Public Roads (1965) *Calibrating and testing a gravity model for any size urban area*, Government Printing Office. Washington, D.C.

M. Chisholm (1971) Forecasting the generation of freight traffic in Great Britain, in M. Chisholm, A. E. Frey and P. Haggett (Eds.) *Regional forecasting*, Butterworths, London, pp. 431–442.

* E. L. Cripps (1970) A comparative study of information systems for urban and regional planning 1: Scandinavia, Working Paper 10, Urban Systems Research Unit, University of Reading.

E. L. Cripps and A. E. Cater (1972) The empirical development of a disaggregated residential location model: some preliminary results, in A. G. Wilson (Ed.) *Patterns and processes in urban and regional systems*, Pion, London, pp. 114–145.

* E. L. Cripps and P. Hall (1969) An introduction to the study of information for urban and regional planning, Information Paper 8, pp. 22–81, Centre for Environmental Studies, London.

N. R. Draper and H. Smith (1966) *Applied regression analysis*, John Wiley, New York.

A. W. Evans (1971) The calibration of trip distribution models with exponential or similar functions, *Transportation Research*, 5, pp. 15–38.

G. J. D. Hewings (1971) Regional input-output models in the U.K.: some problems and prospects for the use of non-survey techniques, *Regional Studies*, 5, pp. 11–22.

G. M. Hyman (1969) The calibration of trip distribution models, *Environment and Planning*, 1, pp. 105–112.

Ministry of Transport (1966) *Portbury*, H.M.S.O., London.

* G. H. Orcutt, H. W. Watts and J. B. Edwards (1968) Data aggregation and information loss, *American Economic Review*, 58, pp. 773–787.

P. O'Sullivan (1971) Forecasting interregional freight flows in Great Britain, in M. Chisholm, A. E. Frey and P. Haggett (Eds.), *Regional Forecasting*, Butterworths, London, pp. 443–450.

W. I. Morrison (1972) An input-output model of Peterborough, unpublished Ph.D. Thesis, Department of Geography, University College, London.

D. A. Quarmby (1967) Choice of travel mode for the journey to work: some findings, *Journal of Transport Economics and Policy*, 1, pp. 273–314; also reprinted in R. E. Quandt (Ed.) (1970) *The demand for travel: theory and measurement*, Heath Lexington Books, Lexington, Mass., pp. 235–295.

J. I. Round (1972) Regional input-output models in the U.K.: a re-appraisal of some techniques, *Regional Studies*, 6, pp. 1–9.

E. Ruiter (1972) Analytical structures, paper prepared for H.R.B. Conference on Travel demand forecasting, Williamsburg, Virginia, to be published.

M. L. Senior and A. G. Wilson (1973) Disaggregated residential location models: some tests and further theoretical development, in E. L. Cripps (Ed.) *Proceedings*, Fifth Annual Conference, British Section, Regional Science Association, Pion, London, to be published.

R. Stone (1967) *Mathematics in the social sciences*, Chapman and Hall, London.

H. Theil (1965) *Economics and information theory*, North Holland, Amsterdam.

A. G. Wilson (1967) A statistical theory of spatial distribution models, *Transportation Research*, 1, pp. 253–269.

A. G. Wilson (1970) *Entropy in urban and regional modelling*. Pion, London.

A. G. Wilson (1973) Further developments of entropy maximizing transport models, *Transportation planning and technology*, 1, pp. 183–193.

A. G. Wilson, A. F. Hawkins, G. J. Hill and D. J. Wagon (1969) Calibrating and testing the SELNEC transport model, *Regional Studies* 3, pp. 337–350; also reprinted in A. G. Wilson (1972) *Papers in urban and regional analysis*, Pion, London, pp. 202–215.

C. B. Winsten (1967) Regression analysis vs. category analysis, pp. 17–19, *Seminar Proceedings*, Trip end estimation, P.T.R.C., London.

PART IV

The Use of Models in Planning

CHAPTER 13

From analysis to problem solving and control

13.1. INTRODUCTION

In Chapters 3–12 we have built up a substantial investment in model building. Now, at last, we are in a position to return to the questions and problems of Chapter 2 and to discuss the use of models in solving planning problems. In terms of the conceptual framework presented in Chapter 2, the models will form the basis of the analytical capability which underpins design and policy-making activities in planning. The rest of this chapter is structured accordingly. In section 13.2 we review our analytical capabilities, mainly to summarize where we have got to (and to see what analysis offers us directly as an aid to problem solving). Then in Section 3.3, we discuss the use of models in design, and in Section 3.4 the problem of evaluation using model outputs. In Section 13.5 we draw some threads together and see what all this means for problem solving. In terms of the conceptual framework of Chapter 2, solving a problem means finding a means of implementation through the public policy instruments which will achieve desired resource objectives and social goals. A number of concluding comments are then made in Section 13.6.

13.2. ANALYSIS AND CONDITIONAL FORECASTING

It is useful to begin by summarizing very briefly the kind of analytical capability which is offered by the preceding chapters. Chapter 7 informs us about population structure, largely by age and sex, and is applicable at a variety of spatial scales. Chapter 8 gives us analogous information by sector for the economy. Chapter 9 gives us models which predict transport flows for a given disposition of transport facilities and the spatial distribution of population and economic activities which generate such flows. Chapter 10 provides the analytical basis for the study of urban activities and their spatial distribution. In Chapter 11 we indicated how the different sub-models can be integrated into a general model structure. Chapter 12 discussed the practical problems of making these models operational. In Chapters 7, 8 and 9 there was relatively little choice in the models offered. In Chapter 10 there was a considerable variety. The actual choice to be made in a particular planning context depends mainly on the problem to be tackled in relation to the state-of-the-art of modelling, but partly, in some cases, on the taste of the user:

given the evidence, which model alternative does he believe is best at the present time? In this chapter we shall assume that such choices have been made and carry on the discussion mainly in terms of model inputs and outputs and their use in the planning process.

Any planning problem will be characterized by some set of variables: the broader the problem, the more variables there will be in the set. Given such a set, and given the associated model system, the first task is to decide which variables are *endogenous* (internal, predicted by the model) to the model and which are exogenous (external, not predicted by the model, possibly required as an input to the model). There are two kinds of exogenous variable: those which are not included in the model because the planner can control them, and those which are not included through ignorance. In the latter case, there may be differing degrees of ignorance and uncertainty, and it may be possible to learn something about the variable and its likely future value by other kinds of analysis. An example of the first kind of exogenous variable is the supply of public housing: the planner can determine how much he can have and where to put it. An example of the second is the birth rate which is input to the demographic model: something can be learned about it by historical analysis, but we are not yet in a position to build a predictive model. (We should also remind ourselves at this stage, of course, that some explicit assessment of uncertainty, or error, should ideally be associated with each endogenous variable.)

Given these distinctions, we can then say that the main use of models in the planning is for conditional forecasting. For a given set of exogenous variables, the model system can be used to forecast the endogenous variables, the forecast being conditional on the given exogenous variables. Thus, typically, forecasts are conditional in two ways: in relation to the setting of the controlled variables, the plan of which the model is testing the impact, and in relation to assumed values of other variables. Usually, the model will be used to test a range of alternative plans (generated by the design process as discussed in Section 12.4), and for a range of possible assumptions (for example, low, medium and high birth rates) for the other variables. This means that a model is likely to be 'run' many times in the context of any particular planning problem.

These concepts can be illustrated by the shopping model of Chapter 4, the main equation of which is repeated here for convenience:

$$S_{ij} = A_i e_i P_i W_j^\alpha c_{ij}^{-\beta} \tag{13.1}$$

Suppose the planning task is to 'best' allocate shopping floorspace in the area, and that W_j is floorspace in zone j. Then, given e_i, P_i, W_j and c_{ij}, the model will predict S_{ij} and hence $\sum_i S_{ij}$, retail sales in each centre j. In this case, W_j is the main planning variable, and the alternative plans will consist of sets of specifications of the W_js. If the planner is using a shopping model alone, he will have to assume values for e_i, P_i and c_{ij} and possibly run the model for a range of such assumptions to test the sensitivity of the model to these. If he is operating in a broader planning context, then in this case e_i and P_i could possibly be obtained from other models and c_{ij} from the transport planner.

It is perhaps useful to summarize briefly the main endogenous and exogenous variables for each model described in earlier chapters.

For the demographic models of Chapter 7, the main endogenous variables are populations by age and sex, and the main exogenous variables are the birth, death and migration rates. The migration rates can themselves be modelled. In this case, the only variables which are even partially under the planner's control are the exogenous variables in the migration sub-model: regional levels of economic development and so on. This situation could change somewhat if population problems have moved to the fore as issues, and Governments may try to affect birth rates by such devices as free provision of contraceptives and by education.

The main exogenous inputs to the economic model of Chapter 8 are the input–output coefficients, which represent the technical structure of the regional economy, the final demand sector (including exports) and the exogenous factor inputs (including imports). The outputs are total products in each sector of the economy. Some of the endogenous variables can be influenced by the planner (by fiscal policies and by regulation) but the nature of the degree of control which can be achieved in this way is far from fully understood.

The volume and spatial distribution of urban activities, and the amount of transport infrastructure provided, are the main inputs to the transport model of Chapter 9, and transport flows are the output. Usually, only the provision of transport infrastructure is taken as the controllable variable for the transport planner and the distribution of activities is provided for him by others. That is, the volume and spatial distribution of activities are provided by the models and associated analyses of Chapter 10. It should be emphasized, of course, that in principle greater efficiency could be achieved by the integration of these two aspects of planning, and the present trend is to attempt to do just that. We saw in Chapter 10 that for residential and workplace locational analysis, the models should preferably be dynamic, and in this case the first exogenous input is the distribution of activities from the previous time period. Then, the range of variables which are exogenous is in this case often determined by the model chosen. This is also true for comparative static cross-sectional location models. In the Lowry model, for example, the distribution of basic employment is exogenous, together with transport networks, but other variables are endogenous. Various prices are exogenous, endogenous or not present at all according to the model chosen. Similarly in this case, it is impossible to offer brief generalizations, and we can only say that the endogenous/exogenous/controllable distinctions must be made carefully on an *ad hoc* basis each time.

13.3. DESIGN

Introduction: basic foci of interest

We have already seen from Chapter 2 that design is conceived in this book as the 'effective generation of effective alternative plans'. A plan is a setting of the public policy instruments. Then, if the designer has a model-based analytical capability available to him, these 'settings' will be values assigned to the 'controllable exogenous variables' (cf. Section 13.2) and he can use his model system to trace the impact of his plan on his system of interest. The model will provide conditional forecasts, and these forecasts, directly or by transformation (see Section 13.4) provide indicators of the extent to which this plan achieves resource objectives and social goals: in short, the extent to which it solves problems.

This is clearly an enormous task, and although the models of this book should provide some help in relation to most elements of the task, the whole design problem is likely to be sub-divided. We begin, therefore, by examining some of the foci of interest for different kinds of designer.

There are perhaps two major dimensions which define a space within which foci of interest can be identified: one is concerned with spatial scale, the other with prime system (or sub-system) of interest. Four spatial scales can be identified: national, regional, urban and local. The system of interest, at any of these scales, may be people-based, resource-based, policy-based or place-based. The spatial scales are obvious, and there are certainly planners operating at each of these scales. We shall discuss examples below. The second dimension perhaps requires a little more explanation. If the designer is *people-based*, it is likely that his focus will be some group of people: the poor, those who work in a certain occupation, etc. For any set of policy instruments, the impacts the planner will be most interested in will be the *package* of impacts on particular people or groups. This package notion, and people-focus, is particularly important, and is easily lost in the midst of separate discussions of models of housing, jobs, residential location, transport and so on. The ultimate absurdity would be, for example, to design perfect housing in a location with highly imperfect access to jobs or services. Even quite extreme examples of this can be found as consequences of planning, and less extreme examples are commonplace. The *resource-based* designer will concentrate on what can be achieved with some specialized resource: housing, transport and so on. The *policy-based* planner and designer will probably work with an agency of government which is responsible for the operation of one or more policy instruments. The *place-based* planner will ask: what can I achieve for this particular place? (This may also coincide with a place-community, though the concept of 'community' has broader connotations and is more likely to be considered people-based. In that case, it may be Webber's (1963) 'community without propinquity' and may be defined by some characteristic other than place.

The planning system as a whole will, of course, operate with a mixture of all these foci. The existence of the foci is probably healthy as it encourages the development of specialist skills; healthy provided they can be co-ordinated, and in the last analysis are people-dominated!

The classification adopted above works through the three layers of Figure 2.2. It also illustrates the essential problem of design, the combinatorial problem: there are, in principle, inordinately large numbers of 'settings', or combinations, of policy instruments, large numbers of alternative plans; these are connected to resource objectives and social goals in the figure through what would be a very complicated network if everything were to be specified in detail. The essence of the integrated design problem is as follows: ideally, we would like to start at the 'social goals' level of the figure and trace paths down to settings of policy instruments which would achieve these goals within given resource constraints, but this is usually impossible because the real world is so complicated; in practice, we have to proceed upwards by model-based impact analysis from policy instruments to social goals.

What the models offer the designer

At the national and regional spatial scales, the models of this book which are most directly helpful to the planner are the demographic and migration models of Chapter 7, the economic models of Chapter 8, and perhaps the transport model of Chapter 9 in relation to inter-urban flows. As we saw in Section 13.2, with respect to the first two of these, the planner has relatively few controllable variables, or at least few whose impact he fully understands (in part, of course, due to the inadequacy of the present models). In an obvious sense, these models will help the national or regional planner to assess in broad terms the resources needed to support the population, and the extent to which these resources are produced in the corresponding national or regional economies. They could also help him to understand the migration of people and economic activity, and to assess the impacts of different kinds of regional development policies. In the case of the inter-urban transport flows, the designer has available to him a good tool for the assessment of impacts of a particular national motorway structure or inter-city rail or air system. In the not too distant future, it may be possible to make the demographic and economic models more 'transport sensitive', so that the secondary impacts of transport plans could also be investigated.

The models of Chapters 9, 10 and 11 will be most useful to the planner whose task is to construct broad strategic comprehensive plans for some urban-regional study area. His inputs (controlled through expenditure on public facilities or land-use regulation) will be such variables as houses by type (H_i^k), jobs by wage (E_j^w), levels of service provision (W_j^s), and transport by mode (c_{ij}^k), and the models will then give him sets of conditional forecasts which represent the impacts of these dispositions of resources. It will tell him, in broad terms, how the whole thing adds together.

The same kind of analysis, and the same models, could distinguish impacts on a particular local area, and so could also be used by the place-focused planner. Since the basic resources are covered, the resource-focused planner is also helped. Some of the models operate at a sufficiently fine level of dis-aggregation to be helpful to the people-focused planner: the disaggregated residential models of Chapter 10, for example, would be capable of informing the designer where poor people would live, given a disposition of housing of different types (and in Section 13.5, we will begin to explore how to *evaluate* this conditional-forecast type of information). It is more difficult to be sure that we have, from the models as discussed so far, the right kind of 'package' information about people-impact. This particular question will be explored further in Section 13.4.

Model-based design in practice

We should begin by noting some design criteria for model systems if they are to be effective for the planner-designer. Above all, he should ideally be able to get quick information back from the system. There is no technical reason why, with modern computers and related peripheral equipment, this this should not be achieved, though relatively little effort, as yet, has been devoted to the problem (cf. Dial, 1972). There is no reason, in fact, why the designer should not get an on-line response in quick time. He feeds-in values of his control variables (doing this by digital means, or, for example, by sketching networks with light pencils on photo-sensitive tables connected to the computer) and receives model outputs, probably directly in mapped form as well as digital outputs.

Because of the extent of the design combinational problem, the systematic solution of problems by computer is unlikely to be achieved except in quite trivial cases. Solutions will arise from the man-machine interaction of the designer and the computer-based model system. The designer will be operat-ing the 'organizing concepts' (cf. Alexander, 1964) of his profession; he will know that transport networks connected in certain ways are feasible and much more 'sensible' than most others and so on. He will also have to experi-ment with ideas which lie outside the present 'principles'. It will be important for him to test a wide range of solutions within his principles. The computer output will then almost certainly lead him to construct and to test new plans which embody the 'best' features (measured as impacts) of the earlier tests. In this way, he should be able quickly to identify good solutions if they exist. (Whether he will necessarily be able to identify the optimum optimorum, because of the combinatoral problems, is another matter: cf. Harris, 1967, Lowry, 1967.) Examples of this sort of procedure will be given in Chapter 14.

13.4. EVALUATION

Introduction

As with the section on design, we can only present an argument at a very general level and illustrate it by example. Evaluation methods enable us to choose between different plans according to some criteria. If the impacts of each plane are analysed with a model system, then the evaluation methodologist has to construct indicators from the model outputs which will then form the basis of the criteria to be adopted. There are three crucial problems to be solved: first, to ensure that the indicators are adequate measures of impact; second, to measure impact on different groups of people and organizations who are affected; and third, to weight different indicators so that they can be combined into a single measure. Briefly, then, these are the problems of *measurement*, *incidence* and *weighting*.

This set of problems will have to be solved, explicitly or implicitly, directly or indirectly, for any planning problem: for each of the spatial scales and foci of interest discussed in the preceding section. We begin, however, with a general and abstract discussion of the problem in the next sub-section and then, in the following one, we discuss evaluation in practice.

Basic principles of evaluation methods

Suppose the state of the system we are trying to plan is changing continually over time. In symbols, let $\Lambda(t)$ be the state of the system at time t. At some initial time t_0, usually the 'present', we know the state of the system, $\Lambda(t_0)$, and we suppose that we can use our powers of analysis to predict future states of the system, say up to same time t_1. Denote by $[\Lambda(t_0), \Lambda(t_1)] = \Omega(t_0, t_1)$ the initial and final states, and all the states for intermediate times. That is, $\Omega(t_0, t_1)$ denotes the whole time path from $t = t_0$ to $t = t_1$. Alternative plans can be numbered $1, 2, 3, \ldots$, and each consists of a series of actions with effects $\Omega(t_0, t_1)$. Denote the time path which results from the implementation of the nth plan by $\Omega^n(t_0, t_1)$. Then the task of the evaluation methodologist is to arrange $\Omega^n(t_0, t_1)$, $n = 1, 2, \ldots$ in order of preference. In general, this is obviously an extremely complicated, and perhaps usually impossible, task.

Suppose, at first, we concentrate on end-states only. So our task is to order $\Lambda^n(t_1)$, $n = 1, 2, 3, \ldots$. Within the state vector $\Lambda(t)$, let $g_1(t), g_2(t), \ldots$ be *indicators* which we use as the basis of developing evaluation criteria. If we can identify such a set, we have begun to solve the measurement problem. Usually, this has to be solved simultaneously with the incidence problem: for the present, let us assume that the indicators are constructed to inform us adequately about incidence. Then the weighting problem, at its simplest, is: how do we find a set of weights w_k such that

$$W = \sum_k w_k g_k(t) \tag{13.2}$$

is a single indicator which we can use for ranking plans. (Note that, from the way we have defined g_k, the w_ks reflect not only weights to be attached to different sectors—housing, health, transport and so on—but also goal achievement for different types of people.)

The simplest way, then, of formally stating the evaluation problem (using end-states only) is: for each plan, $n = 1, 2, 3, \ldots$ find goal indicators $(g_k^n(t))$, weights w_k, such that

$$W^n = \sum_k w_k g_k^n(t) \tag{13.3}$$

is an index which can be used to rank plans.

This problem is best tackled in the framework of welfare economics, and before we proceed further we should see how far we can get within this framework. The measurement, incidence and weighting problems are all solved simultaneously within the framework. The measurement problem consists of identifying the population of individuals with whom we are concerned, $r = 1, 2, 3 \ldots$, say, and the set of goods which can be 'purchased' by each individual, $i = 1, 2, 3, \ldots$, so that x_i^r is the amount of the ith good purchased by individual r. We will use broad definitions of 'good', so that i may be public or private, but we thus go on to make the strong assumption that we can define the price, p_i, for each good i. Its measurement, interpretation, and even definition, may be difficult for a public good. Ideally we should perhaps have price as p_i^r, the price of good i as perceived by person r (in the sense that his behaviour is partially determined by this price), for the case where markets do not exist to ensure an equal price across the board (or to take account of market imperfections). In effect, we have already made such assumptions in the definition of the prices of transport goods in Chapter 9. Further, we should also bear in mind that it may be fruitful to rewrite and re-interpret the definitions given so far, and the theories which follow, in the formalism of Lancaster (1965). Meanwhile, we will work within the simplest possible assumptions which allow us to demonstrate the principles of the welfare economics approach to the evaluation problem.

The incidence problem is not a problem until we aggregate later: at present we are working directly with individuals. The weighting problem is solved within this framework by working with money units. We let M^r be the income of rth individual, and we measure the impact of any plan by measuring the compensating variation in income which would take any affected individual back to his old utility level.

We assume that it is possible to define a utility function

$$U^r = U^r(x_1^r, x_2^r, \ldots, M^r) \tag{13.4}$$

for the rth individual which records his preferences in that he purchases quantities of goods (x_i^r) at prices (p_i) so as to maximize U^r in equation (13.4) subject to

$$\sum_i x_i^r p_i = M^r \qquad (13.5)$$

We can assume that all income is spent, without loss of generality, by taking one of the goods as either 'savings', or 'money'. This last device is particularly useful when a complete enumeration of goods is unnecessary, or impracticable. Formally, we can write the solution to this maximization problem as

$$x_i^r = x_i^r(p_1, p_2, \ldots M^r) \qquad (13.6)$$

for each good i, and this is the individual demand function for the ith good.

Suppose now, that as a result of the implementation of some plan, the prices are changed from p_i^0 at time t_0 to p_i^1 at time t_1. How do we measure the impact of this change? Initially, we work in terms of small increments and explore the consequences of price changes from (p_i) to $(p_i + \delta p_i)$.

By differentiating equation (13.5) partially with respect to p_i (that is, keeping the other p_is fixed), it can be seen that

$$\frac{\partial M^r}{\partial p_i} = x_i^r(p_1, p_2, \ldots, M^r) \qquad (13.7)$$

Thus, for the set of small changes, the change in individual rs income is

$$\delta M^r = \sum_i \frac{\partial M^r}{\partial p_i} \delta p_i \qquad (13.8)$$

so

$$\delta M^r = \sum_i x_i^r \delta p_i \qquad (13.9)$$

This can be used to calculate the individual's compensating variation in income for the change.

It is rarely possible in evaluation, any more than it has proved in model building, to carry through the analysis at the individual level. Suppose, then, we group individuals in sets $r \in R(n)$, the group of individuals of type n. Then, under suitable conditions, we can aggregate the results already obtained. The demand equation, (13.6) becomes

$$x_i^n = \sum_{r \in R(n)} x_i^r = x_i^n(p_1, p_2, \ldots, M^n) \qquad (13.10)$$

where M^n is now income for the group, and equation (13.7) and (13.9) become

$$\frac{\partial M^n}{\partial p_i} = x_i^n(p_1, p_2, \ldots, M^n) \qquad (13.11)$$

and

$$\delta M^n = \sum_i x_i^n \, \delta p_i \qquad (13.12)$$

respectively. These equations can either be considered to result from the maximization of a social welfare function for the group:

$$W^n = W^n(U^1, U^2, \ldots) \qquad (13.13)$$

where U^r on the right-hand side ranges over $r \in R(n)$, or a group utility function

$$U^n = U^n(x_1^n, x_2^n, \ldots, M^n) \qquad (13.14)$$

The conditions under which different sorts of aggregation are possible and appropriate are set out by Green (1964).

At this point, it is useful to explore the consequences of a single price change, and to define the concept of *consumers' surplus*. We illustrate the concept at the group n level of aggregation. Then

$$\delta M^n = x_i^n \, \delta p_i \qquad (13.15)$$

if p_i goes to $p_i + \delta p_i$ but all other prices remain fixed. These changes are shown on Figure 13.1. The term $x_i^n \, \delta p_i$ on the right-hand side of equation (13.15) is the area ABCD on Figure 13.1. If p_i increases, δp_i is positive and so

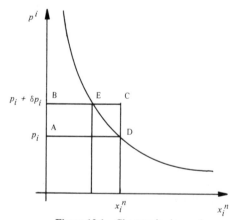

Figure 13.1   Changes in demand

δM^n is positive and vice versa. This statement must be carefully interpreted: equation (13.15) holds for a given utility level, and so δM^n is the change in income which maintains this utility level in the new situation. Thus, for a price increase, more income will be needed; for a price decrease, less. The second is the situation we will face if we are using this method to measure the benefit of some investment which has reduced price. δM^n will be negative in this situation but, if it is not actually taken away, it represents the money which is made available for additional expenditure. Thus, if δB^n is the benefit to group n resulting from a change,

$$\delta B^n = -\delta M^n = -x_i^n \, \delta p_i \tag{13.16}$$

For a price change from p_i^0 to p_i^1, we can obtain the total benefit B^n, by integration

$$B^n = -\int_{p_i^0}^{p_i^1} x_i^n \, dp_i \tag{13.17}$$

This is the shaded area in Figure 13.2.

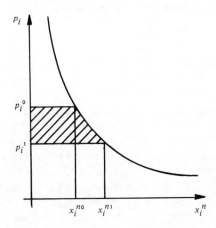

Figure 13.2   Change in consumers' surplus

Consider now the shaded area in Figure 13.3. This shaded area is known as the *consumers' surplus* since, at any price greater than p_i^0, some people would still have been prepared to buy the good, and the shaded area represents the surplus of this group of consumers because the price is actually p_i^0. It can now be seen by inspection that the shaded area in Figure 13.2 is the difference of the consumers' surplus in the old situation and that in the new, and so the measure of benefit in equation (13.17) is the change in consumers' surplus. In equation terms, if $C.S.^n$ is consumers' surplus for example, then, from Figure 13.3,

$$C.S.^n = \int_{p_i^0}^{\infty} x_i^n \, dp_i \tag{13.18}$$

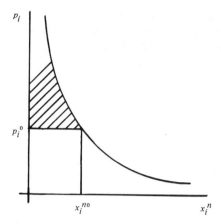

Figure 13.3   Consumers' surplus

and

$$B^n = -\int_{p_i^0}^{p_i^1} x_i^n \, dp_i = \int_{p_i^1}^{\infty} x_i^n \, dp_i - \int_{p_i^0}^{\infty} x_i^n \, dp_i = \Delta C.S.^n \qquad (13.19)$$

Thus, consumers' surplus can be identified with the compensating variation in income. (Certain stringent conditions apply. Also, in some circumstances it is useful to define the equivalent variation in income. For a discussion on both points, see Wilson and Kirwan (1969), and Neuberger (1971).)

One of the major difficulties with the use of the consumers' surplus as a measure of benefit, and hence as a goal indicator, is that our knowledge of the demand curve is usually incomplete and, indeed, is often restricted to the two points D and E on Figure 13.1. However, for small changes, an approximation can be used which avoids this difficulty and which leads to a useful formula: we take the chord ED in Figure 13.1 to be a straight line, and then comparison with Figure 13.2 shows that

$$\Delta C.S.^n = \text{ABED} = \tfrac{1}{2}(x_i^{n0} + x_i^{n1})(p_i^0 - p_i^1) \qquad (13.20)$$

(using the formula for the area of a trapezium).

The consumers' surplus which results from a series of price changes can be considered as the sum of a number of terms of this form:

$$B^n = \Delta C.S.^n = \frac{1}{2} \sum_i (x_i^{n0} + x_i^{n1})(p_i^0 - p_i^1) \qquad (13.21)$$

We can use the concepts developed above to help us choose between alternative plans as follows. Suppose for the mth plan, we have capital investment C^m, and we have estimated benefits B^{nm} as in equation (13.21) for ach group affected n, for plan m. Then

$$B^{*m} = \sum_n B^{nm} \qquad (13.22)$$

.re total benefits for plan m. Suppose our main interest is still end-state valuation. Then, we could assume that B^{*m} represented the benefits of plan n, say for the first year of operation of the plan which has 'cost' C^m. Then B^{*m}/C^m represents the 'first-year rate of return', and our evaluation criterion might be to choose the plan with the greatest first-year rate of return.

It is fairly straightforward to generalize this procedure so that it deals with the time period $t = t_0$ to $t = t_1$. Suppose this whole period to be divided into single years. Then let $C^m(t)$ be the costs of the mth plan in the tth year, and let $B^{*m}(t)$ be the total benefits in that year. Some rate of discount, or interest rate, ρ is needed. (For a discussion of how such rates are determined, see Prest and Turvey (1965), Wilson, (1966)). Then a sum of money A, received at t_0, say, is worth £A while at t_0, is worth £$A/(1 + \rho)$ if received at $t_0 + 1$, $A/(1 + \rho)^2$ if received at $t_0 + 2$ and so on. So, we can define the *net present value* of the mth plan as

$$NPV^m = \sum_{l=0}^{t_1 - t_0} \frac{B^{*m}(t_0 + l) - C^m(t_0 + l)}{(1 + \rho)^l} \qquad (13.23)$$

Typically, ρ will be the prevailing rate of interest, and we can say that if

$$NPV^m > 0 \qquad (13.24)$$

then the mth plan is worth carrying out, and if we are comparing alternatives we might choose the one with the greatest NPV and implement it, provided that inequality (13.24) is satisfied.

As the value of ρ is slowly increased, NPV^m in equation (13.23) decreases. It is sometimes convenient to find the value of ρ, say ρ_0^m for which NPV^m is zero. This is known as the *internal rate of return* for the mth plan. An alternative evaluation criterion is then to choose the plan with the greatest internal rate of return.

In this discussion, we have assumed equal weights, equal marginal utilities of money, for each of our groups n. As we shall note in our comments below, welfare economics does not deal with distributional questions. These issues could be reflected in the above discussion by noting that, in equation (13.22), weights might be attached to the terms B^{nm} on the right-hand side. Not surprisingly, then, we cannot avoid some remaining issues of value.

In this presentation, we have enumerated goal indicators by specifying the range of goods which can be purchased and the way in which they are valued. We have distinguished different groups of people. By valuing the goods in money terms, we have implicitly solved the weighting problem. We have been able to calculate the costs and benefits resulting from one or more price changes. Unfortunately, for a number of reasons, this framework is not usually applicable. We discuss some of these reasons in turn.

(1) The behavioural basis of the theory presented here is acceptable in outline: utility functions are simply ways of recording preferences (and quite 'odd' preferences can be so recorded). However, there are considerable practical difficulties in the definition of urban 'goods': housing, jobs, transport and so on. Further, it is also likely that individuals making choices are faced with more complex constraints than a single budget constraint: time constraints, linkage constraints (you can only 'buy' some activity by also 'buying' another, like a trip to the place of that activity) and social barriers, are three examples.

(2) The theory is based on individual behaviour, and most of our models are more aggregative. The consequences of aggregation are not well understood. Can we work with group utility functions, for example, or should we seek a social welfare function?

(3) Another assumption which underpins the behavioural basis of the welfare economics' framework is that goods are produced and sold in perfectly competitive markets. This is obviously untrue in general, and particularly false for 'urban goods'. There are at least three interrelated reasons why markets are imperfect in practice.

(a) Because of *indivisibilities* or, more generally, *increasing returns to scale*, some goods are produced in situations where mergers could take place and monopolies be formed.

(b) Because of *externalities*: the purchase or use of a good involves people other than the producer in costs or benefits.

(c) The people involved have *imperfect information*.

Goods which involve increasing returns to scale can be produced under public regulation or control; externalities can sometimes be handled through fiscal policies, but not always; imperfect information is a fact of life (which we attempt to take into account in building our *models of behaviour*, one reason why model predictions appear to be sub-optimal or to represent 'irrational' behaviour).

(4) There may be a range of plans which produce the same B^{*m}, but which have different *distributional* consequences—the B^{nm}s are different. Welfare economics cannot make the political decision on distribution which then arises. Of course, any distribution which results from a plan may be modified by the fiscal policies of the government of the day so that they can obtain a more 'equitable' distribution. This is another reason why it is particularly important to distinguish the *incidence* of costs and benefits in any calculation.

(5) Many 'urban' goods are public or semi-public goods. This makes it difficult to measure or estimate appropriate *prices*.

We can draw a number of conclusions from our review of the difficulties. First, since welfare economics is the best underpinning framework we have,

ore research in the field is worthwhile. Second, it is also worthwhile to
make the models available 'connect' to a welfare economics formulation,
as we have tried to do with the transport model in Chapter 9 and the residential location model in Chapter 10. Third, since the difficulties are so
severe, we shall have, for the time being, to adopt a second-best practical
position in many cases and fall back on our earlier concept of goal indicators.
t is to these practical considerations that we now turn.

We can adopt Hill's (1966) *goals' achievement matrix* for our purposes, to
make explicit the measurement, incidence and weighting problems associated
with evaluation in terms of goal indicators. Suppose we can enumerate goals
or, more precisely, goal indicators) by an index $g = 1, 2, 3 \ldots$. With each
indicator, we associate a weight α_g. Suppose we distinguish groups in the
population by an index $n = 1, 2, 3 \ldots$ and we associate another weight, β^n,
with each group. We assume that each goal indicator can be computed
according to its impact on each group, and that 'costs' (not necessarily in
money units of course) and 'benefits' associated with each group are computed separately. Thus, for each goal indicator, we compute $(C_g^n, B_g^n), n = 1,$
$2, 3, \ldots$. These quantities can be recorded as in Table 13.1. We add another

Table 13.1.   Hill's goals achievement matrix

Goal indicator $g =$			1		2	
Goal weight:			α_1		α_2	$\cdots$
Group $n =$	Group weight	Cost	Benefit	Cost	Benefit	
1	β^1	C_1^1	B_1^1	C_2^1	B_2^1	
2	β^2	C_1^2	B_1^2	C_2^2	B_2^2	
$\vdots$	$\vdots$	$\vdots$	$\vdots$	$\vdots$	$\vdots$	

superscript m to indicate the mth plan, and then the aggregate value-indicator
for plan m is

$$W^m = \sum_g \sum_n \alpha_g \beta^n (B_g^{nm} - C_g^{nm}) \qquad (13.25)$$

The weights can be adjusted by the decision-makers in the political process.
Then the plan with the highest W^m can be chosen. (The weights, of course,
can be chosen to reflect the fact that the goal indicators will often be measured
in different units, as well as to reflect values.) An alternative method of setting
out costs and benefits (though this time with a greater emphasis on measure-
men in money units) is provided by the *planning balance sheet* of Lichfield
(1966).

There are considerable difficulties whether we go for a fully fledged cost benefit analysis (say in the manner of Lichfield's planning balance sheet) or a goal achievements' matrix (in the manner of Hill). In the first case, many costs and benefits will be difficult to measure: Lichfield includes these, but as letters rather than numbers; in the second, agreed sets of weights (given that agreement will be demanded among politicians who disagree on policy) will be hard to come by. However, in spite of these difficulties, it is worth going through the procedure, unmeasured variables and all, for the light it sheds on the structure of the problem and the nature of the decisions to be made.

It should be emphasized at this stage that since it is more difficult to compare goal achievements between sectors, for example, between transport and health, plans more often than not are constructed for particular sectors, and the evaluation process is then entirely concerned with applying some procedure such as Hill's entirely within a sector. Thus, below, we briefly review such evaluation methods as they might involve the models of Chapters 7–11 in turn.

Evaluation in practice

For the demographic and economic models of Chapters 7 and 8 there is little we can add to the discussion of Section 13.2. There are relatively few variables either under the planner's control at all, or, if they appear to be under control, such that the effects are fully understood. It is correspondingly difficult to define goal indicators in these sectors. To what extent is demographic growth a good thing? Do high-gross migration flows indicate a healthy mobility in the population, or are they symptoms of some malaise? On the economic side, it is not even as clearly acceptable as it once was to say that maximum feasible growth is the desired policy. Such policies must now be checked against such things as pollution and resource-depletion constraints. Thus, the state of the planning art in these sectors is such that our goal indicators are likely to be simple: population and economic growth *targets*, for example, and the models will certainly help to chart paths towards any given targets and say whether the targets are feasible within given time periods.

It is in the transport sector that most progress has been made towards using the framework of welfare economics, at least within the sector. Consider, for illustrative purposes, a one-mode, one-person type situation, and a model that estimates T_{ij} as a function of c_{ij}s. This is interpreted as a demand model which shows, among other things, how the T_{ij}s vary with cost. Thus, if a new transport facility reduces costs from c_{ij}^0 to c_{ij}^1, then the argument which produced equation (13.21) can be used to produce an estimate of the benefits of the new facility as

$$B = \tfrac{1}{2} \sum_i \sum_j (T_{ij}^0 + T_{ij}^1)(c_{ij}^0 - c_{ij}^1) \qquad (13.26)$$

If the model distinguishes different person types, then the benefit measure can be similarly disaggregated, as in equation (13.21). In the SELNEC Transportation Study (1972) benefits were calculated using these methods for car owners and non-car owners separately.

We should recognize that the transport model can produce many other 'goal indicators' which are useful in a variety of ways: improvements in 'accessibility' for different groups in different locations, for example, or indices of congestion in different parts of each network, which will be useful to the engineers. The reader is referred to the great variety of published transportation studies for more details: see, for example, Tressider *et al.* (1968) or SELNEC Transportation Study (1972).

Next we look at residential and workplace location, the first of the location sectors discussed in Chapter 10. This provides us with an example to illustrate another method of constructing goal indicators in relatively unadvanced parts of the field: the use of *standards*. It might be argued, for example, that housing should meet a minimum standard for a given size of household, and the planning task is then to ensure that no-one is under the minimum. This method is relatively unadvanced because, clearly, there is a considerable arbitrariness in standard-setting; however, the committees of distinguished men who set standards are helping to set weights within a goals achievement matrix.

To use this method, it would be best to use the T_{ij}^{kw} model of Chapter 10, and to define 'house type', k, such that it reflected standards. Then, for a given distribution, H_i^k at prices p_i^k, for a job distribution E_j^w and transport costs c_{ij}, the model will allocate people to houses by type, and will say something about who is going to sub-standard housing and why. This will offer the designer clues as to how to improve his plans.

The state-of-the-art, however, is such that even simpler procedures are often used: sub-standard housing is identified as slum housing and scheduled for demolition. New housing is built, usually not on the same site, and people re-allocated according to 'filtering' processes which can be quite complicated. The model will predict the outcome of such processes for a given distribution H_i^k, and there are various ways in which goal indicators could be constructed to reflect this. One example would be: mean percentage of income within an income group which has to be devoted to housing (as distinct from the 'hypothetical' or 'historical' q^w which is fed in initially).

Since T_{ij}^{kw} is predicted as a function of p_i^k, it should also be possible to use the equation (13.21) method to get an economic measure of the consequences of some plan. A formula analogous to (13.26) for the transport case would be

$$B^w = \frac{1}{2} \sum_i \sum_j \sum_k (T_{ij}^{kw0} + T_{ij}^{kw1})(p_i^{k0} - p_i^{k1}) \qquad (13.27)$$

using an obvious notation for benefits to income group w. One of the main problems in applying this formula is that many people are not paying, or organizations charging, market prices. Those prices which are market-determined will be partly functions of those which are not. Ideally, p_i^{k0} should be the market prices which would have obtained initially under perfectly competitive conditions, and p_i^{k1} similar prices after the change. B^w in equation (13.27) would then be the correct measure of benefit, and any subsidy questions, or change in subsidy questions, could be dealt with explicitly and separately. However, it is difficult to know how to calculate p_i^{k0} and p_i^{k1} as pseudo-market prices. Under certain circumstances, the shadow prices predicted by an economic residential location model such as the Herbert–Stevens model may help. Indeed, if this model is being used, the value of Z, or the change in the value of Z after a plan has been implemented, directly provides a measure of benefit.

Before we leave the discussion of residential and workplace location, we will briefly note a quite different kind of evaluation procedure (Wilson, 1972)). This involves making some assumptions about the likely behaviour of the supply side in a perfect market economy. For a given income group, we would expect the individuals in this group to display a variety of preferences and hence, if the supply side responded accordingly, a variety of choices. If c defines a journey-to-work cost range, and p a house-price range, we would compute

$$\phi^w(p, c) = \sum_{p_i^k \in p} \sum_{c_{ij} \in c} T_{ij}^{kw} \qquad (13.28)$$

as the frequency distribution into (p, c) groups for income group w. We might expect this distribution to be something like a bivariate normal distribution, or at least a *smooth* one. If, on examining the model prediction of $\phi^w(p, c)$, or indeed the 'observed' value of it, we note 'gaps' in the distribution, then we may call these *opportunity gaps* due to supply-side deficiencies and invoke general theorems of economics to say that welfare could be improved if these gaps were filled. Using this indicator, the designer can then obtain quite specific ideas about what is needed in some respects.

The planning of the distribution of shopping centres using a model of the form

$$S_{ij} = A_i e_i P_i W_j^\alpha \, e^{-\beta c_{ij}} \qquad (13.29)$$

raises and illustrates some interesting points in evaluation methodology. Suppose W_j reflects the distribution of shopping facilities; W_j^0 in some initial situation, W_j^1 after some plan has been implemented. It has been well known since Hotelling's (1929) example of ice-cream men on a linear beach that the competitive equilibrium and the welfare equilibrium can be very different. Figure 13.4(a) shows the welfare equilibrium with ice-cream men at first and

Figure 13.4   Ice-cream men on a linear beach—Hotelling (1929)

third quartile points and, with an even density of people assumed, people travelling the minimum mean distance for ice-cream. Figure 13.4(b) shows the competitive equilibrium which has resulted from each ice-cream man in turn moving nearer to the centre of the beach in an attempt to obtain more than half of the sales. The real world is much more complicated, of course, but the situation in which a planner constructs W_i^1 to fulfil welfare objectives and the one in which shopkeepers determine W_j^1 as individual profit maximizers are likely to reflect some of the differences between Figures 13.4(a) and (b). The real-world situation, as well as having the complexities of two dimensions and a non-homogenous spread of purchasing powers (the $e_i P_i$ of equation (13.29)), will also have increasing returns to scale (reflected by the magnitude of α in equation (13.29)) so that some agglomeration can provide benefits to both shopkeeper and consumer.

How then, do we construct good indicators for this problem? If we write

$$W_j^\alpha = e^{\alpha \log W_j} = e^{\beta \cdot (\alpha/\beta) \cdot \log W_j} \tag{13.30}$$

and take $(\alpha \log W_j / \beta)$ as a benefit to be set against travel cost c_{ij}, then perhaps we should try to arrange W_j^1 such that

$$Z = \sum_i \sum_j S_{ij} \left(\frac{\alpha}{\beta} \log W_j^1 - c_{ij} \right) \tag{13.31}$$

is a maximum, with S_{ij} given by equation (13.29)? We may also wish to impose additional constraints, such as Lowry's minimum-size constraint:

$$W_j^1 \geqslant W^{\min} \tag{13.32}$$

We have now defined a fairly complicated non-linear mathematical programming problem in the variables W_j^1. It is interesting to compare this kind of formulation with more standard linear-programming formulations. For example, choose S_{ij} such that

$$Z = \sum_i \sum_j S_{ij} c_{ij} \tag{13.33}$$

is a minimum subject

$$\sum_j S_{ij} = e_i P_i \tag{13.34}$$

and

$$\sum_i S_{ij} = W_j \tag{13.35}$$

That is, S_{ij} is taken as the solution to the transportation problem of linear programming, and then the W_js would be manipulated further to reduce Z. The use of the gravity model for S_{ij}, in equation (13.29) rather than the linear-programming scheme given in equations (13.33)–(13.35) simply reflects real-world complications and imperfections: the variety of goods and specialist needs, lack of perfect information and so on.

Of course, it is much more usual to use the shopping model of equation (13.29) in a planning process with simpler goal indicators: turnover per square foot for each shopping centre, improved accessibility (say using a Hansen measure) for residents of particular areas, and so on.

Some other services can be modelled in a similar way to shopping and have similar evaluation methods; others, as we saw in Chapter 10, are more susceptible directly to mathematical programming formulations, and in such cases the model provides the evaluation methodology.

It is more difficult, as ever, to discuss the economic activity sector and associated evaluation criteria. The models in this sector are crude and are not in themselves particularly helpful in offering hints about related evaluation criteria. In seeking criteria, on the one hand we must in principle look at the form of the production function of each organization, including the effect of its linkages with other organizations, in relation to the demand for its product; on the other hand, it will also be useful to examine the social consequences of the organization's development, for example, as a job provider. Some of these questions are tackled at a regional level with the input–output model and an associated target-achieving evaluation methodology. Most of the other questions must await improved models.

It only remains to comment on evaluation methods as applied when a general model is used. Since a general model will contain components for each of the sectors discussed above, the previous discussion again applies here. However, the need for a general model, which has continually been emphasized, relates primarily to the suspected interdependence of the major urban and regional sectors. A general model, therefore, should be able to predict secondary- and higher-order consequences of planned changes which are aimed mainly at one sector. Thus the residential location model will tell us about the consequences of transport network changes. These secondary- and higher-order changes can then be measured by relating them to the appropriate goal indicators for each sector.

13.5. PROBLEM SOLVING AND CONTROL

The reader will by now have a good idea of the potential contribution of the model-based analyst to problem solving. The purpose of this section is twofold: first, to act as a reminder that the planner will often *have to* focus on a particular problem, and that the analytical basis needed then has to be built using the *methods* of this book, but not necessarily taking a model straight 'off-the-shelf' without further thought; and second, to re-emphasize the time dimension in the planners' task and the associated on-going control problem.

Perhaps the most important point to remember about building an analytical package as a problem-solving aid is that the correct level of resolution should be identified together with an associated error measure. Answers to problems can sometimes be quite clear in situations where the error may be quite high. In the case study in Section 14.2, for example, a minimum feasible amount of some quantity was identified, and the model prediction was one-*tenth* of this. Even with an error of, say, 200%, the analyst could still confidently state that the minimum was unlikely to be attained.

The second comment on problem solving connects us directly to the discussion on control: there will not be many situations for which the analysis is free of uncertainty and error (due either to basic ignorance of model or mechanisms of change, or to 'unpredictable' future changes in taste, technology, values etc.). This suggests that it is safest to work with the concept of 'best answer to this problem at this time', and to be prepared continually to revise plans either as a result of improved and revised analyses or more inventive designs, or as a result of some unforeseen 'environmental' change. The importance of any particular problem, and the uncertainties associated with the corresponding plan, will help to determine the appropriate investment in research on this topic. This point also allows us to take up a commonly voiced criticism of model-based planning: that decisions will not 'wait for' the models to be developed. The answer is: O.K., take the decisions, but on as temporary a basis as possible, keeping as many options open as possible, and let us revise later with more information and using improved analytical techniques.

We conclude, then, that for situations of any complexity at all, developing in various ways through time, plans should be *rolling plans* which are revised at intervals. Then, in effect, we are devising a control system for the system being planned. Consider the task of urban development control as represented by Figure 13.5. The boxes enclosed by the dotted line in the Figure can be considered to be the city's control system, the current plan being based on the latest available analysis and design, leading to a current setting of the controlled variables. At this point, it is convenient to pause and to ask what we know about the theory of control.

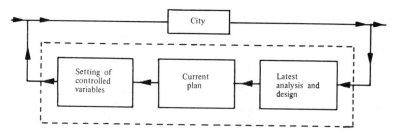

Figure 13.5   The planning system as a control system

We should emphasize at the outset that 'control' is not being used in any machine-like deterministic sense. By 'control', we simply mean the planning system operating to achieve social goals. Perhaps the most crucial element in the theory of control is Ashby's (1956) law of requisite variety. The variety of a system is, formally, the number of states it can get into; less formally, it is a measure of the complexity of the system. The law of requisite variety then states that a control system must have, at least, the variety of the system which it is attempting to control. In many ways, the law is quantified common sense, and is intuitively obvious but it is, nonetheless, very important. A city, for example, is an extremely complex high-variety system. Only a planning system with correspondingly high variety *could* control it.

We should note, of course, that the definition of variety depends on the level of resolution at which the system is viewed. Even allowing for a coarse level of resolution at which to plan the city, it is clear that most planning systems, in practice, are of much lower variety than the system they are trying to control. The advantage of using a model-based analysis system, within the scheme outlined in Figure 13.5 is that this increases the variety of the control system: the control system adopts, as it were, the variety of the model system, which reflects that of the city itself, and hence provides the information (another word for 'variety' in this context) necessary for effective control.

We can further illustrate this using some ideas of Beer (1972) from his book, *Brain of the Firm*. He argues that the most effective control system which has ever evolved in nature is the *central nervous system* (CNS) of the human body, and that we can learn much about the nature of control by studying its organization. Figure 13.6 represents a Beer CNS-type control system for an organization with activities A, B, C, ... There are five levels in a control hierarchy, numbered 1 (the lowest) to 5 (the highest). At the 1-level, the basic activity is directly controlled; the 2-level coordinates these by organizing an exchange of information; the 3-level is the management level; it implements the current production plan. Level-5 is the cerebral, thinking, level: it reviews problems (or information received from below), transmits solutions (as amendments to the plan). Level-4 is a giant switch and filter: it receives

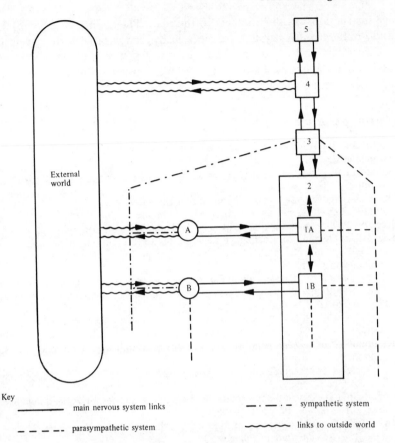

Key

main nervous system links   — · — · —   sympathetic system

— — — — —   parasympathetic system   ～～～～～   links to outside world

Figure 13.6   A CNS-type control system. (Based, with permission, on Stafford Beer, *Brain of the Firm*, Penguin Press, 1972, Figure 22, p. 168.)

information from above, below and from the outside world, and 'decides' what to transmit to whom. The A, B, C, ... production activities may also have contacts with the external world as shown. The solid lines on the Figure are the main communication channels. These are supported by additional channels: the 'sympathetic' which is usually excitory in its action, and the parasympathetic which is normally inhibitory. For the details, the reader is referred to Beer's book. The important point to note for our present purposes is that the level-4 part of the control system is critical to the whole operation, and Beer argues that *it is usually almost entirely missing from most management systems*. In a planning system, we would expect level-4 to contain the model-based analysts whose work is the main subject of this book. They feed digested information and reports to the decision-makers at level-5, and receive instructions or amendments to the plan. The counterparts of levels 3, 2 and 1 in the planning system are more easily recognizable as the development controllers and the doers. Thus, Beer's structure, and especially his discussion of level-4, is likely to be most useful to anyone who is setting up a model-based planning system.

13.6. REFERENCES

C. Alexander (1964) *Notes on the synthesis of form*, Harvard University Press, Cambridge, Mass.

* K. J. Arrow and T. Scitovsky (1969) *Readings in welfare economics*, Allen and Unwin, London.

W. R. Ashby (1956) *Cybernetics*, Chapman and Hall, London.

*S. Beer (1966) *Decision and control*, John Wiley, London.

S. Beer (1972) *Brain of the firm*, Allen Lane: the Penguin Press, London.

R. Dial (1972) Demand forecasting for new options and technology, paper presented to the Highway Research Board Conference on Travel demand forecasting, Williamsburg, Virginia.

* C. D. Foster and M. E. Beesley (1963) Estimating the social benefit of constructing an underground railway in London, *Journal of the Royal Statistical Society*, Series A, **126**, pp. 46–92.

* J. K. Friend and W. N. Jessop (1969) *Local government and strategic choice*, Tavistock, London.

* J. de Graaff (1967) *Theoretical welfare economics*, Cambridge University Press, London.

H. A. J. Green (1964) *Aggregation in economic analysis*, Princeton University Press, Princeton, New Jersey.

B. Harris (1967) The city of the future: the problem of optimal design, *Papers, Regional Science Association*, **19**, pp. 185–195.

M. Hill (1966) A goals' achievement matrix in evaluating alternative plans, *Journal of the American Institute of Planners*, **34**, pp. 19–29.

H. Hotelling (1929) Stability in competition, *Economic Journal*, **39**, pp. 41–57.

K. J. Lancaster (1965) A new approach to consumer theory, *Journal of Political Economy*, **74**, pp. 132–157.

N. Lichfield (1966) Cost–benefit analysis in town planning—a case study: Swanley, *Urban Studies*, **3**, pp. 215–249.

* N. Lichfield (1970) Evaluation methodology of urban and regional plans: a review, *Regional Studies*, **4**, pp. 151–165.

I. S. Lowry (1967) Comments on Britton Harris, *Papers, Regional Science Association*, **19**, pp. 197–198.

* L. Martin and L. March (Eds.) (1972) *Urban space and structures*, Cambridge University Press, London.

* E. J. Mishan (1971) *Cost-benefit analysis*, Allen and Unwin, London.

H. Neuberger (1971) User benefit in the evaluation of transport and land use plans, *Journal of Transport Economics and Policy*, **5**, pp. 52–75.

A. R. Prest and R. Turvey (1965) Cost–benefit analysis: a survey, *Economic Journal*, **75**, pp. 683–735.

SELNEC Transportation Study (1972) *A broad plan for 1984*, Town Hall, Manchester.

* J. C. Tanner (1968) A theoretical model for the design of a motorway system, *Transportation Research*, **2**, pp. 123–141.

J. O. Tressider, D. A. Meyers, J. E. Burrell and T. J. Powell (1968) The London transportation study: methods and techniques, *Proceedings Institution of Civil Engineers*, **39**, pp. 433–464.

M. Webber (1963) Order in diversity: community without propinquity, in L. Wingo (Ed.) *Cities and space*, Johns Hopkins Press, Baltimore, pp. 23–54.

A. G. Wilson (1966) Cost–benefit analysis in the local government sector, *Local Government Finance*, **70**, pp. 314–319 and 345–351.

A. G. Wilson (1967) Forward financial planning in local government, *Local Government Finance*, **71**, pp. 437–446.

A. G. Wilson (1972) Some recent developments in micro-economic approaches to modelling household behaviour, with special reference to spatio-temporal organization, Paper 11 in *Papers in urban and regional analysis*, Pion, London, pp. 216–236.

A. G. Wilson and R. Kirwan (1969) Measures of benefits in the evaluation of urban transport improvements, Working Paper 43, Centre for Environmental Studies, London.

CHAPTER 14

Planning with models: two examples

14.1. INTRODUCTION

It is already clear that models can be used in urban and regional planning processes in a great variety of ways. To the present time, however, practitioners in the field have perhaps been more concerned with model development *per se* and less with inventing new ways of using the models. Thus, most current uses have been concerned with simple conditional forecasting, as discussed in Section 13.2. For the purposes of this book, on the principles of model building, relatively little is to be learned from describing detailed processes of model calibration and conditional forecasting and, in any case, if such a task were to be attempted, the result would be another book rather than a chapter of this one. Nonetheless, the reader should seek the appropriate knowledge and experience of practical model building by reading as many relevant reports and papers as possible. In this chapter, we concentrate on two examples which illustrate the use of models in planning: the main feature of each being that the effect of the use of the models on the final decision or plan can be traced.

The first example is concerned with the location of a major regional facility in the U.K., a port, and it illustrates that, for some kinds of problem in planning, the use of a model can give a clear-cut answer in spite of possibly large errors on the model's predictions. The second example is concerned with transport planning in the Greater Manchester area, officially known as the SELNEC area (South East Lancashire, North East Cheshire). This example illustrates the use of a model with a more complicated planning problem, the design of the best modal networks; though initially, one of the tasks, as in the first example, was to evaluate one major public transport project.

14.2. A PROBLEM IN PORT INVESTMENT LOCATION

The Harbours Act of 1964 in the U.K. required major investment proposals to be approved by the Minister of Transport, who would be advised by the National Ports Council for such purposes. In May 1964, the Port of Bristol Authority (P.B.A.) submitted for approval Stage I of the Portbury project, which was estimated to cost £27 m (at 1963 prices) for nine new deep-water berths, of which two were for bulk cargo and seven for general cargo. In May 1965, the National Ports Council recommended to the Minister that the scheme should be approved.

The Portbury scheme was an exceptionally large one, and the Government decided to carry out its own investigation (Ministry of Transport, 1966). The basic forecasts underpinning the P.B.A. submission had been supplied by the Authority itself, its own resources being supplemented by those of consultants. The National Ports Council, in carrying out its own appraisal, had performed a discounted cash flow (d.c.f.) analysis using these forecasts. There had been some disagreement between the P.B.A. and its consultants on some figures, and the rate of return on the project (over a 50-year period) was found to be nil if the consultants' forecasts were used, and 7·5 % if the P.B.A.'s forecasts were used (Ministry of Transport, 1966, p. 2). The crucial difference was the forecast for overseas exports. The 1964 figure for Bristol was 0·196 m tons per annum; the consultants' forecast figure for 1980 (with Portbury) was 0·465 m tons, while the P.B.A. forecast was 2·600 m tons. The corresponding figures for imports were not the subject of any substantial disagreement. It was decided to investigate these forecasts by alternative means in an attempt to 'decide' between the P.B.A. and their consultants' forecasts.

This was made feasible because new data became available shortly before the Minister had to make her decision: a survey of flows of goods to and from all U.K. ports had been carried out in 1964 by Martech Ltd. for the Port of London Authority, and their results were made available to the Ministry's Economic Planning Group. This gave observed values of T_{ij}, the flow of goods (by weight) from zone i of the U.K., through port j (exports), or to zone i from port j (imports). The U.K. was divided into 41 zones, and 25 ports were included in the survey. Data was available for goods by type, but was used in aggregate form because of shortage of time.

Two kinds of analysis were carried out on the data: first, a so-called radial analysis and second, a gravity model of the flows was built. Although only the second is a model-building exercise, both will be described because of the way they complement each other in relation to the planning problem, and because it illustrates a kind of supporting analysis which is often useful for model-based work.

Suppose d_{ij} is the distance (centroid to centroid) from zone i to port j. Then, the radial analysis consisted of the calculation of $P_{1j}(d)$, $P_{2j}(d)$ and $P_{3i}(d)$, where d is a distance *range*, 0–25, 25–50, 50–75 and so on, and the variables are proportions of all exports through j which originate in 'ring d' around port j, the production of all exports originating in ring d around j which pass through j, and the proportion of exports originating in zone i which pass through ports lying in ring d around i. Similar variables can be defined for imports. For $p_{1j}(d)$ and $p_{3i}(d)$, it was also convenient to define the corresponding *cumulative* percentages $P_{1j}(d)$ and $P_{3i}(d)$. Thus, using an obvious notation:

$$p_{1j}(d) = \frac{\sum_{\substack{i \text{ s.t.} \\ d_{ij} \in d}} T_{ij}}{\sum_i T_{ij}}$$ (14.1)

$$p_{2j}(d) = \frac{\sum_{\substack{i \text{ s.t.} \\ d_{ij} \in d}} T_{ij}}{\sum_{\substack{i, j \text{ s.t.} \\ d_{ij} \in d}} T_{ij}}$$ (14.2)

$$p_{3i}(d) = \frac{\sum_{\substack{j \text{ s.t.} \\ d_{ij} \in d}} T_{ij}}{\sum_j T_{ij}}$$ (14.3)

$$P_{1j}(d) = \sum_{d' \leqslant d} p_{2j}(d')$$ (14.4)

and

$$P_{3i}(d) = \sum_{d' \leqslant d} p_{3i}(d')$$ (14.15)

Tables were published of $P_{1j}(d)$, $p_{2j}(d)$ and $P_{3i}(d)$. All showed gravity-like decay features with distance, and with a surprisingly rapid decay. The mean distance travelled for exports was 66 miles and for imports 36 miles. It was discovered that two-fifths of all Britain's sea-going exports travel less than 25 miles, and two-thirds less than 75 miles. For London, 79% of exports originating in the local area used the port; for Liverpool, the corresponding figure was 81%.

These were encouraging results to support the development of a gravity model. The model used (which will be described for exports only, though an equivalent model was also run for imports) was

$$T_{ij} = A_i O_i X_j^a d_{ij}^{-b}$$ (14.6)

with

$$A_i = 1 \bigg/ \sum_j X_j^a d_{ij}^{-b}$$ (14.7)

where

$$O_i = \text{total exports originating in zone } i;$$
$$X_j = \text{total exports handled by port } j;$$
$$a, b = \text{parameters}$$

and the other variables have already been defined. Thus the model is a singly constrained spatial interaction model in which X_j^a is being used as an attractiveness factor; a and b are parameters to be estimated.

Five goodness-of-fit statistics were computed

$$G_1 = \sum_j (X_j - X_j^{\text{obs}})^2 \qquad (14.8)$$

$$G_2 = \sum_i \sum_j (T_{ij} - T_{ij}^{\text{obs}})^2 \qquad (14.9)$$

$$G_3 = \frac{\sum_i \sum_j T_{ij} d_{ij}}{\sum_i \sum_j T_{ij}} \qquad (14.10)$$

and G_4 as the R^2-statistic comparing the vector X_j with X_j^{obs} and G_5 as the R^2-statistic comparing T_{ij} with T_{ij}^{obs}. The calibration procedure used was the simple one of running the model, and calculating G_1–G_5, for a 'grid' of (a, b) values. G_1 suffered from the 'bogus calibration' problem discussed in Chapter 12: it was zero for $a = 1$, $b = 0$. However, values of a and b were found in a straightforward manner which more or less minimized G_1 and G_2 and were such that G_3 coincided with the actual mean distance. For exports, $a = 1.00$, $b = 1.25$ gave the best fit, and for imports, $a = 0.75$, $b = 1.75$. All four 'best-fit' R^2s were greater than 0.95.

The model was then used to produce forecasts. This could only be done on a crude basis, as no figures were available for expected increase in export production (the O_is) by 1980. An expected average national increase from 1964 to 1980 had to be applied in each region. The increases were 84% for exports and 56% for imports. Unfortunately, this meant that the published forecasts were simply the *model* estimates increased by 84% and 56% for exports and imports respectively. The results are shown for all 25 ports in Table 14.1.

Even though the forecasts were made on a very simple basis, some confidence (at least in terms of general guidance) could be attached to the results because the model had fitted the 1964 data reasonably well; also, an alternative figure for Bristol exports was produced, of 0.263 m tons, to be compared to the consultants' estimate of 0.465 m tons and the P.B.A. figure of 2.600 m tons. Clearly, the model forecast was much nearer to the consultants' than that of the P.B.A. Indeed, since the largest errors in a gravity model are associated with the smallest flows, it was possible to be generous and argue that the model's prediction was 'compatible with' that of the consultants', even though the latter was considerably higher. It was equally clear that it was not compatible with the P.B.A. figure, the minimum needed to get a good rate of return.

The next step was to seek help from the radial analysis. If the P.B.A. figure were to be accepted, where would the shortfall come from? The radial analysis showed that the bulk of it would have to come a long distance from Bristol: the Midlands, and even the London area. The Government paper (Ministry

Table 14.1.   Results of the gravity model analysis [a,b]

	Exports			Imports		
(1)	(2)	(3)	(4)	(5)	(6)	(7)
Port	Actual total 1964	Model total 1964	Forecast 1980	Actual total 1964	Model total 1964	Forecast 1980
1. King's Lynn ..	59·3	35·4	65·3	380·0	221·6	344·6
2. Felixstowe ..	108·4	47·6	87·8	193·5	97·8	152·1
3. Ipswich	49·6	25·6	47·2	490·7	248·6	386·6
4. Harwich.. ..	272·1	124·7	229·9	445·3	212·1	329·8
5. Yarmouth ..	78·7	34·7	64·0	240·5	92·2	143·4
6. Leith	97·1	88·6	163·4	956·6	1253·6	1949·3
7. Grangemouth ..	366·2	233·6	430·8	762·3	550·3	855·7
8. Glasgow.. ..	736·9	965·0	1779·5	1803·8	1746·0	2715·0
9. Newcastle ..	234·6	238·9	440·5	721·5	834·3	1297·3
10. Sunderland	25·6	19·0	35·0	51·5	65·0	101·1
11. Tees	961·9	1284·0	2367·7	1215·4	1181·9	1837·9
12. Hull	970·3	650·5	1199·5	3961·7	3656·2	5685·4
13. Immingham ..	98·7	54·5	100·5	1160·4	420·9	654·5
14. Goole	210·5	209·7	386·7	435·3	980·8	1525·1
15. Grimsby.. ..	62·1	34·1	62·9	372·4	177·2	275·5
16. Manchester ..	650·4	1029·0	1897·5	3351·6	4387·5	6822·6
17. Liverpool ..	4481·2	4546·9	8384·5	7712·6	8143·5	12663·1
18. Shoreham ..	12·4	7·1	13·1	241·7	719·1	1118·2
19. Dover	286·2	123·2	227·2	447·7	260·4	404·9
20. Southampton ..	362·7	286·7	528·7	904·8	984·0	1530·1
21. Bristol	196·3	142·5	262·8	3184·2	3182·9	4949·4
22. Newport ..	549·9	586·4	1081·3	440·0	374·7	582·7
23. Cardiff	96·1	101·5	187·2	551·8	427·2	664·3
24. Swansea	447·8	462·3	852·5	572·5	482·9	750·9
25. London	4443·7	4527·2	8348·2	13,511·3	13,408·2	20,849·8

[a] All totals are given in thousands of tons. The national average increases used in obtaining the forecasts are 84 % and 56 % for exports and imports respectively. The actual figures in column (2) differ slightly from those in Annex 3 because of rounding.

[b] Reproduced by permission of the Controller of Her Majesty's Stationery Office, from *Portbury*, Ministry of Transport, 1966.

of Transport, 1966, p. 8) noted: 'To sum up, if Bristol attracted the whole of the increase in deep-sea and medium-sea exports of the Midland region (say 500,000 tons) and was successful in attracting one-third of that region's existing exports of that type (say 330,000 tons), and if these tonnages were entirely additional to the gravity model's estimate of 260,000 tons for Bristol in 1980, which strictly speaking they are not, it will be evident that a further 1·5 m tons of exports would still be required to be diverted from the ports to which they would otherwise flow in order to reach the Port of Bristol

Authority's figure of 2·7 m tons.' It was also noted that any major diversion would lead to increased inland haulage costs.

Thus, the model and related analyses made out a solid case against supporting the P.B.A. figures and project. The P.B.A. did not accept that this 'financial' method of evaluation was valid for a major port. They argued (i) that a large part of the country's export expansion would be in the Midlands and London, that (ii) the M4 and M5 motorways gave Bristol a good chance of attracting much of this and (iii) there was a case for having a third major liner terminal in addition to London and Liverpool 'as an insurance against the ever-present risk of congestion and dislocation in the country's two principal ports.' It was also argued that the Portbury development would help the Severnside region in general and would encourage expansion there.

Unfortunately for Bristol, not only was the model-based argument about export figures presented above against it, other features were also. The scheme was expensive: an average cost of £3 m per berth as against a more typical figure of £1·6 m (and this could only be reduced if the 9-berth scheme was expanded to 25 berths so that the cost of a large new entrance lock could be 'shared' more). The trends in the direction of Britain's trade flows seemed increasingly towards Europe and thus militated against Western ports such as Bristol. At the time of the analysis (1966), the container 'revolution' was just beginning to happen, and it was by no means obvious that many new berths would be needed if much future general cargo traffic were containerized. The regional development argument was not accepted either: it was argued (Ministry of Transport, 1966, p. 9) that to make up the shortfall in exports would require a population increment in the Bristol region of 3 million, or for an equivalent amount in imports, an increment of 1·25–1·5 million, and neither seemed possible by 1980, given an existing 1964 population of 857,000. Thus, there was a strong case supporting the Minister's decision in 1966 to turn down the P.B.A.'s submission, and model-based analysis played a crucial part in this.

14.3. A CASE STUDY IN URBAN TRANSPORT PLANNING

The only field of planning in which the use of models is common is that of urban transport planning. It remains relatively difficult, however, to find case studies which illustrate the planning structure as conceptualized in this book, for reasons which are discussed in the concluding comments in Section 14.4. Here, we discuss the SELNEC Transportation Study (1972), concentrating on the use of the model rather than the model itself. The model used in the study was more or less that described in detail in Sections 9.3–9.7, and therefore no further description is needed here.

The survey for the study was carried out in 1965/66, and the analytical work began in 1967. It is appropriate to begin with a description of the organization of the analytical and planning work in the study, since they are closely intertwined: the tasks of data analysis and model building are so time consuming in a pioneering study (the SELNEC Study was pioneering for its staff and for the area at least), that the planning process has to be structured so as to accommodate this work. The analysis part of the study consisted of a survey to provide data for model calibration, the calibration process itself, and the execution of a number of model runs to make conditional forecasts and to provide outputs for the evaluation of alternative plans. The design task was to specify alternative model networks, highway and public transport (the latter considered as one network, but made up mainly of rail and bus components). The policy task was to choose between these and to recommend a single plan.

The design stage was carried out in three phases. First, alternative networks were drawn up without model-based analytical help (during the data analysis and model calibration phase). Towards the end of this phase, a preliminary version of the model became available for the journey-to-work in the morning peak period only, and the first round of alternative networks was tested using this model. A full range of evaluation outputs could not, of course, be obtained using this restricted model, but useful information was obtained on loadings in different parts of the modal networks. This information was used to generate some preliminary conclusions and formed the basis of the second phase of the design work: some sections of the original plan were dropped, others were modified and new ones were added. (In ideal circumstances, of course, full evaluation output would have been used as a basis for new design work.) This second phase of design work was carried out in parallel with the further development of the model and by the end of the phase the model was operating an all-trip purposes and a full economic evaluation, using the methods of Section 13.4, was carried out. The appraisal of the alternatives in the light of this evaluative information led to a third design phase: a plan was constructed which had some of the best features of several second-phase alternatives. This was tested and evaluated using the model, found to be satisfactory in its major features, and recommended as the plan for 1984 for the region.

We can now examine the kinds of issues involved in design in more detail. This study provides a good, and rare, example of one which attempts to generate and to evaluate a wide range of alternatives. We shall attempt to give the full flavour of the exercise without giving details of the geography which would be of very local interest only.

The first design phase was mainly concerned with public transport alternatives. The Greater Manchester area is well endowed with radial rail lines: there were 14 connecting outlying towns and suburbs with central Manchester, northern ones terminating in the northern part of the city centre, southern ones in the southern part. The main public transport facilities, however, were provided by an extensive bus system. The analysis work in the SELNEC Study had been preceded by M.A.R.T.S., the Manchester Area Rapid Transit Study (1967-A, 1967-B, 1968), which had explored in some detail the feasibility of constructing one rapid transit (R.T.) rail line, north–south and through central Manchester, therefore this was very much in mind as one of the public transport options. This proposal had not, however, been evaluated using a model. The same firm of consultants who had conducted the M.A.R.T.S. Study were asked to carry out a rail planning study within the umbrella of the SELNEC Study to investigate the possibility of other rail options (de Leuw, Chadwick, O hEocha, 1968). Two other kinds of alternatives emerged: the upgrading of the services on the existing radial rail lines, and the possibility of a central area tunnel which would, for the first time, link the northern and southern lines into central Manchester. The idea of a tunnel had, of course, first been raised in connection with the R.T. line, since its central section would be underground. But now alternative alignments for the tunnel were investigated. The public transport rail options to be investigated, therefore, were combinations of these three main features: the north–south R.T. line, upgrading the existing rail system, and building one or more tunnels in central Manchester to improve the connectivity of the system and to improve central area distribution for rail commuters.

Various combinations were tested using the morning-peak journey-to-work model and the following kinds of conclusions emerged:

(1) Some combinations were obviously under-utilized and were eliminated.

(2) The R.T. line generated enough traffic to warrant further investigation.

(3) As an alternative to the R.T. line, a busway in the same corridor should be investigated.

(4) The upgraded rail system could have its design improved using information from traffic flows gained in the tests.

(5) That some central area tunnels merited further investigation as a means of connecting links in the upgraded rail system.

These provided the guidelines for the second phase of public transport network design (de Leuw, Chadwick, O hEocha, 1969). In each phase, the bus network was designed to maintain and to improve existing services, and to provide a feeder system for the rail lines. Relatively little work was carried out in the first design phase on the highway network. The SELNEC Transportation Study had been preceded by the publication in 1962 of the SELNEC Highway Plan (1962) by a Committee of local authorities in the area. This Plan had been produced virtually without a budget constraint, and so was a very dense 'library' of possible road schemes. It was tested with the journey-to-work model and found to be more or less satisfactory in an engineering sense, though there was still some peak period congestion. (A 'minimal' highway network, the existing network plus committed schemes, was used in the first phase model-testing of the public transport alternatives.)

By the start of the second design phase, guidance had been obtained from the Ministry of Transport on the likely investment budget for all facilities in the period covered by the Study, 1966–1981, something in the range of £175–200 m. The original SELNEC Highway Plan, if implemented in the same period, would cost £500 m. Thus the second phase of design consisted of (i) refining alternative rail networks for further testing in the light of earlier results, (ii) paring down the SELNEC Highway Plan and to this was added (iii) an examination of possible new technologies.

The cheapest rail alternative was the upgraded existing rail system (approx. £24 m); to this could be added a tunnel (for approximately an additional £18 m); the R.T. line would be coupled with the upgraded rail system and, of course, a particular tunnel alignment at a total cost of approximately £82 m. The matching highway networks in each case were the 'maximum' (to make up the budget, though considerably less than the Highway Plan of 1962), the 'intermediate' and the 'minimum'. The new links which were retained in the highway network from the 'library' were mainly those which improved suburban connections. Conversely, many radial links were dropped on the assumption that the rail system could carry this traffic. The 'new technology' review suggested only that central area distribution would be facilitated by moving-pavement *Passenger Conveyors* in certain parts of the central area, and these were added to one of the networks to be tested.

Seven model runs were carried out to evaluate the alternatives thus generated in the second design phase. Use benefits were calculated using the methods of Section 13.4, and to these were added operator and community benefits: improvements in operating costs, accident costs and so on. The benefits and capital costs were estimated separately for highway and public transport users, and the results are summarized in Table 14.2.

Test 1 gives a reasonable overall rate-of-return, and the size of the public transport benefits indicates that a high rate of return is obtained from the upgrading of the existing rail system, which is why this feature was retained in all subsequent networks. Test 2 gave a relatively low rate-of-return: although the R.T. line ridership was reasonably high, the additional benefits were not sufficient to maintain a greater overall rate-of-return. Test 7 was inserted at this point to see what would happen if the maximum highway system were combined with the R.T. system, to check if congestion in the minimum highway system in test 2 was somehow depressing the benefits. The rate-of-return remained fairly low.

Test 3 investigated an alternative disposition of services in the upgraded rail system but, with aggregate indicators, it was impossible to distinguish the results from test 1. In test 4, a travelator, a central area passenger conveyor, was added to the upgraded rail system at a cost of £5 m. This produced a significant increase in public transport benefits indicating a high rate-of-return, especially on the travelator itself.

Table 14.2.   Costs and benefits of main alternatives[a]

(£m)

Option	Highway benefits	P.T. benefits	Total benefits	Highway capital cost	P.T. capital cost	Total cost	First year rate-of-return %
1. Max. highway/upgr. rail	11·1	9·8	20·9	154·8	24·1	178·9	11·7
2. Min. highway/R.T.	2·9	12·4	15·3	99·4	82·1	181·5	8·5
3. Max. highway/Alt. upgr. rail	11·1	9·1	20·2	154·5	20·3	174·8	11·6
4. Max. highway/upgr. rail + travelator	12·6	9·8	22·4	152·3	25·8	178·1	12·6
5. Int. highway/upgr. rail + tunnel	7·4	10·0	17·4	126·1	42·7	168·8	10·3
6. Alt. int. highway (busway)/upgr. rail	8·2	9·8	18·0	139·5	24·2	163·7	11·0
7. Max. highway/R.T.	7·5	12·4	19·9	126·9	82·1	209·0	9·5

[a] These numbers are taken, with permission, from A broad plan for 1984, SELNEC Transportation Study, 1972.

In test 5, the tunnel was investigated (on a different alignment to the R.T line's tunnel). A heavy traffic loading on the tunnel was found, with a reason able, though by no means the highest, overall rate-of-return. In test 6, the busway was investigated as an alternative to the R.T. line. The overall rate of-return was reasonable, but as it offered an improvement over tests 1 and 2 (and, it was thought, not over 5 if the service frequencies of trains in the tunnel were changed), it was not proceeded with any further.

At the end of this second phase of design and evaluation, the following conclusions were drawn.

(1) The upgraded rail system was a good investment.

(2) The travelator was a useful addition.

(3) The R.T. line might just be financially viable with the ridership which was predicted but it could only be included, for budget reasons, if the minimum network were to be adopted on the highway side. This seemed extremely congested, even in off-peak times, and so the R.T. line was rejected for the recommended plan.

(4) The busway was rejected.

(5) There was high predicted traffic in the tunnel, and this also had the specific advantage that it helped reduce car trips to central Manchester. Further, it was felt that the rate-of-return in test 5 was disproved by unduly low train frequencies which had been used for tunnel trains. Accordingly, the tunnel went into the recommended plan.

(6) The only highway network which performed satisfactorily in engineering operational terms, and which generated the highest rate-of-return, was the 'maximum' highway network. Accordingly, it was decided to retain this, and to extend the time horizon from 1981 to 1984 so that the budget would expand to accommodate it.

The third phase of design, then, was to assemble a recommended plan based on these conclusions. It contained the upgraded rail system, central area travelators, the tunnel and the 'maximum' highway network. Since the time horizon had been adjusted to 1984, certain changes had to be made to the model inputs. This done, the plan was tested with the model with the result shown in Table 14.3. Although this table has the same format as Table 14.2, the results are not directly comparable because of the changes to the model inputs. Nonetheless, it can perhaps be taken as a measure of the further design refinements that the overall rate-of-return is now 13·2 %.

Table 14.3.   Costs and benefits for recommended plan: SELNEC T.S. (1972) [a]

Option	Highway benefits	P.T. benefits	Total benefits	Highway capital cost	P.T. capital cost	Total cost	Rate-of-return %
Recommended plan for 1984	16·84	10·44	27·28	159·26	48·20	207·46	13·2

[a] These numbers are taken, with permission, from *A broad plan for 1984*, SELNEC Transportation Study, 1972.

Two features of this description stand out in the present context: first, ongoing phases of design have been guided by model runs, and could only be effectively guided with such model outputs; and second, the final outcome, the recommended plan, could not have been predicted at the outset as a result of using non-model methods.

In many ways, the SELNEC Study illustrates some of the best features of the use of a sophisticated model in a planning study. However, there are other general lessons to be learned, and critical comments to be made, and these are taken up in the next section.

4.4. CONCLUDING COMMENTS

In Sections 14.2 and 14.3, case studies were presented of the use of models in two planning studies, and it is clear that model-based analysis, in each case, made a considerable contribution. However, it is vital not to be complacent. In this section we undertake a more critical review of the outputs of the two studies, and see if some general conclusions to facilitate future progress can be drawn.

We should begin by getting a feel for what the outputs of the studies mean. In the *Portbury* case, this was really done in the presentation in Section 14.2 through the radial analysis: if the model prediction of exports through Bristol was incorrect, where could the additional goods come from? It was possible to support the conclusions of the model. The proposed solution to the Portbury problem as defined was clear: not to build the facility at that time.

The SELNEC Study is more complicated, and the published report contained relatively little comment on model outputs. Since it is instructive for the reader to become familiar with 'back-of-envelope' explorations of the meanings of model outputs and evaluation indicators, we attempt such an analysis of the outputs of the SELNEC cost–benefit analysis as presented in Tables 14.2 and 14.3, and see what this might suggest for further planning work.

Perhaps the biggest single difficulty is that a plan consists of a large number of specific projects, and yet our evaluation of alternatives is based on a single indicator for each plan, the first year rate-of-return. The information in Table 14.2, together with a substantial assumption, at least allows us to examine separately the contributions of the highway and public transport parts of the network. The benefits and costs in Tables 14.2 and 14.3 are measured relative to some base 'minimum investment' network. But, if we make the assumptions that the contributions of highway investment and public transport investment are very large to highway users and public transport users respectively, then we can proceed as follows. Take tests 2 and 7 in Table 14.2, for example. From test 2 to test 7, the highway budget has increased by £27·46 m and the highway benefits by £4·57 m p.a., and this suggests a first year rate-of-return on this highway investment (from the 'minimum' to the 'maximum' network) of $27{\cdot}46/4{\cdot}57 = 16{\cdot}7\%$, a good figure. Test 2 directly gives highway benefits of £2·88 m p.a. for investment in the 'minimum' highway network of £99·41 m, suggesting a rate-of-return of only 2·9% on this initial investment. This immediately throws up a puzzle which the analyst needs to resolve: why should the first £99 m of investment generate only 2·9% return, and the 'next' £27 m, 16·7%? Was the first pool of projects badly selected? We shall return to this question below.

Note, incidentally, that test 5 gives very similar *highway* benefits to test 7 in spite of a considerable difference in *public transport* investment, suggesting that our assumption about separability may not be a bad one.

We can now examine public transport first year rates-of-return. Test 3 shows that benefits of £9·13 m p.a. are generated from an investment of £20·33 m in the upgraded rail system, suggesting a high rate-of-return of 45% on this investment. The rate-of-return on the R.T. line can be estimated roughly by comparing tests 1 and 7. An additional public transport investment of £58·03 m produces additional benefits of only £2·62 m p.a., suggesting a low rate-of-return of 4·5%. The tunnel can be investigated by comparing tests 3 and 5. An additional investment of £22·36 m produces benefits of £0·82 m p.a. and a rate-of-return of 3·7%. The travelator can be investigated by comparing tests 3 and 4. £5 m of investment produces £0·68 m p.a. in public transport benefit, and a rate-of-return of 12·5%, but also extra highway users benefit by reducing time from car park to office which could take the rate-of-return to nearer 40%.

We have thus arrived at the following situation: highway investment rates-of-return seem high *once the first £99 m has been spent*; public transport rates-of-return are very high for the less-capital-intensive projects, such as the rail upgrading and the travelator, but rather low for expensive projects. The highway result seems particularly odd, and we should seek to explain that first. It seems to arise as follows. Each term in the user benefit formula contains the factor $(c_{ij}^0 - c_{ij}^1)$, the difference in costs before and after the investment. For the minimum investment, because of the growth of car-ownership from 1966 to 1981 and corresponding increase in demand, the 1981 situation is just as congested as the 1966 situation for both peak and off-peak periods. Thus, the users' benefit, measured by the equation (13.26) formula, gives a small or zero contribution for most links. With more investment, the congestion, at least in the off-peak periods, is reduced, and more user benefits are collected. This suggests that the analyst still has a problem in benefit measurement (the use of equation (13.26) as an approximation for one based on equation (13.19) in a situation where the population is changing is probably wrong) rather than that the law of diminishing returns has been turned upside down in this case (for further information, see Neuberger (1971)).

There are also fundamental questions to be raised about the low rates-of-return on more expensive public transport investment. The justification for including the tunnel in the recommended plan was that it would help take away car traffic from the centre of Manchester. There is a hint here that the opportunity cost of not having it may be considerably greater than is reflected in the evaluation procedures used: it may be competing with the most expensive projects in the highway pool on which the rates-of-return are also very low, and so, if an overriding objective is to maintain the city centre, and if this conjecture were true, then investment in such projects as the tunnel would be well worthwhile.

This is a convenient place to mention one more criticism of the evaluation procedure itself: that it concentrates too much on what can be measured. At the present time, this criticism must be accepted. In the SELNEC case, for example, it would be nice to have, as a part of the transport report, a detailed account of the impact on the environment of the different highway and public transport projects, even though such impacts could not be quantified in such a way that they could be added into the cost-benefit analysis. The evaluation framework could then be expanded in the direction of Hill's goals' achievements matrix; though, to be fair, this had already implicitly happened to some extent in the SELNEC decision-making procedure.

So what would the next steps be in each of the case studies we have explored? In the *Portbury* case, the decision makers may have been happier if a wider range of alternatives had been explored, though this would have meant carrying out something like a national ports' planning study. The implications of this will be explored further below. Refinements to the model would be needed on types of good, specialist facilities offered at different parts in relation to different overseas ports, the impact of containerization and so on. In the SELNEC case, although the study examined more alternatives than is customary, yet others could have been examined, on a more systematic basis. We have also identified a number of problems with the evaluation procedure: we would like further information on the impact of particular projects within a plan (and our 'back-of-envelope' calculation gave some clues on the sort of information we would like and how it might then affect the design process); we identified problems associated with the user benefit formula when the 'environment' of the plan is changing (and we discovered this because of puzzles arising from our back-of-envelope calculations); and there are the old problems of intangibles. It would also be an improvement if we could embed the whole procedure in a better time structure so that our analysis procedure gave us time streams of costs and benefits. This might also allow us to say something about phasing. Ideally, we would like to be able to classify trips by geographical type (centre–suburban, suburban–suburban and so on, person type and purpose) and to obtain year-by-year evaluations of the impact of each project within each modal network being tested; all this within the framework of an improved evaluation methodology.

In conclusion, we comment on the practical aspects of model-based planning studies of this kind, beginning with the SELNEC Study as the most substantial of the two cases discussed. There are tremendous start-up costs, partly with obtaining (possibly by survey) suitable data and manipulating it into suitable form for analysis, and partly with the development of appropriate model computer software. These start-up costs for urban and regional agencies could be reduced if the appropriate national agencies existed to support such work. They are also likely to be less of a problem in the longer run as model-based planning studies are set up on a continuing basis, as indeed has now happened to the SELNEC Study.

Even when the state is reached where the data base is organized and the model programmes are running, there remain a number of labour-intensive (as distinct from computer-intensive) and therefore time-consuming activities, as part of the ongoing programme. Perhaps the most important of these is network building. Networks have to be coded in considerable detail, both in order to estimate c_{ij}^ks effectively, and to form the basis of a satisfactory assignment procedure. Figures 14.1 and 14.2 show sections of the coded highway and public transport networks respectively. This shows the amount of detail which has to be represented. The highway trees from one zone for the base-year peak hour network are shown in Figure 14.3. Any suggested change in the network (to build major facilities for a new option, for example) has to be built into the appropriate modal network by hand, and then tested on the computer before it can be used in a model run. It is in this sort of procedure that there is considerable scope for further innovation to make it less labour-consuming.

In the Portbury case, the corresponding continuing study should probably be set up at a national level. The national agency could then interact with Port Authorities within a Lange–Lerner kind of framework (Marglin, 1963, Wilson, 1972). Steps to set up national planning agencies in relation to major regional facilities only seem to be mooted after some major single-region study has been carried out, usually one surrounded by controversy. Another recent example is the Roskill Commission Study on the siting of a third London airport, which has led to suggestions that such studies should be carried out on a national basis.

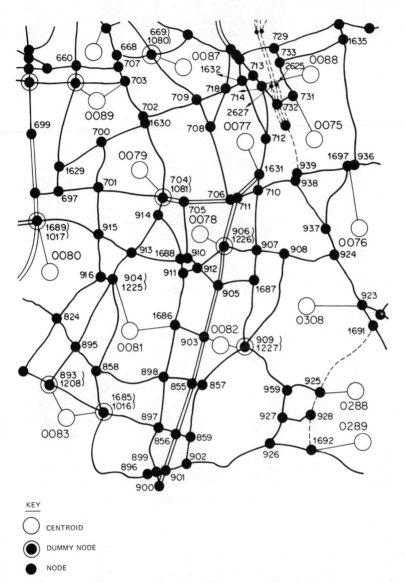

KEY

○ CENTROID

◉ DUMMY NODE

● NODE

Figure 14.1 Section of coded highway network. (Reproduced with permission from Technical Working Paper No. 6: Network Specification and Evaluation, S.E.L.N.E.C. Transportation Study, 1970, Figure 16.)

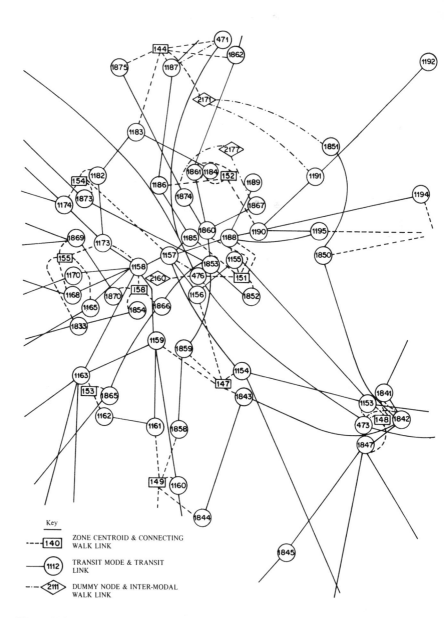

Figure 14.2   Section of public transport network. (Reproduced with permission from Technical Working Paper No. 6: Network Specification and Evaluation, S.E.L.N.E.C. Transportation Study, 1970, Figure 22.)

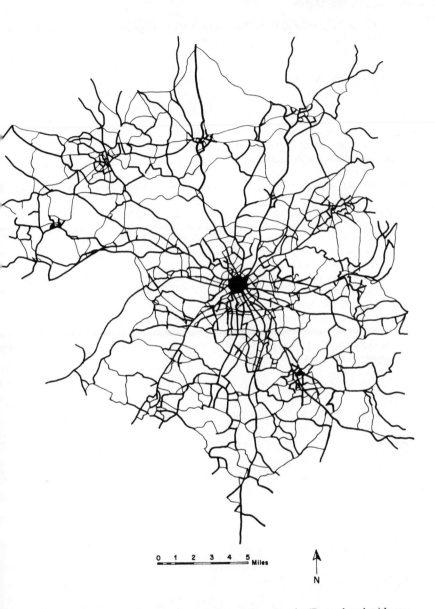

0 1 2 3 4 5 Miles

N

Figure 14.3 Highway tree for sample zone, base year network. (Reproduced with permission from Technical Working Paper No. 6. Network Specification and Evaluation, S.E.L.N.E.C. Transportation Study, 1970, Figure 24.)

14.5. REFERENCES

* D. E. Boyce, N. Day and C. McDonald (1970) *Metropolitan plan making*, Regional Science Research Institute, Philadelphia.

de Leuw, Chadwick, O hEocha (1968) Rail planning study, Technical Working Paper 2 SELNEC Transportation Study, Town Hall, Manchester.

de Leuw, Chadwick, O hEocha (1969) Rail planning study (stage 2), Technical Workin Paper 10, SELNEC Transportation Study, Town Hall, Manchester.

Manchester Area Rapid Transit Study (1967-A) *Volume I: Report of the Workin Party*, Town Hall, Manchester.

Manchester Area Rapid Transit Study (1967-B) *Volume II: Study of rapid transi systems and concepts*, Town Hall, Manchester.

Manchester Area Rapid Transit Study (1968) *Volume III: the first priority*, Town Hall Manchester.

S. A. Marglin (1963) *Approaches to dynamic investment planning*, North Holland Amsterdam.

Ministry of Transport (1966) *Portbury*, H.M.S.O., London.

H. Neuberger (1971) User benefit in the evaluation of transport and land use plans *Journal of Transport Economics and Policy*, **5**, pp. 52–75.

* D. A. Quarmby (1970) Estimating the transport value of a Barrage across Morecambe Bay, *Regional Studies*, **4**, pp. 205–239.

SELNEC Highway Engineering Committee (1962) *SELNEC, A highway plan*, Town Hall, Manchester.

SELNEC Transportation Study (1972) *A broad plan for 1984*, Town Hall, Manchester

* R. Spence (1968) Transportation studies—a critical assessment, *Proceedings, Transpor Engineering Conference*, Institution of Civil Engineers, London pp. 35–44.

A. G. Wilson (1972) National planning for ports, in *Papers in urban and regiona analysis*, Pion, London, pp. 31–45.

CHAPTER 15

Future prospects

15.1. INTRODUCTION

The brief concluding comments below are made under three headings. First, we note that many of the models discussed in this book have a potentially wider range of application than has been indicated. Second, we discuss the connections of the models presented here to ongoing research programmes. Third, we assess the prospects for the future, both in terms of model development and the use of models in planning.

15.2. A NOTE ON THE GENERAL APPLICABILITY OF THE MODELS

Mathematical modelling has developed simultaneously and in parallel in many (previously 'soft') scientific fields in the last 20 years. There is so much in common, that it is not surprising that attempts have been made to develop a *general systems theory* (cf. von Bertalanffy, 1968). In many ways, however, this has not succeeded. It is not yet possible to take models 'off the shelf' in a general systems theory pool which can be easily applied in a specific field such as urban and regional studies. This is probably because the peculiarities and intricacies of the particular field as yet dominate the problem. This may change in the future. It should, however, be emphasized that the general systems field, and mathematical modelling in related sciences such as biology, can be a very fruitful source of ideas for the urban and regional systems model builder. One of the tasks which we should undertake, then, is the reverse process: do other fields have anything to learn from the models of this book? We discuss this briefly, also noting feedbacks the other way for future research, for the models of Chapters 7–11 in turn.

The demographic models of Chapter 7 were applied to human populations at urban and regional scales. They could in principle be applied to any population: of machine tools for example. They could also be used to build more specialized models within the population field: students in a University, manpower in a factory (cf. Bartholomew, 1967) and so on. In other words, birth, death and migration are universal processes and models of these should have a wide applicability. They could be applied to animal populations, and it is not surprising that the continuous variable model of Section 7.6 is closely connected to some of Rosen's (1970) work in biology. This could lead to further applications in ecological studies. The accounting basis for population models described in Section 7.7 also provides an obvious basis for extending this work into other fields.

The input–output process which underpins the economic models of Chapter 8 is also a universal process. The difficulties of extending it to other fields are probably largely the difficulties of identification and measurement of the variables involved and the technical coefficients. There are signs that the model is being used in a context broader than the economic one, for example by integrating economic and ecological models within such a framework (Isard *et al.*, 1972).

Chapters 9, 10 and 11 make frequent use of the family of spatial interaction models described in Chapter 6. These models also have an obvious wide application. Recently, for example, such models have been suggested as the basis for a water resource planning system, simulating the water flows between supply points and usage points (Wilson, 1973). Perhaps the most important point for workers in related fields is to ensure that the level of expertise which has been developed in the urban and regional field is transferred; the recognition that a family of models exists, and the nature of the 'balancing factor' adjustment processes, the use of entropy-maximizing methods to guarantee internal consistency and so on. Sometimes, modelling processes are similar in ways which are not apparent at first sight, and much time could be saved (avoiding parallel and independent development) if such commonalities could be recognized more easily. For example, in the field of input–output analysis, time $t + T$ accounts are sometimes estimated from time t accounts and the time $t + T$ row and column totals. The factoring process involved is exactly the same as the balancing factor adjustment process in spatial interaction modelling. However, the two fields developed separately with different workers producing equivalent theories on the process (Bacharach, 1970, Evans, 1970).

In Chapter 11, we were particularly concerned with knitting together sub-models which had been developed independently. The techniques for doing this, methods of system description using subscript lists, knitting together in an accounting framework and so on, should have a much more general applicability.

Finally, we should also note that some of the calibration methods of Chapter 12 are at present unique to the urban and regional studies field but could be used for similar models in other fields.

15.3. CONNECTIONS TO ONGOING RESEARCH

We begin by criticizing the models presented in broad terms, and then we can identify major research fields corresponding to the categories developed

At the most general level, the main problems are concerned with time and mechanism (or process). The demographic and economic models are dynamic in structure, but the mechanism of change is represented almost entirely in the birth, death and migration rates or technical coefficients and final demand rates respectively. In these cases, the frameworks are sound, but more detail needs to be built into the models on the processes of change. Most of the transport and location models of Chapters 9–11 are cross-sectional equilibrium models. In some cases, this is probably adequate: for the transport model and the shopping model, for example. In other cases, and especially the residential location model, an explicitly dynamic treatment is required. We have attempted to develop the appropriate frameworks for this in Chapters 10 and 11, but again, much more detailed work will be needed in the future on the mechanisms of change.

In summary then, accounting bases provide appropriate frameworks for the development of dynamic models, but much more work will be needed in the future on the processes of change. This is connected to another problem which has been raised in various parts of the book: the aggregation problem. The processes of change are best studied at the most micro-level—the household or the firm, say. But there are very difficult theoretical problems involved in linking new knowledge from research at the micro-level, with our comprehensive models which are inevitably more aggregative. This is likely to remain one of the most fundamental research problems for a long time to come.

In the above remarks, we have tried to sketch out, in a broad way, the most fundamental research problems facing the urban and regional model builder. Two important complementary points should be emphasized. First, much valuable research is being done, and will continue to be done, on the details and further developments of the models as presented here. Next, the second and related point: the fact that substantial ongoing problems can be identified is in itself an indication of the progress which has already been made, and the models currently available are potentially of great use in themselves.

15.4. FUTURE PROSPECTS

The main conclusion to be drawn therefore is that a set of good models already exists for urban and regional analysis, and that these models will be most useful for urban and regional planners operating within the types of framework described in Chapters 2 and 13. Yet this does not reflect the present situation. We saw in Chapter 14 that start-up costs are high, and this has probably inhibited larger-scale use of the available models. There seems to be no doubt, however, that as computer use becomes more commonplace in government (especially urban and regional government), and data systems become more effective and more integrated, model-based planning systems will develop in parallel. Also, increasing interest has been shown, and is continuing, in academic research in these fields, and substantial progress with research problems can be expected to continue.

15.5. REFERENCES

M. Bacharach (1970) *Biproportional matrices and input–output change*, Cambridge University Press, London.

D. J. Bartholomew (1967) *Stochastic models for social processes*, John Wiley, London.

L. von Bertalanffy (1968) *General system theory*, George Braziller, New York.

A. W. Evans (1970) Some properties of trip distribution models, *Transportation Research*, **4**, pp. 19–36.

W. Isard *et al.* (1972) *Ecologic-economic analysis for regional development*, Free Press, New York.

R. Rosen (1970) *Dynamical systems theory in biology, Volume 1*, John Wiley, New York.

* A. G. Wilson (1971) On some problems in urban and regional modelling, M. Chisholm, A. E. Frey and P. Haggett (Eds.) *Regional forecasting*, Butterworth, London, pp. 179–220; also reprinted in A. G. Wilson (1972) *Papers in urban and regional analysis*, Pion, London, pp. 91–132.

A. G. Wilson (1973) Towards system models for water resource management, *Environmental Management*, **1**, pp. 36–52.

APPENDIX 1

Entropy-maximizing methods

The principles and uses of entropy-maximizing methods are described in another book by the author (Wilson, 1970) and only a brief presentation is given here. The methods will be outlined in relation to spatial interaction models, though they could be applied more widely.

The family of spatial interaction models developed in Chapter 6, and frequently used in the rest of the book, were based on the three assumptions (6.1)–(6.3). The basic situation is illustrated in Figure A1.1. Some interaction

Figure A1.1   Basic interaction

between zones i and j is taken as proportional to each of a mass at i, a mass at j, and inversely proportional to some function of the distance (or travel cost) between them. The model is based on a Newtonian analogy.

The entropy-maximizing method changes the basis of the analogy and deals directly with the basic components of the system of interest. Suppose we are concerned with people and, say, the journey-to-work. The Newtonian analogy takes 'residential population' and 'jobs' as masses. The entropy-maximizing method works with individuals, assesses their probability of making a particular journey to work and, essentially, obtains the interaction as a statistical average. We illustrate the method for one case only: the production–attraction· constrained model of Chapter 6. The reader should then be able to see that an analogous method can be used for other members of the family of spatial interaction models, or other 'probability assignment' models, and he can find the details in the book cited above (Wilson, 1970).

Suppose elements of the matrix $\{T_{ij}\}$ satisfy

$$\sum_j T_{ij} = O_i \qquad (A1.1)$$

$$\sum_i T_{ij} = D_j \qquad (A1.2)$$

$$\sum_i \sum_j T_{ij} c_{ij} = C \qquad (A1.3)$$

Consider three levels of resolution at which the system of interest can be described as shown in Figure A1.2 (and, to fix ideas, let us again take the journey to work as an example).

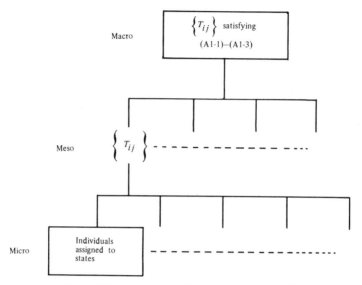

Figure A1.2   Leve's of resolution in the analysis of interaction

At the most detailed, or micro, level, we could assign individuals to particular work trip categories, as indicated in Figure A1.3.

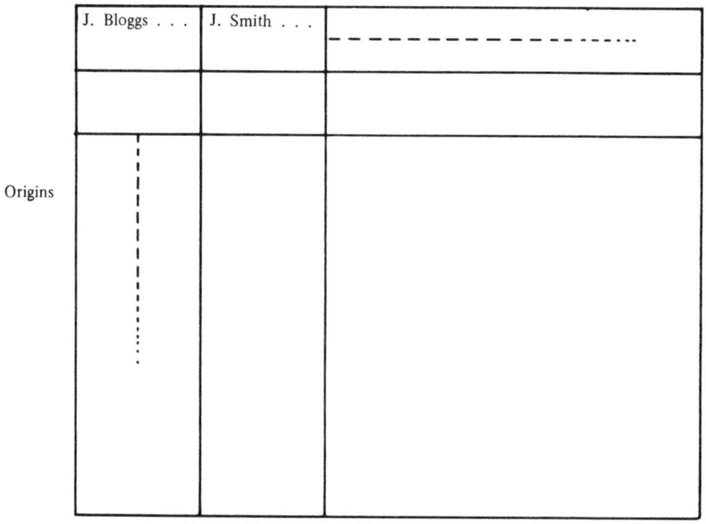

Figure A1.3   A micro state

At the intermediate, or meso level, we are only interested in the total inter-action: counting individuals, as shown in Figure A1.4.

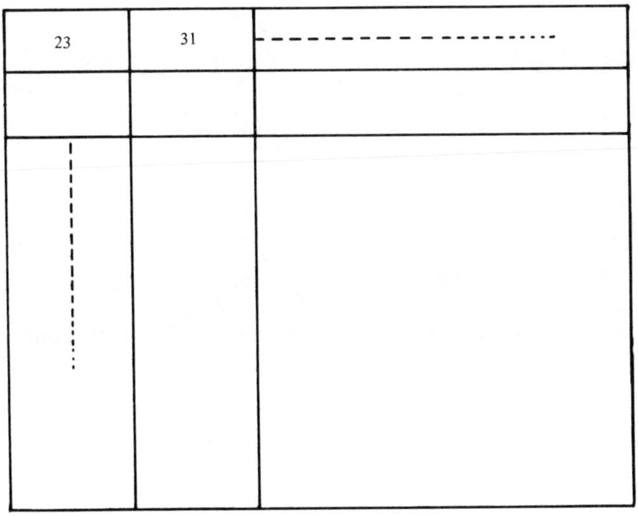

23	31	-- -- -- -- -- -- -- -- -- -- -- ...

Figure A1.4   A meso state

At the macro level, our only restriction is that $\{T_{ij}\}$ should satisfy the given constraints (A1.1)–(A1.3). Clearly, there are many micro-states, assignments of individuals, which give rise to a given meso-state, and many meso-states which give rise to the given macro-state, as indicated in Figure A1.2. We now make the assumption *that all micro-states* (*within the restriction of the overall macro-constraints*) *are equally probable*. Then, the most probable meso-state is that with the greatest number of micro states associated with it.

The number of ways of assigning individuals to the boxes of Figure A1.3 and giving rise to $\{T_{ij}\}$ is $W(\{T_{ij}\})$ where

$$W(\{T_{ij}\}) = \frac{T!}{\prod_{ij} T_{ij}!} \tag{A1.4}$$

It can be shown (Wilson, 1970), that if log $W(\{T_{ij}\})$ is maximized subject to the constraints (A1.1)–(A1.3), then the resulting $\{T_{ij}\}$ has elements given by

$$T_{ij} = A_i B_j O_i D_j \, e^{-\beta c_{ij}} \tag{A1.5}$$

where

$$A_i = 1 \Big/ \sum_j B_j D_j \, e^{-\beta c_{ij}} \tag{A1.6}$$

and

$$B_j = 1 \Big/ \sum_i A_i O_i \, e^{-\beta c_{ij}} \tag{A1.7}$$

ensure that constraints (A1.1) and (A1.2) are satisfied, and β is the Lagrangian multiplier associated with (A1.3). This is the doubly constrained model presented in equations (6.16)–(6.18) except that the general function $f(c_{ij})$ has been replaced by the negative exponential function, $e^{-\beta c_{ij}}$.

A1. REFERENCES

* P. Gould (1972) Pedagogic review: Entropy in urban and regional modelling, *Annals, Association of American Geographers*, **62**, pp. 689–700.

A. G. Wilson (1970) *Entropy in urban and regional modelling*, Pion, London.

APPENDIX 2

The intervening opportunities model

The spatial interaction models used throughout the book have been variants of the so-called gravity model. As an alternative, the intervening opportunities model is available. This is based on an attractively simple hypothesis, that that there is a constant probability that a traveller will be 'satisfied' at the 'next' opportunity. The original intervening opportunities model was developed by Stouffer (1940) with the even simpler assumption that the number of trips from an origin to a destination zone is proportional to the number of opportunities at the destination zone and inversely proportional to the number of intervening opportunities. In its modern form, the derivation is due to Schneider (Chicago Area Transportation Study, 1960).

In order to be able to compute intervening opportunities, we have to develop our notation so that we can identify the rank order of destination zones 'away from' any origin zone. In most discussions in the literature, this is not done explicitly, and presentations are often difficult to follow. Here, we shall define $j(\mu, i)$ to be the μth ranked destination zone (rank being determined by increasing travel cost) away from i. Let $U_{ij(\mu, i)}$ be the probability that a single traveller will continue beyond the μth zone away from i. Let L be the probability that an opportunity will satisfy this traveller when it is offered. Then, to the first order in L,

$$U_{ij(1, i)} = 1 - LD_{j(1, i)} \tag{A2.1}$$

where D_j is the number of opportunities (e.g. jobs if we are modelling the journey to work) in zone j. Then, successive probabilities can be combined as follows:

$$U_{ij(\mu, i)} = U_{ij(\mu - 1, i)}(1 - LD_{j(\mu, i)}) \tag{A2.2}$$

From equation (A2.2), we get

$$\frac{U_{ij(\mu, i)} - U_{ij(\mu - 1, i)}}{U_{ij(\mu - 1, i)}} = -LD_{j(\mu, i)} \tag{A2.3}$$

We can now define $A_{j(\mu, i)}$ to be the number of intervening opportunities from i up to and including $j(\mu, i)$. Then, equation (A2.3) can be written

$$\frac{U_{ij(\mu, i)} - U_{ij(\mu - 1, i)}}{U_{ij(\mu - 1, i)}} = -L(A_{j(\mu, i)} - A_{j(\mu - 1, i)}) \tag{A2.4}$$

If we can assume continuous variation of opportunities, equation (A2.4) can be written, using an obvious notation, as

$$\frac{dU}{U} = -L\,dA \tag{A2.5}$$

and this integrates to

$$\log U = -LA + C \tag{A2.6}$$

where C is a constant of integration. Thus, in terms of the zonal variables again, equation (2.6) can be written

$$U_{ij(\mu,\,i)} = k_i\,e^{-LA_{j(\mu,\,i)}} \tag{A2.7}$$

where k_i is a constant. If these are O_i travellers leaving i, then $T_{ij(\mu,\,i)}$, the number of trips from i to $j(\mu, i)$ is, in terms of the probability $U_{ij(\mu,\,i)}$,

$$T_{ij(\mu,\,i)} = O_i(U_{ij(\mu-1,\,i)} - U_{ij(\mu,\,i)}) \tag{A2.8}$$

This, using (A2.7) twice, for $U_{ij(\mu-1,\,i)}$ and $U_{ij(\mu,\,i)}$ gives

$$T_{ij(\mu,\,i)} = k_i O_i(e^{-LA_{j(\mu-1,\,i)}} - e^{-LA_{j(\mu,\,i)}}) \tag{A2.9}$$

Note that

$$\sum_\mu T_{ij(\mu,\,i)} = k_i O_i(1 - e^{-LA_{j(N,\,i)}}) \tag{A2.10}$$

if there are N zones. $e^{-LA_{j(N,\,i)}}$ should be sufficiently small that it can be neglected, and so k_i can be taken as 1. Then equation (2.9) can be written

$$T_{ij(\mu,\,i)} = O_i(e^{-LA_{j(\mu-1,\,i)}} - e^{-LA_{j(\mu,\,i)}}) \tag{A2.11}$$

and this is the usual statement of the intervening opportunities model.

One of the main differences between this and the gravity model is that it is not wholly multiplicative and this makes it less convenient (although 'convenience' only counts as a test 'other things being equal'!). Many of the developments which are applied to the gravity model in Chapter 6 could be applied to the intervening opportunities model. For example, a generalized cost c_{ij} could be used for ranking zones. The reader could, if he so wishes, replace many of the spatial interaction models of this book with a corresponding version of the intervening opportunities model. The place of the intervening opportunities model within an entropy-maximizing framework is discussed in the book cited in Appendix 1 (Wilson, 1970, especially Appendix 3).

A2. REFERENCES

Chicago Area Transportation Study (1960) *Final report*, Chicago.
S. A. Stouffer (1940) Intervening opportunities: a theory relating mobility and distance, *American Sociological Review*, **5**, pp. 845–867.
A. G. Wilson (1970) *Entropy in urban and regional modelling*, Pion, London.

APPENDIX 3

The algebra of the contragredient (or companion matrix) transformation

All the references checked so far on companion matrixes seem inadequate in explanation in the sense that they take many results in linear algebra as given. This appendix attempts to spell out the results in more detail.

Let $e_1, e_2, \ldots e_n$ be the *basis* of some n dimensional vector space. Then a vector x has *coordinates* $(x_1, x_2, \ldots x_n)$ in this space, and

$$x = x_1 e_1 + x_2 e_2 + \ldots + x_n e_n \tag{A3.1}$$

We can think of this basis as

$$
e_1 = \begin{pmatrix} 1 \\ 0 \\ 0 \\ \cdot \\ \cdot \\ \cdot \\ 0 \end{pmatrix}
\quad
e_2 = \begin{pmatrix} 0 \\ 1 \\ 0 \\ \cdot \\ \cdot \\ \cdot \\ 0 \end{pmatrix}
\quad
e_3 = \begin{pmatrix} 0 \\ 0 \\ 1 \\ 0 \\ \cdot \\ \cdot \\ 0 \end{pmatrix}
\quad
e_n = \begin{pmatrix} 0 \\ 0 \\ 0 \\ \cdot \\ \cdot \\ \cdot \\ 1 \end{pmatrix}
\tag{A3.2}
$$

Suppose we now transform to a new basis $e_1^*, e_2^*, \ldots e_n^*$. The coordinates of this basis with respect to the first basis system are

$$e_i^* = \sum_j \hat{T}_{ji} e_j \tag{A3.3}$$

and it can be shown that the new coordinates of x, written as x^* are

$$x^* = Tx \tag{A3.4}$$

or

$$x_i^* = \sum_j T_{ij} x_j \tag{A3.5}$$

In (A3.3) $\hat{T}_{ji}$ is the (ji)th element of the *inverse* of T in (A3.5). The new basis, and the coordinates, are said to transform *contragrediently*.

Suppose a linear transformation with respect to the first basis is given by the matrix A, so that a relationship between vectors y and x may be expressed as

$$y = Ax \tag{A3.6}$$

In the system with respect to the new basis, this relationship is

$$\mathbf{y^* = A^* x^*} \tag{A3.7}$$

But,

$$\mathbf{y^* = Ty} \tag{A3.8}$$

and

$$\mathbf{x^* = Tx} \tag{A3.9}$$

So, substituting from equations (A3.8) and (A3.9) into equation (A3.6) we have

$$\mathbf{T^{-1}y^* = AT^{-1}x^*}$$

so, pre-multiplying by T

$$\mathbf{y^* = TAT^{-1}x^*} \tag{A3.10}$$

so, comparing (A3.7) and (A3.10)

$$\mathbf{A^* = TAT^{-1}} \tag{A3.11}$$

shows how $\mathbf{A}$ transfers into $\mathbf{A^*}$ under the shift to a new basis given by $\mathbf{T}$.

Suppose now that a_{ij} is the (ij)th element of a matrix $\mathbf{a}$ in equation (7.94). We wish to find a transformation $\mathbf{T}$ such that, with a new basis, $\mathbf{TaT^{-1}}$ is a more convenient form. The most familiar of such canonical transformations is the diagonalization of a matrix. This can be achieved by taking each column of $\mathbf{T}$ as the eigenvectors of $\mathbf{a}$. In this case, however, it is most useful to obtain the *companion matrix* of $\mathbf{a}$: what Birkhoff and MacLane (1953) call the 'first natural form' of a matrix. This is done as follows.

We seek a vector (given in the *old* coordinates) so that we can take

$$\mathbf{f}_1 = \alpha, \qquad \mathbf{f}_2 = a\alpha, \qquad \mathbf{f}_3 = a^2\alpha, \qquad \ldots \mathbf{f}_n = a^{n-1}\alpha \tag{A3.12}$$

(in the old coordinates) as the *new basis*. (For the *new coordinates*, we shall have

$$\mathbf{f}_1^* = \begin{pmatrix} 1 \\ 0 \\ 0 \\ \vdots \\ 0 \end{pmatrix} \qquad \mathbf{f}_2^* = \begin{pmatrix} 0 \\ 1 \\ 0 \\ \vdots \\ 0 \end{pmatrix} \cdots \mathbf{f}_n^* = \begin{pmatrix} 0 \\ 0 \\ \vdots \\ \vdots \\ 1 \end{pmatrix} \tag{A3.13}$$

in the usual way).

Let T be the matrix of the transformation from the old basis to the new, so that

$$\mathbf{a^* = TaT^{-1}} \tag{A3.14}$$

The coordinate transformations are given by

$$\mathbf{x}^* = \mathbf{Tx} \tag{A3.15}$$

in the usual way. Let $\hat{\mathbf{T}}$ be the transpose of $\mathbf{T}^{-1}$. Then

$$\mathbf{f}_i = \sum_j \hat{T}_{ij} \mathbf{e}_j \tag{A3.16}$$

so that the columns of $\hat{\mathbf{T}}$ are the elements of $\mathbf{f}_i$ in the old coordinates as given in (A3.12). This enables $\mathbf{T}$ to be obtained.

From (A3.12), we see that

$$\left.\begin{array}{l} \mathbf{f}_2 = a\mathbf{f}_1 \\ \mathbf{f}_3 = a\mathbf{f}_2 \end{array}\right\} \tag{A3.17}$$

and so on. Thus in the new coordinates

$$\left.\begin{array}{l} \mathbf{f}_2^* = a^*\mathbf{f}_1^* \\ \mathbf{f}_3^* = a^*\mathbf{f}_2^* \end{array}\right\} \tag{A3.18}$$

We can use (A3.13) directly to obtain a^*: from the first of the (A3.18) equations

$$a^* \begin{pmatrix} 1 \\ 0 \\ 0 \\ \vdots \\ 0 \end{pmatrix} = \begin{pmatrix} 0 \\ 1 \\ 0 \\ \vdots \\ 0 \end{pmatrix}$$

This means that the first column of a^* must take the form

$$\begin{pmatrix} 0 \\ 1 \\ 0 \\ \vdots \\ 0 \end{pmatrix}$$

Similarly, the second equation tells us that the second column of a^* must be

$$\begin{pmatrix} 0 \\ 0 \\ 1 \\ 0 \\ \vdots \\ 0 \end{pmatrix}$$

and so on up to and including the $(n-1)$th row. The final column can be specified arbitrarily and we take it in the form

$$\begin{pmatrix} -\beta_n \\ -\beta_{n-1} \\ \vdots \\ -\beta_1 \end{pmatrix}$$

for convenience. Hence

$$\mathbf{a}^* = \begin{pmatrix} 0 & 0 & 0 & -\beta_n \\ 1 & 0 & 0 & -\beta_{n-1} \\ 0 & 1 & 0 & -\beta_{n-2} \\ \vdots & \vdots & \vdots & \vdots \\ 0 & 0 & 0 & -\beta_1 \end{pmatrix} \qquad (A3.19)$$

Since the elements of the new basis must be linearly independent, any other vector can be expressed in terms of it. In particular, we can express $\mathbf{a}^n\boldsymbol{\alpha}$ in this form. We can write

$$\mathbf{a}^n\boldsymbol{\alpha} = -\beta_1\boldsymbol{\alpha} - \beta_2\mathbf{a}\boldsymbol{\alpha} - \ldots - \beta_n\mathbf{a}^{n-1}\boldsymbol{\alpha} \qquad (A3.20)$$

in the old coordinates. In the *new* coordinates, the same equation would be

$$\mathbf{a}^{*n}\mathbf{T}\boldsymbol{\alpha} = -\beta_1\mathbf{T}\boldsymbol{\alpha} - \ldots - \beta_n\mathbf{T}^{n-1}\boldsymbol{\alpha} = -\beta_1\mathbf{f}_1^* - \beta_2\mathbf{f}_2^* - \ldots - \beta_n\mathbf{f}_n^* \qquad (A3.21)$$

However, we know that the left-hand side can be written

$$\mathbf{a}^*\mathbf{f}_n^*$$

and this shows that $\beta_1, \beta_2 \ldots \beta_n$ in (A3.21) can be identified with $\beta_1, \beta_2, \ldots \beta_n$ in (A3.19). (Note that Rosen (1970) has the signs wrong in his polynomial (4.2.10) on p. 94 for all the βs.) (A3.20) can be written

$$(\mathbf{a}^n + \beta_n\mathbf{a}^{n-1} + \beta_{n-1}\mathbf{a}^{n-1} + \ldots + \beta_1)\boldsymbol{\alpha} = 0 \qquad (A3.22)$$

The βs turn out to be related to the characteristic roots (eigenvalues) of $\mathbf{a}$.
We can see this as follows: let $g(a)$ be the polynomial

$$g(a) = a^n + \beta_n a^{n-1} + \ldots + \beta_1 \qquad (A3.23)$$

then $(-1)^n g(\lambda)$ is the characteristic polynomial of $\mathbf{a}^*$. (Since *similar* matrices have the same eigenvalues, $\mathbf{a}$ also has the same characteristic polynomial.) (Birkhoff and MacLane, p. 318.) The characteristic polynomial is

$$g(\lambda) = \det(\mathbf{a}^* - \lambda\mathbf{I}) \qquad (A3.24)$$

and an expansion of the determinant shows that the above stated result is correct. Thus, the βs are $(-1)^n$ times the coefficients of the characteristic polynomial and can be found from **a** directly.

We now, at last, have a scheme of calculation:

(1) Given **a**, find the characteristic polynomial, and hence the β_is using (A3.24) and (A3.23).

(2) (A3.22) are then a set of n linear equations in α which can be solved for the elements of α.

(4) The column vectors $\alpha, a\alpha, a^2\alpha, \ldots a^{n-1}\alpha$ then form the columns of the matrix $\hat{T}$ which gives the transformation from the old basis to the new.

(4) We can then get the *coordinate* transformation **T**, since

$$\mathbf{T} = \hat{\mathbf{T}}'^{-1} \tag{A3.25}$$

where $'$ indicates transposition.

We then have all the equipment to put the equation system in canonical form using the companion matrix.

A3.1. REFERENCES

G. Birkhoff and S. MacLane (1953) *A survey of modern algebra*, Macmillan, London.
R. Rosen (1970) *Dynamical systems theory in biology*, Vol. 1, John Wiley, New York.

Author Index

Subject Index